ROMANCE READING ON THE BOOK

ESSAYS ON MEDIEVAL NARRATIVE PRESENTED TO MALDWYN MILLS

Maldwyn Mills

ROMANCE READING ON THE BOOK

Essays on Medieval Narrative

presented to Maldwyn Mills

Edited by

JENNIFER FELLOWS, ROSALIND FIELD,

GILLIAN ROGERS and JUDITH WEISS

CARDIFF
UNIVERSITY OF WALES PRESS
1996

© The contributors, 1996

All rights reserved. No part of this book may be reproduced, stored in a retrieval system, or transmitted, in any form or by any means, electronic, mechanical, photocopying, recording or otherwise, without clearance from the University of Wales Press, 6 Gwennyth Street, Cardiff, CF2 4YD

British Library Cataloguing in Publication Data

A catalogue record for this book is available from the British Library.

ISBN 0-7083-1241-1

Typeset by Action Typesetting Limited, Gloucester
Printed in Great Britain by Dinefwr Press, Llandybïe, Dyfed

Contents

List of illiustrations	vii
List of contributors	viii
Preface	xi
List of abbreviations	xii
Biographical sketch JAMES OGDEN	1
A list of the writings of Maldwyn Mills 1962–1994 DESMOND SLAY	6
Introduction ROSALIND FIELD and JUDITH WEISS	11
1 *The Wars of Alexander*: from reality to romance W. R. J. BARRON	22
2 The branching tree of medieval narrative: Welsh *cainc* and French *branche* CERIDWEN LLOYD-MORGAN	36
3 Madness in *Sir Orfeo* DEREK PEARSALL	51
4 Cloaking desire: re-reading *Emaré* MARGARET ROBSON	64
5 Malory's Mordred and the *Morte Arthure* P. J. C. FIELD	77

6	'Illuminat vith lawte, and with lufe lasit': Gawain gives Arthur a lesson in magnanimity GILLIAN ROGERS	94
7	No poet has his travesty alone: *The Weddynge of Sir Gawen and Dame Ragnell* STEPHEN H. A. SHEPHERD	112
8	*The Awntyrs off Arthure*: jests and jousts ROSAMUND ALLEN	129
9	The pattern of Providence in *Chevelere Assigne* DIANE SPEED	143
10	'A damsell by herselfe alone': images of magic and femininity from *Lanval* to *Sir Lambewell* ELIZABETH WILLIAMS	155
11	Looking behind the book: MS Cotton Caligula A.ii, part 1, and the experience of its texts JOHN J. THOMPSON	171
12	MS Porkington 10 and its scribes DANIEL HUWS	188
13	Rate revisited: the compilation of the narrative works in MS Ashmole 61 LYNNE S. BLANCHFIELD	208
14	'Prenes: engre': an early sixteenth-century presentation copy of *The Erle of Tolous* CAROL M. MEALE	221
15	Robert Parry's *Moderatus*: a study in Elizabethan romance JOHN SIMONS	237
16	*Bevis redivivus*: the printed editions of *Sir Bevis of Hampton* JENNIFER FELLOWS	251
Bibliography		269
Index of manuscripts cited		291
General index		295
Tabula gratulatoria		305

Illustrations

Plates

Plate 1	MS Brogyntyn II.1, fo. 52^v: scribe L/M/N	194
Plate 2	MS Brogyntyn II.I, fo. 23^r: scribe K	195
Plate 3	MS Brogyntyn II.I, fo. 89^r: scribe O	196
Plate 4	MS Brogyntyn II.1, fo. 90^r: scribe I/P	197
Plate 5	MS Brogyntyn II.1, fo. 138^v: scribe J	200
Plate 6	MS Brogyntyn II.1, fo. 139^r: scribe Q	201
Plate 7	The presentation miniature in MS Ashmole 45	222
Plate 8	Drawing of Henry VIII from Wolsey's patent for Cardinal College, Ipswich	225
Plate 9	The opening of *The Erle of Tolous* in MS Ashmole 45	227
Plate 10	The conclusion of *The Erle of Tolous* in MS Ashmole 45	229
Plate 11	A woodcut from Pynson's edition of *Bevis* (*c.* 1503)	253
Plate 12	The title-page of *The Famous and Renowned History of Sir Bevis of Southampton* (1689)	263
Plate 13	An illustration from Andrew Lang's *Red Romance Book* (1905)	267

Tables

1	Collation, contents and scribes of MS Brogyntyn II.1	190–1
2	Contents of MS Ashmole 61	216–17

Figure

1	MS Cotton Caligula A.ii, part 1 – contents and physical make-up	174–8

Contributors

ROSAMUND ALLEN teaches Old and Middle English, and medieval literature, at Queen Mary and Westfield College, University of London. She has published on the medieval English mystics, on Arthurian and other narratives and on John Gower.

RAY BARRON was a student at St Andrews, Yale and Strasbourg, taught at Aberdeen, Manchester and Shiraz, and is currently an honorary research fellow of the University of Exeter.

LYNNE BLANCHFIELD gained her doctorate from Aberystwyth in 1992 and has since taught medieval literature in a variety of contexts. She currently teaches Shakespeare and other literature for the Open University and elsewhere.

JENNIFER FELLOWS studied at London and Cambridge and now works as a freelance editor in academic publishing; she is Assistant Editor of *Medium Ævum*. Her own published work is mainly on Middle English romances and on the theory and practice of editing medieval texts.

PETER FIELD has been at the University of Wales, Bangor, since the dawn of time and is now a professor of English there. Although he has written academic pieces on authors from Laȝamon to Pope, nothing has ever succeeded in distracting him from Malory for long.

ROSALIND FIELD (no relation of the above!) is a lecturer in English at Royal Holloway, University of London. She has degrees from the Universities of Cambridge and York, and has published on Chaucer and on *Pearl*, as well as on Anglo-Norman and Middle English romance.

DANIEL HUWS was Keeper of Manuscripts and Records at the National Library of Wales from 1981 to 1992.

CERIDWEN LLOYD-MORGAN has been working as an archivist

in the Department of Manuscripts, National Library of Wales, since 1981. Her medieval research is mainly on Arthurian literature and on the influence of medieval French literature on Middle Welsh prose texts.

CAROL MEALE is a reader in Medieval Studies at the University of Bristol. Her research interests include late medieval literature, especially romance, book production and the reception of texts, patronage and readership, and women's cultural history.

JAMES OGDEN is a senior lecturer at the University of Wales, Aberystwyth, with research interests in Shakespeare and in seventeenth-century literature, especially Milton.

DEREK PEARSALL is Gurney Professor of English at Harvard University and has published extensively on Chaucer, Langland, Gower, Lydgate and medieval romance.

MARGARET ROBSON studied at London and York. She has taught at the University of York and at the University of Wales, Aberystwyth. Her interests are in medieval romance and in feminist and psychoanalytic theory.

GILLIAN ROGERS is English Faculty Librarian at the University of Cambridge and a former postgraduate student of Maldwyn Mills at Aberystwyth. Her research interests centre on the Middle English Arthurian romances and their transmission in the sixteenth and seventeenth centuries.

STEPHEN SHEPHERD is an associate professor of English at Southern Methodist University, Dallas, Texas. His principal area of research interest is in Middle English romance.

JOHN SIMONS studied under Maldwyn Mills both as an undergraduate and as a postgraduate. He has taught at the University of Exeter and at King Alfred's College, Winchester, and is currently head of the School of Humanities and Arts at Edge Hill College, Ormskirk.

DESMOND SLAY was formerly Rendel Professor of English Language and Literature, and head of department, at the University of Wales, Aberystwyth. He is a past president of the Viking Society for Northern Research and a Knight of the Order of the Falcon (Iceland).

DIANE SPEED is a senior lecturer in the Department of English at the University of Sydney, with research interests in medieval romance, exemplum, hagiography and salvation history.

JOHN THOMPSON is a lecturer in English at the Queen's

University of Belfast. He is generally interested in the development of effective learning and teaching in higher education. His research interests are primarily in the writing, dissemination and reception of late medieval English texts and manuscripts.

JUDITH WEISS is a Fellow of Robinson College, Cambridge, where she directs studies in English. She has published on medieval English and Anglo-Norman romance, chronicle and saints' lives.

ELIZABETH WILLIAMS lectured in medieval English at the University of Leeds until she took early retirement in 1991. She also pioneered a course there in children's literature. Her main studies now are in medieval romance, folk-tale and ballad.

Preface

The editors would like to thank the University of Wales Press, and especially Ned Thomas and Liz Powell, for their friendly co-operation in bringing this project to fruition. Our thanks too to the many subscribers who, in demonstrating the affection and esteem in which Maldwyn is held, have made publication possible.

We are grateful to the following libraries for permission to reproduce from manuscripts and rare books in their keeping: the Bodleian Library, Oxford (Plates 7, 9–11), the British Library, London (Plate 12), the National Library of Wales, Aberystwyth (Plates 1–6) and the Public Record Office, London (Plate 8).

This volume would not have seen the light of day had it not been for the enthusiastic collusion and innocent subterfuges of Vivien Mills. We owe much to her friendliness, her encouragement and her sheer delight in the opportunity to involve so many of Maldwyn's friends in this tribute to him. We deeply regret that she did not live to see its publication.

December 1995   J. L. F., R. P. F.,
                        G. E. R. and J. E. W.

Abbreviations

ANTS	Anglo-Norman Text Society
Briquet	*Les Filigranes* (see Briquet 1968)
CFMA	Classiques français du moyen âge
CPR	*Calendar of Patent Rolls*
DNB	*Dictionary of National Biography* (see Stephen et al. 1885–)
EETS	Early English Text Society
ES	Extra Series
OS	Original Series
SS	Supplementary Series
IMEV	*Index of Middle English Verse* (see Brown and Robbins 1943)
MED	*Middle English Dictionary* (see Kurath, Kuhn et al. 1952–)
PMLA	*Publications of the Modern Language Association of America*
SATF	Société des anciens textes français
STC	*Short-Title Catalogue ... 1475–1640* (see Jackson et al. 1976–91)
STS	Scottish Text Society
Supplement	*Supplement to the Index of Middle English Verse* (see Robbins and Cutler 1965)
VCH	*Victoria History of the Counties of England*
Wing	*Short-Title Catalogue ... 1641–1700* (see Wing 1948–51)

All references to the works of Chaucer are to *The Riverside Chaucer* (Benson 1987).

Biographical sketch

JAMES OGDEN

Maldwyn's interest in romances possibly derives from the adventures of his own early life. He was born in Cardiff on 25 June 1926. His parents separated when he was about a year old, and thereafter he saw very little of his mother and not much of his father; his upbringing was entrusted to five spinster aunts who lived together in the Adamstown district of the city. Maldwyn loved this 'amiable and indulgent quintet', and in his turn looked after them as they grew older. Prominent among his early memories are family visits to the cinema, and attendance at the local Baptist chapel, the former more to his taste than the latter.

Maldwyn's formal education began at the Moorland Road School, Splott, and continued with a scholarship to Cardiff High School. Here he developed an interest in geography, which is sometimes seen again in the pinpointing of localities mentioned in the romances; his edition of *Horn Childe* even has a map of Northumbria. In those days you could not read Geography at the University of Wales's college in Cardiff, and without much difficulty the scholarly senior English master at Cardiff High, William Dyfed Parry, persuaded him to read English instead. As a result of hearing him reading aloud 'The Lotos-Eaters' Mr Parry also tried to persuade him to 'get rid of your appalling Cardiff accent'. Fortunately Maldwyn offered some resistance, and there has been a recurrent rumour among students that he is a foreigner.

There was a war on, and Maldwyn's undergraduate years at Cardiff were interrupted by military service from November 1944 to January 1948, which took him to India and Singapore, serving in the army education corps. The army showed its sense of self-preservation in deciding that he was 'not officer material'. On his return to Cardiff, Maldwyn took the English Department's 'Medieval Option' with Professor E. C. Llewelyn, George Thomas and Charles Elliott, graduating with first-class honours in 1950. He read for his MA with Kathleen Williams, a brilliant young member of the department, and wrote a dissertation on eighteenth-century poetic theory and practice. Then the judgement of Llewelyn, passed on by George Thomas, 'bloody fool to study eighteenth-century poetry when he could read Old French', brought him back to medieval studies. George himself became one of Maldwyn's most helpful advisers. But probably the best-known member of the Cardiff department at that time was the Shakespeare scholar S. L. Bethel, who offered Maldwyn the part of the bear in his production of *The Winter's Tale*; Maldwyn turned him down, considering Bethel's view of the bear's role too frivolous. His theatrical career at Cardiff did, however, include the role of the bearish Ajax in *Troilus and Cressida*, and he was the producer of *The Silent Woman*. Later, at Oxford, he played the pastor Kroll in *Rosmersholm*.

Before leaving Cardiff, Maldwyn embarked on an ambitious comparative study of Old French and Middle English romances, and in 1953 he found himself with the choice of taking a Stopford Brooke Memorial Scholarship to London University or a Meyricke Scholarship to Jesus College, Oxford. He chose the latter, where he could have been supervised by Professor J. R. R. Tolkien, but decided rather to go to Mrs D. R. Sutherland for Old French and to G. V. Smithers for Middle English. It was Smithers who suggested he should do an edition of the six *Lybeaus* manuscripts for his D. Phil., and who obliged him to bring greater philological rigour to his studies. It was at Mrs Sutherland's lectures that he met Vivien Spice: they fell in love, and were married after her graduation in 1955. Vivien was a convert to Roman Catholicism, and after their marriage Maldwyn also converted. They have been blessed with three children: Dafydd, born in 1960; Peter, born in 1961, who died tragically in 1983; and Lora, born in 1964. As Maldwyn has often said, he owes much to Vivien's knowledge, wisdom and encouragement.

Maldwyn's teaching career began as assistant master at Merchant Taylors' School, Liverpool, in 1956. Here he was happy enough for a while, but to pursue his main interests he needed a university post, and in 1959 he was appointed assistant lecturer in English at the University College of Wales, Aberystwyth. Here at that time medieval studies were especially strong, with the Old Icelandic scholars Gwyn Jones as head of department, and Desmond Slay as unofficial second-in-command. There were also distinguished medievalists in other departments, notably Hywel Emmanuel (Classics), Edmund Fryde (History), David Hoggan (French) and, briefly, John Ellis (German). Maldwyn's teaching immediately and for much of his career concentrated on two honours courses, 'Chaucer and his Contemporaries' and 'Medieval English Texts'; over the years he progressively modified the content of both, and in 1973 the latter course became 'Middle English Romances'. He has also collaborated on a number of other courses, especially those on contemporary cinema and on Elizabethan and Jacobean drama, and he has attracted to the department some excellent research students. As a teacher Maldwyn has the rare gift of combining enthusiasm for his subjects with clarity of exposition. Both students and colleagues have enjoyed hearing him describe small but significant differences in versions of a narrative, and have shared his delight in the humour and humanity of medieval pictures and carvings. The conclusion is no less true for being obvious: gladly would he learn, and gladly teach.

With the encouragement of generally sympathetic heads of department – Gwyn Jones, Arthur Johnston, Jim Nosworthy, Desmond Slay and Brean Hammond – Maldwyn's research led to impressive publications and a personal chair at Aberystwyth in 1979. His chief critical endeavour has been the rehabilitation of romance, and his chief scholarly works the editions of *Lybeaus Desconus* for the Early English Text Society (1969), *Fragments of 'Guy of Warwick'* for Medium Ævum Monographs (with Daniel Huws, 1974), and *Horn Childe and Maiden Rimnild* for the Heidelberg series of Middle English Texts (1988). *Lybeaus* and *Horn Childe* replaced very old and unsatisfactory editions, and offered reliable texts and commentaries; *Fragments* presented newly discovered manuscripts. Reviewers[1] had some difficulty in finding anything wrong with these works, and one of them complained of Maldwyn's 'somewhat cavalier use of square brackets' in the text of *Lybeaus*. The consensus of opinion on *Lybeaus* and *Horn Childe* was that with such admirable editions scholars could now assess the merits of these romances for themselves, and need no longer accept the dismissive comments of literary historians; so it is worth emphasizing that Maldwyn's work was founded on a better appreciation of the romances as literature. The idea that they deserve to be known to students as well as scholars lies behind the editions of *Six Medieval Romances* (1973) and of *Ywain and Gawain, Sir Percyvell of Gales and The Anturs of Arther* (1992) for the Everyman series. In the Introduction to the former there is an emphatic rejection of the critical view, perhaps deriving ultimately from Chaucer, that the literary effects of these romances are the by-products of a haphazard mode of writing; for example, the repetitions of *Emaré* are defended as creating a sense of order in the heroine's dangerous world, and a Shakespearean awareness of the strange patterns in human life. Articles in the learned journals which similarly realized the ideal of the scholar–critic include those on *Sir Gawain and the Green Knight* (*Modern Language Review*, 1965, reprinted in an anthology of the best studies of the poem, 1968) and *Havelok the Dane* (*Medium Ævum*, 1967 and 1976). The second essay on *Havelok* characteristically argues that oddities in the story of the hero's return to Denmark are created less by the author's faulty recollections than by his thoughtful elaborations. In his essay on Raymond Chandler's *Farewell My Lovely* (*Watching the Detectives*, 1990) Maldwyn's mature understanding of the use of sources, and his acute sense of the possibilities of narrative, were applied to detective fiction, another genre which has had less than its share of intelligent criticism.

As this sketch has hinted, Maldwyn has not spent all his life in the study. He has happily given his time to family, friends, students and the wider academic community. In 1988 Maldwyn organized a highly successful conference at Gregynog on Romance in Medieval England; this proved to be the first of a lively biennial series. Once when he was acting head of department the figure of C. S. Lewis appeared to him in a dream, urging him to 'finish *Horn Childe*', and prompting speculation about whether academic league tables are studied by the heavenly host. Anyway Lewis can rest in peace; that book was finished, and others, and we hope there will be more.

Maldwyn remained at Aberystwyth right up to his retirement in 1993, when the department held the ritual farewell dinner. Such occasions are not always happy; old colleagues remember ancient feuds, while young ones have modern preoccupations. But this one was enjoyed by all. It began with the showing of an excerpt from *King Kong*, a film Maldwyn did *not* see with his aunts when it first appeared, though of course he remedied that later. It ended with a young colleague remarking on Maldwyn's resemblance to Father Christmas in appearance and behaviour. An old colleague cannot take quite such a rosy view. I remember Maldwyn's talent for satire, and many occasions for its use; often enough academic life has seemed, in his phrase, 'much ado about learning and the advancement of nothing'. Still, it is true that such satire has rarely been pointed at individuals; rather, Maldwyn has come to us bearing the gifts of scholarship, benevolence and laughter.

Notes

1 Of *Lybaeus*: A. J. Bliss, *Studia Neophilologica*, 42 (1970) 491-4; G. C. Britton, *Notes and Queries*, 17 (1970), 365-7, and *Year's Work in English Studies*, 50 (1971), 86-7; A. S. G. Edwards, *English Studies*, 53 (1971), 251-3; and V. J. Scattergood, *Yearbook of English Studies*, 2 (1971), 236-7. Of *Fragments of 'Guy of Warwick'*: R. W. McTurk and D. J. Williams, *Year's Work in English Studies*, 55 (1976), 109. Of *Horn Childe*: Jennifer Fellows, *Modern Language Review*, 86 (1991), 970-1; and S. Powell, *Year's Work in English Studies,* 69 (1991), 153. Of *Six Medieval Romances*: G. C. Britton, *Notes and Queries*, 22 (1975), 452-4; R. Allen, *Year's Work in English Studies*, 54 (1975), 93-4. This is not meant for an exhaustive list.

A list of the writings of Maldwyn Mills 1962–1994

DESMOND SLAY

1962
Review of *Sir Launfal*, ed. A. J. Bliss (London, 1960), *Medium Ævum*, 31, pp. 75–8.
'The composition and style of the "Southern" *Octavian*, *Sir Launfal*, and *Libeaus Desconus*', *Medium Ævum*, 31, pp. 88–109.

1963
'A medieval reviser at work', *Medium Ævum*, 32, pp. 11–23.

1965
'Christian significance and romance tradition in *Sir Gawain and the Green Knight*', *Modern Language Review*, 60, pp. 483–93.

1966
'A note on *Sir Launfal* 733–744', *Medium Ævum*, 35, pp. 122–4.
Review of *Sir Eglamour of Artois*, ed. Frances E. Richardson, EETS 256 (London, 1965), *Medium Ævum*, 35, pp. 269–73.
'The huntsman and the dwarf in *Erec* and *Libeaus Desconus*', *Romania*, 87, pp. 33–58.

1967
'Havelok and the brutal fisherman', *Medium Ævum*, 36, pp. 219–30.

1968
'Christian significance and romance tradition in *Sir Gawain and the Green Knight*' (1965) reprinted in *Critical Studies of 'Sir Gawain and the Green Knight'*, ed. Donald R. Howard and Christian Zacher (Notre Dame, University of Indiana Press), pp. 85–105.

1969
Ed. *Lybeaus Desconus*, EETS 261 (London, Oxford University Press for the EETS). 302 pp.

1970
Review of '*Sir Amadace*' *and* '*The Avowing of Arthur*', ed. Christopher Brookhouse (Copenhagen, 1968), *Medium Ævum*, 39, pp. 63–6.
Bibliographical entry on Geoffrey Chaucer in Potthast's *Repertorium fontium historiae medii aevii* (Rome), III, pp. 235–6.

1971
Review of *The Siege of Jerusalem in Prose*, ed. A. Kurvinen (Helsinki, 1969), *Review of English Studies*, n.s. 22, p. 247.
Review article on *A Manual of the Writings in Middle English 1050–1500*, Fasc. I, ed. J. Burke Severs (New Haven, Conn., 1967); Hanspeter Schelp, *Exemplarische Romanzen im Mittelenglischen* (Göttingen, 1967); Dieter Mehl, *Die mittelenglischen Romanzen des 13. und 14. Jahrhunderts* (Heidelberg, 1967) and the English-language edition *The Middle English Romances of the Thirteenth and Fourteenth Centuries* (London, 1968), *Medium Ævum*, 40, pp. 291–303.

1973
Ed. *Six Middle English Romances*, Everyman's University Library (London, Dent; Totowa, NJ, Rowman and Littlefield). xxxiii + 224 pp. (Reprinted 1982, 1988; reissued 1992.)

1974
Ed. with Daniel Huws, *Fragments of an Early Fourteenth-Century 'Guy of Warwick'*, Medium Ævum Monographs, n.s. 4 (Oxford, Society for the Study of Mediæval Languages and Literature). 110 pp.
Geoffrey Chaucer, *Troilus and Criseyde*, Everyman's University Library, ed. John Warrington [1953], revised with an introduction by Maldwyn Mills (London, Dent; New York, Dutton). xvi + 337 pp. (Reprinted 1987, 1981; reissued 1988.)

1975
Review of John Stevens, *Medieval Romance: Themes and Approaches* (London, 1973), *Medium Ævum*, 44, pp. 320–4.

1976
'Havelok's return', *Medium Ævum*, 45, pp. 20-35.

1977
Review of C. Luttrell, *The Creation of the First Arthurian Romance: A Quest* (London, 1974), *Medium Ævum*, 46, pp. 300-6.

1978
Review of Urs Dürmüller, *Narrative Possibilities of the Tail-Rime Romance* (Bern, 1975), *Medium Ævum*, 47, pp. 152-6.

1982
Review of *Cambridge University Library MS Ff.2.38*, introd. Frances McSparran and P. R. Robinson (London, 1979), *Medium Ævum*, 51, pp. 246-50.

1984
Review of Anne Wilson, *Traditional Romance and Tale: How Stories Mean* (Ipswich, 1976), *Powys Review*, 15, pp. 76-7.

1985
Review of *The King of Tars*, ed. Judith Perryman (Heidelberg, 1980), *Medium Ævum*, 54, pp. 301-2.

1987
Review of *The Legend of Arthur in the Middle Ages: Studies presented to A. H. Diverres by Colleagues, Pupils and Friends*, ed. P. B. Grout et al. (Cambridge, 1983); Valerie Krishna, *The Alliterative Morte Arthure: A New Verse Translation* (Washington, DC, 1983), *Modern Language Review*, 82, pp. 910-11.

1988
Ed. *Horn Childe and Maiden Rimnild*, Middle English Texts 20 (Heidelberg, Winter). 144 pp.
Review of *The Changing Face of Arthurian Romance: Essays on Arthurian Prose Romances in Memory of Cedric E. Pickford,* ed. Alison Adams et al. (Cambridge, 1986), *Studies in the Age of Chaucer*, 10, pp. 111-14.

1989
Review of *Octovian*, ed. Frances McSparran, EETS 289 (London, 1986), *Medium Ævum*, 58, pp. 324-5.

1990
'Chandler's cannibalism', in *Watching the Detectives: Essays on Crime Fiction*, ed. Ian A. Bell and Graham Daldry (Basingstoke, Macmillan), pp. 117-33.

1991
Ed. with Jennifer Fellows and Carol M. Meale, *Romance in Medieval England* (Cambridge, D. S. Brewer). viii + 228 pp.
'Introduction', ibid., pp. 1-3.
'Techniques of translation in the Middle English versions of *Guy of Warwick*', in *The Medieval Translator II*, ed. R. Ellis (London, Centre for Medieval Studies, Queen Mary and Westfield College, University of London), pp. 209-29.
Review of *Medieval English Romances*, ed. Diane Speed (Sydney, 1989), *Notes and Queries*, 236, pp. 522-3.

1992
Ed. *Ywain and Gawain, Sir Percyvell of Gales, The Anturs of Arther*, Everyman's Library (London, Dent; Rutland, Vt, Charles E. Tuttle). xl + 210 pp.
'Structure and meaning in *Guy of Warwick*', in *From Medieval to Medievalism*, ed. John Simons (Basingstoke, Macmillan), pp. 54-68.

1994
'*Sir Isumbras* and the styles of the tail-rhyme romance', in *Readings in Medieval English Romance*, ed. Carol M. Meale (Cambridge, D. S. Brewer), pp. 1-24.
'The illustrations of British Library MS. Egerton 3132A and Bodleian Library MS. Douce 261', in *Essays and Poems presented to Daniel Huws*, ed. Tegwyn Jones and E. B. Fryde (Aberystwyth, National Library of Wales), pp. 307-27.
Review of Piero Boitani and Anna Torti, *Poetics: Theory and Practice in Medieval Literature,* the J. A. W. Bennett Memorial Lectures, 7th ser., Perugia, 1990 (Cambridge, 1991), *Modern Language Review,* 89, pp. 961-2.

Recordings

Horn Childe. Read by Maldwyn Mills. Recorded at BBC Radio Bristol, 1990. Published by The Chaucer Studio, University of Adelaide.

Sir Gawain and the Green Knight. Several readers, including Maldwyn Mills (Guide). Recorded at the 7th International Congress of the New Chaucer Society, University of Kent at Canterbury, 1990. Published by The Chaucer Studio, University of Adelaide.

Introduction

ROSALIND FIELD and JUDITH WEISS

Maldwyn Mills's scholarly career has been characterized by his interest in medieval romance. In particular, he has sought to rehabilitate Middle English romance and rescue it from the low critical esteem in which it was formerly held, by generations of critics who assumed the model for the genre had been established conclusively by continental French writers, and who explained any insular differences as owing to incompetent imitation. He has been ahead of his time in drawing attention to the literary qualities of romances, revealing as skilful what had been patronizingly dismissed as haphazard, and reminding us of their potential for engaging with the most central issues in human experience.

Over the last thirty years there has indeed been a sea change in attitudes to the romances of medieval England, so much so that the cynical may think there is a danger in hailing as great works of art some that have hitherto been justly neglected. The capacity of medieval romance to reconstruct legendary or traditional figures, such as those from classical or Celtic sources, by placing them in contemporary medieval settings, viewing them against medieval values and concerns or moralizing them in the service of a didactic message, is viewed no longer with disdain but with sympathy: it is an example of the flexibility of the genre that it can accommodate and revitalize the old, and present the familiar as new, sometimes even disturbingly so. But Pearsall's article in this volume on *Sir Orfeo*, as well as reminding us of the change within his own teaching experience, also reminds us of the necessity of careful discrimination between the well-wrought poem and the potboiler. It exemplifies, as well, the benefits of paying minute and sympathetic attention to brief and anonymous works whose structures and artistic skills may at first alienate or elude us because of their unfamiliarity.

These more sympathetic attitudes to individual romances have been accompanied by an increasing awareness of the difficulties of trying to define the genre, and a willingness not to be narrowly prescriptive but as generously liberal as romance itself is in what it can encompass. In their papers, Speed and Blanchfield demonstrate the affinities of romance with hagiography and pious exemplum and consider whether we should not, rather, be talking of romance mode, as argued here and elsewhere by Barron.[1] There have also been significant advances in our knowledge of how romances were written, compiled and produced. We know far more than was known at the start of Maldwyn's career about the manuscripts containing these narratives: about the social and historical backgrounds to them, and their possible, or likely, or certain, patrons and dedicatees. We know more about the scribes who copied them, so often reproved for bungling and ignorant changes, not so often appreciated for the care with which they selected and compiled texts, sometimes in careful collaboration. Blanchfield aptly quotes Murray Evans's warning on the danger of literary critics ignoring these codicological matters, which may destroy their arguments with a well-aimed blast of fact.

In this collection in honour of the editor of *Lybeaus Desconus* and *Horn Childe*, it is fitting that many papers address single works, enlarging our knowledge of their sources, their variant versions and their contexts of production, and fitting them into a wider literary and cultural background. For in the careful re-evaluation of a single romance often lies new direction in criticism, and an enlargement of the canon of familiar texts. This essentially pragmatic approach underpins the recent growth in theoretical discussion of romance and of romances, and in such a varied genre theory needs to be continually tested by reference to new and well-informed readings. In a collection of this kind, the suggestive juxtaposition of several such papers allows for the emergence of more general observations. Together they cover a wide range, from the reality of the classical hero, Alexander, to the popularity of the legendary local hero, Bevis, from the classical sources of the medieval romance to its sixteenth- and seventeenth-century descendants. This also draws attention to the movable borders, geographical and cultural, of the study of romance. The Middle English romances cannot – certainly should not – be considered in a linguistic and cultural vacuum. Here they are placed in relation to their antecedents in Welsh and French, to sources in classical history and French romance, to their progeny amongst the romances of the Iberian peninsula.

Romance, of course, tends to deal in heroes – and one strand of the literary criticism of the last thirty years has seen the maturing and development of the hero as constituting a pattern integral to most, if not all, romances.[2] That such a pattern was still informing late Renaissance specimens of the genre can be seen from Simons's discussion of the sixteenth-century Anglo-Welsh romance *Moderatus* (by Robert Parry), whose protagonist develops from a spineless, silly courtier into a competent and courteous knight. Yet romance is also good at accommodating new interpretations of traditional heroes. Speed shows how the *Chevalier au Cygne* cycle can be reshaped to present a hero whose career exemplifies the operation of Providence in human history, an optimistic philosophy surprisingly rare amongst the romances considered here. Barron shows us an Alexander rather different from the one in the pages of Arrian, one whose historical and legendary exploits have been transferred into an alliterative poem which still celebrates the exotic and heroic but has profound reservations about the *desmesure* of its central character and his pretensions to divinity. From time to time he seems diminished into merely a cunning and daring folk-hero, more like a Reynard than a Roland. A figure comparable to Alexander, his fellow-Worthy Arthur, also receives ambivalent or downright unsympathetic treatment in several romances of the late fourteenth and the fifteenth century, some of which place king and court in the Anglo-Scots border setting of Inglewood Forest, and several of which consciously denigrate Arthur in favour of his nephew, Gawain. Rogers remarks of *The Awntyrs off Arthure*, *The Weddynge of Sir Gawen and Dame Ragnell* and *Golagros and Gawane* that 'all three poems treat Arthur with a curious mixture of praise and blame'. Allen perceives contemporary territorial struggles on the north-west borders of England and Scotland as influencing the pejorative portrait of Arthur in the *Awntyrs*. Shepherd goes further and detects the deliberate importation of degrading and risible elements by the poet of *Weddynge* in his picture of the Arthurian court, as part of an irreverent parody. If there is a 'proper' hero to be found, it is not amongst the knights at all but in the unlikely figure of the Loathly Lady, Dame Ragnell, intelligent, witty and playful.

The tale of Dame Ragnell provides one of the many examples of the intertextuality that is such a marked feature of Arthurian romances. Here source studies have been enlarged by an awareness of texts which demand to be read in their particular literary context to illuminate their full effects and achievement. For Allen, the *Awntyrs* offers a parodic inversion of the Dame Ragnell story, which Shepherd in turn argues is itself, in the *Weddynge*, an inversion, with a humorous closure exploiting the comic potential of a well-established genre. His reading of the *Weddynge*, as well as offering new suggestions as to its date and authorship, proposes a new and more respectful view of it as a careful, not careless, burlesque of aspects of other Arthurian poems like the *Awntyrs* and the *Avowynge*; it 'creatively adapts' passages of the Wife of Bath's Tale and deliberately provides false conclusions as a joke, as well as portraying a most undignified Arthur. Thus a romance previously considered a poor thing, in a defective text, is rehabilitated as a poem with a command of irony and allusion.

Rogers opens her study with a quotation from the *Weddynge*, but is less concerned with its comic aspects than with the theme she discerns running through it and two other cognate romances, the *Awntyrs* and *Golagros and Gawane*: Arthur as moral backslider, saved, counselled and shown up by a nephew superior in every way. The theme can be traced back to earlier works like the Vulgate *Merlin* and is used by the Scottish author of *Golagros* to create an imperialistic king (English by implication) greedy for land, aggressively in pursuit of unjust conquests. Romance in the fifteenth century thus offers an opportunity to examine problems of kingship, of law and of public as well as private morality. A 'black' Arthur may also be a product of the historical context in which an Arthurian romance was written and circulated. Both Rogers and Allen illumine the ways in which the issue of feudal land tenure and law become moral concerns in *Golagros* and the *Awntyrs*. Allen focuses particularly on the Border politics possibly lying behind topographical references in the *Awntyrs*: territory annexed by the English was re-appropriated by James I of Scotland when he resumed power. In its sympathetic attitude to Galeron, dispossessed by Arthur, the romance reveals itself to have been commissioned by or directed towards a powerful local family, the Nevilles, who were in alliance with James. Though seeking to identify figures and occasions of romance too closely with historical ones can be a risky and ultimately unsatisfying business, it can also serve to remind us of the long-standing claim of historicity in insular romance, first incorporated by Anglo-Norman writers and then taken over by Middle English ones, and supported by a precise sense of place. It may well be that through its local references the *Awntyrs* is, in Pearsall's words, 'drawing out a contemporary historical significance in a traditional story'. It certainly uses the story to press the broader historical reminder of the responsibilities of rule and the slipperiness of fortunes of war. Another discreditable aspect of Arthur, the Herod figure who initiates the May Day massacre in Malory's *Morte Darthur*, is investigated by Field. Such villainous behaviour seems surprisingly inconsistent with Malory's usual conception of the king and appears to be a flaw, which nevertheless is of value as a clue to the development of his work. Postulating as source a lost, fuller version of the alliterative *Morte Arthure*, Field suggests that Malory's child-murderer is a relic of the 'black' Arthur of earlier accounts. His study, like those of Rogers and of Allen, is not primarily concerned with the alliterative *Morte*, yet all three attest its importance in the development of later Arthurian romance.

The way romance eludes definition is in part caused by the multiplicity and heterogeneity of the stories it uses, offering as they do a range of structures as well as of material. Amongst the romances considered in this volume are both classical stories like that of Alexander, with its firm Aristotelian structure of beginning, middle and end, and vernacular ones like the Celtic stories, 'free' as Lloyd-Morgan puts it, of 'Aristotelian restraints'. Such tales are episodic: leading off in many directions, eventually returning, like branches, to the main tree trunk, though they can break off and become autonomous. Lloyd-Morgan compares early, multi-authored, Welsh works like the *Mabinogi* and French examples of 'branching' narrative, such as the *Roman de Renart*, also the product of several hands, and considers later, single-authored romances still using the same technique, which Vinaver characterized as 'the poetry of interlace'.[3] Speed, considering a different, many-branched group of tales, studies 'the narrative processes allowing a poem to operate independently of the cycle'. The 'branching-off' development explored by Lloyd-Morgan is here illustrated by the Middle English *Chevelere Assigne*.

If, as Lloyd-Morgan argues, the concept of the branching narrative develops separately in French and Welsh tradition, Celtic influence upon the materials of the so-called 'Breton *lai*' is undisputed. Problems of definition remain: a *lai* is often much the same as a short romance, but we are still in the realms of the episodic, since the *lai*, though usually standing alone, can refer to, or even depend upon, a larger narrative framework, as is the case with Marie de France's *Chevrefoil* or with the *Folie Tristan*. Marie uses this short and concentrated form to explore the emotional and psychological dilemmas of her heroines and heroes, often by means of powerful symbols. Middle English 'lays of Bretayn' repeat like a formula insistence on Breton origins, musical accompaniment and the nomenclature of the *lais* but in other respects are mostly far from their atmosphere and concerns. Four studies in this volume address 'lays of Bretayn': Pearsall on *Sir Orfeo*, Robson on *Emaré*, Williams on versions of *Lanval*, and Meale on *The Erle of Tolous*. *Orfeo* notably transforms Pluto and Proserpina into fairies and sets their court inside the Celtic Otherworld. Two centuries later than Marie de France, this poem seems closest to hers in its aspirations and accomplishment. Close in some ways too, if we accept Robson's reading, is *Emaré*, whose heroine can be seen as the tale's prime mover as she 'shapes events to her desired end'; the imprisoned lady in *Yonec*, who is granted lover (and finally son) through the strength of her desires, comes to mind. But *Emaré* is not, except for its cursory finale, in the least Breton, British or Celtic in material or atmosphere. The same could be said of *The Erle of Tolous*, loosely based as it is on events in the reign of the Emperor Louis the Pious. Its didactic message that, despite all provocations and trials, the sanctity of the marriage bond must be preserved also seems far from the ethos of Marie's *lais*. Emaré is a striking example of that rarity, a woman as the principal figure in a romance. Usually she is read by critics in relation to Chaucer's and Gower's Constance and to other passive victims and calumniated wives like the empress in *The Erle of Tolous*. There has, however, been a tendency in recent feminist criticism to re-read romances with new attention to the woman's role as threatening or challenging male authority.[4] So, in another example of the fluidity of romance, in its ability to sustain radically new interpretations, Robson turns the usual view of *Emaré* on its head. Her late twentieth-century feminist analysis of the 'calumniated wife' figure reveals a version of female power disguised as weakness. The masochism of the heroine is seen as a device by which she actually becomes agent rather than victim. At the end of the romance, Emaré becomes 'the dispenser of order', while appearing to conform to masculine notions of feminine behaviour. This interpretation is supported by new work currently being done on the lives of female saints, reminding us that romances do not exist in a literary vacuum.[5]

In its potentially incestuous relations between father and daughter, analysed in psychological terms by Robson, *Emaré* conforms rather well to patterns of latent 'family dramas' in romances, principally those of adolescents struggling to escape their parents. The 'family drama' of *Sir Orfeo* is concerned on the other hand with the relationship between husband and wife when one of them is afflicted with what, in modern terms, would be called 'schizophrenic alienation'. Pearsall sees the actions of Orfeo, once his wife is abducted, as a deliberate attempt to imitate her unrecognizability and her exile in order to share it, to change in order to approach and recover her. This seems a far cry from the classical story behind *Sir Orfeo*, though the interpretation may be latent in that story, and it is once again one of the strengths of romance that it can use and reinvigorate traditonal tale in this manner.

Among the *lais* discussed in this volume, it is only the English versions of the Lanval story that go directly back to Marie de France, and Williams shows us, by close comparison of the figure of the fay in the original with that in *Sir Landevale*, Thomas Chestre's *Sir Launfal* and the Percy Folio's *Sir Lambewell*, how the changing tastes of later centuries have dictated different attitudes to magic, the supernatural, and the sensuality of women. Editors and critics of romances are now less inclined than they once were to reconstruct a recension based on a hypothetical archetype, and more inclined to accept the individuality of variant texts.[6] So, here, there are fruitful insights to be gained by considering each of the English Lanval romances in its own right as conveying a different response to the story. The Middle English versions prefer their fairies less innocent, more ostentatious and glamorous, but the uneasy post-Renaissance attitude to the magical is evinced in the Percy version, which tries to suppress the fairy element and make it less voluptuous, in short to make the heroine respectable. In comparison, Marie de France's female (on several levels) text challenges, and defeats, the efforts of these English adapters, in ways which reveal the gender-based tensions of the genre in medieval and post-medieval England.

Our knowledge of the historical and cultural contexts within which romances were produced has also been much enlarged by studies of the manuscripts and printed copies which contain them. Studying the physical existence of romances, scholars are continually aware of the alarming fragility of our material evidence. The very qualities that encapsulate the appeal of romances, their fictionality, their popularity and their flexibility, were those that sent them to the margins of medieval literary culture; it is a truism of English literary history that only one manuscript of *Sir Gawain and the Green Knight* survives, against over a hundred of *The Prick of Conscience*. Studies in this volume of Malory, *Sir Orfeo*, *The Weddynge of Sir Gawen* and others serve as reminders of the arbitrary nature of the material we investigate. Yet what information can be painstakingly extracted from the surviving manuscripts all contributes to a broader picture of the conditions, scribal activity, publication, dissemination and audience that led to the existence and survival of these texts.

A group of contributions to this collection leads us to consider how romances in mixed compilations relate to other forms of narrative, and on what principles scribes may have gone about selecting them. The historical background to a manuscript, its patron, or dedicatee, and their intellectual circle, may all have a bearing on our appreciation of the romances within it. The grouping of romances in a single manuscript may lead to a reconsideration of too narrow a definition of the genre. Blanchfield's study of MS Ashmole 61 shows that placing the romances in this manuscript in their context with other narrative works reveals a compilation with a purpose. The scribe, Rate, evidently set out to assemble 'family-based' narratives with a strong moral and religious emphasis and seems to have regarded romances as no different from other works in this respect. His audience (he may have been a household chaplain in Leicestershire) presumably shared this view and perhaps also the prejudices which made him intensify the pietistic elements in one romance and introduce anti-Semitic variants into devotional texts.

We may not always gain a greater respect for scribal tastes in the process of discovering more about the manuscripts for which they were responsible, but we may for those scribes' competence. Though both Allen and Shepherd draw attention to error and defective texts much in need of correction, the studies of Meale, Huws and Thompson redress the balance by uncovering evidence of careful scribal ordering, co-operation or collaboration. In Huws's collation and analysis of the miscellany MS Porkington 10 (a.k.a. Brogyntyn II.1) he reveals the planning of the book and examines the evidence available of the cultural context of a romance text. The number of scribes at work on this miscellany offers a range of abilities and authority, from those unaware of the destination of their work, to that of the two main scribes, whose work indicates the presence of a personal taste – whether of scribe or patron – which results in, amongst other things, the inclusion of the unique text of *Syre Gawene and the Carle of Carelyle*. Enquiry into the local evidence of ownership establishes both the Welshness of the manuscript and the permeability of the Welsh border, attested also by Simons's essay.

Thompson's study and collation of MS Cotton Caligula A.ii attempts to reconstruct the processes of compilation behind it, and reveals the care with which a scribe would treat the work of an identifiable author, in this case the three romances apparently by Thomas Chestre, which are retained as a single series with a standardized visual appearance. The scribe also appears to have been experimenting with the visual layout of tail-rhyme romance. In this 'household volume' Thompson discerns the compilers' interest in current events, from the short items used as fillers. Comparison of this manuscript with other London manuscripts suggests a politically motivated revision of a poem referring to Lord Cromwell, a further indication of the socio-literary context within which romance was to be found at this date.

London seems also to have provided the milieu of the scribe, artist and readership of the sixteenth-century MS Ashmole 45. This surprisingly *de luxe* production of a romance, at a period when English romances were being far more cheaply turned out by the printing presses, is illustrated by a presentation miniature. Meale shows how this would have required careful co-ordination between scribe and artist, and perhaps the support of a stationer in consultation with the purchaser. She investigates the political and intellectual circles of the family into whose hands the manuscript fell a generation after its genesis and speculates that its unusual illustration indicates a commissioned marriage-gift from husband to wife. In this case, we would have a rare example of a woman – and, furthermore, as appears from details of the illustration, a member of the bourgeoisie – actually owning an English romance.

It was, of course, the tastes of the bourgeoisie that kept the romances going throughout the sixteenth century, despite humanist and Puritan disapproval. Some of the most popular figures in

English romance had thus necessarily to be developed and refined for later tastes in ways which seem comically at variance with their original conception. Guy of Warwick and Bevis of Hampton, though constantly disparaged by men of letters, had a vogue which extended many centuries byond their creation. Fellows demonstrates that *Bevis* was probably rewritten specifically for the press in the sixteenth century, and in the process attempts were made to modify the character of the hero who, in both Anglo-Norman and Middle English versions of the story, was a somewhat harsh and loutish figure. Against his original grain, Bevis becomes more preoccupied with honour and *largesse* and treats his mistress with unexpected tenderness. Such tinkering still leaves the atmosphere of the romance as a whole unaffected, and it continued to be extremely popular until mid-seventeenth-century taste demanded that it be completely recast, with Bevis as the perfect gentleman. By now, the matter and ethos of Middle English romance was completely alien to most readers.

The longevity of the genre was assured by its appeal to a changing audience, from the Anglo-Norman nobility down to that hybrid class detected by Simons, readers who were well-educated but still happy to read about chivalric adventures, especially if they were blended with the more refined pastoral ethos of the courtly novella made fashionable by writers like Lyly. Their less cultured cousins were presumably still enjoying the adventures of Bevis and Guy. Medieval romance survived for so long because it successfully adapted itself, in two opposite directions: it became more popular, but also more sophisticated or at least more genteel. Cheap and accessible to all in an age of print, or beautifully presented in a bespoke illustrated manuscript, it had something for everybody.

Those who know Maldwyn Mills will of course remark here that the history of popular romance does not end with the era of the chapbook but continues unabated into the present day, reappearing most robustly in those films of gothic horror that he so enjoys. We can only offer this volume to him in the hope that it will not elicit that characteristic cry: 'What new Horror is this?'

Notes

1   Barron 1987: 2–5.
2   See, e.g., Brewer 1988a: 8.

3 Vinaver 1971: ch. 5.
4 E.g. Fisher and Halley 1989.
5 Wogan-Browne 1994.
6 Fellows 1991: esp. 16.

1

The Wars of Alexander: from reality to romance

W. R. J. BARRON

The fascination of the Alexander legend is that, more than for any other medieval story-matter, the underlying reality is available to us, and the process by which it was transmuted into romance can be traced across the centuries through a multitude of versions in many languages, Eastern as well as Western. Since it flourished equally in the heroic age and in the age of romance, its transmutations may have something to teach us about the vexed question of the relationship of the epic and romance genres. An English version late in the evolutionary process and markedly neither heroic nor romantic, the alliterative *Wars of Alexander*, may suggest how the English romances, so various in kind, uneven in quality, difficult to categorize for comparative study, relate to the classic models on which our conception of the genres is based.

Between the life of Alexander (356–323 BC) and the Middle English text lie some nineteen centuries. The life is richly documented. Through our historical sources for Philip of Macedon's reign, we know something of the youth of Alexander, his tutoring by Aristotle and his early military career. But his great adventure of world conquest was recorded in detail by a number of eye-witnesses: by Callisthenes, Aristotle's nephew and pupil, keeper of the official record unfortunately broken off by his execution for treason; in personal memoirs by Ptolemy, one of Alexander's generals and future ruler of Egypt; by Nearchus, his admiral, and Onesicritus, his helmsman; and by Aristobulus, an engineer in his train. Their accounts and the verbal evidence of other eye-witnesses were used by the Alexandrian historian Cleitarchus, a near-contemporary. Only fragments of these primary accounts survive; the extant histories were not written until three to five centuries after Alexander's death. Of these, modern scholars have preferred the Greek

Alexandri anabasis of Flavius Arrianus Xenophon, governor of Cappadocia under Hadrian early in the second century AD. He is often at odds with his near-contemporary Plutarch and the other classical historians who represent the vulgate tradition stemming from Cleitarchus – notably Quintus Curtius Rufus, who wrote under Augustus in the first century AD. Both traditions claim to draw on eye-witness accounts; often when two eye-witnesses are cited on the same event they disagree. Reality is a hard bird to snare![1]

The bald facts of Alexander's life are so incredible that it would not be surprising if they encouraged fantasies. The eye-witnesses were interested not in the fantasy of the great adventure but in the political reality of a world-conqueror whose posthumous reputation they sought to enhance or denigrate in the political in-fighting over the division of his vast empire. Each projected the Alexander in whom he wanted to believe; and no doubt they believed they had seen what they wanted to see. As politics faded into legend, each age remade Alexander in the image of its needs, its interests, its ideals, its morality, and Alexander took his place among the Nine Worthies as a universal icon. The vital force in that process was the charisma of the hero – whether seen historically as a leader of men driven by a vision of a new world-order, a romantic adventurer seeking personal glory in exotic realms, a demi-god struck down in his hour of triumph, or an exemplar of aspiring and fallible man falling from the wheel of Fortune.

The medieval tradition of the Alexander legend derives only very indirectly from the classical tradition, through the Greek prose pseudo-Callisthenes compiled by a native of Alexandria in the third century AD, partly from literary sources and partly from Egyptian popular tradition. This haphazard compilation, diversified in various recensions, was given a degree of academic respectability and a wide currency in a number of Latin translations, notably that by Julius Valerius (*c.* AD 320) and the *Historia de preliis Alexandri Magni* of Leo, archpresbyter of Naples (*c.* 950). French writers seized on both in the first years of the twelfth century, their early versions being ultimately amalgamated in the massive *Roman d'Alexandre*, by Alexandre de Paris, where the hero is presented as the embodiment of chivalric ideals. In the second half of the twelfth century, the Anglo-Norman poet Thomas of Kent went back to an epitome of Julius Valerius, the earliest Latin version of the pseudo-

Callisthenes, for the main source of his *Roman de toute chevalerie*. Other vernacular versions carried the legend of Alexander, already widespread in Asia and Africa, all over Europe. In the tradition they represent, Alexander is portrayed as charismatic leader, epic warrior, courtly prince, ideal ruler, emphasis shifting with the audience for which each version was prepared.[2]

But there was another tradition, which moralized the legend as the pseudo-Callisthenes tradition was progressively romanticized. It was rooted in the pro and anti factions in Greece, even within Alexander's army, in the contention for fragments of his empire after his death (each faction glorifying or vilifying his achievements in their assaults on each other) and in the inevitable backlash against his giant reputation as the reality on which it was based faded from memory. Certain aspects of his career laid him open to criticism: his absolute authority, essential in a campaign of thousands of miles into unknown and hostile territory, resulting in the torture and execution of those accused – justly in some cases – of treason against him; his all-night drinking parties, part of the Greek tradition of solidarity between military comrades, in the course of which he murdered one of his closest friends and insulted others; his multiple, political marriages, which led to accusations of sexual excess; his adoption of some of the administrative structures and cultural usages of his captured territories, in furtherance of an internationalism which would unite East and West, which led Greeks to see him as corrupted by barbarian values. The Stoic philosophers judged him as either fundamentally weak or bad, attributing his prosperity to Fortune, his downfall to excesses caused by the effects of absolute power upon a weak personality. Medieval moralists, whose admiration for Aristotle and his pupil Callisthenes, executed by Alexander, predisposed them to accept the denunciations of Diogenes and Seneca and later the Fathers of the Church, merely substituted for Fortune the power of God to raise him and cast him down.

The variety of forms in which the Alexander legend exists rules out the possibility of tracing the process of romanticization and moralization stage by stage across the centuries. But by contrasting an early stage, Arrian's history, which represents a conscious attempt to determine the facts of Alexander's life by critical comparison of the available records, with a comparatively late, popular, to some degree degenerate version in *The Wars of Alexander*, more of the process may become apparent. It is already far advanced in

Leo's *Historia de preliis*, of which the *Wars* gives a faithful, though incomplete, version in some 5,600 lines, made sometime in the century before 1450, elaborating battle passages, extrapolating expressions of feeling, and displaying occasional verbal vividness which suggests that the material was imaginatively realized, not merely translated.[3] Despite its division into books in the classical manner, the narrative shows little sense of temporal or geographical sequence, switching erratically from region to region, from one stage of Alexander's career to another. Other medieval versions are similarly casual in sequence, the incoherence apparently originating with the pseudo-Callisthenes. Episodes in Alexander's life were often treated as emblematic of stages in the heroic career paralleled in the lives of other heroes of legend, literature, even folklore. I have chosen here only some of the most characteristic.

Arrian acknowledges Philip of Macedon and his wife Olympias as Alexander's parents; but when, during his conquest of Egypt, he visits the shrine of Jupiter Ammon to consult the oracle said to have been consulted by Perseus and Heracles, Arrian comments: 'Alexander longed to equal the fame of Perseus and Heracles; the blood of both flowed in his veins, and just as legend traced their descent from Zeus, so he, too, had a feeling that in some way he was descended from Ammon' (93).[4] Arrian is merely acknowledging contemporary beliefs which made little distinction between claims of descent from a hero, a demi-god or a god. Plutarch repeats a story that Philip spied on Olympias in bed with Jupiter Ammon in the form of a snake. Some historians say Ammon acknowledged his son; Arrian leaves it uncertain. The modern mind inevitably wonders whether Alexander himself believed in his divine ancestry – the source, perhaps, of his superb self-confidence – or merely encouraged popular belief as an instrument of policy.

In the alliterative poem, Alexander is fathered by Anectanabos, king of Egypt, who, foreseeing by necromancy the Persian conquest of his country, flees, disguised as a 'clerk', to Macedon. The god Serapis promises that Anectanabos will avenge Egypt's defeat by eventually returning as a young conqueror. At Alexander's birth, earthquakes and other prodigies mark the advent of a hero, and Philip accepts him as his son. His heroic stature is shown by the rapidity with which he learns from Aristotle – 'In foure or in fyfe ȝere he ferre was in lare / Þan othire at had bene þare elleuyn wyntir' (633–4)[5] – and the rumbustious way he treats any other teacher: 'Him wald he kenely on þe croune knok with his tablis' (639). At 11 he surpasses all in practice of arms. When Anectanabos, asked what he sees in the stars, says that he foresees his own death at the hands of his son, Alexander pushes him into a ditch to disprove prophecy – and so fulfils it! Later Ammon gives him advice in dreams.

A historical figure inspired to emulate the heroes and demi-gods from whom he claims descent! From our perspective, the overtones are those of epic, of combatants before the walls of Troy watched over by protective deities, Achilles provided with new arms through the agency of his goddess mother. In the *Wars* we have a royal shape-shifter posing as a 'scholar' of the black arts, a prophet who creates expectation of a divine lover, fulfils it himself and prophesies the birth of a conqueror who is to reincarnate and avenge him. It sounds like medieval romanticization of the original idea; but the Anectanabos episode originates with the pseudo-Callisthenes in third-century Alexandria, and the spirit is that of Greek romance. There has been a shift of values, but those of the pseudo-Callisthenes are no less real by the standards of the age. The English poet, whether or not he fully appreciated the values, has preserved the central idea of a precocious boy mysteriously sired by a deity, without showing undue interest in the element of necromancy, or contempt for the pagan beliefs involved.

But he is less perceptive in his appreciation of the influence of Alexander's belief in his divine or semi-divine nature upon his assumption of his heroic role. Arrian records the self-consciousness with which he associated himself with the heroes and demi-gods of Greek tradition. On crossing the Hellespont into Asia, Alexander marched to Troy, and there 'offered sacrifice to Athena, patron goddess of the city; here he made a gift of his armour to the temple, and took in exchange, from where they hung on the temple walls, some weapons which were still preserved from the Trojan war' (36). Whether or not he saw himself as a successor to earlier Greek heroes battling against an Asian power, legend quickly cast him in that role, having him offer sacrifice on the tomb of the first Greek to set foot on Asian soil in the Trojan war, to ensure better luck in his own mission (35–6). Emulation of earlier heroes is given as an explanation of some of his most difficult feats, such as the march from India to Persia along the waterless coast of modern Pakistan, where earlier invaders of India (Semiramis and Cyrus), had lost all but a handful of their forces. When his followers force him to turn back in the headwaters of the Punjab, he says: 'Are you not aware that if Heracles, my ancestor, had gone no further than Tiryns or Argos ... he would never have won the glory which changed him from a man into a god, actual or apparent?' (188-9). The English Alexander, by contrast, seems embarrassed by suggestions of his divinity, preferring to emphasize his inherent ability. When the oracle of Apollo hails him as Heracles he denies the claim (2300-15). When he succeeds Darius, and the Persians hail him as a god, he replies: 'Feyne of ȝoure wordis! / I am a coruptible kyng & of clay fourmed!' (3586-7).

The English poet recognized the value of the grand gesture in establishing heroic status, but provides an interesting contrast to the hero-test recorded in Arrian. When Alexander is faced at the outset of his Asian conquests with the Gordian Knot, divinely contrived as proof that the man who can unfasten the yoke from the cart is destined to be lord of Asia, Arrian records: 'Some say that Alexander cut the knot with a stroke of his sword and exclaimed "I have undone it!", but Aristobulus thinks that he took out the pin – a sort of wooden peg which was driven right through the shaft of the wagon and held the knot together – and thus pulled the yoke away from the shaft' (63). So already in Arrian there are conflicting accounts of a key episode, suggesting contrasting clues to Alexander's personality. The nature of the Gordian Knot puzzled later ages, when wagons were differently yoked, so other hero-tests were substituted. In the *Wars* it is the taming of Bucephalus, a fierce beast no one could ride in Plutarch and Arrian, but which kneels to let Alexander mount. The English version takes naive pleasure in elaborating the taming episode: the wild horse is fed on the flesh of criminals; Alexander, passing its cage, is struck by the half-gnawed corpses lying about and puts in his hand; Bucephalus licks it and kneels in homage, leading Philip to predict that the boy will succeed him. So, despite the naivety of the treatment, the function of the hero-test in revealing potential greatness survives, but the qualities revealed are those of the popular hero whose innocent fearlessness wins the attachment of a helpful beast. The essential interest of the element, and the grotesque details, go back to the pseudo-Callisthenes. Note how the kneeling of the horse has survived, reinterpreted in function and meaning.

The hero's confidence under test is a sign of his belief in his status as demi-god. Other signs, in the case of the historical Alexander, included his trust in portents, such as an eclipse of the moon portending victory within the month. His reaction to unusual phenomena suggests that he sees them as manifestations of divine favour, but his piety is combined with pragmatism: when the omens are unfavourable for an assault on the Scythians, he ultimately overrules the seers and gives the signal for attack; and he tacitly accepts the seers' suggestion that his murder of his comrade Cleitus in drunken rage was due to his neglect to sacrifice to Dionysus, though without attempting to deny his personal guilt.

Such manifestations of pagan belief seem bound to attract the disapproval of medieval moralists. But some could be harmonized with aspects of their own system of belief, such as the conception of dreams as divinely inspired for human guidance. So in the *Wars*, when Alexander, in despair at the stubborn resistance of Tyre, dreams that he holds a ripe grape yielding much wine, a clerk foretells victory. The general ambivalence of the moralists was shared by the theologians, whose mystical interpretation of biblical history tended to reduce great figures of the past to symbolic types. Their view of Alexander, coloured by the historical account of him in Maccabees and extrapolated from prophetic allusions in Daniel, was as the foreordained destroyer of Persia and predecessor of the Seleucid Antiochus, oppressor of the Jews, the type of Antichrist. Their disapproval largely obliterated the comparatively favourable view by the Jewish historian Josephus, who invented a dream in which God promised Alexander that he should conquer the Persian empire, and detailed the reverence he paid to God's high-priest when he made sacrifice in the Temple of Jerusalem. Augustine interpreted Alexander's reverence as an attempt to add Jehovah to his polytheistic pantheon, while others attributed his respect for the city as due to divinely inspired awe of a holy place – evidence of God's omnipotence over tyrants.

The Jerusalem episode, invented by Josephus, features in the *Wars*, where Alexander demands aid from the bishop of Jerusalem in the siege of Tyre, is refused and marches on Jerusalem. Angels advise that he be received as victor, and the ceremonies of welcome include many Christian features. Alexander kneels before the mitred bishop to honour the God who has once appeared to him in sleep similarly attired, is shown in the Temple Daniel's prophecy that the Greeks should destroy the Persians, and offers a boon to the bishop, who asks leave to continue in his own faith and that the Persians shall become Jews also. The blurring of Jewish and Christian traditions casts Alexander in the role of the benevolent pagan, without pressing the issue of his spiritual status to the point of open disapproval.

So much for the nature of the hero; now for the hero in action. So far as personal prowess is concerned, Alexander appears in Arrian like some archetypal hero of epic: 'an unmistakable figure in magnificent armour, attended by his suite with an almost ecstatic reverence' (39). Alexander's instinct is always to engage the enemy leaders, and, centuries after the event, Arrian records their hand-to-hand encounters in terms which Homer might have used of Hector and Achilles, or Virgil of Aeneas and Turnus. And there are signs that Alexander was conscious of and cultivated the heroic parallels. His personal heroism was part of his charisma, inspiring and shaming his followers.

In all courtly versions of the legend, Alexander's personal prowess bulks large, but in the alliterative text it has diminished in scale and in heroic character. When Alexander, aged 12, invades the Peloponnesus, King Nicholas spits in his face; in hand-to-hand combat of great alliterative violence, Alexander cuts off his head and wins general submission. But his valour is more often displayed in less epic fashion: he ventures alone into Darius' camp, at supper thrice secretes the golden cup set before him, and when recognized rides off in triumph, having spoiled the Philistines. When Alexander, only three cubits tall, is challenged to single combat by the Indian king Porus, six cubits, he kills him. (Alexander was in fact below average height, Porus over seven feet tall; they became allies after the king's defeat.) The legend has been transmuted with overtones of Tom Thumb or Jack-the-Giant-Killer, of the folk-hero using wit and daring as much as valour.

There is a similar contrast in oratory, vital faculty of the epic hero as courtly conversation is of the romantic hero. Alexander's speeches are an important part of his leadership: on the eve of a battle he speaks to his officers politically and tactically, to the men bluntly and emotively. The English Alexander is briefer, his oratory characterized by the wit of a folk-hero, using alliterative proverbs which ridicule the pretensions of his enemies, as when he rejects Darius' demand for tribute:

> For sais ȝour lord, þe lefe hen þat laide hire first egg,
> Hire bodi nowe with barante is barely consumed,
> And is Darius so of his dett duly depryued.
>
> (1016–18)

Oratory is an adjunct of the hero's charisma, his power over those around him; but the natural world is a challenge not susceptible to his control. Penetrating into regions remote from the Mediterranean world, Alexander encountered all sorts of natural wonders – such as a desert stream which, without visible rainfall, became a raging torrent in a few moments, sweeping away his camp; all have natural explanations, which Alexander sought as he sought the sources of rivers, made special voyages to study the estuaries of the Indus, Tigris and Euphrates, exported Asian oxen to Greece to improve the native breed, and freely admitted his mistake in thinking the Indus the source of the Nile because both had crocodiles in them. His motivation was akin to that of the scientific discoverer; but Arrian recognized that the fantastic facts, especially of the wonders of India, licensed the fabulists of that and later ages to invent travellers' tales, 'in the belief that none of the absurd stories they tell about India are likely to be brought to the test of truth' (166).

In the *Wars* it is the spirit of the fabulist that dominates rather than that of the scientist. The natural wonders in Arrian are sometimes worked into the plot: Alexander is able to cross the River Granton (Arrian's Granicus) at night because it is frozen then, even in summer, but it breaks up under the fleeing Persian forces, drowning 300,000 of them – the alliterative poet is always generous with numbers! In India Alexander's men are plagued by heat, thirst, 'crabbid snakis, / And oþire warlaȝes wild' (3922–3), but Alexander shows little interest in them except as military hazards. In India he sees an uncouth beast with a head like a horse, catches him by using a naked virgin and burns him to death – hardly a scientific attitude! Encountering a basilisk, he sets a mirror before it, causing it to kill itself. Reaching the Red Sea, he ascends in an iron chair raised by four griffins and descends into the sea in a glass box. These famous incidents, repeatedly elaborated, even moralized – the celestial journey, for instance, typifying Alexander's aspiring pride - are treated in the English version simply as exotic adventures reduced, like all the wonders of the East, to a romantic gloss. In historical accounts such wonders typify the unknown regions to be conquered and the dangers to be faced in the pursuit of the imperial dream. The solid substance of that dream is the cities founded by Alexander, some seventy of them, from the Egyptian Alexandria, a centre of world civilization, to Alexandria the Furthest and other lost sites beyond Samarkand. Though he did not reach the great Eastern Ocean of his imagination, the extent of Alexander's conquest was unparalleled, its cohesion rooted in his conception of the marriage of East and West, a fusion of races and cultures which he began by appointing native leaders to offices of trust, by marrying Greeks to Asian women, recruiting Persian youths into his army, adopting Persian dress and the custom of prostration - revolutionary ideas in which, ironically, lay the future dissolution of his empire.

The *Wars* initially acknowledges the imperial dream when Alexander announces, on assuming the crown of Macedon, that all nations shall serve him (1114-17); thereafter it is alluded to only in passing. Writing for a provincial English audience whose sense of world geography and classical history was no doubt as vague as his own, the alliterative poet could hardly be expected to make much of an imperial concept so different in scale and structure from the familiar feudal state; or, in an age when the Islamic threat still persisted, to approve a fusion of Eastern and Western cultures. Yet the shadow of Alexander's vision still faintly persists.

Interracial marriage was designed to be a key factor in turning that dream into reality. At the great multiple wedding at Susa which symbolized the union of East and West, Alexander himself married a daughter, no longer young, of the dead Darius - the whole context suggests marriages of policy rather than affection, though his earliest marriage with Roxane, daughter of a minor Bactrian chieftain, history interpreted as a love-match (148). In general, Alexander's relations with women seem to have been based on respect, as when he appointed a woman governor of a province where female rule was traditional, or dismissed a party of Amazons to prevent them being abused by his troops.

Not a whisper of romance as we or medieval courtly literature understand it; marriage as a dynastic factor sounds more like the feudal reality against which the *roman courtois* reacted. Quintus

Curtius shows Alexander, corrupted by oriental influences, gradually slipping into sexual licence, and the anti-Alexander faction accused him of every form of lechery. With the coming of *amour courtois* a more positive treatment was felt necessary, and the episode chosen was that of the non-historical Queen Candace, who, enamoured of Alexander, manoeuvres him into embarrassing and dangerous situations. In courtly versions their love is mutual, and in one Alexander's celestial journey ends when the griffin car lands in the grounds of her palace, with the inevitable sequel. This was more than even some authors of romance could stomach: the Spanish *Libro de Alexandre* omits it, while Thomas of Kent's *Roman de toute chevalerie* makes Alexander the plaything of a designing woman and adds a sermon on the wiles of her sex. The English poem avoids romance by its preoccupation with plot and machinery, such as Candace's revolving boudoir. The effect is of *roman d'aventure* rather than *roman courtois*.

For the historical Alexander the most vital relationship seems to have been with male comrades, from the beloved Hephaestion to the many common soldiers he knew by name. His relationship with Hephaestion draws no more comment from Arrian than other homosexual affairs noted for their political rather than their personal significance; but he approves the trust that led Alexander to hand his physician Philip the letter he had received accusing him of plotting to poison the king and, while he read it, drink the medicine Philip had just given him. Arrian states that 'Alexander was always capable of putting himself on a footing of equality and comradeship with his subordinates' (229); but their failure to support him when his troops revolted, and the violence to which their drinking-bouts increasingly led, signalled the collapse of the unique fusion of aristocratic structure and democratic spirit on which Alexander's remarkable achievements rested.

One has only to think of Arthur's relationship to the Round Table company, or Charlemagne's to his *douzepers*, to see how the triumph and collapse of Alexander's military brotherhood might have appealed to writers of either epic or romance. The *Wars* begins promisingly when, after taming Bucephalus, Alexander claims his own establishment and chooses twelve boys as his lieutenants (817–18), but thereafter Alexander dominates almost to the exclusion of his comrades. The episode of Philip the doctor remains, however – no doubt because such a display of trust between leader and follower remained meaningful.

In both epic and romance the hero is often in rivalry with himself, the loftiness of his aspirations courting the danger of excess, of *demesure* or *ofermode*. Significantly, Arrian saw Alexander as 'to an extraordinary degree, the slave of ambition' (226) and commented: 'In drink, too, he ... tended to barbaric excess' (134-6). The question of when enough is enough became crucial in India, when Alexander insisted on pressing on eastward despite the resistance of his men, one of whom advised: 'Sir, if there is one thing above all others a successful man should know, it is *when to stop*' (191). The English Alexander shows no moderation in military matters, destroying the city of Thebes with the utmost ferocity, but draws no disapproval from the poet – who nonetheless treats fully the debate on worldly values. Meeting the Gymnosophists, Alexander pities their poverty and offers them whatever they wish – they choose immortality, reminding the conqueror of his own mortality. He says his spirit is stirred by a higher spirit, as the sea by winds (4148-95).

To the moralists, the suddenness with which Alexander was struck down at the height of his triumph demonstrated the transience of worldly glory. But to his contemporaries his death in Babylon at the age of 32, possibly from typhoid, had heroic overtones. His farewell to his followers (253) was one of the great emotional scenes of history, and his heroic charisma surrounded his death with elements of mythology – warnings from Chaldaean seers not to enter Babylon, ominous portents – almost before his body was cold. Arrian's conclusion mingles historical and mythical components of the emerging hero-legend (256), sugggesting that, like his birth, his death was not that of an ordinary mortal.

In the *Wars*, Alexander meets late in his career a phoenix, which foretells that he will live one year and eight months more; it will not say who will kill him. Alexander weeps and laments. Both manuscripts of the *Wars* are incomplete; but in the poem's source, the *Historia de preliis,* Alexander, poisoned by Antipater, attempts to drown himself, giving instructions for the future of his unborn child by Roxane and dividing his empire among his followers; his death is attended by portents. The survival of the political realities – including the poisoning, of which contemporaries were convinced – is remarkable at such a distance in time. But the moralists have the last word: on seeing his golden tomb at Alexandria, philosophers comment on the transitory nature of his achievements and the vanity of human aspirations.

As a world-conqueror struck down at the height of his achievement, Alexander took his place among the Nine Worthies on the wheel of Fortune. Even in his own age the knowledge that he and his enterprises were fated gave a legendary perspective to historical accounts. Arrian, commenting on a conflict of evidence, regrets the power of myth to transform fact (203), and that Alexander had no Homer to fix his legend for all time (36). In the *Wars* the shadow of the wheel of Fortune is cast upon the narrative from the beginning. Mocked by Darius as a child, Alexander reminds him of the swiftness with which it can turn. And at the point of death Darius turns the warning upon him, for God wills that pride should have a fall:

> Me þink my lyfe as to þe len3th is like to þis werkis,
> þat þis coppis opon kellwyse knytt in þe wo3es;
> With þe lest winde of þe werd þat þe web touches,
> þe note anentes ilk ane & all to no3t worthis. (3428–31)

Here, too, poetic fame is seen as impervious to Fortune (2246–7).

In Aristotelian terms Alexander's life is itself romance: superior abilities achieving superb feats but without being able to avoid ultimate failure or those flaws and excesses that draw the criticism of lesser men – history poised, like romance, between myth and mimesis.[6] But it was a life lived under the influence of myth and legend, if classical accounts of the extent to which Alexander modelled himself on Greek demi-gods and heroes are accurate. The readiness with which his self-projection was accepted by his biographers no doubt reflects the extent to which eye-witnesses were subject to the same influences. The values expressed, fundamentally heroic, remain valid over the centuries, progressively intermingled with elements of fantasy, exoticism and didacticism. In the *Wars* heroic values have begun to fade, superseded by the wit and daring of the folk-hero. The genre characteristics of *roman courtois* are merely incidental, but the persistence of the romance mode from life to a form of literature remote in time, milieu, and manner of expression is demonstrated by the survival of key episodes in which its essence is expressed in human terms.

A last example. When his forces were dying of thirst in the desert, soldiers found a trickle of water and brought it to Alexander in a helmet; he poured it away. Arrian comments: 'So extraordinary was the effect of this action that the water wasted by Alexander was as good as a drink for every man in the army' (218–19). Homerized, I take it, this would be a scene in epic, an heroic act symbolizing powers of leadership by example. But it survives, unchanged in content or meaning, in the homely diction of the *Wars*, as the 'litill drysnynge of dewe was droppid fra þe heuen' refused by Alexander even to save his own life when others, Macedonians *and* Persians, must die of thirst:

> þan slike a comfurth þam enclosed for his kynd wordis
> As all þe water of þe werd ware in þaire wambs hellid.
> (3940—1)

Notes

1 On the sources of the Alexander legend, see Merkelbach 1954; on the relationship of Arrian to the other 'historical' accounts of Alexander's life, see Bosworth 1988.
2 The astonishing diffusion of the Alexander legend during the Middle Ages is recorded in Cary 1956, a remarkable book, to which I am much indebted.
3 The source of the *Wars* was, according to Cary and the most recent editors (see below n. 5), some text of the I³ recension of the *Historia de preliis*. Only one episode (1628–99), describing Alexander's encounter with the high-priest of the Jews, has no counterpart in the *Historia*.
4 References to Arrian are to the excellent and accessible translation by de Sélincourt (1958).
5 References to the *Wars* are to Duggan and Turville-Petre 1989.
6 Aristotle's classifications in the *Poetics* are helpfully discussed in Frye 1957, and briefly outlined in relation to medieval romance in Barron 1987.

2

The branching tree of medieval narrative: Welsh *cainc* and French *branche*

CERIDWEN LLOYD-MORGAN

Both Welsh *cainc* and French *branche*, meaning literally a branch of a tree, were used during the Middle Ages to refer to a narrative or part of one. In this paper I propose to explore the meaning and usage of the term in each literary tradition, with particular reference to romance, and to attempt to establish whether or not, in view of the evidence for other types of literary cross-fertilization between France and Wales, there is any connection between the two.

In Welsh one of the earliest examples of the word *cainc* occurs in Llyfr Du o'r Waun, the Black Book of Chirk (Aberystwyth, National Library of Wales, MS Peniarth 29), copied in the mid-thirteenth century from an earlier exemplar.[1] Here *cainc* appears with its literal meaning: 'traws*keyg* a kerho o kallon e pren' ('a crossbranch grows out from the heart of the tree'). Both the older singular form, *keyg*, and the later *cangen*, derived by back-formation from the plural *cangeu*, are attested from the thirteenth century in texts of the Welsh Laws, in the portions relating to the value of different kinds of trees, so that there is no doubt that the meaning is the literal one of the branch of a tree.[2] But a figurative meaning, the idea of a part or division of something less concrete than a tree, seems to have soon developed, one of the earliest examples being *Pedeir Keinc y Mabinogi*, the Four Branches of the *Mabinogi*, the title given to a group of four early Middle Welsh tales.[3] Although the dating of these tales is still uncertain, dates in the eleventh and twelfth centuries have been suggested for them in their present form.

The Four Branches are comprehensible as separate narratives but they are linked by their closing formulae, which indicate that each is in fact part of a larger whole:

Ac yuelly y teruyna y geing hon yma o'r Mabynnogyon. (p. 27)
A llyna ual y teruyna y geing honn o'r Mabinyogi. (p. 48)
Ac yuelly y teruyna y geing honn yma o'r Mabinogy. (p. 65)
Ac yuelly y teruyna y geing honn o'r Mabinogi. (p. 92)

And so ends this present branch of the *Mabinogion*.
And this is how this branch of the *Mabinogi* ends.
And so ends this present branch of the *Mabinogi*.
And so ends this branch of the *Mabinogi*.

The problem of whether this *Mabinogi*, the whole to which the individual *ceinciau* or branches belong, was made up of these same four branches as we know them, or whether, and to what extent, they have evolved away from their original shape, is still a subject of debate. As early as 1928, W. J. Gruffydd noted the significance of the word *cainc* here, and used it to support his hypothetical reconstruction of the original form of the *Pedeir Keinc*: 'the term *cainc* supposes that the mabinogi is one whole dealing with the life of one hero, but divided into different episodes called "branches" which are in themselves complete'.[4] More recently, Dr Sioned Davies has suggested that the number of branches of the *Mabinogi* need not have always been four, and, stressing the evidence for oral delivery of the tales, speculates as to a possible connection with another semantic field of *cainc*, namely a song or tune, a usage attested from at least the fourteenth century.[5]

However, it is not the archaeology of specific texts that concerns us here, but, instead, the literary implications of *cainc* and its semantic equivalents. Nonetheless, the use of the closing formulae quoted above shows that *Pedeir Keinc y Mabinogi*, at one period of their history at least, were considered to be parts of a whole, four branches of a single 'tree', whether they were added by a single final redactor, whose work lies behind the two main manuscript versions preserved in Llyfr Gwyn Rhydderch, the White Book of Rhydderch (Aberystwyth, National Library of Wales, MS Peniarth 4-5) and the Llyfr Coch o Hergest, the Red Book of Hergest (Oxford, Bodleian Library, MS Jesus College 111), or whether they belong to an earlier stage of development, when the tales may have existed in a rather different form.

The image suggested by *cainc* is that of a tree, and such an image is a particularly appropriate one within the context of Middle Welsh prose tales, since these tend to present a number of episodes or narrative sequences leading off from a main narrative 'trunk' to which they may not always return but to which they can be traced back.[6] The image of the tree represents the untrammelled narrative development, free of Aristotelian restraints, that is so characteristic of early Welsh prose tales. Nonetheless, it is in the *Pedeir Keinc*, and there alone, that *cainc* is used *explicitly* within a text to describe its divisions, though in neither of the main manuscript versions is the term used to describe the four sections seen as a unit: *Pedeir Keinc y Mabinogi* is, in fact, a modern title which does not occur in the medieval manuscripts. By contrast to this modern usage, the mid-thirteenth century White Book gives no general title at all, whilst the Red Book of Hergest simply prefaces the first branch with 'llyma dechreu mabinogi' ('here is the beginning of the *Mabinogi*') (col. 710). As Ifor Williams noted, of the other tales in the Red Book and White Book which together are now conveniently if inaccurately described as the 'Mabinogion', each has a closing formula not unlike those used in the *Mabinogi* proper, but they consistently avoid the use of *cainc*.[7] Instead, more general terms denoting 'story', such as *chwedyl* or *ystorya*, are employed. It is clear that the word *cainc*, like *mabinogi*, helped to set *Pedeir Keinc y Mabinogi* apart from the other prose tales. Whereas the latter were seen as individually autonomous, despite sharing some characters or motifs, the *Pedeir Keinc* were apparently perceived as four related tales to be taken together. It is significant that, whilst the order of the other tales varies from the White Book to the Red, the order of these four stories is respected.

Since the term *cainc* does seem peculiarly appropriate for describing the narrative structure of other Welsh prose tales, it is striking that it is not used in any remotely similar *literary* context anywhere else in the corpus of Middle Welsh prose narrative. Other figurative uses of *cainc* do occur, however, and not only in the musical field already mentioned. The phrase *keingev caryat* ('branches of love') is found in a mid-fourteenth-century manuscript of religious prose, *Llyvyr Agkyr Llandewivrevi*, the Book of the Anchorite of Llanddewibrefi (now Oxford, Bodleian Library, MS Jesus College 119).[8] Around 1400, in *Gramagedau'r Penceirddiaid*, where the art of poetry is codified, *cainc* is used repeatedly in a series of triads. *Cerdd dafod*, poetry, is thus divided into three 'branches': 'Teir keing yssyd o gerd dafawt, nyt amgen, klerwryaeth, teulwryaeth a prydydyaeth' ('There are three branches of *cerdd dafod*, namely *klerwryaeth, teulwryaeth* and *prydydyaeth*'). Each of these three branches within *cerdd dafod* is then subdivided into three further branches.[9] In each of these instances the 'branch' refers to a part or division of a larger whole. But if, despite the existence of such figurative usage outside the narrative tradition, *cainc* was not used in any of the Middle Welsh tales apart from the *Mabinogi*, it could be because this usage had already become archaic, or because no other group of texts possessed the same relationship, the same degree of narrative overlap between them, however restricted that continuity may be in the *Pedeir Keinc* themselves. It is true that today the tales of *Peredur, Owein* and *Gereint* are usually grouped together, and often described as the 'three romances', but this is a purely modern practice, resulting from a recognition that these tales correspond to three *romans* by Chrétien de Troyes, and neither this misleading title nor even the grouping of them has any basis whatsoever in the manuscripts themselves. In the White Book, *Peredur* is separated from *Owein* by *Breudwyt Macsen Wledig* and *Lludd a Llefelys*; and the Triads, saints' lives and poetry intervene between *Owein* and *Gereint*.[10] In the compiling of so important a medieval compendium as the White Book, then, these three texts, despite their having in common an Arthurian setting and possible French influence, were not regarded as an obvious group. Similarly, in the Red Book of Hergest, although *Peredur* follows on from *Owein, Breudwyt Maxen, Lludd a Llefelys* and the *Pedeir Keinc* then intervene before we reach *Gereint*.

If there is no other group of Middle Welsh tales comparable with *Pedeir Keinc y Mabinogi*, nor do we have any single native text long enough to allow of division into 'branches'. Certain major textual divisions can be found in the longer of the surviving texts, in *Owein* and *Peredur* for example. In the former, a break occurs between the conclusion of the tale of the lady of the fountain and the final section concerned with the Du Traws, and this break is emphasized in the Red Book by beginning a new paragraph with a large initial,[11] whilst in the White Book version of *Peredur* there are two major breaks noted in this way.[12] However, in both these texts, although the sections created by these breaks are linked only loosely with the preceding or following episodes, such sections still form an integral part of a single narrative about one principal hero. Thus the relationship between the various sections within each text is quite different to that between individual branches of the *Mabinogi*, where, in their present form, each branch focuses on a separate character or small group of characters, even if there may be some slight overlap or cross-referencing.

Although redactors of Middle Welsh prose narrative apparently avoided the use of *cainc* outside *Pedeir Keinc y Mabinogi*, equivalent terms are found in other Western European literatures. As a textual division, however, its use seems largely confined to France. I have been unable to trace any comparable examples in the literatures of Wales's closest neighbours, Ireland and England, with whom close contact and cross-fertilization might be expected. Turning to continental Europe, I have found no evidence of this usage in the Spanish or Italian traditions, but in Germany an isolated example appears in Wolfram von Eschenbach's *Parzival*. At the end of book xiii he states: 'an den rehten *stam* diz maere ist komen',[13] where *stam* clearly refers to the main 'trunk' of the narrative, to which Wolfram is about to return. In other words, although the term is semantically different from *cainc*, the image is still that of a tree. Nevertheless, Wolfram is referring only to different parts of a single narrative; the phrase quoted above is a transition formula drawing the audience's attention not only to the end of one portion of the narrative but also to the shift back to the main focus of the story.

Apart from such isolated examples, the use of tree imagery descriptive of literary structure appears to be rare in Western European tradition outside France. There, by contrast, *branche* is employed extensively, from the mid-twelfth century onwards. One of the earliest examples occurs in the *Roman de Thèbes*, composed *c*. 1165. A colophon to one of the surviving manuscripts, Paris, Bibliothèque Nationale, MS f. fr. 375, reads: '*Explicit* li sieges de Tebes et de Thioclet et de Pollinices li tierce branke.'[14] A similar *explicit* occurs at the end of the mid-twelfth-century *Roman de Troie*, which follows the *Roman de Thèbes* in the same manuscript: 'Ci faut de Troies et de Thebes li quarte [branke] et puis li sieges d'Ataines.'[15] For the scribe of this manuscript, Perrot de Nesle, a *branke* seems to have signified one text in a compendium. Although the texts in question may have affinities, inasmuch as the *Roman de Thèbes* and the *Roman de Troie* are based, albeit freely, on Latin sources, and have a similar setting and mood, the links between them are far less close than those between the branches of the *Mabinogi*. Although the *romans d'antiquité*, including these two, were regarded as a group even as early as the late twelfth century, by the poet Jehan Bodel, this was because of their setting in a classical past, which distinguished them from the other two major groups in contemporary French literature, the *chansons de geste*, with their French heroic background, and the Arthurian romances of the *matière de Bretagne*.[16]

Another early, and extremely well-known, use of *branche* occurs in the *Roman de Renart*, a corpus of narratives concerning Renart the fox, which had first begun to appear in the second half of the twelfth century.[17] The term is adopted by the various poets who, throughout the thirteenth century and beyond, contributed their own 'branches': it appears sometimes in the rubric preceding each section of the text, regularly within the branches themselves, and above all in opening and closing formulae:

> Ceste branche est bone et petite
> Et bien faite, s'ele est bien dite. (Br. v, 5389–90)

> De ceste branche n'i a plus. (Br. vi, 5550)

> Un prestres de la Croiz en Brie ...
> a mis son estuide et s'entente
> a faire une novele branche
> de Renart. (Br. x, 9253–6)

Here *branche* seems to be used in a way not unlike that of *cainc*, in so far as it describes portions of the narrative whose content is related. Nevertheless, in the *Roman de Renart*, by contrast to the *Pedeir Keinc*, these portions focus entirely on the exploits of a single principal protagonist, within the same general context each time and accompanied by a supporting cast selected usually from the same pool of animal characters. But here, as in the *Pedeir Keinc*, each branch can also be taken alone without reference to the others, even though some familiarity with the others helps to provide a fuller context to the events and to illuminate certain cross-references. In the case of the *Roman de Renart*, however, the genesis of the text was different from that of the *Mabinogi*, for the earliest branches of the *Renart* were consciously built on by later contributors, who adopted the existing pattern and simply grafted further branches on to the narrative tree, a process which could continue indefinitely.[18] Although there is little or no firm evidence about the origins and development of the *Pedeir Keinc* apart from that provided by the texts in their present form, there is nothing to indicate that they were composed in the same fashion as the *Renart*. However, the comparison does raise questions as to why the *Mabinogi* was left with only four branches whilst the *Renart* was allowed to grow freely, and whether there were once other *ceinciau* which have disappeared.

In considering the use of the branch in French, A. S. C. Ross concluded that it 's'applique à des compositions à auteurs multiples';[19] but while this is demonstrably true of the *Renart*, it is not true of the *Roman de Thèbes*. The *Perlesvaus*, an Arthurian Grail romance composed by a single author in the early thirteenth century, is explicitly divided into eleven branches.[20] This division, unique in French Arthurian romance, is observed in all the surviving manuscripts, and the term occurs within the text, notably in the opening formulae which begin each branch except the first, for example:

> Or comence ci l'autre branche du saint Graal. (Br. ii, 567)

> Du saint Graal recommence ci une autre branche, si comme l'autorité del escriture le nos tesmoigne. (Br. vii, 2924–5)

Furthermore, the division into branches is closely related to the content, so that the longer the branch, the more important its content is likely to be.[21] The *Perlesvaus* is of particular interest from a Welsh standpoint as it was translated into Welsh, as the second part of *Y Seint Greal*, at the end of the fourteenth century.[22] The Welsh translator, however, has ignored the branches. At the points in the Welsh text which correspond to the division into branches in the *Perlesvaus* no word equivalent to *branche* is used, not even *rann* ('part', 'division') which is used to describe the two separate sections of *Y Seint Greal*, that is the first part, translated from *La Queste del Saint Graal*, and the second, based on the *Perlesvaus*. As a rule the actual break between branches is observed but is not distinguished from those within the branches themselves. Within native Welsh narrative tradition transition formulae are often used to link episodes or mark the passage of time between incidents, and such formulae are employed at similar junctures in *Y Seint Greal*, but again no distinction is made between major and minor textual pauses or divisions, and at no point is *cainc* or any of its semantic equivalents used.[23] It is far from clear why the translator so consistently avoided the term *branche* when he so often translated mechanically and literally. He cannot have been ignorant of the indigenous use of the term, for he repeatedly demonstrates his familiarity with the subject-matter, narrative techniques and style of earlier native tradition.[24] He makes use of formulae, for example, that appear in *Pedeir Keinc y Mabinogi*, and picks up at least one term, *ynys y kedyrn* ('the Island of the Mighty'), which is only otherwise attested in the second branch of the *Mabinogi*; there is also evidence that the translator had access to the version of *Peredur* found in the Red Book of Hergest, which is separated from the *Pedeir Keinc* by only thirteen columns of the manuscript.[25] It is possible, however, that even allowing that the term may have seemed archaic to him, his very familiarity with the *Pedeir Keinc* made him uneasy about adopting the term *cainc*, if, perhaps, he did not wish his audience to assume any link or similarity between *Y Seint Greal* and the *Pedeir Keinc*. He may also have recognized that the use of *cainc* in the Welsh context was different from that of *branche* in the French *Perlesvaus*. In the *Pedeir Keinc* the term linked four texts which had, in their present form, a certain degree of narrative autonomy, but in the *Perlesvaus* the branches are divisions of one single romance, each branch building upon the preceding ones and quite unable to stand alone, as each one relates adventures which are interconnected in various ways.[26] For the translator of *Y Seint Greal* the idea of a 'branch' may have seemed inappropriate for internal divisions and was thus avoided. Furthermore, since in so doing he reduced the major textual divisions of the *Perlesvaus* to the same status as minor ones, it is possible that he rejected the concept of major breaks, or indeed of two degrees of pause within a text, in favour of a single, undifferentiated series. This procedure has the advantage of bringing his narrative closer to the practice in earlier Welsh romances with French antecedents, such as *Gereint* and *Peredur*, where, although breaks occur and may even be marked by some kind of formula, the nature of the division itself is not explicitly described in the text and is thus less striking than in the *Perlesvaus*.

It is clear that the nature of the *branche* in the *Perlesvaus* is quite different from that in the *Roman de Renart*, and it seems that the way in which the term itself is used by the redactor of the *Perlesvaus* is a new development. In his discussion of the term,

Cedric Pickford tends to blur the distinction, for he states that 'la "branche" a désigné d'assez bonne heure une ramification, une subdivision d'un livre ou d'une oeuvre entière'.[27] It is worth noting, however, that French redactors use the term with increasing vagueness as time passes. Brunetto Latini, writing *c*. 1265, uses it as an apparent synonym for 'parties' when advising the budding *romancier* to order his material rather than simply letting it flow out: 'tu ne dois pas conter le fait mot a mot ensamble si comme il fu, ains le te covient deviser par parties, et dire une branche chi et autre la'.[28]

In such contexts it is difficult to distinguish the 'branches' from the separate threads which make up the *entrelacement* that is so characteristic of the narrative structure of later prose romances in French. In the early thirteenth-century *Prose Lancelot* the meaning of *branche* seems to be moving in this direction, as Ferdinand Lot noted as early as 1918: 'Le terme "branche" ... s'entend d'un *conte* tout entier, consacré à un seul héros, conte rentrant, à son tour, dans un ensemble plus vaste.'[29] Lot's definition is confirmed by the following examples from the earlier, non-cylic *Prose Lancelot*:[30]

> Si se taist d'aus toz li contes et parole de monseignor Gauvain por ce que il aquesta de ceste queste. Et neporqant chascuns de ces vint chevaliers a son conte tot antier, qui sont branches de monseignor Gauvain, car ce est li chiés et a cestui les covient an la fin toz ahurter, por ce que il issent de cestui. (Vol. I, 365.35–366.3)

> ... Cil quatre mestoient en escrit qanque li compaignon lo roi faisoient d'armes, si mistrent en escrit les avantures monseignor Gauvin tot avant, por ce que c'estoit li commancemenz de la queste, et puis les Estor, por ce que do conte meïsmes estoient branche, et puis les avantures a toz les dis huit compaignons. Et tot ce fu del conte Lancelot, et tuit cist autre furent branches de cestuit. Et li contes Lancelot fu meïsmes branche del Greal, si qu'il i fu ajostez. (Vol. I, 571.24–31)

Although the manuscript tradition of the *Prose Lancelot* is both extensive and complex, where *branche* occurs its meaning and usage do seem consistent from one exemplar or version to the next, for the term refers to a narrative thread relating the adventures of one particular knight. It is the constant interweaving of such threads that makes up the *conte*, the 'story' or corpus of tradition, though the *entrelacement* does not necessarily correspond to the division into branches.[31] This is neatly summed up in one version of the *Prose Lancelot*, preserved in two thirteenth-century manuscripts, where both Perceval and Lancelot are described as having their own *conte*, which can in turn be seen, from a different point of view, as *branches* of a far larger and more important conte, that of the Grail story:

> Et le grant conte de Lancelot couuient repairier an la fin a perceual qui est chies en la fin de toz les contes as autres cheualiers. Et tuit sont branches de lui por ce quil acheua la grant queste Et li contes Perceual meismes est une branche del haut conte del graal qui est chiez de tous les contes car por le graal se traueillent tuit li bon cheualier dont lan parole de celui tans.[32]

An analogous, though not identical, use of the term occurs as late as the sixteenth century in the early printed editions which bring together in one volume the three major French Grail romances in prose, the *Perlesvaus*, *La Queste del Saint Graal* and *Li Estoire del Saint Graal*.[33] In these editions, of which the second is apparently a reprinting of the first with different woodcuts and a few minor changes, the *Estoire* occupies the first volume and the other two romances the second, ending with the *Queste*. However, the last paragraph of the *Perlesvaus* is omitted and replaced by a brief account of the birth of Galaad, before the *Queste* proper begins with the words: 'Cy commence la derraine branche du sainct greaal' (sig. PP. 5ᵛ, fo. ccxii). This shows that although the internal references to the *branches* of the *Perlesvaus* have been retained, to the printer the *Queste* was a 'branch' of a corpus of material. Each romance could easily be read on its own, but was still to be regarded as part of a larger whole. However, the term is also used by him with the simpler and more concrete meaning of a part of a book, for in the colophon to the *Queste* and to the second volume of the edition he states:

> Cy fine le derrenier volume de la queste du sainct greaal faisant mention de plusieurs merueilleuses aduentures ... qui a este la derreniere branche de cestuy liure. (sig. TT. 6, fo. ccxxxi)

By the early sixteenth century, therefore, *branche* was being used to denote any part or division of a whole, a simple figurative use which was already attested in the thirteenth and fourteenth centuries. In the early thirteenth-century *Vengeance Raguidel*, for example, *branche* suggests the 'other part' or 'other half':

> L'autre branke del ju parti
> Est que vos me laissiées monter
> Si nos conbatrons per a per.[34]

In the mid-thirteenth century, Brunetto Latini, in discussing the ordering of narrative, prescribes a division of the *conte* into six 'parties' or 'branches', and uses both terms interchangeably. Thus the prologue is described as the first branch or part of the *conte*, to be followed by 'le fait, le devisement, le confermement, le deffermement et la conclusion', and each of these six branches is then discussed.[35] Similarly the book of the *Menagier de Paris*, composed c. 1394, describes the seven deadly sins in terms of branches of a tree: 'Orgueil est la racine et commencement de tous autres pechiez. Le pechié d'orgueil a .v. branches. C'estassavoir: inobedience, jactence, ypocrisie, discorde, et singularité.'[36] Each branch is discussed in turn, and each of the other sins is subdivided into branches in the same way. In these instances, where *branche* does not refer to a division of a literary text but is employed for purposes of clarification within a text, the usage is comparable rather to the Welsh use of *cainc* in *Gramadegau'r Penceirddiaid* than to that in narrative literature such as the *Pedeir Keinc*.

Examination of the use of *branche* in the French tradition between the late twelfth and the late fourteenth century suggests an evolution in meaning, hand in hand, perhaps, with changes in the narrative literature itself. Our earliest example of extensive use of the term is the *Roman de Renart*, which is episodic in form, and where *branche* is used to isolate and define these episodes. By the earlier thirteenth century, however, a subtler, more complex narrative structure – the *entrelacement* characteristic of the prose romances – had become the norm. *Branche* now came to indicate the set of adventures undertaken by a particular knight, whose own tale then weaves in and out of that of others to form the complete fabric of the narrative. As the prose romances increased in bulk – notably the later reworkings of the early thirteenth-century Vulgate Cycle – the threads became less precisely drawn. The longer the narrative became, the greater the need to subdivide it into portions of more manageable size, and so *branche* came to denote no more than a part of division.

This raises another question with regard to the Welsh translator of the *Perlesvaus*, and his decision not to retain the division into branches as such. Could it be that he was aware that by his time, the last years of the fourteenth century, the meaning and usage of *branche* in the French tradition had changed, and that it was inappropriate to use the term in the way the redactor of the *Perlesvaus* had done at the very beginning of the thirteenth century? This seems unlikely, however, since at no point does the translator betray any extensive knowledge of French literature. On the contrary, apart from one or two indications that he had access to the *Prose Lancelot*, he seems singularly ill-informed about French literature in general, as witness his insensitivity to the significance of *chevalerie* and *courtoisie*.[37] His abandonment of *cainc* both as a term and as a textual division must therefore stem from other considerations, most probably, as I have already suggested, a disinclination to use it because of its close association, if not identification, in the contemporary Welsh mind with *Pedeir Keinc y Mabinogi*.

It is, moreover, highly unlikely that there was any direct connection between the use of *cainc* in Welsh, and *branche* in French. Since the *Pedeir Keinc* are thought to have achieved their present written form some time between 1050 and 1120, they almost certainly predate the mid-twelfth-century *Roman de Thèbes*, the earliest French text to employ the term.[38] The *Pedeir Keinc* are also much earlier than the period when borrowing from French literature became common, namely the thirteenth and fourteenth centuries. Furthermore, there is no evidence to suggest that the *Roman de Renart*, perhaps the best-known of the earlier French texts to use *branche*, was ever known in Wales. Although many other French texts became available in Wales, in the original or in translation, there is nothing to indicate that this was true of the *Renart*. Nor is there any evidence to suggest that the concept of the branch as a textual division could have travelled in the opposite direction, from Wales to France. Consequently, we can only conclude that the idea of the branch as a textual division arose quite naturally and independently in these two countries. This is perfectly consistent with the extension of the meaning of the word for a tree-branch, in many Western European languages, to take on a range of figurative meanings, from that of a simple part or division of a whole to that of a genealogical line. The concept of the family tree composed of many branches is of great antiquity and common to many languages: Latin *stirps*, Italian *stirpe* and *ramo*, Spanish *rama*, and Irish *géag*, for example; in the Middle Ages the biblical 'Tree of Jesse' was a familiar image in written texts and in visual media such as stained glass in churches. It is not surprising, therefore, that the image of the tree, and especially that of the branch, should have come to be used quite independently in literary contexts in both Wales and France during this period: it is far more remarkable that so convenient a term should have been so little used in the languages of their neighbouring countries.

The French use of the branch as a textual division gradually disappears with the end of the Middle Ages, and this may be attributed to changes in the nature of narrative itself, notably the move from a text shaped by a number of different hands over a period of years to that composed by a single author. Although in France verse texts are attributed to single authors from the twelfth century on, the compilers of the large prose romances, where the branch was an important structural element, were often anonymous and their work continually reworked by subsequent, often unnamed, redactors or 'editor-scribes'. In the Welsh tradition, meanwhile, the concept of a single author in complete control of his material was very slow to develop in the field of narrative. With the advent of printing, which allows multiple copies of texts without textual variants, without an editorial input by generations of subsequent scribes, the text becomes much more stable. The recognition of the text as the work of a single author, whose words must be respected, leaves far less room for extension and adaptation by later copiers, but the medieval narrative, especially in prose, by its nature and its mode of transmission allowed considerable freedom in this respect, and it is in that context that the figurative use of the branch as a textual or narrative division was appropriate and flourished.

Notes

1   Evans 1909: fo. 97.17–18. On the dates of Welsh manuscripts mentioned here, see Huws 1992: 19–21.
2   See, e.g., Williams and Powell 1961: 98; Richards 1990: 85. Modern Welsh makes a semantic distinction between the two forms, *cainc* being used nowadays only for a tune or melody, whilst *cangen* can denote

branches of banks, shops, associations and the like, as well as the branch of a tree.
3 All references will be to Williams 1974.
4 Gruffydd 1928: 324.
5 Davies 1989: 13–15. *Cainc* meaning a song or tune is attested in the poetry of Dafydd ap Gwilym: see Parry 1979: 376.36. See also above n. 2.
6 Lloyd-Morgan 1981: 230–1.
7 Williams 1974: xlii-xliii.
8 Morris-Jones and Rhŷs 1894: 86.3.
9 Williams and Jones 1934: 6.
10 For a full description of the White Book and its contents, see Huws 1991: 1–37.
11 Thomson 1968: line 782.
12 Evans and Jones 1973: cols. 152.3, 165.27. For discussion, see Lloyd-Morgan 1981: 196ff.; Lovecy 1991: 171–82.
13 Leitzmann 1965: III, 77.30.
14 Constans 1890: II, 266. For details of the manuscript, which bears the date 1288, see ibid.: II, ii–vii.
15 Ibid.: II, iv.
16 'N'en sont que trois materes a nul home vivant: / De France et de Bretaigne de Ronme la grant' (Brasseur 1989: I, lines 6–7). This text was composed in the last years of the twelfth century: see ibid.: I, x: 'Quant à la Chanson des Saisnes, elle est certainement antérieure ... à la fin de 1202, et pourrait ... ne pas avoir été commencée avant 1180'; cf. Foulon 1958: 16–18.
17 Reference will be made to Roques 1948–72.
18 See, e.g., Foulet 1914: passim; Flinn 1963: 7–173.
19 Transcript of proceedings of the Colloque sur le roman arthurien en prose au 13ème siècle, Institut Français du Royaume Uni, January 1963, p. 8. Ross also refers to the division into branches of the *Roman d'Alexandre*, but the terminology in this case is not original, being first applied to the text by Paul Meyer. See Armstrong et al. 1965: xvii.
20 Nitze and Jenkins 1972.
21 Kelly 1974: esp. 37–89.
22 The only complete published text is Williams 1876, the translation of the *Perlesvaus* occupying pp. 171–433. For discussion, see Lloyd-Morgan 1978; 1991: 195–8, and references there given.
23 See Lloyd-Morgan 1978.
24 Ibid.: 157–76.
25 For *ynys y kedyrn,* see Williams 1876: 192.39; cf. Williams 1974: 30–2. On the use of the Red Book text of *Peredur*, see Lloyd-Morgan 1978: 161n., 172n. The same scribe, Hywel Fychan, was responsible

for copying both *Y Seint Greal* in Aberystwyth, National Library of Wales, MS Peniarth 11 and the native prose tales, including *Pedeir Keinc y Mabinogi*, in the Red Book of Hergest. See Lloyd-Morgan 1978: 41–5; Charles-Edwards 1980.

26. Cf. Kelly 1974: 43.
27. Pickford 1959: 144.
28. Carmody 1948: 356.13–15.
29. Lot 1918: 13.
30. Kennedy 1980.
31. Colloque sur le roman arthurien (see above n. 19): 8; see also Kennedy 1986: 156–201.
32. Paris, Bibliothèque Nationale, MS f. fr. 751, and London, British Library, MS Lansdowne 757.
33. *LHystoire du Sainct Greaal,* published by Jehan Petit, Galiot du Pré and Michel Le Noir (Paris, 1516); *Cest lhystoire du Sainct Greaal*, published by Le Noir (Paris, 1523). Copies of both editions are preserved in the British Library, and of the second in the National Library of Wales. For a facsimile of the 1516 edition, see Pickford 1978. See also Swanson 1934.
34. Friedwagner 1909: lines 898–900.
35. Carmody 1948: 333.1–3.
36. Brereton and Ferrier 1981: 21.8–10.
37. On his knowledge of the *Prose Lancelot*, see Lloyd-Morgan 1994: 169–79; on his treatment of *chevalerie* and *courtoisie*, see Lloyd-Morgan 1978: 125–39.
38. On the date of *Pedeir Keinc y Mabinogi*, see, e.g., Charles-Edwards 1970: 263–98; Davies 1989: 6.

3

Madness in *Sir Orfeo*

DEREK PEARSALL

I remember first becoming familiar with the Middle English poem of *Sir Orfeo* over thirty years ago when I was teaching it as a set text at King's College, London. I had no idea why it should have been set, or why I was teaching it, but I tried to make the best use of it I could in giving students a grounding in Middle English philology. I remember that the word *owy* (95, 491, 561), as a possible Kentish dialect form, was a very exciting feature of the poem,[1] and we also spent time on the rounding of Old English long *eo*. 'Literary qualities' figured as briefly in my lectures as they do in Bliss's introduction to his edition of the poem, and my own individual contribution to the study of the poem consisted principally of scornful attacks upon its artlessness and naivety. I was withering in my contempt for a poet who insisted on deriving his hero's ancestry from 'King Pluto' and 'King Juno' (43-4) and who tried to convince us that 'Traciens' was simply a name for modern-day Winchester (49-50), and particularly scathing about the happy ending and the hackneyed device of the Faithful Steward.

In subsequent published visitations of the poem, I can perceive traces of these old attitudes, but I can also detect a kind of bemusement or grudging acknowledgement of the power of the poem to enthral its reader despite its apparent lack of the formal and artistic skills that are supposed to be essential to poetic success. It has taken me a long while to realize that any analysis of those skills according to which *Sir Orfeo* falls short must be a bad analysis or must have chosen the wrong skills to analyse. For in truth *Sir Orfeo* is a small poetic miracle, and I shall devote this essay, dedicated to a scholar who understands more than anyone of the inner workings of this kind of romance, to trying to determine what is the secret of its power of enchantment.[2]

The assumption with which I begin is that medieval English romances like *Sir Orfeo*, in so far as they draw their narrative materials from traditional stories such as folk-tales, fairy-tales and myths, are potential treasure-houses of meaning. That potential may be realized in various ways, for instance through the drawing-out of a contemporary historical significance in a traditional story (as in the alliterative *Morte Arthure*) or through the use of a traditional story to ask questions about some of the 'givens' of the romance ideology of chivalry (*Sir Gawain and the Green Knight*) – or not realized at all. Though romances have access to the energies of traditional stories, and to their power of embodying in memorable narrative form certain important and deep perceptions of human experience, the texts that survive may be examples only of the choking of those precious conduits of meaning with various kinds of debris. To preserve such a distinction of value between individual poems, whilst recognizing the mysterious strength of the narrative resources upon which they draw, is important in differentiating between a well-wrought poem like *Sir Orfeo,* drawing upon a myth of ancient pedigree, and a potboiler like *Sir Degare*: the latter reinvents itself as a traditional story, and has a surplus of meaning in relation to the archetypal family drama, but it has no intrinsic interest and no power of enchantment.[3] *Sir Orfeo* demonstrates further that the intrinsic quality of a poem may not be fully communicated in all its extant copies. The poem survives in three texts, two of which (London, British Library, MS Harley 3810, early fifteenth century, and Oxford, Bodleian Library, MS Ashmole 51, late fifteenth century) miss the point with sufficient frequency, decisiveness and unanimity to make it clear that the grasping of the point in the third (Edinburgh, National Library of Scotland, MS Advocates' 19.2.1, the 'Auchinleck' manuscript, *c.* 1330–40) is evidence of its authenticity and not merely of one's subjective preference.[4] The manuscripts of *Sir Orfeo* are not examples of the beauties of *variance*, so enthusiastically celebrated by Cerquiglini, or of the need to view all the witnesses to the text of a popular romance as examples of recomposition equally or necessarily worthy of attention.[5] The Auchinleck text of *Sir Orfeo* is simply a very good text of a poem written by a very good poet; the other manuscripts are irredeemably less good.

For convenience, and for the sake of securing certain footholds in following the progress of the poem's meaning, I shall divide the narrative of *Sir Orfeo* into four phases: loss, mourning, grace and restoration.

Loss

No reason is given for the carrying-away of Heurodis. Neither she nor her husband has done anything wrong for which they need to be punished, and their love was not in any way suspect or to be doubted. Heurodis, though cruelly brusque in her certainty that they must part – 'Do þi best, for y mot go' (126) – acknowledges with touching directness the long amity of their love:

> Allas, mi lord Sir Orfeo!
> Seþþen we first to-gider were
> Ones wroþ neuer we nere,
> Bot euer ich haue y-loued þe
> As mi liif, & so þou me. (120–5)

Orfeo echoes even more movingly the language of Ruth to Naomi in the Book of Ruth i.16 (language which Hardy's Gabriel and Bathsheba also remembered) in affirming the strength and indivisibility of their love:

> Whider þou gost ichil wiþ þe,
> & whider y go þou schalt wiþ me. (129–30)

Heurodis did of course choose to go and laze about in the garden in the middle of the day and fall asleep under an 'ympe-tre' (70), but it would be as excessively severe to criticize her for idleness as for not keeping up with her reading in Celtic legend and remembering how dangerous it was to sleep under trees.[6] The desire to find someone to blame, even to find Orfeo negligent in some respect, is nevertheless strong in some readers, as we shall have cause to remark.

Whatever has happened to Heurodis has happened irrevocably; she is already a different person. Orfeo, in one of the formal rhetorical sets of antitheses for which the poem is notable (102–12), contrasts her past self with her present self, itemizing the superficial manifestations of a change – in demeanour, skin, complexion, fingers and eyes – which has made her quite other, alien, unrecognizable.

Heurodis herself, her anguish momentarily stilled, recognizes the change that has overtaken her, speaking of being returned to what she calls, with touching homely remembrance, 'our owhen orchard' (163) but acknowledging in her last words how she has become part of another 'ous', the company of the king of fairy. To speak of her as having 'gone mad' is a tempting form of words, and it is the way the two maidens put it who report the news, that the queen 'awede wold' (87) and needs to be restrained (the suggestion of wilfulness and not mere modality in *wold* is not out of place). The strongest sense is of a force that makes her want to be away:

> Ac euer sche held in o cri,
> & wold vp, & owy. (95-6)

She has to be held forcibly in her bed, as if the physical restraint will prevent what has already happened (for she is already 'gone') from happening.

Heurodis is terrified, but her terror seems to be not of the fairy king and the abduction but of the return to normality. She acknowledges, though she is now 'other', what her former life was, but she cannot wait to get away from it. When she speaks of the fairy king, his company, his kingdom, it is of an experience of transcending beauty that she speaks. Her attempts to resist (140, 154) are as if they were non-existent, for in truth she is already 'of another mind'. I am irresistibly reminded of the look of terror, submission and acquiescence that one sees in the face of Mary in some late medieval pictures of the Annunciation.[7] This too is the visitation of an irresistible supernatural power, a spiritual ravishing, where the activity of will or choice is hopelessly entangled in the impossibility of countermand. The area of experience that is spoken of here is the threshold between the human and the divine, that liminal space of known and unknown, explicable and inexplicable, that Spearing has spoken of as the favourite hunting-ground of another poet, the *Gawain* poet, and that is commonly filled with revelations, visions, dreams, and apparitions of the divine.[8] There is no suggestion of divine power in *Sir Orfeo*, of course, or indeed of diabolical powers, only the common ground of unknowableness.[9] One reason why Celtic legend of the 'Otherworld' was so useful to the Middle Ages was that it provided a metaphor for this unknowableness, for a supernatural power that was neither part of Christianity nor, like classical mythology, by tradition systematically allegorized.

When Orfeo attempts to protect Heurodis by positioning troops around the 'ympe-tre' (186), he knows, in his heart, that the attempt is hopeless. The certainty of Heurodis' going is acknowledged in his obedience to the fairy king's command that she must be under the tree at a certain time; there is grief but no surprise when she is effortlessly twitched away. Orfeo's 'ten hundred kniʒtes' and 'scheltrom' on each side (183, 187) are reminiscent in their pathetically literal ineffectuality of the attempt by Satan in *Piers Plowman* to fortify Hell against the approach of Christ (C xx.281–94); both are attempts to subdue the supernatural, to control it through the usual apparatus of power, and both misunderstand the relation between the two in the same way. It is not that there is any conscious allusion to the Harrowing of Hell, any more than there was to the Annunciation; the link is in the attempt to find stories and metaphors that will communicate and thereby control something of the bewilderment at the operation of forces that seem to lie beyond human control. The bewilderment in *Sir Orfeo* is at the manner in which a loved person can become, without any sign of essential change in body or mind, completely alien, as if 'possessed' by another (but not 'possessed by the Devil': this is a language that is scrupulously avoided in *Sir Orfeo*).[10] It is the experience of all those who have been confronted with schizophrenic disorder or a related mental illness in someone they love: this is someone I knew; this is someone I do not know.

Mourning

The second part of the poem (197–280) is full of swooning and weeping and the rituals of mourning unburied loss. Orfeo's decision to abandon his kingdom and leave it under the rule of his steward is narrated with sufficiently plausible circumstance to make one fear that a New Historicist will come along one day and prove that *Sir Orfeo* is a poem about parliamentary power and legitimate succession. The reason for Orfeo's decision to live alone in the wilderness is both explained and not explained, like everything in the poem. It is explained in terms of his vow never again to look upon a woman – which I suppose is to be construed as an act of self-denial, or a denial of that will, that pride of life, that might lead Orfeo to love another if he were tempted. This is Orfeo's own explanation, and it is as unsatisfactory as most explanations one gives of one's behaviour in such crises. There is also a tendency to read Orfeo's sojourn in the wilderness as some kind of expiation, though it is hard to know what sin is being expiated.[11] Customarily, in medieval romance, running wild in the wilderness, as with Yvain and Lancelot, is an act of despair and self-abasement at some offence against the code of love, but Orfeo's is a calculated decision, not a madness.[12]

Two words, however, strike the reader who is prepared to believe that the detail of the poem is worth attending to. One is the 'sclauin' or pilgrim's mantle that Orfeo takes upon himself instead of other clothes (228), and the other is the reference, much later in the poem, to the king having gone for ten years 'en exile' (493). Orfeo seems deliberately to have made himself into an exile from the world of men, determined to live as a *peregrinus* like the Seafarer of the Anglo-Saxon poem, who was also living out an experience of irremediable loss.[13] He is not a pilgrim in the usual sense, since he travels to no shrine; rather, his journey is away from the world, a going-away into the unknown, a deliberate imitation of Heurodis' going-away. Like her, as we are told in another memorable rhetorical set-piece of parallel antitheses ('He þat had ... Now ...', 241–56), he has undergone irrevocable change, from what he was to what he is; he is unrecognizable.

There is, as I have said, a temptation – and there would always be such a temptation, in a medieval English poem – to read this as a penitential act, a deliberate act of expiatory self-denial done to appease a wrathful God. But the poem uses no such language and invites no such interpretation. And I think it would be 'modern' to speak of it as Orfeo's 'return to Nature', a seeking-out of the roots of his being; modern readers often see *Sir Gawain and the Green Knight* in this way, as if Gawain needed to mature through a healthy confrontation with non-courtly reality in the form of mountainous landscapes, ice, snow and green giants. It seems, rather, simply that Orfeo is attempting to repeat, as far as he can, his wife's experience, so that he may, as far as he can, share it.[14] This is not allegory, but it is close to allegory, and in a less fully narrative mode the crossing-over into allegory, and the interpretation of Orfeo's self-exile as the withdrawal into the wilderness for purposes of spiritual meditation (probably on the transience of earthly existence), would be swiftly accomplished. But that does not happen here.

Orfeo has one thing that his wife did not have, apart from the power of choice, and that is his harp. His skill as a harper was mentioned at the beginning of the poem, as was the fact, later, that it was the one thing he took with him into the wilderness. Now, at the nadir and dark midwinter of the story,[15] when Orfeo's life has fallen into decay and all hope seems gone, hope returns through the harp. It is Orfeo's harping that brings the wild beasts and birds to sit around him while he plays (and depart without molesting him when he has finished) and so symbolizes the power of music to bring harmony to brute creation. It is not just the power of music, but Orfeo's power, his ability to bring about in others the experience of order and harmony that they may have lost or that they may not have known. In *King Lear,* it is music that helps to restore 'th'untuned and jarring senses' of the king (IV.vii.16), and in *The Tempest* Prospero declares 'a solemn air' to be 'the best comforter / To an unsettled fancy' (V.i.57–8) and what will cure Alonso's brains, now boiled within his skull. Shakespeare refers to the restorative *effect* of music; in *Sir Orfeo* the power of music is the expression of an inner harmony within Orfeo and the hope of restoration that he carries always with him.[16]

Grace

The mystery at the heart of the poem is the initiation of that process of restoration which is engineered through the waking vision of the fairy hunt. Orfeo receives a gift which is the reward for, though not apparently the consequence of, his fidelity and hope. In this imaging of the liminal world between the known and the unknown, it is the poem's subtle skill to leave a tenuous thread between cause and effect, between human powers of choice and the consequences of those choices (Chaucer is similarly skilful in tempting us to discern this thread in the pattern of events in the Knight's Tale).

The sighting of the fairy company comes in three phases, the first two muted, veiled, inconsequential: the first, the hunt, passes with 'dim cri and bloweing' (285), half-heard between waking and sleeping, fading into nothingness, repeating itself endlessly since no beast is ever caught (287); the second, the fairy dance, is again like a distant tapestry in a poem by Keats, the knights and ladies dancing 'In queynt atire, gisely, / Queynt pas & softly' (299–300). In the third, the falcon-hunt of the fairy ladies, each falcon kills its prey, and Orfeo comes suddenly back to laughing vitality. It is a paradoxical moment for the modern reader, that life should be renewed through such death, and we might think we should prefer the corresponding moment of grace in *The Rime of the Ancient Mariner,* which comes when the narrator blesses involuntarily all the slimy creatures of the sea. Hunting, the joy of the chase, and the joy of the kill, is something that we just have to learn to appreciate and share if we are to understand its metaphorical functioning in medieval poetry, whether here or in the deer-hunt in *Sir Gawain and the Green Knight.*

The renewed sense of life is what brings Orfeo face to face with Heurodis, 'his owhen quen' (322). Neither can speak:

> ȝern he biheld hir, & sche him eke,
> Ac noiþer to oþer a word no speke.
> For messais þat sche on him seiȝe,
> Þat had ben so riche & so heiȝe,
> Þe teres fel out of her eiȝe.
> Þe oþer leuedis þis y-seiȝe
> & maked hir oway to ride
> – Sche most wiþ him no lenger abide. (323–30)

This is the poem's climax (note the repeated rhyme), and I am afraid it is sorely spoilt by Bliss's punctuation, which I do not reproduce. Complaining that Sisam, whose punctuation I do reproduce,[17] mispunctuates the passage by placing full stops after lines 324 and 327 instead of after line 326, Bliss explains in his notes to this passage that 'Orfeo and Heurodis do not speak to each other, not because of any enchantment, but because she is full of pity at the sight of his misery'. This, even if it were completely intelligible, would still be completely wrong. The reason that Orfeo and Heurodis do not speak to each other, even though they recognize each other, is that they are on opposite sides of a great divide, between those who live in this world and those who live in the other world of schizophrenic alienation. But even though Heurodis cannot speak, she can feel compassion for the one she loved, and her tears begin the undoing of her prison-house, the ending of her inaccessibility and alienation. Tears, the ability to weep, are always the mark of humanity in traditional story-telling, just as the freezing of their tears is the mark of the outcast state of Fra Alberigo and the other inhabitants of Ptolomaea in the lowest circle of Dante's Hell (*Inferno*, XXXIII.94-9). The tears are not the consequence of anything that Orfeo or Heurodis did, or a reward for faith, but a gift of grace. The other ladies see the tears and, knowing that Heurodis is slipping away from them, make her ride away. Orfeo, newly determined, follows, first twitching his *sclauain* about him and hanging his harp on his back (343-4), as if to mark the beginning of the last stage of his pilgrimage of hope.

Restoration

The castle of the king of fairy is both paradise and limbo, very beautiful on the outside, and very terrible on the inside, being full of the unmoving bodies of the undead, frozen in the positions in which they were snatched into the Otherworld. The imagery is powerful but enigmatic, not entirely explicable in any terms, but I think the dominant impression is of men and women driven out of their minds through pain and suffering, alienated from life, that 'þouȝt dede, and nare nouȝt' (389).[18] The association of the beauty of the outside, and the terror of the inside, is reminiscent of the terrible beauty of Heurodis' first experience of the fairy king and suggestive of the compulsive power of the alienating experience.

But the power of the Otherworld over Heurodis is already undone, and Orfeo's arrival at the castle and his exchange with the porter at the gate and then with the king have a refreshing normality, particularly in the reference back to the practice of minstrels (382-4, 429-34) that was described in the prologue (27-8), and in the comforting reminder of the supposed practice of the one we are listening to. This is a world we are more familiar with, the world of castles, kings, minstrels, and promises that must be kept. The fairy king is 'brought to order' by Orfeo's music, and his court gathers at Orfeo's feet just as the animals did, the menace of the Otherworld, like that of the irrational world, tamed into harmony. The king's response to Orfeo's request for his wife is oddly prosaic and unoutraged: you and she would make a very ill-matched pair, he says, as if all that had to be thought about was the impression that they will make on the neighbours. It is as if he is already aware that his power has been taken away from him by the superior magic of Orfeo's harmony and by the civilized ordering of a society which renders that harmony in the making and keeping of promises.[19] Orfeo knows this too, and his summons to the king is a confident invocation of that higher mysterious law that he knows the king must obey. Heurodis is made free, that is, made whole. The king's acknowledgement of what he must do is brusque:

> Þe king seyd: 'Seþþen it is so
> Take hir bi þe hond & go:
> Of hir ichil þatow be bliþe!'   (469–71)

It echoes the brusqueness of Heurodis' earlier acknowledgement of what she had to do (126), what she, at that time, was 'bound' to do. The Harley and Ashmole MSS both miss this point resoundingly by having the king admit that what Orfeo has said is true and having him further congratulate Orfeo on being a true man (H 430–1, cf. A 456–7). This is no part of the proper behaviour of the lord of unreason, who must be shown to be 'bound' to do what he does.

The harp is the link too into the closing episode of the faithful steward, which works perfectly in completing the release of tension by deflecting it into a subsidiary field of action and in thus completing the expression of the joy of restoration and reunion. The steward treats the disguised Orfeo generously because he is a harper, like his long-dead master, recognizes the harp when Orfeo plays, and through his truth to his promise (569) is the hero of the wonderfully prolonged and deferred second happy ending. Orfeo's long series of conditional clauses, in which he finally, conditionally, makes the steward his heir, winds up the tension of expectation to an almost unbearable degree so that the moment of recognition, when it comes, is one of uncontrollable joy, as the steward crashes over the upturned table to throw himself at his master's feet:

> Ouer & ouer þe bord he þrewe,
> & fel adoun to his fet.   (578–9)

These are tremendous lines.

It is not the purpose of this essay to turn *Sir Orfeo* into an allegory of madness and recovery, or to argue that its subject is what we might call a nervous breakdown or schizoid episode and the appropriate therapy for restoration. On the other hand, the conditions that we name thus, though they may be to some extent historically constructed and to a large extent historically perceived, are not peculiarly modern conditions but part of the condition of being human. The profound and alienating distress of such illnesses, the suddenness and inexplicability of their onset, cry out for narratives of explanation, hope and restorative power. Part of the strength of *Sir Orfeo* as a poem is the generation through narrative, through formal and aesthetic means, of an artistic tension and resolution which can be talked about in formal and aesthetic terms. But the special strength of the poem, as I argue, is its power of calling on experience of some of the most terrifying fragilities of the human mind and some of the most mysterious tenacities of the human heart.

Notes

1 Bliss 1954: xx. All quotations are from this edition.
2 After I had completed the draft of the present essay, I came upon A. C. Spearing's superb study of *Sir Orfeo* (Spearing 1987: 56–82), which anticipates, in its last paragraphs, much of my main argument. But I have left what I wrote substantially unchanged, since there are important differences of detail and emphasis.
3 The distinction I make, between 'story' and 'poem', is a familiar one, and similar to the distinction between pre-existing 'shape' and 'verbal realisation' in Brewer 1980: 3.
4 Scribal mangling of key passages in the poem can be inspected in Bliss's parallel-text edition (Bliss 1954), e.g. at lines in Harley and Ashmole corresponding to Auchinleck 241–56, 558–74.
5 Cerquiglini 1989: esp. 111–12. This is not to deny that *variance* is important in the texts of many Middle English romances: see Fellows 1991; but the attempt by Longsworth (1982: 3) to argue that the three different versions of *Sir Orfeo* 'represent three distinct and equally authentic realizations of the romance' is slight and unconvincing.
6 'Heurodis fell through sloth', says Penelope B. R. Doob in her very determined Christian-allegorical reading of the poem (Doob 1974: 178). For the dangers of sleeping under trees, and the general influence of Celtic legend in this version of the Orpheus story, see Bliss 1954: xxxii–xxxix, and the other sources cited there.
7 In choosing from the five Laudable Conditions of the annunciate Virgin, artists often went for the more dramatic effects of *conturbatio*: see Baxandall 1972: 49–56.
8 Spearing 1970: 104. In Celtic legends, entry to the Otherworld is often quite literally realized as a doorway, a threshold or *limen,* as here when

Orfeo follows the fairy company 'in at a roche' (347, 349). See Bliss 1954: xxxix.

9 John Block Friedman, whose study of the Orpheus story is otherwise generally very useful, interprets the visitation of the fairy king as a diabolical seizure by the lustful noonday demon (Friedman 1970: 184–90).

10 For a discussion of medieval understanding of madness as a form of demonic possession, the punishment for moral turpitude, see Doob 1974: 12–17. Doob unfortunately wants to read *Sir Orfeo* in just this way, as a Christian allegory of Heurodis' fall and resurrection through Orpheus–Christ (ibid.: 178).

11 For an example of the reading of the poem as a Christian exemplum of humble and penitential submission rewarded with divine mercy, see Louis 1967: 245–52.

12 This is where the early essay by D. M. Hill, so suggestive in many ways, seems to go astray, in interpreting Orfeo's sojourn in the wilderness as an image of madness and 'the hunt as part of a pictorial representation of the threat of insanity in the form of hallucination' (Hill 1961: 144).

13 For the idea of the *peregrinus*, see Whitelock 1950: 261–72.

14 As Spearing puts it, in a remarkable passage, the poem seems to suggest that madness can be cured 'only if the healer has the love and courage to be willing to go through madness himself, to commit himself, naked and vulnerable, to the wilderness and the other world and its central citadel' (Spearing 1987: 82).

15 I am thinking of the episode in the Franklin's Tale when the deep midwinter of hopelessness is likewise the moment of the first burgeoning of hope (*Canterbury Tales*, V.1243–55).

16 The power of music to cure madness is an important theme in Spearing 1987. More generally, Seth Lerer suggests that, since it is Orfeo's musical and narrative performance that brings about restoration, 'the poem argues for the place of artistry in civilization and for the place of music and poetry in life' (Lerer 1985: 93). This, though not too farfetched, does make the poem sound a little like a memorandum to an Arts Funding Council.

17 Sisam 1921: 23. For commentary on the punctuation of the passage, and useful discussion of the whole scene, see Owen 1971.

18 The best and most suggestive account of the origins of this passage is Allen 1964. It is worth remarking that 'apparent death and the reanimation of the dead' are discussed by Freud as important features of 'the uncanny' in his essay 'The Uncanny', written in 1919 (repr. in *Penguin Freud Library* 1985: 335–76): see pp. 347, 369.

19 The situation is reminiscent of the Franklin's Tale, where Chaucer simi-

larly portrays the triumph of the good magic of love and truth over the bad magic of illusion. Arveragus' confidence in the power of truth is not as unequivocally represented as that of Orfeo, but it is striking that the Franklin's Tale, presented as a Breton *lai*, so closely reproduces this element in the form. For Chaucer's possible knowledge of *Sir Orfeo*, see Loomis 1941; for the view that promises are the special mark of humane and civilized society, see Arendt 1958: 243-7.

4
Cloaking desire: re-reading *Emaré*

MARGARET ROBSON

In this article I intend to explore the romance *Emaré*. My argument is that in this tale the commonplace motif of the 'calumniated wife' is used both to mask and to betray the strategy of feminine masochism which the heroine adopts as a method of coping with patriarchal restrictions on female desire. I argue that *Emaré* demonstrates the most typical form of feminine masochism, the subservience which Chaucer has Custance articulate:

> I, wrecche womman, no fors though I spille!
> Wommen are born to thraldom and penance,
> And to been under mannes governance.[1]

I shall begin by making some comments on the critical reception of *Emaré*, which has tended to focus on its similarities to 'patient Griselda' stories. For example, Shirley Marchalonis writes:

> In the two romances with female heroes, *Emaré* and *Lay Le Freine*, the women, like the chivalric heroes, are tested, but for a different set of qualities. Women do not have to prove their worth as fighters or their loyalty to the class. Feminine virtue is passive: women, it seems, must endure rather than act.[2]

Dieter Mehl's laudatory portrait of the suffering Emaré is as much a political statement on what 'good' women should be as a piece of criticism: they should, emphatically, be beautiful; being useful is also a help. He writes:

> The whole poem is a glorification of the heroine, who, wherever she goes, awakens love and admiration. Not only her deeds and her practical skills ... but especially her perfect beauty are outward expressions of her

goodness. Even the wicked old queen has to admit that she never saw such a beautiful woman, but it is a sign of her vicious character that she cannot recognize this beauty for what it is, but thinks it must be the mark of a devil.[3]

There is, of course, nothing wrong in that: as Toril Moi has remarked, feminist criticism is avowedly political.[4] The difference beween explicitly and implicitly political criticism is that the latter seems to work against women's interests. Mehl's comments, which have no avowed political connections, nevertheless work on the assumption that the 'heroines' (all 'heroines'?) are 'good'. His approval of the calumniated lady of *The Erle of Tolous* makes this clear: 'Her spirited rejection of the two knights who want to tempt her into adultery clearly shows how abhorrent the thought of any extra-marital relationship appears to her.'[5] Marchalonis, commenting here on *Lay Le Freine,* also makes plain the 'good girl' model:

> Her decoration of the marriage bed with her own cherished mantle is an act of love and generosity that is almost stunning. Her act of devotion apparently cancels out her sin; she is rewarded with an identity, the husband she loves, and the stability and safety of marriage.[6]

Such tales, then, are read as narratives of passive virtue triumphant. What such readings indicate, however, is approval of feminine masochism: whilst Marchalonis's reading seems to recognize – albeit implicitly – that masochism is a ploy which allows Le Freine access to sexual and social security, Mehl appears simply to be admiring the masochistic woman.

Although the strategic adoption of masochism might be understandable, from my point of view as a woman reader I find it difficult simply to like stories where the heroine – such as the saintly Griselda – is passive to the point of stasis. I have always thought of *Emaré* as an extremely irritating tale: her prissy goodness – so commended by Mehl – and the fact that her sufferings 'entitle' her to get her man have always seemed to me to be an execrable pattern for a girl. The construction of 'the heroine' does not appear to allow for a woman to be (what critics encode as) 'sinful'. What I have wanted is for women to do something wrong and still to be the 'heroine'.

Though it is not possible to recreate these long-suffering heroines, it is possible to re-read them; I take as my model in this attempt Judith Fetterly's position of the 'resisting reader'.[7] I hope to show that Emaré's adoption of the masochistic strategy is an effective means of opposing patriarchal legitimacy.

Writing on feminine masochism, Karen Horney notes:

> The influence that these ideologies exert on women is materially strengthened by the fact that women presenting the specified traits are more frequently chosen by men. This implies that women's erotic possibilities depend on their conformity to the image of that which constitutes their 'true nature'.[8]

Emaré has been read as a passive heroine *par excellence*: her very name leads one to infer that she is such. She is subjected to an incestuous proposal from her father, is cast out, then becomes the subject of malicious slander by her mother-in-law, followed by another exile. She suffers patiently and has her man restored to her at the end because she has endured so humbly. Or so goes the received version of the tale. Like the similarly calumniated eponymous heroine of *Le Bone Florence of Rome* (whose name also embodies notions of her 'goodnes'), Emaré is said to approach sanctity through her humility and forgiveness.[9] Her magic robe is the outward sign of her inward grace, as is her beauty.[10]

However, I would argue that Emaré can be read not as the passive plaything of the tale (and of men), but as its prime mover: events are shaped to her desired end, and that is shaped by her desires, which are projected on to the other characters in the story. Structurally – and psychologically too – she is the dominating force; whenever she appears in the narrative, so does bewitching desire. She is the bearer of the magic talisman, the cloak, which is effectively a kind of love-charm: it is the cloak that bewitches, more than her beauty. It has been suggested that in earlier versions of the tale Emaré, and not her father, was given the cloth from which the robe is made, as a love-charm by a supernatural agent.[11] The bearer of a love-charm is not necessarily a romantic innocent. The archetypal bearer of the bewitching garment is Aphrodite, whose magic girdle makes her irresistible.[12] Aphrodite is, above all, an inspirer of sexual passion – but then so too is Emaré, a fact which is not given the emphasis it deserves.

I shall begin, then, by examining that part of the narrative which deals with the incestuous proposition. I argue that the repressed narrative here reveals the daughter's desire for her father. What is explicitly emphasized in this tale is others' desire for Emaré, whilst she remains blameless. Rosalind Coward's observations on women's displacement of sexual desire seem particularly apposite here. She writes:

> Thus as a girl child assumes a position in the adult world, a strong feeling of guilt is attched to infantile sexuality, however unconscious the experience may be. Sexuality has usually to be someone else's responsibility, not an activity desired by the female body and acted on and secured by the female person. Instead female sexuality becomes centred on attracting, on making another person assume responsibility for women's desire.[13]

Here, rather than the beautiful woman being blamed, blame attaches to the father and the mother-in-law: the fact that it is the parents (for here the mother-in-law functions as a rival mother-figure) who are 'guilty' would seem to indicate that the tale does indeed include a narrative of the child's guilty sexual feelings. The absence of the (natural) mother – a trope which is, as Jennifer Fellows has pointed out, a commonplace of medieval romance[14] – and the eventual elimination of the rival mother suggest a narrative which is as implicitly anti-feminist as it is explicitly. As a feminine strategy, masochism serves to secure the one woman by denying that security to the other.

The incestuous proposition which opens the action of the tale occurs after Emaré is given the magic talisman, the robe. The description of the cloth occupies eighty lines (88–168), which is a substantial portion of the narrative; it is a far more detailed account than any other person, place or thing merits. As I have already remarked, the robe functions as a love-charm: it both represents explicitly sexual love and inspires it. What is also important to note is that the cloth is made by one woman and then given to another; and the one who made it made it as a love token.

> In the fowrthe korner was oon,
> Of Babylone the sowdan sonne,
>   The amerayles dowghtyr hym by.
> For hys sake the cloth was wrowght;
> She loved hym in hert and thowght,
>   As testymonyeth thys storye. (157–62)

What is notable in *Emaré* is that the cloth, fashioned by the sultan's daughter, is effectively a message from one woman (more precisely, a daughter) to another. Where sexual knowledge is illicit, then silent communication may take the place of speech, and women weave, rather than write or speak, their messages: thus Procne and Philomela use and interpret the work of their hands.[15] The pairs of lovers depicted on the cloth created by the sultan's daughter are lovers who are forbidden to love each other. The narrative, then, is one of forbidden love and, more specifically, love forbidden to daughters. The daughter's desire for her father, I shall argue, is displaced on to the father's desire for his daughter via the magical agency of the robe, itself covered with portraits of forbidden love.

The forbidden love with which we are presented here is that of Sir Artyus for his daughter, though this incestuous proposition is not, according to my reading, as straightforward as it appears to be. Elizabeth Archibald, in the context of the Constance stories, notes that in earlier versions the daughter was in love with her father and was punished for her masturbatory fantasies by mutilation of the hands.[16] My thesis is that *Emaré* echoes this type of incestuous desire and that her desire for the 'forbidden' love is displayed by her adoption of the love-charm, the magic robe. It is notable that from the point when she receives it (241-6) she is always represented as wearing it until the final reconciliation with her father (1009-20). It is only at this point, when she has made what Peter Brooks describes as a 'correct erotic object choice', that she can leave aside the robe/her projecting of desire on to others, and receive him as her father and not as an object of desire.[17]

The idea that daughters fantasize about being seduced by glamorous strangers (who are, in fantasy, their fathers) is a commonplace of psychoanalytic investigation.[18] It has also been argued that women are supposed to harbour incestuous desire towards their fathers:

> Women are encouraged to commit incest as a way of life ... As opposed to marrying our fathers we marry men like our fathers ... men who are older than us, have more money than us, more power than us, are taller than us, are stronger than us ... our fathers.[19]

And, as Maldwyn Mills has pointed out, the similarity between the narrative treatments of Emaré's father and of her husband is remarkable

> when we compare the author's treatment of the actions of the heroine's father and of her husband. We might have expected a very sharp differentiation here: the father is one of the monsters of the story – an ageing lecher, who treats Emaré quite ruthlessly when she will have nothing to do with him; the husband, on the other hand, is its Prince Charming. But by applying very similar motifs to each, the author makes them seem curiously alike.[20]

They are alike in the position which they occupy seen from the vantage-point of the controlling view, that is, from Emaré's point of view: they are men whom she desires.

The narration of the father's incestuous desire for Emaré only seems curious if we do not accept that hers is the controlling consciousness. Her father first sends for her after he has been given the cloth which has already dazzled him:

> The cloth was dysplayed sone;
> The emperour lokede therupone,
>   And myght hyt not se;
> For glysteryng of the ryche ston
> Redy syght had he non,
>   And sayde, 'How may thys be?'
> The emperour sayde on hygh,
> 'Sertes thys ys a fayry,
>   Or ellys a vanyté!' (97–105)

Sir Artyus' comment 'Sertes, thys ys a fayry, / Or ellys a vanyté!' is later inverted by the mother-in-law: on first beholding Emaré wearing the robe she remarks: 'Sone, thys ys a fende, / In thys wordy wede' (446–7). Both the 'parents' recognize that the robe is magical – a recognition which is not given to anyone else in the tale. For the mother, illicit love is an evil, whereas for the father the possibility of it is enchanting. It should be noted, though, that it is only after the father has expressed his enchantment that the pictures of the forbidden lovers are described:

> And when he wolde wende
> He toke hys leve at the hende
> And wente forth on hys way.

> Now remeveth thys nobyll kyng:
> The emperour aftur hys dowghtur hadde longyng,
>   To speke wyth that may.
> Messengeres forth he sent
> Aftyr the mayde fayr and gent. (184–91)

The narrative is explicit that the cloth has already inspired the father with a desire to see his daughter, and the sight of her is then reported as inspiring incestuous desires:

> Byfore her owene fadur sete,
>   The fayrest wommon on lyfe;
> That all hys hert and all hys thowghth
>   Her to love was y-browght:
> He byhelde her ofte sythe.
> So he was anamored hys thowghtur tyll,
> Wyth her he thowghth to worche hys wyll,
>   And wedde her to hys wyfe. (221–8)

However, as Thelma Fenster has pointed out, the recognition of incestuous desire – usually displayed as the father's desire – is often mutual. Writing on *La Manekine* she observes:

> Otto Rank's warning that the inclination towards incest must not be seen as one-sided is more than apt. When Joie blushes at her father's entry into her chamber, therefore, there is a sense in which she does 'know' his intentions, even though at the level of the persecution story she continues to appear faultless. At that level the reader is allowed to concentrate on the innocence of the blush and to ignore that it can also signify desire.[21]

First he has the robe to bewitch him, then he sees his daughter. Suffice it to say that, obviously, one who is 'dazzled' cannot see clearly, and what one tends to see when so situated is a type of mirage; either what one wants to see, or what someone else suggests one might see. Again, it is the activity of looking/seeing that is indicative of the magic at work, for her father is described as staring at her (225); his inability to look elsewhere is a common feature of lover's rhetoric: 'I can't take my eyes off you.' His actions here are those of a lover, not a father. His councillors, who have not been so bewitched because they are not the objects of Emaré's desire, are, though, obedient to his will that the marriage should be sanctioned:

And called hys counseyle nere.
He bad they shulde sone go and come
And gete leve of the pope of Rome,
To wedde that mayden clere.
Messengerres forth they wente,
They durste not breke hys commandement. (231-6)

The father's desire that this incestuous relationship be sanctified suggests a similarity between this tale and those where the proposition is sanctified by the mother's dying wish that the husband should only remarry someone as beautiful as she is.[22] The Grimm brothers' *Allerleirauh* (*Of Many Different Kinds of Fur*) is such a tale. What might also be signified here is the daughter's desire to take the mother's place. The motif is emphasized in this tale with the mother-in-law's elimination through permanent exile. Emaré forgives her father and he returns to the fold.

The incestuous proposition operates in several ways at once: first, it displays – and displaces – the daughter's desire for her father, a desire which he recognizes and reciprocates. Secondly, what it does is to draw the boundaries between licit and illicit desire: it is on this distinction that I intend to focus now.

As Freud has remarked, incest is the most deep-seated and ancient taboo; he further remarks: 'the basis of taboo is a prohibited action, for performing which a strong inclination exists in the unconscious'.[23] However, incest is prohibited not by natural law (physically, it is perfectly possible) but by man-made law: having been made by men, it can be revoked by men, especially fathers, who are typically controlling figures. The ultimate earthly controlling father in medieval Christendom is the Holy Father, the Pope, and it is to him that Sir Artyus appeals for permission to recreate the law. All the responsibility for sexual desire and sexual activity is placed with the father: the repression of active female sexuality is so deep-seated that no aspect of it is permitted to escape the mechanisms of patriarchally constructed society. Emaré's illicit desire for her father, when recognized and returned by him, can be legitimated. However, neither the tale nor its heroine is concerned with male legitimacy: what we are presented with in the end is female authorization.

There is a constant pull in *Emaré* between what is desirable and what is licit: the dichotomy between the desirable and the licit is even controlled topographically. The father sends to Rome for legitimation, and at the end of the tale he and Emaré's husband make their penitential journeys to Rome. Neither her father nor her husband does meet or receive penance from the Pope after his arrival in Rome, because she is the one who awaits them there and who dispenses the law at this point (835–40, 949–66). As I have pointed out, exactly the same motif occurs in *Le Bone Florence of Rome*. There is something else, though, to be said about this dialectic, and that is that the men appeal to masculine law to sanction desire: the Pope grants the father's request that he should be allowed to marry his daughter. When he has the authority to marry Emaré and tells her of this, then she refuses him. In the narrative she makes her appeal to divine law (1251–64); but it is the law of God, divine law, as mediated through his representative the Pope, that has been granted to her father. Her desires lie outside such legitimating structures: when she is given the place of the mother, then she no longer desires him. This might perhaps say something about the view which is being presented of desire itself: that in fact desire, from the perspective of a woman who accepts male law, is illicit. I would suggest that 'the absent mother' is absent because a mother is not seen to be a sexy creature: women tend to be split into wives and mothers – and then mistresses and daughters. Legitimacy effectively unsexes women.[24] The desiring girl, then, cannot take the place of the mother, as this would serve only to efface her sexual nature. What Emaré has to do, then, is once more to become illicit.

Rather than assent to male law, Emaré becomes an outcast, though again the narrative constructs her as blameless, for it is on her father's orders that she is put to sea:

> The emperour was ryght wrothe
> And swore many a gret othe,
>   That deed shulde she be.
> He lette make a nobull boot,
> And dede her theryn, God wote,
>   In the robe of nobull ble. (265–70)

The masochistic woman is represented both as punishing herself for her illicit desires and as making herself an even more desirable partner because of her obedience to the ultimate male authority,

God, unmediated by earthly men. Her position, in this context, is disobedience masked as obedience: all the legitimating structures operate on behalf of the father – he is the king and has authority for this marriage from the Pope. Emaré's refusal to comply with male law is a refusal which is – eventually – construed almost as saintly. The price to be paid for the refusal of male control by appealing to divine law is the adoption of masochistic practices, whether that is the extreme form displayed in the lives of the female saints, or a passive form, such as that adopted by the patient Griselda. In the first type the female body is mutilated, whereas in the second it is more often effaced. Until the very end of the tale Emaré is displayed wrapped in the dazzling robe: we seldom 'see' her; what we do see is a mobile expression of illicit desire.

Illicit desire has to be accommodated in some way by patriarchal society. My argument is that it is accommodated by reference to divine law. It is therefore of crucial importance that we examine the occasions where women's disobedience is finally accepted as a type of higher obedience. As I have noted, the lives of female saints provide radical examples of this higher obedience. I would tentatively suggest that such women have to be made 'saints' because they are persistent refusers of male dictates: such powerful women cannot be allowed to be shown (or read) as subverting male authority for the simple reason that authority cannot be represented as fragmented. Either authority is absolute (has absolute power behind it), or it can be evaded or even actively challenged. Thus, women's denial of earthly male authority can only be allowed on the basis that some male sanctions it.[25]

What is extraordinary in *Emaré* is that in the end her activities, her desires, are not sanctioned by male law, divine or otherwise: as I have noted, she becomes the dispenser of order. Emaré, then, has succeeded in attaining her desires. Her departure from her father leads her to another man who is (constructed) like her father – and, like him, bewitched by her – but unlike her father in that he is not taboo. Her seduction of him mirrors the desired seduction of her father:

> The kyng loked her upon,
> So fayr a lady he sygh nevur non:
> Hys herte she hadde yn wolde.
> He was so anamered of that syghth,
> Of the mete non he myghth,
> But faste gan her beholde. (397–402)

The objection to the match again comes from a mother, who is, necessarily, presented as evil as she poses a threat to the achievement of the girl's desires. From a feminist point of view, possibly the most disquieting aspect of the adoption of masochistic practices is the way in which such strategies alienate those women who do not adopt them themselves. Emaré's victory over the men means that she becomes the centre of the (formerly) male world. It also means that, because she has managed to do this, she is read as a saintly woman. As a ploy which ensures control, the seduction of man using bewitching techniques, coupled with ultimate obedience, is a success. Emaré is centralized as a heroine because she appears to conform to masculine notions of feminine behaviour.

Resisting the idea that Emaré is an archetypal 'good girl' is difficult: she is a heroine, she suffers and forgives – she must be saintly. But she also ends up as a controlling agent of her own, and others', sexual destiny.

Notes

1 *The Canterbury Tales*, II.285–7. All line references for *Emaré* are to the edition in Mills 1973: 46–74.
2 Marchalonis 1980–1: 90.
3 Mehl 1968: 136.
4 Moi 1988: xiv.
5 Mehl 1968: 88.
6 Marchalonis 1980–1: 92.
7 Fetterly 1978. See, e.g., the following: 'The questions of who profits, and how, are crucial because the attempt to answer them leads directly to an understanding of the function of literary sexual politics ... As readers and teachers and scholars, women are taught to think as men, to identify with a male point of view, and to accept as normal and legitimate a male system of values one of whose central principles is misogyny. Clearly, then, the first act of the feminist critic must be to become a resisting, rather than an assenting reader and, by this refusal to assent, to begin the process of exorcizing the male mind that has been implanted in us' (ibid.: xx–xxii).
8 Horney 1973: 36.
9 Heffernan 1976. Heffernan comments: 'For both Florence and Emaré, beauty, symbolic of moral perfection, is also the basic cause of suffering' (ibid.: 33). Florence is accused of adultery by her brother (ibid.: lines 1291-1305), who then beats her; her sufferings are similar to those inflicted on female saints (ibid.: lines 1512–18). She is later accused

of murder by a rejected suitor (ibid.: lines 1636ff.). As in *Emaré*, the men then arrive at the convent where Florence is domiciled, confess and are forgiven by her (ibid.: lines 1996ff.).
10 Arthur 1989: 84.
11 French and Hale 1930: 428 (note to line 168).
12 Graves 1955: I, 67-71.
13 Coward 1984: 194.
14 Fellows 1993a: 54.
15 The motif of women communicating through the use of sewn, woven or embroidered cloth is an interesting one which has not previously been emphasized. There is great stress laid on Emaré's skill with her hands: 'Of her hondes she was slye' (67; cf. 382, 730), but the association of women's handicrafts with sexual messages has been ignored. The archetypal practitioner of weaving is the 'good' wife Penelope, who uses it as a means of delaying a sexual relationship. By contrast, Clytemnestra, the 'bad' wife, who has already taken a lover, weaves a garment for Agamemnon's homecoming which becomes his shroud. Procne's message to Philomela is woven. Le Freine's message to her sister is the cloth in which she was abandoned. Where women's ability to communicate through speech is denied – as is literally the case with Procne – this is a means which lends itself to them because sewing is (usually) seen as a feminine preserve. Bynum comments on the fact that cooking was perceived to be so much a woman's business that it was not merely arcane but threatening (Bynum 1987: 190). The same is not true of sewing – partly because it is not as obviously life-threatening as poisoned food is: the assumption, made by Mehl (1968: 136), that sewing is an innocent and laudable pastime is not always borne out. The rhetoric of enchantment – spells are either 'cooked' (the witches' brew) or 'woven' (the magic garment) – indicates that such activities are a feminine preserve, and a dangerous one at that. The motif of the woman sewing remains – even in much later, realistic fiction – a telling one: in Elizabeth Gaskell's *North and South*, the scene (ch. 26) where Mrs Thornton unpicks her own initials from her best linen as a prelude to sewing in those of her (expected) daughter-in-law (and rival) is an extraordinarily concise way of indicating her recognition of her own displacement.
16 Archibald 1985-6.
17 Brooks 1984: 104.
18 Kestenberg 1975: 149.
19 Herman and Hirschman 1977: 740.
20 Mills 1973: xiv.
21 Fenster 1982: 46-7.
22 Mills 1973: 197 (notes to lines 52-4).

23 Freud 1960: 31-2.
24 The split between the sexy mistress and the boring wife is given verbal expression in Chrétien de Troyes's *Cligés*: 'De s'amie a feite sa dame, / Car il l'apele amie et dame, / Et por ce ne pert ele mie / Que il ne l'aint come s'amie, / Et ele lui tot autresi / Con l'en doit amer son ami' (Micha 1978: lines 6633-8): 'Of his sweetheart he has made his wife; but he calls her his sweetheart and his lady, so that in this way she does not lose his love as his sweetheart; and she loves him too just as one should a lover' (Owen 1987: 183). The crucial distinction to be made, though, is between the mother and the childless woman. Emaré herself is not subjected to any sexual attentions after she has been rescued from the sea with her son (lines 685-732) - after, in fact, she has become a mother. Guenevere is, of course, childless - and remains a romantic heroine throughout her life. Criseyde too is childless, as is Iseult. 'Bad' mothers, such as Morgause of Orkney, are allowed to remain sexual, but mothers such as Elaine of Corbenic are not. See Luce Irigaray's comments on this issue (Whitford 1991: 36, 51). T. H. White's portrayal of Elaine of Corbenic in *The Once and Future King* strikes me as true to expectation of a 'good' mother.
25 In fact, in the saints' lives male authority is represented as continuous. Typically what happens is that men either carry out one another's orders or take over from one another where appropriate. In Osbern Bokenham's life of St Christine there are four judges involved in torturing her; when one dies, the next takes over (she is tortured continuously for fourteen years): see Serjeantson 1938. In *The Golden Legend*, St Lucy is given to the judge by her betrothed for persecution, and the men of the town gather to rape her on the judge's orders (Ellis 1900: II, 133-4). Similarly, Agnes is given to the provost by her father because she refuses to marry a pagan (ibid.: II, 247). St Christine is represented as being given to a judge after the death of her father (ibid.: IV, 96). See also the life of St Barbara (ibid.: VI, 202), given to a judge because she refuses to worship her father's idols. The rhetoric employed by Virginia's father in the Physician's Tale suggests that the figure of the father and that of the judge are interchangeable here too. The father says: 'Take thou thy deeth, for this is my sentence' (*The Canterbury Tales*, VI.224); Virginia asks him - not the persecuting judge - for mercy, which he denies, condemning her to death himself.

5
Malory's Mordred and the *Morte Arthure*

P. J. C. FIELD

One of the most surprising passages in Malory's *Morte Darthur* comes at the end of the first section of the first tale,[1] when King Arthur attempts to frustrate a prophecy that a child born on May Day will destroy him. He has boys born on that day sent to sea in a ship which is wrecked and drowns nearly all of them, but Arthur's son Mordred, who is destined to destroy him, survives:

> Than kynge Arthure lette sende for all the children that were borne in May-day, begotyn of lordis and borne of ladyes; for Merlyon tolde kynge Arthure that he that sholde destroy hym and all the londe sholde be borne on May-day. Wherefore he sente for hem all in payne of dethe, and so there were founde many lordis sonnys and many knyghtes sonnes, and all were sente unto the kynge. And so was Mordred sente by kynge Lottis wyff. And all were putte in a shyppe to the se; and som were four wekis olde and som lesse. And so by fortune the shyppe drove unto a castelle, and was all to-ryven and destroyed the moste party, save that Mordred was cast up, and a good man founde hym, and fostird hym tylle he was fourtene yere of age, and than brought hym to the courte, as hit rehersith aftirward and towarde the ende of the MORTE ARTHURE.
>
> So, many lordys and barownes of thys realme were displeased for hir children were so loste; and many putte the wyght on Merlion more than on Arthure. So what for drede and for love, they helde their pece.

The reader must assume that the ship is the unmanned ship of traditional story,[2] which allows perpetrators of such deeds to claim technical innocence of their victims' deaths, and that Arthur put the babies into the ship intending them to drown.

The surprising thing about the passage is that it puts King Arthur in such a bad light. Not only is Malory uncensorious in general; he also takes particular pains to portray Arthur as admirable. The most substantial study of characterization in the *Morte Darthur* describes Malory's Arthur as:

> a just, unselfish, strong ruler, and father of his people, his virtues far outweighing his one weakness of undue partiality to his nephew Gawain. This character . . . is built up by the greatest number of changes devoted to any personage except Lancelot, and in its contrast to the picture provided by the sources, of a somewhat ineffectual, fiercely passionate monarch, it presents the greatest originality in characterization which can be attributed to Malory.[3]

This effect was produced by consistently adapting material from seven or eight sources across the length of a substantial book.

The passage quoted from the *Morte Darthur*, however, portrays a child-murderer whose depravity is increased by his conspicuous resemblance to that byword for infamy, King Herod, in his most infamous act, the Massacre of the Innocents. Herod too was faced with a prophecy about the imminent birth of a boy who might supplant him, and attempted to frustrate the prophecy by ordering the killing of all newborn male children in his country. Herod too brought about the deaths of all the children except the subject of the prophecy, who was carried off to another country, where, until the danger passed and he could return to work out his destiny, he was 'fostird' by 'a good man'. (The only description of St Joseph in the Nativity story is as 'a just man'.)[4] In this context Mordred takes on unexpectedly flattering associations,[5] and Arthur, rather than (as one might expect) Mordred, begins to look like Antichrist.[6] Since Arthur does nothing even approaching this in wickedness anywhere else in the *Morte Darthur*, we have a discrepancy that demands explanation.

The respect Malory expresses throughout his book for his 'French books' makes it natural to suggest first that he unthinkingly reproduced material from his French source,[7] which for this part of his story is one of the components of the thirteenth-century French Post-Vulgate Cycle, its *Suite du Merlin*. Artus's part in the corresponding episode of the Post-Vulgate *Suite*,[8] however, is much less discreditable:

> Artus reminds Merlin that the time is coming when the child who will destroy the realm is to be born, and says he will have all boys born in

that month collected and looked after until he decides what to do with them. His subjects, poor as well as rich, send him their boys.

King Lot and his wife put their newborn son Mordres in a splendid, specially made cradle, and despatch him and a suite of knights and ladies from the city of Orquenie. A terrifying storm drives their ship on a rock, drowning all except the child, who floats away in his cradle. A fisherman in a small boat finds him and takes him home secretly to his wife. After debating what to do (but not discussing killing the child), they finally take him to the castle of their lord, Duke Nabur le Desreez, hoping for a reward. The duke rewards them and decides to bring the child up with his infant son Sagremor and knight them together when they reach the proper age.

Artus meanwhile decides to have the other boys killed, but in a dream an imposing figure denounces him for this. If he persists, God will make an example of him; he must instead put the boys into an unmanned ship with the sails set, and Christ will show that he can protect them. Artus does so, and the boys arrive safely at the castle of King Orians in Amalfi.[9] An elderly knight just back from Logres guesses who they are, and on his advice the king has them brought up in a secluded castle.

Meanwhile in Logres the barons find out what Artus has done, and ask Merlin to explain. He tells them the king was trying to frustrate a prophecy about the birth of a child who would cause a battle in which every fighting man (*preudome*) in Logres would die, and that their children will be returned safe and sound in ten years' time. This makes peace between Artus and his barons and averts serious trouble for the country.

In Malory's source, therefore, Artus never has the chance to kill Mordres. He only decides to kill the other boys after apparent hesitation, and promptly has his warning dream and repents. He is shown momentarily as someone willing to massacre babies and for much longer as someone who will not, and never looks much like Herod: the separateness of the stories of Mordres and the other boys prevents it.[10] His sending the babies to sea is not an attempt at murder but obedience to a supernatural command. Malory did not therefore take the idea of Arthur as willing mass-murderer or second Herod from his source.

That being the case, it is difficult to see how this book came to include notions so contrary to the rest of it. Perhaps they might have come about by accident. Malory's creative urge plainly included a drive to retell the authentic story of Arthur and his knights, which could sometimes at least override his desire to present the characters he liked in a good light.[11] He does not, for instance, shirk the 'fact', well established in Arthurian tradition, that his favourite character, Lancelot, commits adultery with his friend's wife, and so brings about his own death and that of almost everybody else. Malory apparently found the illicit affair distasteful but, rather than omitting it, he abbreviated it drastically, as he did with the Mordred episode. With the Mordred episode, the reduction ratio is about twenty to one, and haste, carelessness and savage compression together might have produced effects Malory did not intend or notice.

Simple carelessness seems unlikely. Malory certainly took trouble to understand the whole episode before shortening it. Only in that way could he have combined the two ships into one, the three 'good men' (fisherman, duke and king) into one, and brought the duke's castle forward in the narrative to be the site of the shipwreck. He also had clearly in mind the place of this incident in the larger narrative, casually particularizing the precise day of the ominous birth, which the source only specifies some dozens of pages earlier.[12] Even a careful author, however, might be distracted from the results of a complicated task by the effort involved, so a précis designed to preserve the plot line might produce a narrative dominated by fact, a quasi-chronicle whose objective literary characteristics were morally neutral. That, however, seems unlikely too. Malory habitually compressed his French sources, but the resulting narrative, whatever other chronicle-like characteristics it possesses, usually has a strong moral thrust.[13] The generally increased moral stature of his Arthur is one component of this. Moreover, in the episode now being considered, Malory's source included much that would have reinforced his urge to give his story a moral perspective: it is full of religious and moral judgements, including an explanation of why people might send children to sea in an unmanned ship: 'Il ne porront pas soffrir quil morissent deuant eus.'[14] That explains the action as a form of cowardice, a vice Malory seems particularly to have despised. Among the source's many other moral observations, none is more emphatic than its condemnation of the intended murder of the children. The speaker in Artus's dream tells him that God, who has made him 'the shepherd of his lambs', will be so offended if Artus persists in his intention to kill these 'holy and innocent creatures' that he will punish Artus with a fate that will be a warning to posterity for ever. Even if Malory overlooked the biblical echoes in that, he would have to have been extraordinarily distracted not to have noticed that the action that the French Artus would *not* commit, but which he himself was attributing to his Arthur, represented a degree of moral depravity rarely plumbed in life or literature.

Nor is it likely that Malory would have invented the parallels between Arthur and Herod without noticing them. In fifteenth-century England, the Massacre of the Innocents was one of the best-known events of history. Everyone was reminded of it once a year by a feast-day that struck a sombre note during the twelve joyful days of Christmas, and many were reminded again on the feast of Corpus Christi while watching miracle plays, in which the ranting of Herod seems to have been one of the high points.[15] In the world of medieval romance in particular, it has been persuasively argued that familiarity with the Herod story is an interpretative key to *Havelok the Dane*.[16]

The number of things that Malory would have had to fail to notice or refuse to respond to in order to create his child-killing episode accidentally is so large as to make the idea difficult to credit. It is surprising that he did not simply omit the entire episode, as he often did with parts of his sources that he did not like or did not need. The *Morte Darthur* begins by leaving out two-thirds of the French *Prose Merlin*. It is hard to see how it would have been damaged by losing the attempt on Mordred's life. Whereas Lancelot and Guenevere's adultery provides the mainspring of the plot and what is arguably the major theme in much of Malory's own book and in his most important source, the French Vulgate Cycle, the mass-murder and Herod ideas serve no obvious purpose, either in the action as a whole or locally, except to blacken Arthur's character and complicate the relationship between him and Mordred. Neither idea is developed later either in Malory's own story or in that of any of his known sources. The Vulgate story is driven sufficiently by two factors: that Mordred is Arthur's sister's son, so that Arthur makes him regent when he leaves the kingdom; and that he is ambitious and treacherous, which drives him to usurp Arthur's throne. Mordred being Arthur's own son, although it does not add much to the plot, serves thematic functions by showing sin bringing about its own punishment and provides contrasts with other illegitimate sons in the story: Galahad, Tor and others, including on some interpretations Arthur himself. Having Arthur try to kill Mordred, however, adds little to plot or theme. It could have provided Mordred with a motive or excuse for trying to kill the father who had tried to kill him, and the attempt, particularly if it involved other children, could make Arthur deserve his fate more than he might be felt to deserve it for a sin (incest) that, although grave in itself, he believed to be the lesser, and notoriously easily excused, sin of adultery. Neither Malory nor any of his known sources, however, shows much interest in developing these aspects of the story.

There is, however, a further possibility, which is best addressed by considering the elements in the story that have no counterpart in the *Suite*. It is easy enough to guess how most of them came into being. Malory's insistence that only the gentry's sons were under threat, where his source spoke of both rich and poor, may show a preference for a story set wholly in knightly society. That Arthur issues his command 'on pain of death' may be a stroke of authorial intutition about character derived from the actions being related. Mordred may have been taken up as jetsam rather than flotsam because Malory read his source's *rive* as 'shore', rather than, as the original context requires, as 'river' or 'sea'. Malory may have changed the ending to one of contained political tension because he felt that, after what had happened earlier, the reconciliation in the French story was unbelievable.

The longest element not in the *Suite*, however, is harder to explain. it is the assertion that a good man 'founde hym, and fostird hym tylle he was fourtene yere of age, and than brought hym to the courte, as hit rehersith aftirward and towarde the ende of the MORTE ARTHURE'. As Eugène Vinaver remarked in the commentary to the standard edition, there are four texts Malory might have called 'the MORTE ARTHURE' – the final tale in his own book, its two principal sources (the Old French *Mort Artu* and the English stanzaic *Le Morte Arthur*), and the English alliterative *Morte Arthure* – but none of them gives an account of Mordred being brought to court at 14, or any other age.[17]

It is unlikely that the *Mort Artu* ever included an account of Mordred coming to court. The text varies so little in the many surviving manuscripts[18] that it would be unreasonable to explain the inconsistency in Malory's book by postulating a variant containing an incident as marginal to its story as the arrival of Mordred at court, particularly as the incident would have been retrospective. Since Mordred is already a Knight of the Round Table in the *Prose Lancelot*, it would have had to have been set at least two romances back in the time-scheme of the Vulgate Cycle. Something similar applies to the English stanzaic *Le Morte Arthur*, which is essentially a much-abbreviated version of the *Mort Artu*. It would be surprising if anyone had added to its pared-down and fast-moving story anything as peripheral as the arrival of Mordred at court in a notionally distant past. It would certainly have been at odds with the original inspiration of the poem, and a later *remanieur* who wanted to add it would have had, in addition to other difficulties, to cast the extra material in a moderately complicated stanza-form. Malory's last tale is broadly a conflation of the latter part of those two romances. Since his Mordred too is a knight of the Round Table long before the tale begins, it is difficult to see what would have been gained by its including Mordred's arrival at court.

These objections, however, do not apply to the alliterative *Morte Arthure*, which, as the major source of Malory's 'Tale of King Arthur and the Emperor Lucius', is his most important English source. As Vinaver observed, it alone among Malory's major sources implies that Mordred spent his youth at Arthur's court: early in the poem, Arthur calls Mordred 'my nurree of olde' and 'a childe of my chambyre' and says he has disciplined and chosen him for high office.[19] One of Malory's probable minor sources, *The Awntyrs off Arthure*, also says that Mordred was brought up at Arthur's court,[20] but too briefly to be the source of what Malory says about Mordred's upbringing. The passage on Mordred's upbringing in the *Awntyrs* might be based on a version of the alliterative *Morte*: the lines that immediately precede it certainly are.[21] A number of factors points to the alliterative poem as the work Malory had in mind. It has often been suggested that the only surviving manuscript of the alliterative *Morte*, the Thornton MS (Lincoln Cathedral Library, MS 91), is a shortened version of the poem as originally composed.[22] Although that view has not been universal, one scholar even contending that Malory used the Thornton MS itself,[23] a fuller version of the poem could well have included (late on, as Malory's wording requires) a passage recalling Mordred's arrival at court. Because the alliterative poem is relatively autonomous compared with the *Mort Artu* and the stanzaic poem, and its elaborate set-piece descriptive passages make it relatively slow-paced, such a passage would not be as out of place there as in the other two romances.

Moreover, Malory apparently had the alliterative poem in mind shortly before he composed this episode. In an episode taken from the

Suite du Merlin, he tells of the arrival of an embassy from the Roman emperor, who demands tribute from Arthur.[24] This is clearly the beginning of a story that had long been established as part of the legendary history of Britain, the story of Arthur's Roman war.[25] The surviving versions of the *Suite*, oddly enough, nowhere relate the rest of the story, but the entire story forms the plot of the alliterative *Morte*. Reproducing a fragment of the story from the *Suite* apparently brought to Malory's mind a passage from the alliterative poem's version of it. His Arthur tells the ambassadors: 'on a fayre fylde I shall yelde hym my trwage, that shall be with a sherpe spere othir ellis with a sherpe swerde. And that shall nat be longe, be my fadirs soule Uther!' Vinaver, who thought Malory wrote his second tale first and his first tale second, asserted that the first sentence was 'an obvious reminiscence of the corresponding scene' in 'Arthur and Lucius'.[26] Even if his view of the order of composition of the *Morte Darthur* were true, Vinaver's assertion would be hard to defend. There are actually two corresponding scenes in 'Arthur and Lucius': one in which the ambassadors make their demands, and another in which Arthur gives his reply. In neither does Arthur make an ironic joke about tribute or even use the word *trewage*; nor does he do so in the corresponding scenes in the Thornton text of the alliterative *Morte*.[27] The nearest approximation to the passage quoted comes later: in both texts, when Arthur despatches the corpses of the Roman commanders to Rome, he makes a grim joke about the bodies being the *trybute* the Romans demanded.[28]

However, although the passage quoted does not echo the Thornton text of the alliterative poem, something very like its first sentence could well have appeared in Arthur's formal reply in a lost fuller version of the second scene with the ambassadors. When Arthur sends the corpses to Rome in 'Arthur and Lucius', Malory's style takes on something of the archaic diction, alliteration and humour of alliterative poetry, all of which stylistic features derive from the corresponding scene in his source. In the first sentence above, diction, rhythm and alliteration also seem to echo the style of alliterative poetry, although the words and the alliterating patterns do not appear in the corresponding scenes in the Thornton MS text. Furthermore, if something like that sentence stood in a fuller version of Arthur's reply to the ambassadors, the way his ironic speech despatching his enemies' corpses to Rome echoed his (now lost) original response to their demands would be highly characteristic of the alliterative poem, which put great emphasis on making and fulfilling vows.

The second sentence quoted above is also uncharacteristic of Malory. Its word-order is archaic, and it provides the only instance in the *Morte Darthur* of swearing by someone's soul. It too may come from the alliterative *Morte*, even though it has no counterpart in the Thornton text. The only point in any of Malory's major sources at which Arthur swears by his father's soul seems to be in the *Mort Artu*, when, just after an ominous dream about the wheel of Fortune, Artus refuses the advice of the archbishop to withdraw from imminent battle with Mordred and to wait for Lancelot.[29] There is no evidence that Malory had the *Mort Artu* in mind in either of his first two tales – the first sign of its influence is his reference to Lancelot saving Guenevere from the fire at the beginning of the third tale – but the alliterative poet certainly used the *Mort Artu*'s dream of the wheel of Fortune, expanding it into a spectacular episode that is one of the high points of the poem.[30] He could easily have remembered and used Artus's oath from the next episode. There is a real possibility, therefore, that both the sentences quoted might derive from a lost fuller version of the alliterative *Morte Arthure*.

If the child-killing episode is reconsidered in the light of these things, it will be seen that the narrator's assertion about Mordred that a good man '*f*ounde hym, and *f*ostird hym tylle he was *f*ourtene yere of *a*ge' forms a passable line of alliterative verse. This must be decisive. If Malory's memory conjured up here, for the second time in a few pages, a memorable alliterative line from the story he was telling, we must surely assume that the *Morte Arthure* he refers to here is the alliterative poem of that name. It follows that Malory cannot have used the *Morte Arthure* in the Thornton MS, because it does not contain the alliterative line he remembered, which is why the line has not been identified before.

It may be possible to take matters further by considering two other passages in the alliterative *Morte* that have implications for Mordred's childhood, but which Vinaver overlooked. In the first of them, almost at the end of the poem, Gawain calls Mordred a 'fals fosterede foode'.[31] Since *foode*, like *nurree* in the previous passage, primarily means a foster-child, the phrase might be tautology qualifying the earlier assertion that Mordred was fostered by Arthur. It would say in effect 'something must have gone wrong with the fostering', that Mordred had not responded as he should to an upbringing in the chivalric ethos provided by the household of the greatest of all the kings of Britain. That, however, would not fully explain the third passage, in which, later still, the narrator describes Mordred as a 'churles chekyne'.[32] That might be no more than a reflex insult, a denial of membership of his class to one who was thought to have disgraced it, a product of the impulse that makes quarrelling knights shift to second-person-singular pronouns; but it is surprisingly specific, and not a normal accusation between knightly enemies in the *Morte Arthure*.

An alternative hypothesis can be put forward that would explain the oddities in these passages and in the passage in Malory more satisfactorily. That hypothesis is that the alliterative poet reworked the very passage from the *Suite* that Malory used. The poet was very well-read – his best editor has described him as having 'poured a life-time's reading into his poem'[33] – and if he had access to a copy, the serious-mindedness of the Post-Vulgate Cycle would have appealed to him. We may suggest that he altered the story to have Mordred fostered not by the duke but by the fisherman, who would be the poet's 'churl' and Malory's 'good man' (or better, *goodman*, 'a worthy man not of knightly status').[34] If in the poet's story, as in Malory's, Mordred was 14 when he was brought to Arthur's court, several key words about his upbringing define themselves in secondary, although in each case well-recorded, senses. Readers will already have grasped from the context that as a *child* (of a king's chamber) Mordred is not a baby but a young man in service, but similarly as a *norree* he is not a nurseling but a ward, and as a *foode* not a fosterling but 'a young man, especially a young warrior'.[35] All three terms, however, would still imply that their subject was a beneficiary who owed a debt of gratitude to his benefactor, which was the more binding in that he would be old enough to know it.

If this is the picture of Mordred evoked by the poem, then the 'false fostering' that Gawain speaks of will not be a tautology. It will refer primarily not to a failure by Mordred to respond to the ethos of Arthur's household, but to Mordred's having been fostered by someone of the wrong social class. It may even be that *churles* is plural, meaning the fisherman and his wife: that – like Kay but more so – Mordred had become villainous through having imbibed the milk of a *vilaine*.[36] That such a meaning will be uncongenial to the egalitarian twentieth century is no reason for rejecting it.

The apparent fragment of alliterative verse in the *Morte Darthur* is not the only thing about that anomalous passage that may have been brought about by a lost fuller version of the alliterative *Morte Arthure*. Such a lost version could explain several of the features of the passage that have no counterpart in the *Suite du Merlin*. The alliteration in 'begotyn of lordis and borne of ladyes' might have been inspired by it; the threat of death would be characteristic of the terrifying Arthur of the poem, who threatens to have the ambassadors hanged, drawn and quartered if they do not follow his commands to the letter; and even the ending on a note of political tension might have been inspired by the disaster that is impending in the poem in a way that it is not in the *Suite*. Most important of all, the influence of the alliterative poem may explain both why Arthur's character is blackened in this episode when Malory consistently improved it elsewhere, and why he did not cut the episode out of his story altogether.

The first issue is straightforward: something so uncharacteristic is more likely to be the product of conflation than of gratuitous invention. In this first tale, moreover, Malory is much given to supplementing his 'French book' from minor sources, most of which seem to have been in English.[37] For the most part these minor sources give him only supplementary details of events, and names for characters anonymous in his major sources. He probably felt they lacked the authenticity, whatever that was, of his major sources, most of which were French cyclic romances. Among English Arthurian stories, however, the alliterative *Morte* seems to have come near to the French romances in Malory's esteem: he retold its story almost in full as his second tale, making only such changes as would harmonize it with the rest of his book. Since he apparently knew it when he composed his first tale, it is reasonable to suppose he would have taken supplementary material from it when the opportunity arose. If, when working up the child-killing episode from the French *Suite*, he remembered some of the same events being related in an English source he valued, it must have seemed an ideal opportunity for producing the most authentic version of this part of the Arthurian story.

The second issue can be addressed partly from the same evidence: the authenticity that Malory attributed to the alliterative poem must have pushed him towards incorporating what it said into his book even when it was uncongenial to him. There may, however, have been a secondary cause: that what he took from the alliterative *Morte* helped him make an incident that contributed to his book *as he then expected it to be*. That may not be quite the book we now have. The book we have is indebted above all to the most popular of the French romance cycles, the Vulgate Cycle, and next to the second most popular, the *Prose Tristan*. When composing his first tale, however, Malory may not have known either of them very well. The Vulgate *Queste del Saint Graal*, the fourth Vulgate Cycle romance, is the major source that Malory was to follow most closely and which, to judge from the title he gave it, he admired most, but in this tale he confused two of its three principal characters with other Arthurian characters whose names sounded similar.[38]

When Malory was writing his first tale, however, the French romance to which he will have been closest must have been his major source. That source was part of the Post-Vulgate Cycle, a set of romances notable for its severe morality, including its stress on retribution for sin. By the time he reached the child-killing passage, Malory had already reproduced from his source an account of the incestuous conception of Mordred, and the revelation to Arthur that his incest would cause his own death and the death of all his knights.[39] Malory, as we have seen, also knew the alliterative *Morte Arthure* well, and some powerful passages in that work also stress retribution for sin.[40] The child-killing passage may therefore be an attempt to conflate major and minor sources so as to develop that theme. Malory's 'as hit rehersith aftirward' looks like a promise to re-emphasize that theme of retribution for incest later by relating Mordred's arrival at court as part of an account of the downfall of the Round Table. He may already have planned to base that account on the *Queste del Saint Graal* and the *Mort Artu*, but those romances could easily be read as saying that the deaths of Arthur and his knights were primarily caused by Arthur's incest, even without the help of the Post-Vulgate *Suite* and the alliterative *Morte*. Malory might have planned to make more of the theme in other ways as well, although in the event he did not do so, despite echoing the alliterative poem from time to time in his last tales. It may have influenced what his final tale says about Arthur winning the Holy Cross, Arthur's epitaph, Ector's threnody for Lancelot, and the last words of the story.[41]

There are still uncertainties left. Even if we were certain that the child-killing episode was produced by conflating the corresponding passage in the *Suite du Merlin* with a lost fuller version of the *Morte Arthure*, it would still be difficult to say what, apart from the fragment of verse Malory remembered, was in that passage in the alliterative poem. We certainly cannot subtract from Malory's episode everything that has a counterpart in the *Suite* and say that the rest appeared in a similar form in the original *Morte Arthure*. He might have needed no other stimulus than a memory of the alliterative poem's picture of ruthless royal self-assertion. Its mountains of adult corpses might have led his imagination to a shipload of dead children, its breaches of the laws of war to a breach of the more fundamental taboo protecting the innocent and helpless. Arthur's assertiveness in the poem might have been enough to make Malory imply that his motives are wholly selfish, whereas the *Suite* seems to suggest that Artus really cares for his country, perhaps even more than for himself.

On the other hand, there is a real possibility that a lost fuller version of the alliterative poem described Arthur as a mass child-killer and second Herod. The poet certainly did not share Malory's distaste for blackening Arthur's character: his picture of Arthur is sufficiently critical to have led one scholar to argue that the poem was a satire on an authoritarian king bent on overseas conquest.[42] Portraying Arthur as a child-murderer and even, perhaps implicitly, as a latter-day Herod, would stretch the characterization of Arthur in the poem as we have it but would not be incompatible with it. In a poem arguably written to show Arthur as an imperious tyrant, an echo of Herod would fit very well with some of the things seen in his wars, such as his threat to kill every man in Lorraine and Lombardy who obeyed Lucius' laws, the deliberate devastation of civilian property in his Italian campaign, and his death-bed command that Mordred's children should be killed and their bodies be thrown into the sea.[43] The lost material might even, as suggested above, have been partly based on the very passage from the *Suite* that Malory used.

Although we cannot be certain, it is a reasonable guess that Malory abandoned his first intentions for his story as he got to know his other 'French books' better, because of what he felt to be their greater authority. When he found Mordred appearing as an adult in most of the tales he was telling, he may have had practical difficulties in finding a place in his story for a retrospective account of Mordred's arrival at court; but that difficulty would not have been insuperable, if only because the story of the healing of Sir Urry, the episode that introduces the final tale, includes several retrospective vignettes. By then, however, Malory seems to have developed, partly from his various sources and partly in opposition to them, more complex and arguably theologically more orthodox ideas about the fall of Arthur and his knights. Those ideas left Mordred as little more than part of the machinery, however necessary – which may be why Malory did not give Mordred's past and motives even a few parenthetical lines in the Urry episode to match those on Sir Marrok that record that Marrok's wife turned him into a werewolf.[44]

It may be asked why, if Malory changed his mind about the kind of book he was writing, the *Morte Darthur* still promises to relate Mordred's arrival at court. The obvious explanation is that Malory forgot it, as he forgot his promise in the fifth tale to relate the death of La Beale Isode's hapless suitor Keyhydyns.[45] Leaving in the child-killing episode is a second lapse, because it is plainly incompatible with Arthur's character as presented elsewhere in Malory's book. The duplicated account of the arrival of the Roman ambassadors, the short version from the *Suite* in the first tale, and the long one from the alliterative *Morte* in the second, constitute a third lapse, because they are incompatible with each other, like the double 'first appearance' of Sir Ironside at Arthur's court in the fourth tale.[46] However such duplications may sit in the twentieth-century experimental novel, in the *Morte Darthur* they must be flaws, since Malory as author made such an effort to remove them. He omits the last third of the alliterative *Morte* (which duplicates the story of the death of Arthur that he relates in his eighth tale), the 'Third Book of Tristan de Liones' (which duplicates the Grail quest he relates in his sixth tale) and the Roman war story in the *Mort Artu* (which duplicates his entire second tale), but these smaller duplications in his first tale seem to have been overlooked.

There are ways of coming to terms with such flaws even as literature,[47] but we may regret them the less because they give us clues to something about which we have very little other evidence: the conception and development of the *Morte Darthur*.

Notes

1. Vinaver and Field 1990: 55.19-33. (All Malory references are to this edition, by page and line numbers.) I am grateful to Mr Aidan Clark, Dr Rosalind Field and Professor W. M. Tydeman for suggestions which have improved this paper.
2. Cf., e.g., Chaucer's Man of Law's Tale (*The Canterbury Tales,* II.439, 799, 868); Schlauch 1941; *Emaré* 265-75, 584-719 (Mills 1973: 62, 65); *King Horn* 105-40, 190 (Fellows 1993c: 4-5, 6); and see Fellows 1993c: 269-70.
3. Wilson 1934: 65-79, esp. 65-6, 74, 79.
4. Matthew i.19.
5. For a recent short history of Mordred's character, see Shoji 1993: 53-63.
6. For Mordred as Antichrist, see Rosenstein 1993: 459-74, esp. 461, 466-7.
7. Cf. Wilson 1950b.
8. All known manuscripts of the *Suite* are incomplete, but the source passage survives in Cambridge University Library, MS Add. 7071, fos. 244vb-246vb, and in London, British Library, MS Add. 38117 (the Huth MS), fos. 95vb-99vb (= Paris and Ulrich 1886: I, 203-12).
9. The story has already related that Nabur's son Sagremor will become a knight of the Round Table, and now adds that Orians's son Ascanor will become one too and that he will be nicknamed 'le Lait Hardi'. The Commentary to Vinaver and Field 1990 wrongly says that Orians himself will have that nickname.
10. Dr Rosalind Field points out to me that Mordred himself in this story shows some similarities to the other embodiment of gratuitous evil in the Gospel story, Judas Iscariot, who in medieval legend was also set adrift on the sea as the result of a dream, was brought up by charitable strangers and eventually found his way home, where he not only killed his (unrecognized) father but completed the Oedipus parallel by marrying his mother (Ryan 1993: I, 167-8).
11. See Vinaver and Field 1990: 1260.8.
12. CUL MS Add. 7071, fo. 233va; Huth MS, fo. 79vb (= Paris and Ulrich 1886: I, 159).
13. See Field 1971: 36-102.
14. CUL MS Add. 7071, fo. 246^{rb-va}; Huth MS, fo. 98rb (= Paris and Ulrich 1886: I, 210).
15. Cf. *The Canterbury Tales,* I.3383-4; Davis 1971-6: II, 426; Evans 1970: s.v.; and cf. *OED,* s.v. 'out-Herod'.
16. Speed 1994.
17. Vinaver and Field 1990: 1303 (note to 55.32-3). This note is

unchanged from the previous (1973) edition, which was wholly Vinaver's.
18 See Frappier 1961; Woledge 1954–75: s.v.
19 Vinaver and Field 1990: 1303 (note to 55.32–3); and cf. Hamel 1984: lines 689–92. The primary sense of *nurree* is 'foster-child'.
20 *The Awntyrs off Arthure* 308–11 (Mills 1992: 170). The *Awntyrs* may have given Malory the name of one of his minor characters, Galeron of Galloway (Benson 1976: 41).
21 Mills 1992: 202 (note to lines 305–11).
22 Gordon and Vinaver 1937; Vorontzoff 1937; O'Loughlin 1959.
23 Matthews 1960: esp. 211. For other views, see Wilson 1950a: 47–9; Hamel 1984: 5–14.
24 Vinaver and Field 1990: 48.15–27.
25 It goes back to Geoffrey of Monmouth's *Historia regum Britanniae*.
26 Vinaver and Field 1990: 1300 (note to 48.22–4).
27 Ibid.: 185.8–187.13, 190.13–191.8; Hamel 1984: lines 78–165, 419–66.
28 Vinaver and Field 1990: 225.26–226.8; Hamel 1984: lines 2344–64.
29 Frappier 1936: §162. Arthur does swear by 'l'ame Uter-pandagron [*sic*] son pere' in one of Malory's minor sources, Chrétien de Troyes's *Yvain* (Roques 1955: line 663); cf. Field 1991; but there is nothing to suggest that Malory was thinking of Yvain at this point in his story.
30 Wilson 1950a: 33–40; Hamel 1984: 42.
31 Hamel 1984: line 3776.
32 Ibid.: line 4181.
33 Ibid.: 34-62, at 34.
34 See *OED*, s.v. 'goodman'; and cf. *MED*, s.v. 'god man', esp. later senses.
35 See *MED*, s.vv. 'child', 5-6; 'norri'; 'fode', 3a.
36 For Kay, see Gowans 1988: 108-9.
37 See Wilson 1950a; Field 1991 and 1993a.
38 Vinaver and Field 1990: 1037.8–11 (title of the 'Tale of the Sankgreal'), 92.2–3 (Perceval confused with Pelleas), 180.10 (Galahad confused with Galahalt the Haute Prince). Malory's memory of *Perlesvaus* seems also to have been confused in this tale and clarified later: see Field 1993b.
39 Vinaver and Field 1990: 41.11–30, 44.16–30.
40 E.g. Hamel 1984: lines 3398–3406, 3446–55.
41 Vinaver and Field 1990: 1242.25 and 29, 1259.9–21, 1260.15. For the second, see Withrington 1987; for the others, see Field 1978: notes to lines 2109, 2458, 2498.
42 Matthews 1960.

43 Hamel 1984: lines 429-30, 3150-75, 4320-2.
44 See Vinaver and Field 1990: 1150.27-9.
45 Ibid.: 493.10-11.
46 Ibid.: 326.13-32, 336.28-338.6.
47 See Field 1993a.

6
'Illuminat vith lawte, and with lufe lasit': Gawain gives Arthur a lesson in magnanimity

GILLIAN ROGERS

> Nay, drede you nott, lord, by Mary flower,
> I am nott that man that wold you dishonour,
> Nother by euyn ne by moron. (*WSG* 149–51; Gawain to Arthur)

As a research student of Maldwyn's I set out, in my innocence, with the idea of discussing *all* the English Gawain poems, and worked on several texts that did not find their way into the finished thesis until Maldwyn patiently persuaded me that I could not possibly hope to deal with the whole Gawain canon in one dissertation. Among the abandoned romances that I worked on were *The Awntyrs off Arthure* (*AA*), written after 1375, *Golagros and Gawane* (*GG*), dating to just before the turn of the fifteenth century, and *The Weddynge of Sir Gawen and Dame Ragnell* (*WSG*), composed *c*. 1450, the first two of which deal with the theme of Arthur's unjust sequestration of lands belonging to others, and the third of which uses this motif as a nominal excuse for hostile action against Arthur.[1]

What most interested me in them, however, was the idea that in each, although in very different ways, Arthur finds himself in an untenable position because of his act of unjust sequestration and has to be extricated by Gawain, who in each is the loyal vassal, willingly undertaking the task if it will save Arthur's face and help to maintain his 'worship' – not, however, without considerable cost to himself.

The roots of this situation go right back to the beginnings of his literary career, where, in William of Malmesbury's *Gesta regum Anglorum* (*c*. 1125), and Geoffrey of Monmouth's *Historia regum Britanniae* (*c*. 1138), we find it in its simplest form – Gawain deeply involved in his uncle's affairs, expending all his not inconsiderable energies in upholding his position and, in the latter, dying in his cause.

By far the most extended and impressive treatment of his activities on behalf of Arthur and his kingdom is found in the Vulgate *Merlin*, where, from the moment he first hears of his relationship to Arthur and of his struggles against the Saxons and against his rebel vassals, the young Gawain abandons his carefree life of hunting and amusement, and leads his brothers and innumerable cousins and friends against the Saxons while Arthur is away helping Leodagan against Rion and dallying with Guenevere, and succeeds in holding them at bay, with Merlin's help and advice, until Arthur returns. There is tacit criticism of Arthur in this. How could he spend so long away from his kingdom while it was being overrun by Saxons? In effect, Gawain, guided by Merlin, saves his kingdom for him, and also plays a dominant part in bringing about a reconciliation with the rebel vassals, among whom is his own father, whom he threatens to behead if he does not accord with Arthur. Loyalty to his uncle overrides loyalty to immediate family in a spectacular way here, in sharp distinction to the role decreed for him in the *Suite du Merlin*, where his family loyalties take precedence over almost all others.[2]

But Gawain, throughout his literary career, is not uncritical of his uncle's activities and never hesitates to rebuke him if he thinks he is doing something foolish. He is, indeed, the one knight at court with the licence to do this and emerge unscathed from the experience.[3] This habit of rebuke is seen as early as the opening scene of Chrétien's *Erec et Enide*, where Arthur has conceived the ill-advised notion of hunting the white stag, a proceeding which, as 'Mon seignor Gauvain' points out to him, is bound to lead to trouble, since the one who kills the stag must kiss the fairest lady of the court, and, says Gawain, there are five hundred beautiful damsels here, all with bold and valiant lovers ready to dispute the verdict. Arthur ignores his advice, but later, when he has killed the stag himself and things threaten to turn out as Gawain has predicted, he turns to him again:

> Biax niés Gauvains, conselliez m'an,
> sauve m'annor et ma droiture,
> que je n'ai de la noise cure.

(Gawain, my good nephew, advise me how to keep my honour and my rights, for I have no wish for quarrelling.)[4]

Gawain's criticisms, however, are usually prompted by a desire to save Arthur from the results of his own folly, and thus are a by-product of his deep concern for his uncle's 'wele and wirchipe', of which he is the principal upholder.

It is a small step from this situation to one where Gawain is forced to take action in order to save Arthur from himself. In the three romances I began with, *AA*, *GG* and *WSG*, the initial situation is one in which Arthur has cast land-greedy eyes on another man's possessions. In the second part of *AA*, according to Galeron of Galloway, the owner of the disputed lands, he has 'wonene hem in werre with a wrange [wile]' (421) and given them to Gawain, and Galeron has come to claim them back, vowing that Gawain

> shal hem neuer welde ...
> But he wyne hem in were,
> Withe a shelde and a spere,
> On a faire felde   (*AA* 425-9)

– although in the next lines, oddly, he widens his challenge to include the whole court.

Arthur tacitly acknowledges the justice of Galeron's charge by failing to rebut it, and by granting his request for single combat on the following day. In this instance, Gawain, as the recipient of the said lands, is obviously the most fitting person to undertake the combat, as he himself recognizes, and he insists on being allowed to fight, despite Arthur's deep reluctance to jeopardize his safety in this way.[5] Gawain has, in fact, been put in a false position by Arthur, to such an extent that he finds himself, in order to uphold Arthur's honour, having to maintain the rightness of his cause in the face of its manifest wrongness:

> I wolle fight with þe knighte,
> In defence of my riȝte.   (*AA* 466-7)

When requested by Arthur to give the lands back to Galeron, Gawain does so with a ready will, although the generosity of this is somewhat undermined by the fact that Arthur has already given him other lands to compensate for his loss. And we are bound to ask the question: whose lands were these before Arthur so casually handed them over to him? Seen in the light of the first part of *AA*, where, during a hunt at the Tarn Wadling, the ghost of Guenevere's mother appears to her and to her companion Gawain and launches a bitter attack upon the moral laxity of the court, on Guenevere's pride, vanity and neglect of the poor and (prompted by a question from Gawain) upon Arthur's covetousness in the matter of other people's lands, this casual resolution of the matter can only create a sense of moral unease in the reader.

In *WSG*, the motif of Arthur's unjust sequestration of land only occurs as the immediate reason for Sir Gromer Somer Joure's hostility towards him but, again, the lands have been given to Gawain, and so, once again, he is the most appropriate person to resolve the issue. When Arthur tells him that the answer to the riddle can only be obtained by his consenting to marry the Loathly Lady, he agrees at once, in terms which leave no doubt as to where his loyalties lie:

> For ye ar my kyng withe honour,
> And haue worshypt me in many a stowre ...
> To saue your lyfe, lorde, itt were my parte,
> Or were I false and a greatt coward. (*WSG* 348–52)

He goes through with it, too, much the calmest figure in a court thrown into a frenzy of mourning for him and reduced to shameful suggestions as to how to hush the whole affair up. He is, of course, duly rewarded when the Loathly Lady is transformed back into a beautiful young woman, but he was not to know that this would happen when he agreed to marry her.

Despite his manifestly deep loyalty to Arthur, however, he is not averse to teasing him a little, and so, on the morning after the wedding, when Arthur, perturbed at Gawain's non-appearance in hall and convinced that the Fiend has taken him, knocks apprehensively on the door and asks why he sleeps so long, Gawain replies that he 'wold be glad, and ye wold lett me be' (734), for he is 'fulle welle att eas' (735). He relents immediately, however, and opens the door to show the king why he is so reluctant to rise. His relationship with Arthur, then, is not simply one of blind devotion and loyalty, even though devotion and loyalty are the mainsprings of his action.

This becomes very apparent when we turn to the third of these romances, *GG*.[6] Whereas in *AA* Gawain, trapped in a false position by Arthur's stance towards Galeron, in effect finds himself in collusion with him, in *GG* he takes active steps to circumvent him. The Scottish author of *GG* had absolutely clear-cut ideas about what he was doing when he adapted two sections of a prose version of the First Continuation of Chrétien's *Perceval* to his own purposes, and it is a measure of his originality that he could extract two such unrelated incidents from among so many and see the potential for linking them in the way that he does. For he makes the events of the first episode (1–234) act as a commentary-in-advance on the events of the second (235–end), and he uses Gawain himself as the connecting link between the two seemingly disparate episodes. The juxtaposition of the two brings out the superiority of Gawain's courteous approach to others over Arthur's imperialistic one.

Kay's behaviour in the first episode, while presenting a clear contrast with Gawain's, also foreshadows Arthur's in the second. In the first episode, Arthur decides to go on pilgrimage to the Holy Land, an inspired change of motivation from that in the French source, where Arthur takes fifteen knights with him in a bid to rescue Girflet from the Riche Soudoier's prison. The fact that he is on so holy a mission at the time when he vows to subdue Golagros to his will makes a telling point about the quality of his Christian belief in relation to his worldly ambition. On the way, he and his company run out of supplies and see a city not far away. Kay asks to be allowed to go and ask for *vittale* from its lord. Arthur agrees, but warns him: 'Luke that wisly thow wirk' (58) – futilely, as it turns out. Finding the gates open, Kay goes in and enters a hall, which is deserted save for a dwarf tending the spit. Kay, desperate for food, snatches a leg of the roasting fowl. The dwarf roars out his indignation, and this brings in the very angry, and very formidable, lord of the castle, who vows to make Kay regret his rudeness before he leaves. Kay, hasty-tempered as always, retorts that he does not give a cake for his threats and will pay him back for them. The lord wastes no more time on him, but fells him with a blow and stalks out. Kay creeps out of the hall and makes his way back to Arthur, reporting that it is no use expecting any food from that source.

Gawain advises Arthur to send a milder-mannered man in place of *crabbit* Kay, one who will seek friendship with the lord. He is evidently not thinking of himself in this role, but readily agrees to go when Arthur, realizing that Kay has aroused the lord's ill-will, begs him to 'for the gude rude!' (124), for 'Is nane sa bowsum ane berne, brith for to bynd' (125). Arthur himself thus defines Gawain's role, not only in this first episode, but in the second also.

Gawain's message to the lord of the castle makes clear his own allegiance and his own opinion of his liege lord. He is come, he says, 'Fra cumly Arthur, the king, cortesse and fre' (138). His lord, he continues, wishes to buy food in the lord's town, at whatever price is asked. This is a contrast, *avant la lettre*, to the second episode. Here, Arthur is willing to pay for what he gets; in the second episode, he wishes to take without payment. The lord replies firmly that he does not wish any food to be sold to Gawain's *senyeour*.

> 'That is at your avne will,' said wourthy Gawane;
> 'To mak you lord of your avne, me think it grete skill'
> (*GG* 146-7)

– thereby stating the principle which will govern his actions in the second episode.[7] The lord of the hall, however, has a surprise for Gawain: 'Pase on thi purpos', he says;

> For all the wyis I weild ar at his avne will
> How to luge and to leynd, and in my land lent;
> Gif I sauld hym his awin,
> It war wrang to be knawin;
> Than war I wourthy to be drawin
> Baldly on bent. (*GG* 150-6)

And later, to Arthur, he says:

> Heir I mak yow of myne maister of myght,
> Of all the wyis and welth I weild in this steid ...
> This kyth and this castell ...
> Ressaue as your awin. (*GG* 187-95)

There is a nice irony in this situation, which becomes apparent as the second episode unfolds. Here, in the prologue to the main action, the lord, a kinsman of Arthur's as it turns out, unhesitatingly and unstintingly offers his all to Arthur, who really only wants a good meal and a bed for the night; while in the second episode, Golagros, whose all is precisely what Arthur does want, gives him nothing at all. The lord's generous offer here, in effect stating the ideal lord–vassal relationship, is an addition of the Scottish poet, and is thus part of the deliberate patterning of his poem.

The 'Gawain–Kay contrast', so common a feature of Arthurian romance, is here, unusually, put to good structural and thematic use, and is also extended beyond its usual scope by bringing Arthur into the equation too. As is usual in this motif, Kay's *crabbit* nature, which instantly sets him in opposition to anyone new he encounters, is set against Gawain's pacific and courteous way of approaching strangers.[8] But here, in addition, it is used as a deliberate foreshadowing of Arthur's intransigent attitude towards Golagros, just as Gawain's way of dealing with the unnamed lord of the castle in the first episode foreshadows his treatment of Golagros in the second. Kay, hungry for food, grabs what he wants without asking; Arthur, hungry for land, attempts to grab that belonging to the free and independent Golagros. Kay comes to grief; Arthur, thanks to Gawain, does not. This Gawain–Kay motif occurs again, in the second episode, but in a very different form, as we shall see.

In the second part we see the themes of the first played out on a larger scale, and more seriously. The poet pares the problem down to its barest bones by concentrating his narrative upon one episode, presenting us, in the person of Golagros, with a theme closely related to that of unjust conquest, the reverse side of the coin in fact, that of sovereignty and freedom, the right of the individual lord to rule his lands in his own way, owing no feudal allegiance to any other man.

The omniscient Sir Spynagros is introduced (in place of Bran de Lis in the French version), to act as guide, informant and admonisher of Arthur, an important role which serves to underline the nature of Arthur's activities in this section. When Arthur, continuing his pilgrimage to the Holy Land, sees the magnificent castle set high above the Rhône and asks about it, Spynagros tells him that its lord owes no allegiance to anyone. Arthur is astonished at this, but says instantly:

> He sall at my agane cumyng
> Mak homage and oblissing,
> I mak myne avow! (*GG* 271–3)

This *gab*-like pronouncement elicits a stern warning from Spynagros not to meddle:

> Or he be strenyeit with strenth, yone sterne for to schore,
> Mony ledis salbe loissit, and liffis forlorne. (*GG* 276-7)

And later, when Arthur confirms his vow –

> Yit sal I mak thame vnrufe, foroutin resting,
> And reve thame thair rentis, with routis full ride (*GG* 499-500)

– Spynagros comes back at him with:

> Schir, ye ar in your maieste, your mayne and your myght,
> Yit within thir dais thre,
> The sicker suth sall ye se,
> Quhat kin men that thai be,
> And how thai dar fight. (*GG* 514-18)

Arthur of course pays no heed to his warning. He has vowed to force Golagros to do homage to him, and is determined to achieve this aim –

> Or ellis mony wedou
> Ful wraithly sal weip   (*GG* 297-8)

– a declaration which contains echoes of his widow-making activities in the alliterative *Morte Arthure* (*AMA*).[9] No man dare argue with him – not even, we must assume, Gawain.

Arthur hurries through his pilgrimage with almost indecent haste, and is soon camped outside the city on the Rhône once more, holding a council of his knights to decide what should be done. In another departure from the source, he is advised by a 'vight weriour' (not, this time, Spynagros) to send an embassy to Golagros, 'wise, vailyeing, and moist of valour' (328), to test his reaction to the idea of paying homage to an alien king. If he agrees, he should be received with honour; if he refuses, then he should be besieged.

Gawain, Lancelot and Ewin are chosen to go on the embassy, but do not escape without a lecture from Spynagros as to what to say to Golagros: 'meikly with mouth mel to that myld', he urges, 'and mak him na manance ... And faynd his frendschip to fang', for 'It hynderis neuer for to be heyndly of speche' (354–8). Gawain, one feels, scarcely needs such a lecture, but it serves to underline the point about feudal relationships and the correct way to establish them.

The courteous welcome given to the members of the embassy by Golagros both emphasizes the heinousness of Arthur's intention and gives Gawain a measure of insight into his future opponent's character. At this point, the *GG* poet, like the *Gawain* poet on another occasion when Gawain is about to depart on a dangerous journey, pauses to list Gawain's virtues in an unusually full portrait of him:

> That euer wes beildit in blis, and bounte embrasit,
> Joly and gentill, and full cheuailrus,
> That neuer poynt of his prise wes fundin defasit,
> Egir and ertand, and ryght anterus,
> Illuminat vith lawte, and with lufe lasit.   (*GG* 390–4)

This statement carries no overtones of ambiguity at all and, in the event, proves to be a very precise and accurate description of Gawain's character as expressed in his actions. The phrase 'with lufe lasit' seems a direct reference to the pentangle virtues of Gawain in *Sir Gawain and the Green Knight*, and line 392 might almost have been written as a direct rebuttal of Sir Bredbeddle's claim that Gawain has lost his '3 points' as a result of concealing the lace from him in *The Grene Knight*.[10]

Gawain's honey-tongued message is very unlike that which he delivers on a previous embassy, that to the Emperor Lucius in *AMA*, where his obvious intention is to start a riot. Here, he is all smooth diplomat, delivering a speech in which the true meaning is glossed over under cover of an offer of friendship, and with the sting in the tail. He speaks of Arthur's greatness, of Golagros's might and nobility, says that Arthur will not rest until he has freely secured Golagros's *frendschip*, says that his lord will not stint of prayer and *largesse* to gain it. By 'friendship', of course, Gawain really means 'submission', but so skilful is his speech that this aspect of the matter is made to seem a minor point, of no particular importance.

By making Gawain Arthur's messenger at this crucial moment, however, the poet raises a problem in the modern reader's mind, since this appears to make him, tacitly at least, a supporter of Arthur's unjust claim. There is no indication of his own feelings at this point. But would contemporary readers necessarily have drawn this conclusion? It is possible that they would have seen him simply as the impartial ambassador, the loyal servant of his king, doing Arthur's bidding in the best and most courteous way that he can. For here no moral dilemma of a gift of lands comes between him and his bounden duty as it does in *AA*. One's view of Gawain is thus much clearer and less impeded by moral problems than it is in that romance.

Golagros has no difficulty in interpreting Gawain's honeyed words, and reading 'submission' for 'friendship', but he replies with equal courtesy. He and his forebears have never owed fealty to any man in the past, and if he did homage to Arthur now he would be fit only to hang from a tree. 'Bot', he says:

> sauand my senyeoury fra subiection,
> And my lordscip vn-lamyt, withoutin legiance,
> All that I can to yone king, cumly with croun,
> I sall preif all my pane to do hym plesance. (*GG* 441-4)

He is willing to do anything for Arthur save that which Arthur most desires, give up his freedom:

> I will noght bow me ane bak ...
> I think my fredome to hald,
> As my eldaris of ald
> Has done me beforne (*GG* 449-53)

– a stark contrast to the willingness of the lord in the first part to acknowledge Arthur as his overlord. Despite this firm denial of Arthur's right to deprive Golagros of his lands, the exchange is a most civilized one on both sides, paralleling the equally civilized one between Gawain and Arthur's kinsman in the first part.

Golagros's resistance simply stiffens Arthur's resolve and, ignoring Spynagros's strictures, he sets about getting his own way. Nonetheless, Spynagros's overt criticism of Arthur's tactics, and his own unashamed admiration of Golagros, underline the criminal folly of Arthur's proceedings.

Hostilities commence, with grievous wounds resulting from the various encounters; indeed, the Scottish poet emphasizes the waste and futility of the whole proceeding by having two of the combatants die of heart-attacks, and another of his wounds. Despite his fierce resolve to subdue Golagros to his will, Arthur does suffer at the sight of his knights' travails on the field of battle:

> The roy ramyt for reuth, richist of rent,
> For cair of his knightis cruel and kene   (*GG* 693-4)

– although his sorrow does not move him to stop the fighting of course.

Eventually, Gawain, hearing from Spynagros that Golagros intends to come out himself on the following day, asks to be allowed to encounter him. Arthur grants him the combat, praying God to grant Gawain his 'grace'. Spynagros, not apparently having much faith in Gawain's ability to overcome Golagros, proffers another dose of advice, this time to keep cool and let Golagros become angry and wear himself out first – quite good advice, as it turns out.

Golagros's appearance on the field of battle is described in some detail, whereas the arming of Gawain, given some prominence in the French source, is merely referred to. Instead, we are given Kay's exploit, not, as in the French, abortive and a source of mockery, but successful – just. Desperate to win some glory for himself, he goes out alone, in secret, to seek combat, and, after a strenuous fight with an opponent bent on the same errand, he finds himself the victor, not so much by force of arms as by lack of enthusiasm on the other knight's part. As W. R. J. Barron pointed out some years ago, this triumph of Kay's lends even more point to Gawain's subsequent decision to aid Golagros, since he knows that Kay will seem to have succeeded where he failed.[11] The effect of the omission of Gawain's arming ceremony is to emphasize the emergence of Golagros from his stronghold, his coming out to defend his sovereignty, stately and magnificent – and powerful.

At first, Gawain heeds Spynagros's advice to let Golagros become angry and wear himself out first, and he suffers considerably as a result, to the great alarm and distress of the king, who, to do him justice, is concerned far more for Gawain's safety than for his own honour. But eventually Gawain becomes angry as well, and the two batter away at each other, fairly evenly matched. Seeing them there on the field, neither one gaining the advantage, Arthur suffers a slight change of heart which gives hope for the future, for, while entreating God to spare Gawain, he does also have the grace to pray that the outcome of the encounter be honourable to both the combatants.

At last, after a particularly hard blow from Gawain, Golagros stumbles on a slope and falls, and before he can move Gawain is upon him, demanding that he yield. He is greatly disconcerted at Golagros's firm refusal to do so. None of his forebears has ever been overcome and disgraced, says Golagros. He prefers to die rather than let people see him shamed thus:

> Do furth thi devoir;
> Of me gettis thou na more. (*GG* 1048-9)

Gawain entreats him to change his mind, 'For he wes wondir wa to wirk hym mare wugh' (1067):

> Schir, say for thi self, thow seis thou art schent;
> It may nocht mend the ane myte to mak it so teugh. (*GG* 1068-9)

He urges him to come to the king, and, seeking to comfort him, he offers him the promise of a dukedom if he will.[12] He is way off the mark, of course, but he means well. Golagros will have none of it; he is unyielding in his determination not to trade honour for riches. He sets his freedom far above anything that the Round Table can offer him. He will abide by his destiny.

Gawain, in a quandary, now proves the truth of the poet's earlier description of him as 'with lufe lasit', and begins to fulfil the potential his words and actions had hinted at in the first episode. Moved to pity, he asks an extraordinary question for a knight in his victorious position: 'How may I succour the sound ... Before this pepill in plane, and pair noght thy pris?' (*GG* 1092-3). Even so, he is taken aback at Golagros's prompt reply:

> Lat it worth at my wil the wourschip to wale,
> As I had wonnyn the of were, wourthy and wis;
> Syne cary to the castel, quhare I haue maist cure.
> Thus may thow saif me fra syte;
> As I am cristynit perfite,
> I sall thi kyndnes quyte,
> And sauf thyn honoure. (*GG* 1096-1102)

Such a ready reply may seem to sit, perhaps, somewhat oddly on one who previously had expressed so strong a determination to die rather than to yield, but then Golagros thought he was facing the usual fate of a defeated knight, and would infinitely have preferred to die rather than accept his life under such humiliating circumstances. Gawain's unusual reaction shows him a glimmer of light at the end of the tunnel, a possible way out of the *impasse*.

Because Golagros is concerned for his freedom and his honour, and not for the respect of an *amie* as is his French counterpart, the whole balance of this scene is altered. In the First Continuation of *Perceval*, Gawain's concern is to save the lives of the Riche Soudoier and his lady; here, his quandary is more serious, as his debate with himself shows. Not only is he being asked to trust a knight he does not know, but, if that trust should prove misplaced, he risks imperilling many other knights' lives. But he has tested this knight in battle and knows him to be brave and valiant; in speech he knows him to be courteous. Gawain decides to trust him. His decision resolves the whole disastrous situation: 'I do me in thi gentrice, be Drightin sa deir' (1111), he says simply. In doing so, he is pronouncing judgement upon Arthur's unjust claim to Golagros's lands and sovereignty. He has made his decision, has come down on the side of the independent lord against his own liege lord. He has been promised redress, but he has no sure knowledge that this will be forthcoming. He has only his instinct to guide him, that Golagros is a good and honourable man and will keep his promise.[13]

The reaction of Arthur and his knights to the sight of Gawain being led away is extreme, and is very reminiscent of their several reactions to the idea of harm coming to him in *AMA*. The king weeps, 'As all his welthis in warld had bene away went' (1132) and retires to his tent. His knights, stirred to their depths, cry out in grief:

>   The flour of knighthede is caught throu his cruelte!
>   Now is the Round Tabill rebutit, richest of rent,
>   Quhen wourschipfull Wawane, the wit of our were,
>   Is led to ane presoune;
>   Now failyeis gude fortoune!   (*GG* 1135–9)

Compare *AMA* 2685, where the foraging knights cry out: 'For all oure wirchipe, iwysse, away es in erthe!' when they see how severely wounded their 'wardayne full wyrchipfull' is. And Arthur, kneeling by Gawain's dead body, cries out in passionate grief:

> For nowe my wirchipe es wente ...
> Here es þe hope of my hele, my happynge of armes;
> My herte and my hardynes hale one hym lengede –
> My concell, my comforthe þat kepide myn herte! (*AMA* 3957–60)[14]

This is Gawain seen almost as a mascot, the Round Table's 'luck', and Arthur's source of good fortune. No other knight of Arthur's court seems to elicit this kind of response to the prospect of his loss.

In the castle, Golagros, amid the rejoicing of his people, sets Gawain at the high table with his wife and daughter, and both he and the prisoners taken in the various combats are treated with courtesy. After the meal, Golagros offers his people the choice of having him remain as their lord, though defeated and owing allegiance to another, or of choosing a new, undefeated lord (he presumably has Gawain in mind for this). Their response is overwhelmingly in his favour, thus justifying Gawain's trust in him. Sure of their loyalty, Golagros now tells them of Gawain's act of compassion towards a defeated man. What impresses him most about Gawain's action is that he did it 'In sight of his souerane' (1201). 'It war syn, but recure', he says,

> The knightis honour suld smure,
> That did me this honoure,
> Quhilk maist is of price. (*GG* 1203–6)

Golagros then declares his intention of being 'at his bidding full bane, blith to obeise' (1209), the outcome hopefully envisaged by the 'vight weriour' when he advised Arthur to send an embassy to Golagros. But he is, initially, making this promise to Gawain, and he follows it up with a promise to

> make the manrent with hand,
> As right is, and skill. (*GG* 1218–19)

The guest–host relationship is now reversed. Gawain, by conquest and generosity, has become Golagros's lord. In his submission to Gawain, Golagros pays him one of the simplest, yet also one of the most impressive, tributes that that knight ever receives in the whole of his chequered literary career. 'Schir', he says, 'I knaw be conquest thow art ane kynd man' (1214).[15] This submission has no counterpart in the French. The Riche Soudoier merely packs his lady off to another of his castles, releases his prisoners, and goes off with them to Arthur, to whom he yields. There is no question of him yielding first to Gawain and only afterwards to Arthur, as he does here.[16]

The doubling of the scene in this way is not so much a stylistic defect as the *GG* poet's way of emphasizing the fact that it is not Arthur's aggression that has subdued Golagros, but Gawain's magnanimity. It seems only fitting that Golagros should first pay homage to the knight who has enabled him to preserve life, honour and lordship by subordinating his own honour to that of his conquered opponent.

Late as it is, they go in a happy, laughing party to Arthur's camp 'with grete lightis on loft' (1254). Arthur is not a little alarmed to see them come, and his knights form a line of lances across the road to bar their way. But Spynagros, as always, knows that they come in peace: 'I wait schir Gawane the gay has graithit this gait' (1267), he declares.

Golagros submits freely to Arthur, making his reason for doing so quite clear:

> Because of yone bald berne, that broght me of bandis,
> All that I haue wndir hewyne, I hald of you haill,
> In firth, forest and fell, quhare euer that it standis.
> Sen vourschipfull Wawane has wonnyn to your handis
> The senyory in gouernyng,
> Cumly conquerour and kyng,
> Heir mak [I] yow obeising,
> As liege lord of landis. (*GG* 1316-23)

And he requests that it be made public. At Gawain's suggestion, they all repair back to the castle for nine days of feasting. Before leaving, Arthur restores his freedom to Golagros, absolutely and without conditions.

So, to sum up, Gawain fights Golagros to uphold Arthur's claim to Golagros's lands, but by his decision to agree to become Golagros's prisoner so that Golagros can ascertain his standing with his own people he tacitly acknowledges the injustice of Arthur's position and takes matters into his own hands, exercising his independent judgement of both opponent and situation, thereby resolving the hopeless dilemma at a stroke. Golagros shows his awareness of what this surrender means to Gawain in terms of his own reputation by emphasizing the fact that Gawain yielded himself in full view of his sovereign lord and all his companions of the Round Table. Gawain here, then, takes a positive step in opposition to Arthur, thereby fulfilling, in this late flowering of his literary career, the promise of fruitful reaction against his uncle and liege lord that began to bud as early as Chrétien's *Erec*. The result in this instance is a happy one. Gawain's action sparks off Arthur's reaction. The vassal has given his lord a lesson in magnanimity. Only Gawain, of all Arthur's knights, could have achieved this without incurring Arthur's wrath. The promise of the first part, with its themes of reconciliation through courtesy and of making the lord of the castle 'lord of his own', is borne out in the second, where Gawain's courteous regard for the feelings of others reconciles him to Golagros, who is thus prompted to follow the example of the lord in the first episode and surrender his all, first to Gawain and then to Arthur. Arthur in return is moved to emulate Gawain and makes Golagros too 'lord of his own' once more.

We are left with no such feeling of rightness at the end of *AA*, despite its 'happy' ending of restitution and reconciliation. There is no sense on Arthur's part that he might have been wrong to take Galeron's lands in the first place; indeed, he seems to preen himself on his magnanimity in granting them back to him once Gawain has overcome him. There is no sense, either, that Gawain has learned anything particular from his damaging encounter with Galeron. The lesson of the fearful apparition of Guenevere's mother that rises from the Tarn Wadling in the first part of the romance, its message to the questioning Gawain that 'Your king is to couetous' (265), seems to fall on deaf ears, and it is very evident that Arthur, Gawain and all the companions of the Round Table intend to go on exactly as they have done in the past – until nemesis, the nature of which, based on the events of *AMA*, is clearly spelled out to Gawain and Guenevere at the Tarn by Guenevere's mother, catches up with them.

These two romances, *AA* and *GG*, then, demonstrate two different ways in which the theme of Arthur's unjust conquest could be treated by poets with a serious intent. The *AA* poet juxtaposes a homiletic 'romance' derived from many different, mainly non-

Arthurian, sources, with a seemingly 'typical' romance episode of knightly combat, in which Arthur is described in terms of admiration for his magnificence and his apparent magnanimity towards a defeated opponent, and leaves the reader to draw the moral lesson from the juxtaposition. The *conjointure* is awkward and ungainly, but nevertheless curiously compelling. In *GG*, the two carefully selected episodes enhance and illuminate each other, and the result is a coherent and cogent demonstration of the abuse of kingly power redeemed by an act of true magnanimity. The poet, however, prepares the way for Arthur's acceptance of Gawain's lesson in the way that he describes him throughout, without apparent irony, as *cumly, seymly,* and *kene,* and allows him a moment of grace in which to express the hope that both combatants will emerge unscathed. This ending leaves behind it in the reader's mind no moral uncertainty at all.

> 'Garamercy, Gawen,' then sayd kyng Arthor,
> 'Of alle knyghtes thou berest the flowre . . .
> My worshypp and my lyf thou savyst for-euere
> Therfore my loue shalle nott frome the dyssevyr,
> As I am kyng in lond.'   (*WSG* 372–7)

Notes

1 Gates 1969; Amours 1897: 1–46; Sumner 1924; dates from Severs 1967: 61–5.
2 The Vulgate *Merlin,* translated as *The Story of Merlin* by Rupert T. Pickens in Lacy 1993: I, 167–424.
3 Although Sir Spinagros in *GG* is, exceptionally, allowed this licence, as will be seen below.
4 Roques 1955: lines 308–10; Owen 1987: 1, 5.
5 The *AA* poet seems to be unaware of the tradition, recounted in William of Malmesbury's *Gesta regum Anglorum,* which made Gawain himself lord of Galloway.
6 For a discussion of the possible contemporary political background to this romance, see Alexander 1975: 28ff.
7 Other examples of Gawain making his host 'lord of his own', in the form of 'at your/his bidding ... bain' occur in *Sir Gawain and the Green Knight* 1092 (Tolkien and Gordon 1967: 30); in *The Turke and Gowin* 108 (Hales and Furnivall 1867–8: I, 94); and in *Syre Gawene and the Carle of Carelyle* 458–60 (Madden 1839: 200) and its Percy Folio counterpart, *Carle off Carlile* 302 (Hales and Furnivall 1867–8: III, 287).

8   The archetypal example of this occurs in Chrétien's *Erec*, where Gawain succeeds by his courtesy in bringing the wounded Erec back to court for a much-needed night's rest, while Kay's brusque approach merely earns him a fall (Roques 1955: lines 3945-4137; Owen 1987: 53–5).
9   There are many echoes of *AMA* in this romance, as there are also in *AA*.
10 Hales and Furnivall 1867–8: II, 76.
11 Barron 1974: 179.
12 The theme of 'duke-making' occurs also in *AMA* and in *AA*, both of which seem to have influenced the *GG* poet, notably in his portrayal of Arthur as conqueror. All three poems treat Arthur with a curious mixture of praise and blame, although the ambiguity is greatest in *AMA*, where critics are still trying to decide whether Arthur's wars are just or unjust.
13 By changing the balance of the scene in this way, the poet also removes some of the credibility of motivation. It is difficult to see how Gawain's apparent submission will alter the basic situation. Is Golagros so uncertain of his people's loyalty that he feels he has to ask them whether they prefer him alive and defeated, or dead with honour? Since they will know that he has been defeated as soon as he tells them, how does Gawain's action save him from disgrace in their eyes?
14 Quotations from Hamel 1984.
15 Although Perceval makes a similar remark to Gawain when they first meet in *Perlesvaus* (see Bryant 1978: 137). Hearing Gawain's praise of him, he says: 'Sire ... you never have a bad word for anyone.'
16 In *AA* too Galeron yields first to Gawain and only afterwards to Arthur, although the scene is described in a confused manner, so that no clear message comes across as it does in *GG*.

7

No poet has his travesty alone: *The Weddynge of Sir Gawen and Dame Ragnell*[1]

STEPHEN H. A. SHEPHERD

This is one of those texts that seem to get edited more often than they get written about.[2] There is some agreement among scholars that it is worthwhile and interesting – perhaps not the least reason for which is that it is an analogue to the Wife of Bath's Tale (WBT) or that it shows some interesting connections with Malory – but little has been said about the poem on its own terms. The chief difficulty appears to lie in deciding to what extent the poem is deliberately humorous beyond the necessary irony of its main action – the irony being found in the situation where men embody or act out the answer to the great question of what women desire most *before* they learn the answer. A concomitant difficulty lies in deciding to what extent the poem offers rather clever *faux* doggerel instead of comprising, alas, nothing but the real thing.

Critical comment, though brief, is consequently variable. Derek Pearsall describes the *Weddynge* (*WSG*) as another example of the 'process of degeneration' to which romance plots are often subject through successive copyings. He describes the poem as 'coarse enough,' and notes the 'obvious relish' with which the poet (not infrequently) describes Ragnell's ugliness. Pearsall nevertheless points to a more serious reading when he adds: 'Gawain behaves like a gentleman throughout, as does Arthur.'[3] P. J. C. Field (whose main purpose is to suggest the possibility that Malory is the author) says that 'the *Wedding* is written in a particularly uninspired kind of doggerel'.[4] Nevertheless, he also acknowledges 'the cheerful effect of the jogging verse-rhythms'.[5] Donald B. Sands places the poem under the heading of 'Burlesque and Grotesquerie' in his well-known anthology and observes that 'the *Dame Ragnell* poet seems to have taken delight in grotesque characterization and absurd social situation, and both features are staples of literary humour'.[6] But Sands also says that this is the work of 'an indifferent artist' and that 'it has no aesthetic complexities'.[7] At the same time he suggests the possibility of a moralistic reading, noting that 'the modern reader may sense two things – that the audience had more respect for Gawain than for Arthur and that the King is selfish enough to foist his personal onus off on his nephew and best friend'.[8] Sands also finds cause for serious reflection on the poem's conclusion: 'oddly, the romance ends on a note of pathos: the poet says Gawain, though often wed, loved Ragnell more than he ever loved any woman, but lost her within five years'.[9] John Withrington takes up Sands's terms, finding that the poem's author 'evidently took great delight in burlesquing the seriousness found elsewhere in Arthurian literature, and revelled in the grotesque and comic possibilities offered by his subject matter',[10] and, on a more serious note, adding: 'unusually ... the poem does not have a happy ending. [Gawain's and Ragnell's] life together lasts only five years, and although Gawain marries often, we are told he never loved anyone else quite as much as Dame Ragnell.'[11] Withrington further notes (this time perhaps recalling Pearsall) that 'Gawain's courteous, loyal and cool approach to the demands made upon him reinforce the image of the "verray parfit gentil knight" presented elsewhere in ME romances'.[12]

Such are the kinds of observation made about the poem; none of them is hostile, but none, on the other hand, for all their resulting contrariety, seems to be equal to its author's obvious interest in the poem. It is a pity that, beyond brief notices in their introductions, Sands and Withrington rarely point to specific examples of the burlesque elements they have alluded to. Certainly, the idea that the poem presents some form of burlesque deserves more examination than it has received, especially given claims made at the same time that it is not well written and is lacking in aesthetic complexity. The text as preserved is defective, having a number of unresolved rhymes, and many couplets which lack the corresponding tail-rhyme lines which otherwise characterize the principal verse-form. This makes it difficult to be certain about authorial intentions and no doubt accounts in large part for the limited amount of critical comment to date. That notwithstanding, it is the purpose of this paper to suggest that the text preserves enough evidence intact to demonstrate that its author carefully constructed an allusive and irreverent humour on several levels – structural, thematic, even lexical.

As taxonomic descriptions of *WSG* point out, the poem not only is a 'Loathly Lady' romance analogous to WBT, but also belongs with a corpus of Middle English texts like *Sir Gawain and the Green Knight* (*GGK*) in which a knight (usually Gawain) has his renowned courtesy and martial prowess tested. Further, *WSG* is a member of a sub-group of these texts which sets much of the action in the enchanted environs of Inglewood Forest. Besides *WSG*, that group consists of *The Avowynge of King Arthur, Sir Gawan, Sir Kaye, and Sir Bawdewyn of Bretan* (*AKA*), *The Awntyrs off Arthure at the Tarn Wathelyne* (*AA*) and, closer to *WSG* than the others, the Percy Folio ballad of *The Marriage of Sir Gawaine* (*MSG*).

Gawain-testing and Inglewood are not, however, the only points the poem has in common with others. The poem may also be imitative of distinctive *formal* features found in some poems in the group. For instance, *AA*, *AKA* and *GGK* all conclude by repeating their opening lines; *WSG* is not quite so exact in its repetition as those poems, but parts of the fourth-last and third-last stanzas do recall the opening stanza and the third stanza (italics mine):

> Lythe and lystenyth the lif of a lord riche!
> The while that he lyvid was none hym liche,
>   Nether in bowre ne in halle.
> *In the tyme of Arthoure thys adventure betyd*;
> And of the greatt adventure, that he hymself dyd,
>   That Kyng curteys and royall ...
>
> Nowe, wyll ye lyst a whyle to my talkyng,
> I shall you tell of Arthoure the Kyng,
>   Howe ones hym befell –
> *On huntyng he was in Ingleswod*
> With alle his bold knyghtes good –
>   Nowe herken to my spell! (1–18)[13]

> *Thus endyth the adventure of Kyng Arthoure*,
> That oft in his days was grevyd sore,
>   And of the weddyng of Gawen –
> Gawen was weddyd oft in his days;
> Butt so well he never lovyd woman, always,
>   As I have hard men sayn.

> *This adventure befell in Ingleswod,*
> *As good Kyng Arthoure on huntyng yod;*
>   Thus have I hard men tell.
>   Nowe God, as thou were in Bethleme born,
>   Suffer never her soules be forlorne
>   In the brynnyng fyre of hell!   (829-40)

It should be added here, for what it is worth, that line 4 reproduces verbatim the first line of the Douce text of *AA*.[14] Note also that the opening line is scrupulously, even excessively, alliterative.[15]

AA and a number of other alliterative poems employ concatenation as a form of stanza-linking.[16] Evidence for such activity in *WSG* is admittedly weak, but there appear to be enough traces to give pause for thought; the impression is of an occasional structural formality reminiscent of the concatenating poems (italics mine):

> The dere lept forth into a brere –
> And ever *the Kyng went* nere and nere.
>
> So *Kyng Arthure went* a whyle
> After the dere (I trowe half a myle).   (35-8)

> Unto Carlyll then the Kyng cam,
> Butt of his *hevynesse* knewe no man;
>   His hartt was wonder *hevy*.
>
> In this *hevynesse* he dyd abyde
> That many of his knyghtes mervelyd that tyde.   (132-6)

> 'Fare wele,' sayd Syr Arthoure, 'so mott I the,
> *I am glad I have so sped!*'
> Kyng Arthoure turnyd hys hors into the playn;
> And sone he mett with Dame Ragnell agayn,
>   In the same place and stede:
>
> 'Syr Kyng, *I am glad ye have sped well.*'   (492-7)

> 'Openly I wol be weddyd or I parte the froo,
>   Elles *shame woll ye have!*
> Ryde before, and I woll com after,
> Unto thy courte, syr King Arthoure;

> Of no man *I woll shame* –
> Bethynk you howe I have savyd your lyf;
> Therfor with me nowe shall ye nott stryfe,
> For and ye do, ye be to blame!'
>
> The Kyng of her *had greatt shame*.   (507–15)

> 'Butt do as ye lyst nowe, my lady gaye;
>   *The choyse I putt in your fyst* –
>
> Evyn as ye wolle, *I putt itt in your hand,*
> Lose me when ye lyst, for I am bond –
>   *I putt the choyse in you.*'   (677–81)

> She lyvyd with Syr Gawen butt yerys .v. –
> That *grevyd* Gawen alle his lyfe,
>   I telle you, securly;
>
> In her lyfe she *grevyd* hym never.   (820–3)

It is unwise to make too much of this evidence, and one should hasten to point out that the Percy Folio ballad *MSG* employs considerable 'incremental repetition', which, though characteristic of the ballad form, may suggest that a common ancestor of the two poems employed stanza-linking as a matter of course, and that *WSG* does not necessarily do so as a matter of imitation with ulterior motives.

That said, there is yet another feature of the poem which may just be imitative of the formal preoccupations of a poem like *AA*. The key word in the poem, as in *WBT*, is *sovereynté*, for that provides the answer to the great question of what women desire most. A. C. Spearing has noted that three Middle English poems, *GGK*, Henryson's *Morall Fabillis*, and *AA*, employ or play upon the notion of a 'sovereign mid-point', where the very centre of the poem presents a view of a sovereign enthroned at the centre of his court, or where there is depicted a 'moment of triumph'.[17] In Henryson and *GGK* such moments appear to have been knowingly displaced or transformed to reflect ironic or subversive themes. The 'central sovereignty' of *AA* is, however, unmitigated: the central line, describing Arthur, reads: 'He was þe soueraynest of al, sitting in sete.'[18] Because of the defective condition of the surviving text of *WSG*, it is impossible to determine the original mid-point; a page is lost, moreover, between fos. 136 and

137 of the Rawlinson MS, making for what can only be estimated at sixty-four missing lines. One wonders, nevertheless, whether it is more than just coincidence that, within two stanzas – indeed, within ten lines – of the nominal centre of the poem as it survives, the sovereign delivers to his challenger, Gromer Somer Joure, an effectively triumphant (though ultimately ironic) answer to the great question – and it is, of course, an answer which names sovereignty:

'I saye no more butt, above al thyng,
Wemen desyre sovereynté, for that is theyr lykyng
  And that is ther moste desyre –
To have the rewll of the manlyest men,
And then ar they well (thus they me dyd ken) –
  To rule the, Gromer syre!' (467-72)

(This appears within 1% of the poem's total length away from the centre.)

Of course to accept the possibility of such a feature in a medieval text is as perilous as identifying numerological systems or embedded anagrams; it is all too easy to see what one wants to see. With this in mind, it must be observed that if one accepts Thomas Percy's estimates of the number of stanzas now missing in the analogous *MSG*, then the corresponding stanza there falls almost exactly in the middle, the fifty-fourth of 109;[19] and WBT (not to mention Gower's analogous Tale of Florent) produces the triumphant answer very near to its physical centre.[20] Perhaps, then, the feature comes (if it is truly there) from a common ancestor; perhaps it is but coincidentally central in the surviving poems. And yet, in either case, one still has to wonder how the *WSG* poet can have been unaware of the feature and its structural value in highlighting what amounts to an announcement of the principal irony of the piece. With the employment of an encircling conclusion not found in the other 'Loathly Lady' poems, *WSG* constructs the impression of a symmetry which, after the fashion of a poem like *AA*, is bound to draw attention to the centre of the poem.

This and other evidence adduced so far for ways in which *WSG* may glance at other texts and techniques is tenuous at best. More secure evidence is available from the observations of commentators such as Field and Withrington, who agree that *WSG* appears in two places to recall WBT.[21] The passages in question are as follows:

> 1 Somme sayd they lovyd to be well arayd;
> Somme sayd they lovyd to be fayre prayed;
> Somme sayd they lovyd a lusty man
> That in theyr armys can clypp them, and kysse them than;
> Somme sayd one, somme sayd other   (199–203)

– which recalls WBT:

> Somme seyde wommen loven best richesse,
> Somme seyde honour, somme seyde jolynesse;
> Somme riche array, somme seyden lust abedde,
> And oftetyme to be widwe and wedde.
> Somme seyde that oure hertes been most esed
> Whan that we been yflatred and yplesed.
> He gooth ful ny the sothe, I wol nat lye.
> A man shal winne us best with flaterye.
> (*The Canterbury Tales*, III.925–32)

> 2 'Summe men sayn we desyre to be fayre;
> Also we desyre to have repayre
>   Of diverse straunge men;
> Also we love to have lust in bed
> And often we desyre to wed –
>   Thus ye men nott ken.
>
> Yett we desyre anoder maner thyng,
> To be holden nott old, butt fresshe and yong;
> With flatryng and glosyng and quaynt gyn,
> So ye men may us wemen ever wyn
>   Of whate ye woll crave.
>
> Ye goo full nyse, I woll nott lye!
> Butt there is one thyng is alle oure fantasye,   (408–20)

which recall the same lines again from WBT, with the added feature, as Withrington notes, of recalling the Wife's use of the first person plural.[22]

It should be added that there is a third passage which may recall the Wife's reference, not in her Tale but in her Prologue, to the attractions of the 'conjugal debt':[23]

> A! Syr Gawen, syn I have you wed,
> Shewe me your cortesy in bed –

With ryght itt may nott be denyed! (*WSG* 629-31)

> The thre were goode men, and riche, and olde;
> Unnethe myghte they the statut holde
> In which that they were bounden unto me.
> Ye woot wel what I meene of this, pardee!
> (*The Canterbury Tales,* III.197-200)

It is possible that the poem not only recalls the Wife and her Tale in these three passages but that it does so in a spirit of creative adaptation and imitation. The third passage has a kind of triumphant and teasing irreverence reminiscent of both the Wife *and* the 'wyf' of her Tale; and, even if the third passage does not result from a specific recollection of Chaucer, it is at least consistent with the other two more authoritative examples in being inherently sardonic. The second passage is perhaps the most freely imitative of the three, for it comprises the point in the story where the hag gives to the beleaguered knight the right answer to the great question. In Chaucer, there is no repetition in that answer of what was earlier said about what the *wrong* answers would be. Indeed, all that is said in WBT is that the hag 'rouned ... a pistel in his ere, / And bad hym to be glad and have no fere' (*The Canterbury Tales,* III. 1021-2). By contrast, the second passage in *WSG* in essence recycles the earlier neo-Chaucerian catalogue of wrong answers with the effect of providing Ragnell with an opportunity to tease a rushed Arthur with a delayed answer. The lines already quoted are preceded by the following, which begin with Arthur's request for haste:

> ' ... tell me nowe, alle in hast,
> Whate woll help now, att last –
>   Have done! I may nott tary!'
> 'Syr,' quod Dame Ragnell, 'nowe shalt thou knowe
> Whate wemen desyren moste, of high and lowe;
>   From this I woll nott varaye.' (402-7)

Ragnell then goes on to give the right answer only after fifteen more tortuous lines of 'varying'.

In being so toyed with, Arthur is accorded even less dignity than the subdued knight of WBT, who has the great answer whispered in his ear without much ado. Moreover, in this and the third example, with its jibe about the 'conjugal debt', the imitative element is displaced contextually from that of the Chaucerian model. The effect of this is surely to give to the humour naturally received from the models the added dimension of travesty of literary form. Whether the same can be said for the other seemingly imitative elements remarked earlier remains to be seen. What can be said, however, is that the weight of evidence presented so far suggests that the poem was intended to be read comparatively. If the Chaucerian imitations represent only the later additions of an interpolator (note the disturbed rhyme-scheme in the first two examples), then the least that can be said for them is that the interpolator recognized something already present in the poem which invited the linking of imitation of form with humour.

Just such a link is perhaps more obviously made in the way the poem ends – or, to be more precise, in the way in which the poem refuses to end. There are two false conclusions before the genuine conclusion. In the first, the narrator promises to be brief (as did Dame Ragnell with Arthur):

> Nowe, for to make you a short conclusyon,
> I cast me for to make an end full sone
> Of this gentyll lady. (817–19)

Given the immediate context, one is led to believe that the verb phrase 'make an end' means, to cite the first two senses given by the *MED* definition, '(a) to cause (something) to cease; stop (something); (b) to finish or conclude (a speech, story, etc.)'.[24] It becomes clear in the next line, however, that sense (c), 'to destroy or kill', is now in order (there is the additional implication that the poet kills Ragnell off just to shorten the poem):

> She lyvyd with Syr Gawen butt yerys .v. –
> That grevyd Gawen alle his lyfe,
> I telle you, securly. (820–2)

Then we have three more lines, the last of which promises closure –

> In her lyfe she grevyd hym never;
> Therfor was never woman to hym lever –
> Thus leves my talkyng (823–5)

– which promise is immediately broken:

> She was the fayrest lady of ale Englond,
> When she was on lyve, I understand –
> So sayd Arthoure the Kyng. (826–8)

After this a new conclusion begins, and it is there that we get the close echoes of the opening lines of the poem which suggest imitation of poems like *AA*; but the first false conclusion is also likely to be imitative, in this case presenting a travesty of the way in which any number of romances 'finish off' their principal characters at the end. For example:

> And so Sir Ywain and his wive
> In joy and blis þai led þaire live.
> So did Lunet and þe liown
> Until þat ded haves dreven þam down.[25]

> Now King Orfeo newe coround is,
> & his quen, Dame Heurodis,
> & liued long after-ward,
> & seþþen was king þe steward.[26]

> Whan he was saued sonde,
> Þei made Sir Galeron þat stonde,
> A kni3t of the table ronde,
> To his lyues ende.[27]

Together the two false conclusions of *WSG* smack of deliberate irreverence. Alone, the first might count as merely inept, but followed so egregiously as it is by the second – which itself is not the actual ending and so confounds the otherwise thoughtful circularity of closure implied by its recollection of the opening lines – the impression is of sham ineptitude. To feel sad or perturbed here at the death of Ragnell risks missing the joke.

Better sense can be made of the third and final conclusion, and indeed of the other potentially imitative features mentioned so far, by examining other less formal aspects of the poem's humour. Such things as the false conclusions or the recollections of WBT naturally depend for their comic force upon our familiarity with the normative structural patterns, or perhaps even the very wording, of other related poems. Inevitably, the comparative reading one should engage in in such circumstances will extend beyond form and into such things as theme and tone – though it seems that the reverse has happened in most modern readings of the poem, where the potentially imitative elements tend to be viewed only as evidence of derivation from, or analogy to, better-known texts. It is important to note that nearly all the imitative features here examined could be described as 'half-baked'; they are imprecisely or ironically rendered. However physically central the sovereignty of the poem is, for instance, it remains sham sovereignty. It is not original to the sovereign, its very utterance in fact reflecting a failure of his own authority. While *WSG*, just like other 'testing' poems, questions the integrity of Arthurian excellence, it does so on the level of the ridiculous and antithetical. Sands and Withrington allude to this in their recognition of 'burlesque' elements; the examples about to be considered may therefore seem obvious – but perhaps the other points we have already considered will make the humorous status of those examples seem more secure.

Where a 'testing' poem like, say, *AA* measures Arthurian achievements in personal honour, political justice, *Frauendienst* and charity, *WSG* offers risible and degraded alternatives. The principles of *Frauendienst*, for example, are here degraded, not only by the poem's insistent relish for 'fat and ugly' jokes of the kind remarked by Pearsall, but by such things as Arthur's rude and patronizing dismissal of Ragnell:

> 'Whate mean you, lady? Telle me tyghte,
> For of thy wordes I have great dispyte;
>   To you I have no nede.
>
> What is your desyre, fayre lady?
> Lett me wete, shortly,
>   Whate is your meanyng,
> And why my lyfe is in your hand;
> Tell me, and I shall you warraunt
>   Alle your oun askyng.'
>
> 'Forsoth,' sayd the lady, 'I am no qued!'   (270–9)

The traditional ideal of Arthurian charity is degraded in *WSG* by Arthur's begrudging and remarkably childish response to Ragnell's request, at the end, that Gromer Somer Joure be treated well:

> She prayd the Kyng, for his gentilnes,
> 'To be good lord to Syr Gromer, iwysse,
> Of that to you he hath offendyd.'
> 'Yes, lady, that shall I nowe, for your sake –
> For I wott well he may nott amendes make –
> He dyd to me full unhend!' (811–16)

Sheer stupidity also has its place in the story, certainly among the men. Sands finds that the fact that Arthur and Gawain collect their answers to the great question in books 'to us is funny and may have been so to listeners in the ... fifteenth century'.[28] No doubt, but surely the better part of the joke comes from the fact that Gromer *stops to read* the answers, thereby allowing Arthur to hedge his bets:

> The Kyng pullyd oute bokes twayne;
> 'Syr, ther is myne answer, I dare sayn,
> For somme woll help att nede.'
> Syr Gromer lokyd on theym everychon. (449–52)

Compare the more discerning response of Gromer's counterpart in *MSG*:

> And then he tooke King Arthurs letters in his hands,
> And away he cold them fling;
> And then he puld out a good browne sword
> And cryd himselfe a king. (88–91)[29]

Gawain may remain something of a paragon of loyalty in this poem, as we have seen several commentators observe, but even paragons, it must be remembered, can be inane and platitudinous (no one has ever questioned Dan Quayle's loyalty). Below are some examples of Gawain at his silly best (italics mine).

Arthur speaks first:

> 'Ther that knyght fast dyd me threte
> And wold have slayn me with greatt heatt;
> Butt I spak fayre agayn –
> Wepyns with me there had I none;
> Alas, my worshypp therfor is nowe gone.'
> *'What thereof?'*[30] sayd Gawen. (158–64)

> 'By God,' sayd the Kyng, 'I drede me sore;
> I cast me to seke a lytell more
>   In Yngleswod Forest –
> I have butt a moneth to my day sett;
> I may hapen on somme good tydynges to hytt –
>   Thys thynkyth me nowe best.'
>
> 'Do as ye lyst,' then Gawen sayd,
> 'Whate-so-ever ye do, I hold me payd –
> *Hytt is good to be spyrryng*!' (213–21)

Here Gawain is overwhelmed not just with the prospect of having to 'chese' a 'choyse', but with the very words themselves:

> 'Alas!' sayd Gawen, 'the choyse is hard!
> To chese the best, itt is froward,
>   Wheder choyse that I chese!' (667–9)

If there is any true intelligence manifest among the poem's characters, it is with Dame Ragnell, who not only speaks with wit but, unlike the others, seems always to be conscious of her capacity for raising a smile. And she speaks with a triumphant self-consciousness which at times appears almost to stand outside the world of the story. We have already seen her taunt Gawain with her request for him to 'show [his] courtesy in bed'; and we have seen her tease Arthur by delaying her revelation of the answer to the great question. In addition, elsewhere she insists that her wedding will be public, to which the queen agrees; but the queen still tries to change Ragnell's mind. Ragnell interrupts confidently, returning the queen's words:

> 'I am greed,' sayd Dame Gaynour,
> 'Butt me wold thynk more honour
>   And your worshypp moste –'
> 'Ye, as for that, lady, God you save;
> This daye my worshypp woll I have,
>   I tell you withoute boste.' (581–6)

Ragnell thus distinguishes between temporary honour and the true lasting honour she will receive should, as she alone knows, Gawain grant her sovereignty. Once she is transformed into 'the fayrest creature / That ever [Gawain] sawe', Gawain, aware that he is in the presence of something unnatural, exclaims 'A! Jhesu! ... whate are ye?' (644) Ragnell responds teasingly:

> Syr, I am your wyf, securly! –
> Why ar ye so unkynde? (645–6)

Unkynde no doubt carries the common additional sense of 'unnatural.' Again, Ragnell proves a master of irony. Indeed, in a passage which is very telling (not the least reason for which is that it has been mis-edited in the past) Ragnell displays a capacity not only to construct word-play, but also to deconstruct it. To begin with, she responds to Arthur's complaint about her ugliness with a proverb:

> No force, syr Kyng, though I be foull;
> Choyse for a make hath an owll. (309–10)

The sense of the proverb is that even ugly creatures can choose (and do find) mates.[31] Ragnell then tells Arthur that she will meet him there again when he comes for the answer to the great question. Then – in a unique burst of self-satisfied wit – Arthur says farewell by making punning reference both to Ragnell's ugliness and to her proverb: 'Now farewell,' sayd the Kyng, 'lady fowll' (315). *Fowll* has usually been dropped from the printed editions because, through some scribal error, it appears in the manuscript as the last word of the previous line, giving rise to seeming nonsense.[32] Because of this confusion and the apparent loss of rhyme, editors comment on how incomprehensible is Ragnell's response in the next two lines;[33] but the corrected reading of line 315 reveals in Ragnell's response a commanding comprehension:

> 'Ye syr,' she sayd, 'ther is a byrd men call an owll –
> And yett a lady I am.' (316–17)

Ragnell alludes, with characteristic playfulness, to the two senses available in Arthur's disdainful *fowll*. She takes the word to mean 'fowl' and thus transforms the insult into a reprise of the self-salutary proverb about the owl.[34] This, combined with her assertion that she is after all 'a lady' (and by implication really neither foul nor fowl) hints at her full transformative potential. Arthur seems to understand that he has been bettered, for he immediately responds to her with a new-found civility which seeks her identity instead of imposing one: 'Whate is your name? I pray you tell me' (318).

Clearly, the poem has a command of irony and allusion; and we can see that sometimes such qualities go beyond their usual, predictable manifestations. In the case of the last example, Arthur's punning irony is acknowledged and then dismantled; and, to return to just one feature discussed earlier, the borrowings from Chaucer go beyond a mere echoing of directly corresponding contexts. The third and final conclusion shares in these traits. It is easy enough to agree with Field that Malory is implicated in the conclusion;[35] however, given the poem's imitative and irreverent tendencies, it is likely the conclusion was written not by Malory, but by someone who had read Malory and who could perhaps count on a readership familiar with the *Morte Darthur*:

> And, Jhesu, as thou were borne of a virgyn,
> Help hym oute of sorowe that this tale dyd devyne –
>   And that nowe in alle hast –
> For he is besett with gaylours many,
> That kepen hym full sewerly,
>   With wyles wrong and wraste.
>
> Nowe God, as thou art veray Kyng royall,
> Help hym oute of daunger that made this tale,
>   For therein he hath bene long.
> And of greatt pety help thy servaunt –
> For body and soull I yeld into thyne hand –
>   For paynes he hath strong.   (841–52)

Where Malory's admission that he is a 'knyght presoner'[36] achieves considerable gravity amidst his grand nostalgic evocation of the superior complexities of Arthurian civilization, the admission of 'hym ... that made this tale' rounds off an amusingly knowing little account of ethical deficiency and base ineptitude. The confessional nature of the conclusion even seems inept for its breach of a kind of implied contract of closure established with the previous 'conclusion'. The confessing author is not the real author, his confession is but a travesty of the real thing; he is as much a subject of the real author's mischief as Gawain, Gromer, Arthur, WBT, a formal poem like *AA*, or Malory. Can the final joke then be that the 'author's' imprisonment is a not wholly inappropriate fate and very much a reflection of the fractured integrity of so many aspects of 'his' poem?

Notes

1. The poem is preserved uniquely in Oxford, Bodleian Library, MS Rawlinson C.86, fos. 128ᵛ-140ʳ. The portion of the manuscript containing WSG dates from the early sixteenth century, as does the orthography of the text: see Griffiths 1982. The poem's date of composition is generally held to be no earlier than 1450; one of the inferences to be drawn from the present paper is that the poem is likely to have been written after the completion of Malory's *Morte Darthur* (1470-1).
2. Four published editions and three unpublished are listed in Rice 1987: nos. 1597-1601. The most commonly cited editions are identified below in nn. 6, 10 and 15; for a new edition, see below n. 13.
3. Pearsall 1977: 262.
4. Field 1982: 377.
5. Ibid.: 378.
6. Sands 1966: 323.
7. Ibid.: 324.
8. Ibid. See the contribution to this volume by Gillian Rogers (above pp. 94-111).
9. Sands 1966: 325.
10. Withrington 1991: 2.
11. Ibid.: 2.
12. Ibid.: 9.
13. All quotations from *WSG* are from the edition in Shepherd 1995: 243-67.
14. 'In the tyme of Arthurë an aunter bytydde' (Oxford, Bodleian Library, MS Douce 324, fo. 1ʳ). The line may in any event be formulaic; cf. Tolkien and Gordon 1967: line 2522: 'Þus in Arthurus day þis aunter bitidde'.
15. A caveat is again in order, however, for this may of course be evidence of a common, generally alliterative source. Both Laura Sumner and Lucia Glanville have made this very reasonable suggestion after considering a number of the same pieces of evidence considered to this point here; neither writer, however, considers the possibility of creative imitation: see Sumner 1924; Glanville 1958.
16. The feature is not, however, exclusive to alliterative poems. For a discussion of the feature, see Medary 1916.
17. Spearing 1982: 248.
18. Gates 1969: line 358.
19. Wheatley 1891: III, 324-30.

20 WBT begins at line 858 and ends at line 1264, with the true centre therefore at lines 1061-2; the triumphant delivery of the answer occurs at line 1038 – just 6% of total length away from centre. Gower's Tale of Florent begins at line 1396 (Macaulay 1900-1: I, 74) and ends at line 1871 (ibid.: I, 86), with the true centre therefore at line 1634; the triumphant (though largely implied) delivery of the answer occurs at line 1656 – 5% of total length away from centre.
21 See Field 1982: 375 n. 5; Withrington 1991: 20, 40.
22 Withrington 1991: 50.
23 Cf. Christine Ryan Hilary's note to line 198 of WBT (Benson 1987: 867).
24 *MED*, s.v. 'ende' n. (1), 25 (6).
25 Friedman and Harrington 1964: lines 4023-7.
26 Bliss 1966: lines 593-6 (Auchinleck text).
27 Gates 1969: lines 699-702.
28 Sands 1966: 324.
29 Quoted from Shepherd 1995: 383.
30 I.e. 'How so?', as suggested by context, though the sense 'What of it?' is possible. In either case, the response is ambiguous, suggesting the possibility that Arthur had little or no honour to begin with.
31 Field (1982: 375 n. 5) suggests the possible influence here of the Wife of Bath's Prologue *(The Canterbury Tales,* III.269-70): 'Ne noon so grey goos gooth ther in the lake / As, sëistow, wol been withoute make.'
32 The manuscript thus reads: 'Or elles I wott thou artt lore fowll / Now farewell sayd the kyng lady' (fo. 132[r]).
33 E.g., Sands (1966: 334) says that in line 316 'the lady's remark breaks off'. Withrington (1991: 46) finds that 'lines 316-17 are something of a non-sequitur ... and the clumsy repetition of the owl reference may simply reflect an attempt to fill a gap in the text'.
34 Withrington (1991: 46) corrects line 315 but modernizes the rhyme to 'foul', thus partly obscuring the pun.
35 Field 1982: 376 and n. 13.
36 Vinaver and Field 1990: 110.

8

The Awntyrs off Arthure: jests and jousts

ROSAMUND ALLEN

The Awntyrs off Arthure (*AA*) contains a 'grisly ghost', a prognostication of war, and a bloody encounter between two knights and must have been popular: it is extant in four manuscripts, all dated to the second and third quarters of the fifteenth century. Over the last thirty years it has again enjoyed something of a vogue and has been edited at least seven times, the latest edition being Maldwyn Mills's of the unjustly neglected Ireland-Blackburne MS.[1] The complex textual tradition puzzles editors, while critics have not yet all agreed that *AA* has single authorship and unity of tone; Mills's observation that the romance 'stays in the mind as essentially bipartite' is certainly valid.[2]

Opinion about what the poem is and means has deflected attention from the likely audience of *AA*, and no agreement has yet been reached about the date of composition.[3] These issues are interrelated: if this is not one poem but two (or even three), then the components of the extant work might have been written decades apart for very different readerships.[4] I shall argue here that *AA* as we have it, however composed, was devised at a date which can be fairly exactly plotted to match a specific political moment, and probably as a celebration.

The dramatic arrival of the ghost out of Tarn Wadling in the first part of the poem is more inventive than the joust between Gawain and Galeron in the second half;[5] yet most recent criticism has insisted on the unity of the poem, as a diptych study of the dangers of power.[6] In the first half Guenevere's mother confesses that she abused her wealth and privilege; in the second Galeron admits defeat in battle and renounces his hereditary lands. The link between these two acts of self-abasement is effected by the ghostly mother's prophecy of the downfall of the Round Table.[7] After she has warned her daughter to be charitable and chaste, and stipulated that thirty trentals of masses would expunge the unspecified broken vow which has caused her to suffer torment in purgatory, Guenevere's mother responds to Gawain's question 'How shal we fare ... þat fonden to fight?' (ed. Hanna, 261) with the assertion 'Yaure king is to covetus' (265). She then prophesies that he will be brought down by Fortune, 'that wundurfull quele-wryghte' (271), citing the contemporary plight of France as evidence of Fortune's power to debase. Her enumeration of France's problems slides easily from the immediate Arthurian context into what sounds very like an account of France as known to the audience.

The ghost's prophecy locates the action of the poem within the Arthurian legend at the point when Arthur has returned to Britain after defeating Frollo (275) and all the *douzeperes* of France (277), the point, indeed, where the action of the alliterative *Morte Arthure* (*AMA*) also begins. The Romans will be defeated and Gawain is urged (illogically) to turn to Tuscany (284), where news will come that Britain has been lost to Arthur (290); many of the Round Table will die in Dorset (295) and Arthur will perish 'opon Corneuayle cost' (301). Much of this alludes overtly to the chronicle tradition established by Geoffrey of Monmouth's *Historia regum Britanniae* (*c.* 1137), although the immediate debt is to *AMA*, of which critics have noted verbal and thematic echoes.

In *AMA* Geoffrey's account of Arthur's triumph at Caerleon is modified: after conquering northern Europe, including France, Burgundy, Brittany and Guienne among thirty-one named countries, Arthur returns to Britain, hunts in Wales, where he founds Caerleon, but goes to Carlisle for Christmas and New Year (*AMA* 64ff.); it is there, not at Caerleon as in Geoffrey's version, that the embassy from Rome arrives (*AMA* 78–115). Yet *AA* does not 'fit' the chronology suggested by the intertextual allusions to *AMA*: as in that text, Arthur has conquered France and is near Carlisle; by implication the Roman ambassadors are due to arrive any day now, and in *AMA* after four further weeks Arthur departs to conquer Rome, leaving Britain in Mordred's hands. But in *AA* the one who will destroy all the Round Table (311) is still a child playing ball 'In riche Arthures halle' (309), and presumably the downfall is at least a decade away. Why remind the audience of a familiar story, and apparently call their attention to a particular version of it, only to create a disjunction by means of a time-warp? The context *seems* right but, like the outer section of a picture in false perspective, refuses on closer inspection to frame the text.

I suggest that this misfit is a deliberate device to call attention to a political sub-text in the prophecy. Embedded within the ghost's account of Arthur's campaigns in France (probably, as Hanna says, from *AMA* 26–47)[9] are apparent allusions to English conquests in France from 1415 to 1424. These, together with the specific references to places near Carlisle, establish the poem in the context of the Anglo-French and Anglo-Scottish wars of the first quarter of the fifteenth century and locate it in the Border politics of northern England, the northernmost front of the Hundred Years' War.

When the Scottish knight Sir Galeron of Galloway in *AA* fights one of the English court in single combat for the return of his territory, the fictional situation matches historical actuality. In the period after 1389 there were intervals of truce between England and Scotland, during which legal trade resumed and formal jousts were held.[10] Several tourneys and single combats between Scots and Englishmen were arranged. In 1393 Richard de Redemane, sheriff of Carlisle, and four Scots including William de Halyborton, had an encounter in the presence of the King's Lieutenant, Henry Percy.[11] Two years earlier, the earl of Westmorland and Thomas Colville of the Dale obtained permission to perform feats of arms with certain Scots;[12] in 1407 a party of Scots comprising the earl of Mar, Lord Beaumont and the knights Lindsey, Bekyrton, Cockburn, Cranstone and Forbes had permission to travel through England to engage in jousts, the first of which was against the earl of Kent.[13] Jousts between equal numbers of English and Scots were also held at Carlisle in 1404 and 1414,[14] even though hostilities resumed in 1403 and Carlisle was raided in 1406. Less friendly encounters took place, such as that in 1381 between an Englishman and a Scot presided over by Ralph Neville and his cousin Percy.[15]

These encounters often involve Carlisle, where the Neville family had become prominent since Richard II granted Ralph Neville the fee-farm of Carlisle in 1395. After the Percy rebellion in 1403 Henry IV granted wardenship of the east march and custodianship of Berwick to his son John, future duke of Bedford, and the wardenship of the west march between England and Scotland to Ralph Neville; it passed to Ralph's eldest son, John, and on his death in 1420 to Richard Neville, eldest son of Ralph's second marriage. Richard Neville did not have many tenants or estates on a large scale in Cumberland and Westmorland, but for thirty-five years wielded great power on the west march; he was employed as a fee-paid professional, and employed other professionals under contractual, non-tenurial obligations.[16] The huge tracts of the royal forest of Inglewood, the largest of the royal hunting forests, produced income for the Crown, from which royal grants of timber were made for rebuilding Carlisle after major fires, such as that in 1391; from 1427 Neville was keeper of the king's forests north of the Trent and by 1443 could appoint to all foresterships in Inglewood.[17] In *AA*, lists are set up for Gawain's joust with Galeron, and a palisage is erected 'on Plumton Land' (ed. Hanna, 475) which must correspond to modern Plumpton Wall, a township, about five miles north of Penrith, formerly in Inglewood. In 1457, when Richard Neville's son Thomas was acting as his lieutenant for Carlisle, its castle and the marches, he was paid £66. 13s. 4d. from the lawn of Plumpton in Inglewood.[18] Richard's mother, Joan Beaufort, had granted him for life the lordship of Penrith, three miles south of Plumpton on the Roman road from Carlisle through Inglewood Forest, now the A6.[19] The other local place-name mentioned in the poem, Rondallsete (*Randolfesett*, MS T) Hall is now lost, but Randolfsete (1285) or Randersid Hall is shown on or near the Roman road through High Hesket in 1611.[20]

The Neville family controlled the western Border for some decades. Richard married Alice, only daughter of Thomas Lord Montacute in 1425, and was created earl of Salisbury in 1429; his brother George, Lord Latimer was his lieutenant in the 1430s, as was his son in 1457.[21] Richard's mother, Joan Beaufort, was Ralph's second wife. Her father was John of Gaunt, who had himself been warden of the northern marches up to a year before his death in 1399. She was sister of the duke of Exeter and of Henry Beaufort, bishop of Winchester, and half-sister of Henry IV.

In February 1424 Jane (Joan) Beaufort, one of Joan's nieces and daughter of John, duke of Somerset (d. 1410) married King James I of Scotland. They were married by Bishop Beaufort in the Priory Church of St Mary Overey in Southwark, and the wedding banquet was held in his Palace of Winchester close by.[22] James's return to Scotland had been negotiated from the Scottish side by Archibald, fourth earl of Douglas, and masterminded by Joan's brother, Henry Beaufort, bishop of Winchester. In April James re-entered Scotland after an eighteen-year exile in England, taking homage from his subjects in Durham on 28 March before holding his first court a week later at Melrose.[23] There was a major English raid from Cumberland into Eskdale in 1424, but after this a seven-year truce with Scotland ensued.[24] Richard Neville assisted in the final arrangements for James's liberation.

James's resumption of power may well be signalled in *AA*: the territory listed in lines 418–20 and 678–81 corresponds to his own holdings and those lands he had annexed by 1425. By contrast to other corrupted place-names (and much else too) in the poem, these are remarkably well preserved, as well in fact as the Cumberland place-names. Galeron of Galloway announces that he is

> The grattust of Galway of grevys and of gillus
> Of Carrake, of Cummake, of Conyngame, of Kile,
> Of Lonwik, of Lannax, of Laudoune hillus.   (418–20)[25]

The specific naming of the baronies of Kyle, Cunningham and Carrick points to the part of Ayrshire which Robert III, known as John, earl of Carrick before he became king, had regarded as his own territory; in 1404 he had his youngest son James invested with the title and 'whole lands of the earldom of Carrick' with the barony of Cunningham, the barony of Kyle Stewart, and the lands of Kyle Regis and 'the smaller Cumbrae'.[26] James was then 10 years old, and the investiture effectively marked him as heir to the throne: his eldest brother had died the year before he was born, and his next brother, the earl of Rothesay, had been murdered in 1402. But in 1406 James was captured off the Norfolk coast on his way to France – the shock killed his father – and kept imprisoned in England, at first in some discomfort, until his release was negotiated in 1423. In his last years of captivity he was accorded some dignities: he spent Christmas 1423 with the infant prince Henry VI and would have been a familiar figure in noble circles.

Soon after his return to Scotland James asserted control over the Albany Stewarts, Murdac (Murdoch), duke of Albany and governor of Scotland in James's absence, and his sons. Murdac's younger son Walter intrigued against James with his maternal grandfather, Duncan of the Lennox. First Walter and Duncan, then Murdac and his other surviving son Alexander were executed in 1425.[27] Galleron's claim to the lands 'Of Lonwik, of *Lannax*, of Laudoune hillus' (420) could refer to James's appropriation of the Lennox in

1425. Galeron's territory extends over most of western Scotland from Lennox south, with Lanark (Lonwik) and Loudoun Hill (or the Lowther Hills) as eastern boundaries, and the earldom of Carrick and lordship of Galloway to the south and south-east.[28] Carrick belonged to James.[29]

The fictitious name 'Galeron of Galloway' derives ultimately from French romance.[30] If this name in *AA* did suggest an actual person to the contemporary audience, then this would have been the current holder of the lordship of Galloway, or a contestant to the lordship. The previous holder, Archibald, fourth earl of Douglas, one of the 'Black Douglases' and brother-in-law of James I, died in 1424. After arranging James I's release, and before James returned to Scotland, Douglas went with the earl of Buchan to fight in France on the French side: there he was made duke of Touraine but died at the Battle of Verneuil. Douglas was well known in England, where he was held prisoner from 1403 to 1406. He was lord of large areas of Scotland, and his principal holdings, left in charge of his wife, James's elder sister, were in the borderlands. He had left as his deputy his son, Archibald, earl of Wigtown, who became the fifth earl of Douglas. But Archibald, the fifth earl, nephew of James I, did not inherit his father's extensive lands, even though he supported James, who assigned the lordship of Galloway to his sister, Princess Margaret, away from Archibald Douglas;[31] effectively it was in royal control, and in so far as Galloway had a lord at the time, it was James.

AA seems to reflect the territory James had acquired by 1425; like Arthur in *AA* (265) James was accused of 'covetise'.[32] Galeron has not claimed the earldom of Wigtown, today's Galloway, which *was* in Archibald Douglas's hands in 1425. The earldom of Wigtown lay immediately to the east of the lordship of Galloway and was separated from the border with England at Carlisle by one further lordship, Annandale, much of which was in English hands.

'Galeron of Galloway' denotes Scottish command as seen from an English perspective: after all, he does not quite win. *AA* 416–20 are probably a complimentary response to James's swift assertion of strong kingship shortly after his return to Scotland, overwritten by a statement of English dominance. At the very least, the lines reflect an accurate awareness of Scots politics in the mid-1420s.

Besides the Cumberland and Ayrshire place-names, there are other places mentioned in the poem, largely obliterated by layers of scribal bungling. These identify compensatory lands for Gawain when Galeron's own are restored; they are not in the north-west corner of Britain but in Wales (666); Glamorgan (665); just possibly Ireland: Waterford (669), and Ulster Hall (668); and across the Channel: a baronry in Brittany (670).[33] The references to Wales (and Ireland, if the readings *Ulster* and *Waterford* in 668-9 are correct) may relate to English politics. On 22 May 1425 the custody of the lands of the king's ward, Richard, duke of York, were granted to the duke of Gloucester, while care of the 13-year-old boy was assigned to Ralph, first earl of Westmorland. Richard had inherited the dukedom of York in 1415, and could claim the entailed lands of the earldom of Cambridge; he inherited the earldom of Ulster, was titular lord lieutenant of Ireland, and inherited, with the Mortimer lands on the Welsh borders, a claim to the English throne in 1425. Yet on 26 May 1426 Joan Beaufort, widowed the previous October, petitioned the King's Council for more money than the allotted 200 marks annually to maintain Richard, who had been knighted by the 4½-year-old Henry VI one week earlier at Leicester; she was granted £200 p.a.[34] In 1424/5 Richard of York was betrothed to 9-year-old Cecily, Joan Beaufort's daughter, and though summoned to court in 1428 he grew up among the Nevilles; Richard Neville was eleven years his senior. Richard of York was lord of Glamorgan, having inherited the title in 1422 from his uncle.[35] There was, therefore, in the Neville entourage in Westmorland a holder of lands bearing some similarity to those mentioned in *AA*. Other Neville associations with Wales included the lordship of Gower, one of the estates of John Mowbray, the earl marshal (1389-1432), who married Catherine Neville, eldest daughter of Ralph and Joan Beaufort, on 13 January 1412, and was made duke of Norfolk in 1425. Mowbray had been given into the custody of Ralph Neville in 1410. A reference in *AA* to southern England occurs with the 'Earl (*erlis son*, MS D) of Kent' (482), a walk-on part; the widow of Ralph Neville's eldest son, John, was Elizabeth, daughter of Thomas Holland, earl of Kent: their son Ralph became second earl of Westmorland on Ralph's death in October 1425.

The years 1424-5 are apparently again determined for *AA* by political references in the ghost's prophecy. Guenevere's mother's ghost remarks (with the help of some textual emendation): 'Bretan and Burgoyn is both in your bandum' (276), and then prophesies of Mordred's usurpation:

> In riche Arthures halle,
> The barne playes at þe balle
> Þat outray shall you alle,
> Derfely þat day. (ed. Hanna, 309-12)

Presumably *Bretan* here means 'Brittany'; this may be no more than a very selective résumé of the conquests listed at the beginning of *AMA*. If it has topical meaning, however, 'Brittany and Burgundy are both submissive to you'[36] suggests a period when both were in alliance with England. Brittany was under English control from 1364 to 1380, but not again until 1423. When Henry V died in 1422 John, duke of Bedford and regent of France implemented the Treaty of Troyes (1420) by creating a triple alliance between Brittany, England and Burgundy, which was ratified in a treaty signed at Amiens on 13 April 1423 and cemented by Bedford's marriage on 9 May 1423 to Anne, sister of Philip of Burgundy. Their father, John the Fearless, had been murdered on the bridge at Montereau in 1419; his young son Philip, believing the dauphin to be responsible, had allied himself with the English. A further reference to Burgundy in *AA* is obscured by clumsy or corrupted syntax:

> And [th]a[t] byrne on a blonke with the [birde] abydus
> That borne was in Burgoyne be boke and by belle.   (29-30);
> (emendations from DL; TL)

Either the *byrne* or the horse in line 29 could be the referent for the relative clause in 30, but *birde* (TL)/*quene* (Dlr) is the nearest antecedent in the three manuscripts. In no extant romance does Guenevere come from Burgundy, but the audience would be alert to a reference to a queen (more accurately a duchess) from Burgundy in the English royal family.

The Triple Alliance was short-lived: on 15 January 1426 England declared war on Brittany. The confident tone of line 276 fits the narrow band of time between spring 1423 and the signing of a treaty between Brittany and the dauphinist forces on 7 December 1425. The younger brother of the duke of Brittany, Arthur de Richemont, quarrelled with John of Bedford in June 1424 and offered his services to the dauphin in October that year, becoming constable of France in March 1425. De Richemont may well be intended by the expression 'in riche Arthures halle' (*AA* 309) in MSS D and L, not a genetic pair. He was by then in his early thirties himself, but the *barne* playing in his hall could be a contemptuous reference to the dauphin, actually by then aged 21. De Richemont quarrelled with the dauphin in 1427, and they were not reconciled until after the break-up of the Burgundian alliance in 1435.[37]

There may be two further allusions to the English conquests in France: 'Fraunse have ye frely with yaure fighte wonnen' (274) and 'Gyan may grete þe werre was bigonen; / There is [no lorde] on lyue in þat londe leued' (ed. Hanna, 278–9); but reading *lorde* TL; cf. *lordes* D; *lede* Ir) which again may simply echo *AMA*'s listing of Arthur's French conquests, but would seem to have little point unless it had particular relevance to a contemporary situation. The lines describe English dominance, and must therefore relate either to the 1360s under Edward III or the decade between 1415 and 1425 under Henry V and his brother, John of Bedford. The distress of Guienne (278) could refer to the Black Prince's harsh treatment of Guienne in 1369, but is more likely to be a reference to Aquitaine's (Guienne's) lawlessness in the 1420s; it remained an English possession until 1452.[38] 'No lorde on lyue' (279) probably records France's loss between 1415 and 1420 of many nobles: the dauphin Louis; Louis d'Anjou; Jean de Berry; the dukes of Guienne and Burgundy. In 1424 at the Battle of Verneuil 7,262 French and Scots were slain, including the French commander-in-chief, two vicomtes, and Archibald, earl of Douglas, his younger son, the earl of Mar, and his son-in-law, the earl of Buchan. The Scots in this battle were almost annihilated, and Scottish intervention in France now ceased; the dauphin's army was destroyed.[39] Again, therefore, *AA* seems to carry a specific reference to events in 1424–5.

It is therefore not impossible that *AA* is a poem in honour of the Nevilles: perhaps they or gentry in their affinity were its patrons. Its political message and disregard for romantic love suggest possible clerical authorship (perhaps by one of the religious of St Mary's Priory in Carlisle).[40] If the Neville family entourage was its audience, the poem as we have it would seem an ideal compromise between the sobriety required for a venerable peer and his duchess, and the celebrations of Richard of York's betrothal and Richard Neville's marriage in 1425. It has much that could be applicable to several young folk among the entourage of Duchess Joan. The prophecy in the middle section is a reminder of the responsibilities of rule and the slipperiness of the fortunes of war, and would be poignantly appropriate in a family whose matriarch was half-sister to the regent of France, and aunt of the consort of the Scottish king whose subjects had been fighting the English until the recent truce. *AA* is not inappropriate as entertainment; it is possible to read it as a humorous deconstruction of its own moral. The ghost warns against over-indulgence in material goods; the poem contains three extended descriptions of female and knightly attire, one of a pavilion, and an account of a feast. Of course, these are traditional romance topoi, but they do not usually co-exist with exhortations to abstemiousness, and rarely does a rhetorically correct description of a woman, itemizing the head, eyes and clothing, actually refer to a naked ghost with a toad on her head, a burning gaze out of hollow eye-sockets, and toads and serpents instead of garments (105–21). This is black comedy. Structurally the narrative is parodic, inverting the Loathly Lady story associated with Sir Gawain at Tarn Wadling in two narratives, *The Weddynge of Sir Gawen and Dame Ragnell* and *The Marriage of Sir Gawaine*, analogues to Chaucer's Wife of Bath's Tale and Gower's Tale of Florent. In *AA* Arthur is challenged to restore territory, and Gawain confronts a hideous woman who gives him instruction. But the tale is subverted: the woman arrives before the challenger, she remains hideous, and the moral is not the lighthearted 'give a woman her way', but a daunting reminder of how Lady Fortune will have hers. Instead of a hideous hag who turns into a nubile woman, we have a beautiful woman, Guenevere, facing the 'self' she will turn into after death: 'muse on me as a mirror' (167), says the ghost. In analogous texts like the *Trentals of Gregory* the revenant appears in glory after being saved by intercessory masses, but we are not told what happens when Guenevere has the masses said in the final stanza. This framing of the second section with a reference back to the moral matter of the first once again has a young and beautiful woman (Galeron's consort) displaced by a hideous, old and dead one.

To an audience who could recognize the alteration of the traditional 'Tarn Wadling folk-tale' *AA* would be a clever, almost amusing, poem about transpositions of meaning and circumstance, its reversal of the expected being itself a reminder of the insecurities of life and the instability of reputation. References to other texts about Sir Gawain and the Round Table, especially *AMA* and the second and third fitts of *Sir Gawain and the Green Knight*, establish a larger literary context for this brief poem than its 715 lines could otherwise establish.[41] We know that Joan Neville appreciated literature: she was a lender and dedicatee of books, and could have been an informed interpreter of these intertextual allusions.[42]

The implied audience of *AA* is uneasily aware of the instability of power and wealth. The trappings of power, in the form of the lands, activities and clothes of the upper classes, are enthusiastically presented against a sombre backdrop: pay for your privileges. Guenevere is to give to the poor and buy heaven for her mother with a million masses; Gawain restores lands to Galeron and is rewarded by being invested with other lands in their stead. The uncertain tone perhaps reflects a clerical author under magnate patronage.

AA is set in the western borderlands, which had an ambitious nobility and upper gentry in two powerful magnate families, Percy and Neville, and in gentry families like the rival Dacres and Cliffords, themselves later to become magnate wardens of the march.[43] Its allusion to the literary motifs of late medieval romance and its stylized representation of the dealings of the great suggest that it was devised for a celebration like the knighting and wedding inscribed within the text, or for a betrothal. The poem could have been recited in two parts as interludes at a feast, as a mimed entertainment by young nobles or as an amusement preceding an actual joust. The ghost's prophecy and Galeron's titular lands in *AA* suggest a political moment about 1424–5 and not much later. In the Neville family in the first nine months of 1425 there were at least three aspiring men who would form a suitable audience for an account of a battle for territorial rights: Richard of York, soon to be knighted; Ralph Neville junior, soon to be an earl; and Richard Neville, newly married and forester of several important forests, who might be complimented by the hunt which opens the poem.

If *AA* does refer to the Beaufort-Nevilles, they would have done well to heed its warning about Fortune: James I was murdered in 1437; Mowbray died in 1432; Richard Neville and the sons of Ralph Neville's first marriage were at war over the patrimony in 1448; Richard was beheaded after the Battle of Wakefield in 1460; the Douglases were stripped of their power in 1455 by James II, and the Nevilles lost much of their influence in the north to the Percys in the same decade; Richard of York fell at Wakefield. False Fortune is indeed a 'wundurfull quele wryghte' (271–2).[44]

Notes

1. The published editions are Gates 1969, based on Oxford, Bodleian Library, MS Douce 324 (D); Hanna 1974, based on D, collated with Lincoln Cathedral Library, MS 91 (T), London, Lambeth Palace, MS 491 (L), and the two former Ireland–Blackburne MSS (Ir); Phillips 1988; Mills 1992: 161–82, based on the former Ireland–Blackburne MS now in the Robert H. Taylor collection, Princeton. For discussion of the dates of the manuscripts, see Hanna 1974: 2–8; Doyle 1982: 96–7. Except where noted, references to the text are to Mills 1992, which has the best readings for place-names, but the standard line-numbering of Hanna and other editors is used.
2. Mills 1992: xxvii. For further discussion of the structure of *AA*, see Allen 1987; Fichte 1989; Phillips 1989 and 1993.
3. The readership of *AA* is considered in Lawton 1989.
4. For a proposal that *AA* is a compilation, see Allen 1968: 86–110.
5. For Amours (1897: lxxii–lxxiii), cited by Mills (1992: xxvi), the Galeron episode is a 'stock' story.
6. Spearing 1982: 248–52.
7. Phillips (1993: 71–5) considers this prophetic section as part of a second 'fitte' (lines 261–508, following the Ireland–Blackburne MS divisions), which has desire for territory as its theme.
8. References to *AMA* are to Hamel 1984.
9. Hanna 1974: 40.
10. Summerson 1993: 346.
11. *VCH Cumberland*: II, 263. Richard Red(e)man(e)'s life grant of 40 marks p.a. from Richard II was confirmed by Henry IV in 1400 (Summerson 1993: II, 395).
12. Rymer 1739–45: VII, 703; *DNB*, XL, 273. One of these encounters was against Alexander Lindsey, who had slandered Ralph Neville.
13. Amours 1908: VI, 423–4.
14. Summerson 1993: I, 349, citing Bain 1881–8: IV, no. 452; *CPR 1401-5*, p. 410; Record Commission 1814–18: II, 212.
15. *DNB*, XL, 273; Rymer 1739–45: XI, 334–5.
16. The fortunes of the Nevilles in Carlisle and the western march are outlined in Summerson 1993: II, 406–8. On the politics of the marches, see Musgrove 1990: 140–6.
17. Musgrove 1990: 145–6.
18. A *lawn* or *launde* was an area of grass within the forest cultivated for feed for livestock. Plumpton Laund appears in AA 475 as 'plumtun lone' (Ir), 'plonton land' (L), 'plu*n*ton land' (D) (T damaged). See Summerson 1993: II, 408, 393 on supplies from Inglewood; ibid.: II, 408 on Richard's forestership.
19. Richard Neville became master-forester of the parks of the arch-

bishopric of York in 1423 (*CPR* 2 Henry VI) and was allowed the profit from the *laundes* of Inglewood by his own land and did not hold them of anyone (*CPR*, 1427). 'Launders' mentioned by name in *CPR* are Thomas Lowry (1395) and Thomas Burton (1415).

20 Armstrong et al. 1950-2: 204, citing PRO 'Pleas of the Forest' and John Speed's *Theatre of the Empire of Great Britain* (1611).
21 Summerson 1993: II, 407.
22 Carlin 1983: 118.
23 Brown 1994: 40.
24 Summerson 1993: II, 405. Penrith was burned in 1416 (ibid.: 404).
25 This is the reading of MS Ir, as in Mills 1992, but reading *Laudoune* in line 419.
26 Robertson 1908: I, 115; Amours 1908: VI, 45; Brown 1994: 13-14.
27 Brown 1994: 53.
28 John Macqueen, in a private letter dated December 1985, confirms 'Lennox' as a correct reading but reckons that line 420 should refer to the Lowther Hills, and line 678 to Lochar Moss, north-eastern and south-eastern boundaries of Nithsdale. The place-names in lines 678-81 are horribly corrupt, but again Ir seems to have the best text in line 678; it lacks lines 680-1. Lines 681 and 420 should probably read identically.
29 Brown 1994: 43; Musgrove 1990: 146.
30 In the Second Continuation of Chrétien's *Perceval*, as noted in Phillips 1993: 9.
31 Brown 1994: 78.
32 Ibid.: 5, quoting Sir Robert Graham, murderer of James.
33 These place-names are highly corrupt: at line 667, *Criffones Castelles* (D) is further corrupted to *Gryffones* (T; L omits it altogether), but appears as *Kirfre Castell* in Ir; although Hanna's note to line 667 compares Crieff in Perthshire or Griff Grange in north Derbyshire with D's reading, line 667 is probably to be taken with 666 'þe worship of Wales', and the place-name should probably be sought in Wales. I suggest that 'Caerphilly' or even 'Cardiff' may be the original reading.
34 Nicolas 1834: 194.
35 *DNB*, XVI, 1062, col. 1; XIII, 1022, col. 1.
36 Manuscripts vary: Ir has *in ȝour bandoun*; the rest read *to you* and variously *bowne* (L), *bowen* (D), *bownden* (T). The right reading is *to you boun*, 'submissive to you'; Ir's reading means 'under your control'.
37 In 1423 Sir Thomas Burton claimed expenses for custody of Arthur of Brittany from 1417 to 1420; in March 1423 Thomas Swynbourne, captain of Fronsac, wrote to the King's Council about the disorder in Guienne (Nicolas 1834: 118-21, 46-8).

38 'Þat londe' (line 279) probably refers to France (line 277) rather than to Guienne.
39 Brown 1994: 52. Ralph Neville's son-in-law John Mowbray had fought in France between 1420 and 1424, assisting the Burgundians in 1423 and ravaging Brabant with Humfrey of Gloucester late in 1424; in 1420 he routed the dauphin's forces, killing 5,000 men, including 100 Scots (*DNB*, XIII, 1118). At Parliament in April 1425 he tried to secure precedence over the earl of Warwick, being accorded the title of second duke of Norfolk as a compromise (ibid., 1119).
40 Pearsall (1981: 14–17) argues for monastic authorship of some alliterative texts. Echard (1990) considers *AA* in the context of Latin and Celtic romances.
41 Is Arthur's lament for Gawain in *AMA* (Hamel 1984: 3957–60) parodied in Gawain's grief for his horse, and is his defiant challenge to Death (ibid.: line 3968) echoed as Gawain taunts Galeron (line 513)?
42 For the dedication of the Hoccleve manuscript Durham Cathedral Library, MS Cosin V.iii.9 to Joan, and her loan of two books to Henry V, see *DNB*, XL, 273.
43 Summerson 1993: II, 409, 421.
44 All four manuscripts have *wundurfull*, but the correct reading is wunder (see *OED*, s.v. 'wonder', adj.).

9

The pattern of Providence in *Chevelere Assigne*

DIANE SPEED

Chevelere Assigne relates the folk-tale of the Swan Children. It does so, however, in terms that establish it as a prelude to the chivalric romance of the Swan Knight, which was itself adopted as an ancestral romance to provide a suitably illustrious background for Godfrey of Bouillon, hero of the First Crusade. That the English poem (probably late fourteenth-century) is an adaptation of the first part of the three-part cycle, rather than an independent re-telling of the folk-tale, is evident from its references to the young hero as 'Chevelere Assigne', that is, the 'Swan Knight' of the future, and probably also from the idiosyncratic naming of one of his brothers as 'Gadyfere', seemingly in anticipation of this Godfrey's great-nephew.[1] This essay is concerned with the meaning of the English poem and the narrative processes which allow it to operate independently of the cycle.

The opening lines, not paralleled in other versions, are a prologue proposing a universal truth and launching a narrative which is to serve as proof of it:

> Allweldyngne God, whenne it is his wylle,
> Wele he wereth his werke with his owne honde,
> For ofte harmes were hente þat helpe we ne my3te,
> Nere þe hy3nes of hym þat lengeth in hevene.
> For this I saye by a lorde ... (1-5)

Almighty God, that is, takes good care of his creatures in accordance with his will, for they often experience difficulties they cannot overcome without his help. This truth is demonstrated by the story of a certain lord ... The prologue establishes a frame, or pretext, for the story as derived from the cycle, formulating it as an exemplum to illustrate the working of divine Providence. This frame is formally recalled at the end of the poem with the statement, also not paralleled in other versions, that the children have been saved with the help of God: 'And þus þe botenynge of God brow3te hem to honde' (370).

The theme of the frame has been characterized by Ray Barron as 'divine protection'[2] and by Elizabeth Williams as 'God's protective power'.[3] Barron also identifies the exemplum structure created by the opening and closing lines, but considers that 'no didactic theme is developed in the narration'. Now, although God's protection is clearly a recurrent theme in the poem, it is true that it is not fully developed as the structural theme on which the poem depends: the narratorial voice does not draw attention to it in a thoroughly pervasive way, and not all events are even implicitly related to it. I would argue, however, as suggested above, that the framing theme is in fact the broader one of divine Providence, that the emphasis on the notion of protection ('wereth', 2) against evil ('harmes', 3) in fact broadens into the more general topic of beneficent help ('botenynge', 370), and that all this is possible because of God's omnipotence ('Allweldynge', 1), will for good ('wylle', 1) role as creator ('werke', 2), and sovereign majesty ('þe hy3nes of hym þat lengeth in hevene', 4). Assuming, then, that the expression 'divine Providence' signifies God's supreme goodness, caring and sovereignty, this essay proceeds to trace the generic imperative of the prologue and its attendant theme through the complex of narrative structures that constitutes the poem. The component narratives are identified in terms of the figure who is the actantial subject of each.

The four main players are introduced in a telling sequence at the beginning of the poem proper: the 'lorde', who is actually a 'kynge' called Oryens (5-7); 'his qwene', called Bewtrys, who is beautiful (8); 'his moder', called Matabryne, who will cause great sorrow because she is in league with the Devil (9-10); and Chevelere Assigne, descended from these three (11). The last-named is set apart from the others, who are grouped as 'chefe of þe kynde of Chevalere Assygne' (11). He alone is referred to without explanation, as if he will be familiar to the audience. He is the ultimate focus of the narrative to come; the others are considered first as leading to that end. The two women are each defined first in respect of their relationship to the king ('his'). Bewtrys is then further defined in descriptive terms that suggest she will be primarily a static figure ('is'), with whom others may interact dynamically. Matabryne, on the other hand, is further defined in narrative terms ('cawsed') as the antagonist of one or more of the Christian protagonists in the unfolding action. The story of Oryens takes precedence, over the women whose roles are subordinated to his, and over Chevelere Assigne, whose time has not yet come.

The first event after the introduction is an action led by Oryens, as he takes possession of his kingdom and settles there with his wife (12-14). The action is then carried on in terms of a lack on the part of the king which is to be redressed: Oryens has lands but no heir to inherit them, and this causes him sorrow (15-18). Through the rest of this section (19-36), the king remains the actantial subject of the narrative. He sees a poor woman with twins and feels sorry for her burden. When his wife comments that she must have brought this on herself by sleeping with two men, he rebukes her. That night he makes her pregnant. When he knows this has happened, he understands ('was witty', 35) that this is God's loving gift ('his sonde', 36) and thanks him. The children are subsequently born 'whenne God wolde' (41).

The king's own story is all but over by this point. The greater part of the poem concerns the actions of others, over which the king presides as 'do-nothing' king, like Charlemagne or Arthur in much of the cyclic literature named for them, occasionally speaking or gesturing to mark the official boundaries of the action, but otherwise merely emoting, as the following summary of his role makes clear. Oryens is anxious for good news during his wife's labour (57) and sorrowful when his mother tells him the children are pups (58, 66-7); refuses to allow his wife's immediate execution but allows his mother to imprison her as she will (69-70, 73-4); eventually agrees to the execution (189); tells the surprise champion of the queen what is going on and expresses helpless regret (231-5); rejoices that his wife will have this champion (246-7); points the champion out to Matabryne (250-3); dubs the youth knight (276); responds to the latter's request for a horse and an attendant for the judicial combat with the champion of the queen's accuser (279, 287); and is finally told the truth about his children (346-8). His reaction to this information is not recorded, but the happy promise of the pregnancy at the end of the first section can now be seen by the audience or reader to have been fulfilled – his need for an heir has been met.

Oryens understands that his life is being overseen by a caring God, who knows and meets his needs, and the audience will recognize the operation of Providence. Read paradigmatically, Oryens' story presides over and contains those in which Bewtrys, Matabryne and Chevelere Assigne are the subjects of the action. From this point of view, the narrative as a whole does indeed function as the predicated exemplum.

A difficulty with such an understanding of the poem's structure may, however, be perceived in the final return to the frame (370). The working of divine Providence anticipated in the prologue is now said to have been demonstrated, but in relation to a different focal figure; not the king, but the young Chevelere Assigne, Enyas, along with his siblings. Modern aesthetic expectations might see in this a failure of unity in a work of art, but another view is possible if medieval expectations of exemplum are considered.

Briefly, the term 'exemplum' refers in the medieval context either to a non-narrative instance or to a particular narrative, with a beginning, middle and end, which was related to clarify or justify some point of argument.[4] The latter use is relevant here. Through the Middle Ages, it was customary to assemble stories from all manner of sources, ancient and contemporary, and to re-present them in a form that made them ready for use in the kind of argumentative context that might arise in a sermon or a treatise; the narrative might or might not be accompanied by an explicit moralization.[5] Ultimately the largest collection of exempla was the *Gesta Romanorum*.[6] This collection is thought to have been first composed around the beginning of the fourteenth century, probably in England, possibly in Germany, but over time it was very widely disseminated. In England it assumed a distinct form, manifest now in thirty-eight Anglo-Latin manuscripts and four Middle English ones (plus a fragment), almost all from the fifteenth century. Regularly in these texts, and to a large extent in the continental texts, the exempla begin with the formula 'So-and-so reigned in the city of Rome, a wise emperor, who ...'. The ensuing tale may give the named emperor a central role, but it is just as likely to focus on someone belonging to him – his wife, one or more of his sons or daughters, a subject knight, someone brought into conflict with his laws. In both the English and the continental *Gesta* the meaning of the tale is normally made explicit in an attached moralization of an allegorical kind, in which the emperor is generally understood as

God, overseeing human actions and awarding heaven or hell for eternity.

It is tempting to associate *Chevelere Assigne* with such a tradition in order to explain its narrative structure. In both the poem and the *Gesta* exempla, an adult male ruler is the figure who heads the narrative, but he is not necessarily central to the action that constitutes the bulk of it. He is also the figure through whom, one way or another, the nature of God's work in the world, divine Providence, is explained. That is not to claim that Oryens is a signal for an allegorical reading of *Chevelere Assigne* but, rather, to point out, first, that the partial shift of focus in this exemplum is not out of keeping with generic practice and, secondly, that divine Providence was familiar as the overarching theme in exemplum tradition.

To take this second point a little further. An exemplum, axiomatically, recounted a fictional or historical episode in the larger history of humanity,[7] and the history of humanity for the Middle Ages was the salvation history of the world. Histories in both the classical and the Christian model (Livy's history of Rome, *Ab urbe condita*, and Bede's *Historia ecclesiastica gentis Anglorum*, for instance) insisted that they were written, at least in part, to provide examples for present and future generations to follow or avoid.[8] The foundation text for Christian history was, of course, the Bible. Other texts might appear to supply information about times and places beyond those of biblical narrative, but such information could in fact be seen simply as amplifications of biblical statements about the created world and its movement in time from Genesis to Apocalypse. Every generation of human beings, moreover, whether textualized in the Bible or existing beyond its pages, inevitably repeated the same process of fall and salvation/condemnation, and that similarity meant that any and every story could be understood as an illustration of divine Providence. Similarity evoked typicality and bestowed exemplary validity on fictional and historical narrative alike.

The story of Oryens is thus the key to our recognizing the exemplary nature of *Chevelere Assigne*, but consideration of the other protagonists' stories supports this conclusion.

Bewtrys is the actantial subject of two component narratives. The first is itself a mini-exemplum: Bewtrys unkindly remarks that the mother of twins must have slept with two men, is rebuked by her husband and as retribution gives birth herself to seven children at once. God's gracious gift to Oryens coincides with his punishment of Bewtrys. That the retribution is the work of God is made explicit in two later references to it: first, when an angel sent by Christ (193) explains to the hermit who has raised Enyas and his siblings that they are the children of King Oryens –

> By his wyfe Betryce – she bere hem at ones
> For a worde on þe wall þat she wronge seyde   (196–7)

– and later, when Enyas speaks to Oryens of himself and the other children and explains that Bewtrys

> bare hem at ones
> For a worde on þe walle þat she wronge seyde.   (348–9)

The subsequent suffering of Bewtrys belongs not to this mini-exemplum but to the other narrative component of which she is the subject, the tale or romance of the pathetic heroine who undergoes great trials and is eventually rescued – a paradoxical kind of narrative in which the subject is essentially passive, acted on rather than acting. The compiler of the manuscript in which *Chevelere Assigne* is found, London, British Library, MS Cotton Caligula A.ii, seems to have been particularly aware of this generic presence, for he included also two other romances involving accused queens, *Octavian* and *Emaré*,[9] the latter an analogue of Chaucer's Man of Law's Tale. Divine Providence is evoked strikingly in this part of Bewtrys's story. During the eleven years she spends in the dungeon to which she has been consigned by Matabryne, part of her sustenance is supplied direct by God (88), a miracle usually found in hagiographical writing.[10] At the same time she prays to God, as the one who saved Susannah when she was falsely accused by the elders (in the Old Testament Apocryphal book of Daniel and Susannah), to save her also (90–1). Her eventual rescue is implicitly God's response to this prayer: her son, as the angel tells the hermit, is to avenge his mother because this is 'Goddes wyll' (206). God helps her live through her harsh imprisonment and eventually delivers her.

The story of Matabryne is an account of the Devil's work in the world. Throughout the poem, she is explicitly in league with the Devil (10) and damned (38, 75, 240), as is her henchman Malkedras

(120-1, 142, 145). She is not so much a vicious person, potentially still capable of redemption, as vice personified. Unlike the other three main players, she undergoes no change in herself but merely continues to demonstrate her evil nature until she is forcibly stopped. Arguably, she is not the actantial subject of a narrative in the way the others are, and it is more appropriate to consider her in terms of her role in their respective stories.

Matabryne is obviously the antagonist both of Bewtrys as pathetic heroine and of Enyas and his siblings. Any audience would grasp the horror of her words and actions in themselves, but the narratorial voice makes her wickedness quite explicit, both in the statements of her damnation noted above and in other statements. In her first attempt to destroy her new grandchildren, she

> cawsed moch sorowe,
> For she thow3te to do þat byrthe to a fowle ende. (39-40)

Those who imprison Bewtrys at Matabryne's bidding are 'tyrauntes' (84). Her instructions to Markus are to 'murther' the children (93, 129). When Enyas comes to fight for his mother, Matabryne first attacks him in person, pulling out a handful of his hair, at which Enyas pronounces God's judgement on her (254-7). When she has Malkedras meet him in judicial combat as her champion, her henchman damns himself by blasphemy as he addresses Enyas: '"I charge not þy croyse," quod Malkedras, "þe valwe of a chery"' (329). (The antithetical alignment of Enyas himself with God and right will be discussed below.)

Matabryne's direct attacks on Oryens consist of hard words and bullying, but her physical actions against his wife and children are, of course, effectively actions against him – she is his antagonist also, working to prevent fulfilment of his desire for an heir. Her ultimate destruction is an expression of God's perfect goodness, to which her evil is anathema. Nevertheless, her evil provides occasions for divine Providence to be manifested in the lives of the other characters, just as in the Christian world-view God remains almighty but allows the Devil temporary power in the world, and mankind free will in choice of allegiance.

The most extensive evidence of Providence at work belongs, however, to the story of Enyas, the familiar romance narrative of a displaced prince who endures testing and is eventually restored to his rightful position. Yet at the very outset of his story we meet what is probably the greatest stumbling-block to reading the folk-tale of the Swan Children as a Christian exemplum: namely, the silver chains which encircle their necks at birth, and their double nature, elements central to the folk-tale. Whereas supernatural elements such as the provision of the hermit, the hind and the shield are, as will be seen, presented in terms that relate them explicitly to Christian concerns, no such presentation is attempted with the chains; they remain mysterious: even Matabryne, with her closeness to another supernatural source, wants Malkedras to get them for her only as evidence that he has killed the wearers (137-8), and she is evidently unaware that the children might, rather, turn into swans. Once six of the chains have been seized, however, they are appropriated to the theme of divine Providence in two ways. First, the goldsmith who is ordered to destroy them by melting them to forge a cup finds that when he melts half of one chain the metal multiplies enough to make the whole cup, and he is able to put the rest of the chains aside. The possibility of regarding this fairy-tale-like occurrence as a Christian miracle is raised as the smith's wife observes: 'Hit is þorowe þe werke of God, or þey be wronge wonnen' (170).[11] Secondly, the fact that Enyas is absent when the others are attacked by Malkedras, and as a consequence never loses his own chain, allows him to become his mother's champion, in accordance with expressed Providential plans for Oryens and his family. The operation of Providence in Enyas' escape is not explicit at the time, but its presence in his life is explicit at numerous points before and after that event.

To begin with, when Markus, whom Matabryne has ordered to kill the children, chooses rather to leave them in the forest alive, he does so because he knows God must disapprove of her direction –

> 'He þat lendeth with,' quod he, 'leyne me wyth sorowe,
> If I drowne ȝou today, thowgh my deth be nyȝe!' (99-100)

– and he entrusts them to Christ as he goes off (104). Juxtaposed to his departure, and apparently as a result of Markus' prayer, a hermit finds them and calls on Christ to provide sustenance for them (111). Again apparently as a prompt answer to prayer, a hind appears and they feed on her milk 'whyll our Lorde wolde' (117).[12] Then, as they grow up with the hermit, Christ sends them help (119). As with

Bewtrys in prison, this evidence of Providence concerns basic survival.

Later, the night before Bewtrys is due to be burned, an angel tells the hermit that Christ approves what he has done for the children (193-4), reveals their family background and the fate of the remaining child's siblings, and says that Christ has created the boy Enyas to be his mother's champion (200). The hermit asks eternal God in heaven how this is to happen (201-2) and the angel responds with a command to bring Enyas to court the next day and see that he is christened 'Enyas', for 'Goddes wyll moste be fulfylde' (206). The hermit repeats the Providential words of the angel as he informs Enyas: 'Christe hath formeth þe, sone, to fyȝte for þy moder' (209). As they set out, Enyas invokes the name of God (219), and an angel stays on his shoulder to advise him (221-2). These credentials bestow great authority on Enyas, and the ongoing narrative reinforces this.

Confronted by Matabryne, Enyas swears by God in heaven (256) that she will lose her life for her evil deeds, and he is then duly baptized with the name 'Enyas'. The baptism is marked by great ceremony: it is performed by an abbot; two godfathers and one godmother are appointed; many rich gifts are showered on the youth; and the abbey bells begin to ring without the touch of human hand and continue ringing throughout the forthcoming judicial combat (265-73). The miracle of the bells, like the provision of food for Bewtrys, is usually found in hagiographical writing, and has been found in accounts of fifty saints.[13] On this occasion the bells explicitly indicate the overseeing of Providence: 'Wherefore þe wyste well þat Criste was plesed with here dede' (274).

The process of preparing Enyas for combat after this includes the finding of a mysterious shield, white with a cross (suggestive of the red cross on a crusader's shield), and an inscription saying that it belongs to Enyas (281-2), indicative of divine design. The preparation also includes instruction in combat from another young knight, who concludes by entrusting Enyas to God's care (312). The combat itself draws to a conclusion when Malkedras, ignoring Enyas' warning to stay away from the cross on his shield, is struck by both an adder and a flame shooting out from the cross (328-32), the former piercing him, the latter blinding him. Enyas kills and beheads him,[14] and acknowledges the work of God in bringing about this result: 'Thoo thanked he our Lorde lowely þat lente hym þat grace' (339).

Divine Providence has thus been strongly evoked in the stories of all four protagonists, but the last word on the subject concerns one of Enyas' brothers. To start with, the five intact chains are returned to the swans they belong to, making possible their transformation and baptism (365-8). A religious ceremony often marks the resolution of a romance. In *Havelok* and *Sir Orfeo*, for instance, there is a coronation, celebrating rightful possession of a throne;[15] in *King Horn* and *Florys and Blauncheflour* there is a double wedding, marking the reunion of the lovers and the union of their friends.[16] That the ceremony here is baptism (and a ceremony given extra prominence in so far as it echoes the earlier baptism of Enyas) reflects a particular concern to acknowledge God's sovereignty over the life of the hero and his fellows. The last line of the poem (370), as noted earlier, observes that they have been saved by God's help.

But as the narrative loose ends are tied up, two matters are left outstanding: the fate of Markus, blinded by Matabryne for failing to kill the children, and the fate of the swan whose chain is not recovered, preventing his return to human form. In the version of the tale on which *Chevelere Assigne* depends, Markus in fact has his sight restored after the fighting, when Enyas prays for him, and the English poet may simply have neglected to deal explicitly with him. The swan brother, on the other hand, has a central role in the next part of the Swan Knight cycle, drawing his brother's boat along, so that he must remain a swan here.[17] Both matters are, however, undeniably disturbing as the text stands, particularly the case of the brother. Indeed, the poet appears to have elaborated on his source by having the bird make a bloody attack on itself, and the court turn away 'for rewthe' (363), unable to bear the sight.

An explanation for the attention drawn to this scene may perhaps lie in recourse to the familiar tradition according to which another water-bird, the pelican, nourishes its young on its own blood by piercing itself in a similar gesture, an allegory of Christ's sacrifice of himself for the spiritual sustenance of his people.[18] If such a reading is admitted, the poem comes to an end with a strong emblematic reminder both of the consequences of human sin in the world and of the price paid for human salvation, the ultimate work of Providence.

In orthodox theology the operation of divine Providence does not necessarily involve instant or total correction of wrong, or alleviation of suffering. That the triumph of evil and the persistence of suffering are evident for much of the time-scale of *Chevelere Assigne*, and not entirely over when the poem ends, indicates not a lack of consistent interest in the idea of divine protection but an inclusive concern with the overall operation of divine Providence in the world.

Notes

1 All references are to the text in Speed 1993: I, 149–70. Reference is made to 'Chevelere Assigne' at lines 11, 328, 333 and 369, and to 'Gadyfere' at line 367. The relationship of the English poem to other extant versions of the Swan Children prelude to the cycle was explored in a major article by W. R. J. Barron (1967). Since then, a new edition of the medieval French *Beatrix*, with full collation and discussion of the extant manuscripts, has made a more detailed comparison possible: see Nelson 1977. For a comparison using this edition, see the introduction and notes to the text in Speed 1993: I, 149–58; II, 289–300.
2 Barron 1982: 81, on divine protection of creation; and 1987: 182, on divine protection of the hero. Barron's further remarks are from his 1987 book (loc. cit.).
3 Williams 1991: 196.
4 See, e.g., Burrow 1982: 82–3.
5 The exemplum tradition is discussed in, e.g., Brémond et al. 1982; Mosher 1911.
6 The fullest edition is that of the continental Latin by Oesterley (1872). The Middle English texts have been edited in Herrtage 1879; Sandred 1971. Accounts of the unedited Anglo-Latin branch may be found in Herrtage's Introduction, and in Herbert 1910: 183–229. Statements made here are based on current research towards an edition by Philippa Bright and myself.
7 Even if an animal fable is presented as an exemplum, it is understood to refer to certain kinds of people.
8 See the preface to Livy's *Ab urbe condita*, in Foster 1919; and the preface to Bede's *Historia ecclesiastica*, in Colgrave and Mynors 1969.
9 For editions, see Mills 1973: 46–74, 75–124.
10 See esp. the legend of St Catherine of Alexandria, as given in, e.g., *The South English Legendary* (D'Evelyn and Mill 1956–9: II, 533–43).
11 For the multiplication of materials in hagiographical writing, see Loomis 1938–9: 332–3. Loomis points out, however, that saints' legends usually deal with the increase of food and drink, on biblical models, and has found only three instances of the increase of metal, in connection with the furbishment of churches.
12 This creature fulfils the folk-tale function of 'animal nurse', but the

collocation of hind and hermit, especially in connection with nutrition, can be found in hagiographic writing: see Williams 1991: 196.
13 Loomis 1938-9: 331-2.
14 I think it has not previously been noted that several details of this episode echo details of the encounter between David and Goliath in I Samuel xvii.31-51, including the helplessness of the king, the ignorance but divine appointment of the young hero, the exchange of boasts in which the youth speaks with the authority of God, the fact that his opponent is struck on the head, and the final beheading. In so far as Enyas is a mimesis of David, he is a type of the Saviour himself.
15 For editions, see Speed 1993: I, 25-121, 122-48.
16 For editions, see Fellows 1993c: 1-41, 43-72.
17 In a later version, Robert Copland's *History of Helyas, Knight of the Swanne*, printed by Wynkyn de Worde in 1512 (*STC* 7571), the swan does return to human form some time later.
18 E.g., as carved at the entrance of St Peter's, Monkwearmouth.

10
'A damsell by herselfe alone': images of magic and femininity from *Lanval* to *Sir Lambewell*

ELIZABETH WILLIAMS

When Sir Launfal's fairy mistress arrives in King Arthur's court at the climax of Thomas Chestre's romance,[1] she proceeds to justify her lover's rash boast about her beauty in a way that is both theatrical and self-evident:

> Forþ sche wente ynto þe halle
> Þer was þe quene & þe ladyes alle,
>   And also Kyng Artour;
> Her maydenes come ayens her, ryȝt,
> To take her styrop whan sche lyȝt –
>   Of þe lady, Dame Tryamour.
> Sche dede of her mantyll on þe flet
> (Þat men schuld her beholde þe bet)
>   Wythoute a more soiour. (973–81)

Since the mantle has been described some thirty lines earlier as being lined with white ermine and worn over a garment of 'purpere palle', the image of the stripper provocatively allowing her mink coat to slide down over a silken surface in front of an avid audience is strongly suggested.

This impression is, of course, misleading. Sensuous as the action is, it is also judicially necessary: Launfal's life depends on the public acknowledgement of her beauty. She is also a fairy, and, as Judith Weiss has pointed out in another connection, fairies may perhaps be regarded in sexual matters as 'a special case: they are exotic outsiders, free from social and moral constraints, and may be expected to act accordingly'.[2]

Chestre's poem, in any case, represents only one line of a somewhat complex development which begins with Marie de France's original Breton *lai* of *Lanval*[3] (composed *c.* 1160–5 in French but almost certainly in England)[4] and ends when the latest extant text of the Middle English couplet translation of this was copied into the Percy Folio, under the title *Sir Lambewell,* sometime after 1642.[5] The original form of this translation is not extant: its composition has been assigned to the first half of the fourteenth century,[6] but it survives in no manuscript earlier than the sixteenth. The text usually entitled *Sir Landevale,*[7] preserved in Oxford, Bodleian Library, MS Rawlinson C.86, is generally regarded as the best, and it was from an exemplar very close to this in its readings that Thomas Chestre, later in the fourteenth century, remodelled the lay into the tail-rhyme romance of *Sir Launfal.*[8] Engaging as it is, however, *Sir Launfal* survives in only one manuscript, London, British Library, MS Cotton Caligula A.ii, which, perversely, is earlier than any of the five witnesses to the couplet version which it derives from; but, despite the change of metre, and substantive additions to the plot, Chestre's tail-rhyme text can often be used to clarify readings in the couplet version, which is usually judged to be artistically inferior, but which was still finding readers in the age of printing.[9]

This complex situation is exemplified in the episode of the lady's mantle: she lets it fall in the way described only in the Chestre text and in its ultimate source, Marie's *Lanval*. There is no trace of it in the extant texts of the intermediate couplet version, though its presence in Chestre indicates that it must have been in the original translation. More interestingly, its presence in *Lanval* also shows that it was not merely inserted by a male writer with lascivious intent but was part of the design of the original authoress. That design, however, becomes subtly altered in the process of transmission from text to text; and, if the scenes in which the fairy mistress features are compared, it is possible to chart the radical changes of emphasis that result as the treatment of the fay in particular, and of the female body in general, comes to reflect a whole range of different attitudes to beauty, sensuality, magic and sheer opulence.

It is usual to regard the extant English couplet texts as a group and to separate them from the tail-rhyme *Sir Launfal*, but in view of the latter's often close verbal links with the couplet version, and the very late date of the Percy Folio, for present purposes we may think in terms of a three-stage, chronological development: first the twelfth-century *Lanval* (here designated L); then a fourteenth-century stage, represented by the Rawlinson *Sir Landevale* (R) and often visible also in Chestre's *Sir Launfal* (C); and, finally, a last, late redaction of the couplet text, as seen in the Percy *Sir Lambewell* (P).

By happy coincidence, this triadic sequence is echoed in the three scenes in which the lady becomes the focus for detailed attention: her initial discovery in the tent, her solitary ride through Caerleon, and her climactic appearance in Arthur's court. All three passages have their origin in L, which is more surprising than it might appear, for Marie de France seldom indulges in physical description; as all her poems are short (*Lanval* amounts to only 646 lines in Ewert's text) so much attention to the lady's visual impact on no fewer than three occasions greatly increases its significance.

A. C. Spearing, in the course of an interesting study of voyeuristic moments in medieval love-narratives, has also noted the rarity of such passages in Marie de France, and he makes use of the same three scenes to develop a psychoanalytic interpretation of the story with particular reference to the differences between *Lanval* (known to have been written by a woman) and *Sir Launfal* (known to have been written by a man).[10] The wish-fulfilment element in the story is undeniably strong, though Spearing acknowledges that 'it would be mistaken to suppose ... that Marie intended objective magic to symbolize subjective fantasy'.[11] The actual degree of 'objective magic' conveyed by the descriptions in Marie and the later texts is one of the things that this paper seeks to explore, using surface detail and, where they exist, literary parallels, rather than Freudian analysis, to try and gauge the implications and effect of the three scenes in the different versions. Wider issues relating to gender studies lie beyond the limited scope of this analysis.

On the lady's first appearance there are some very subtle variations in what one might call the subliminal indications that she is magical. In describing the ride Lanval takes out of Kardoel which leads to his meeting with her, Marie de France mentions only that he came to a river and that his horse trembled. An earlier generation of scholars, alert to signs of folklore (and especially Celtic) origins for the Breton *lais*, made much of this, documenting extensive parallels between Lanval's mistress and stories of water-fays and swan-maidens,[12] but as premonitory signals of an imminent magical encounter the water and the trembling horse are minimal. I have written elsewhere of the way in which details of setting and action are enormously increased in the Middle English translation at this point, in accordance with a set of conventions which, by the fourteenth century, would evidently have conveyed a much stronger supernatural ambience.[13] R omits the trembling horse but, despite its general tendency to cut and compress rather than expand, adds that Landevale rode west, 'betwene a water and a forest', that it was 'underntyde', that the weather was hot and that he lay down under a tree.[14] Comparison with other stories shows that, after this set of premonitory signals, a fourteenth-century reader could reasonably expect the two damsels who are then seen approaching from the wood to be magical.

It is part of Marie's dramatic technique to use these handmaidens consistently to herald and enhance the subsequent appearance of their mistress. At this first view they seem to be not so much supernatural as dressed overtly to attract the male:

> Vestues ierent richement,
> Laciees mut estreitement
> En deus blians de purpre bis. (L 57–9)

The tight lacing and rich colour suggest opulence and sensuality rather than magic, the garments accentuating the shapely bodies beneath. Both details survive into the English texts, but the sensual impact is perhaps reduced by the addition of velvet mantles, which are mentioned first, green in R and C, red in P. Whether these contain an additional hint of magic is difficult to determine. Both green and red are said to be 'fairy' colours in Celtic literature, but neither need be.[15] So green may have conveyed a magical *frisson* in the original translation, which, as we have seen, also built up the forewarning machinery. But these subliminal suggestions may well have lost their meaning in the late Percy redaction, which, as we shall see below, is at pains to remove hints of magic but may not have recognized these as such; so, although the noonday heat is retained in P, it may not have been thought significant, and the choice of colour may simply have seemed more opulent or even regal.

The lady reclining in her tent provides a focus of even greater complexity. Again, details change and accumulate from text to text. To deal first with the tent, Marie seems primarily concerned to stress its extraordinary value, declaring that even Semiramis or Octavian could not have afforded so much as 'le destre pan' (L 86).

She then mentions its ropes and poles and an eagle of gold on top, again drawing attention to what it must all have cost. R and P both also mention cost, but this is where R comes into the open and states explicitly that the tent was

> With treysour iwrought on every syde
> Al of werke of the faryse. (R 79–80)

C, interestingly, ascribes the workmanship to the Saracens (C 266), an exotic but not a supernatural source, but P has nothing to correspond to this couplet at all. P's tendency to prefer richness to magic is thus confirmed, but two small hints still remain in all extant English versions. One is a reminder that the scene is set in a forest (R 77, C 262, P 101), often a place of supernatural encounter; the other is the addition of a self-effulgent crystal in the beak, or eyes, of the bird that decorates the top of the tent (R 85–6, P 107–8, C 271–2).[16] Gems that shine with their own light seem more associated with fairy realms than with mortal, however wealthy and fabulous.[17]

The fairy mistress herself, lying in the pavilion, presents a picture that is again both rich and alluring, but by no means as simple as it first appears. To start with Marie does no more than indicate her beauty by means of conventional references to the lily and the new rose (L 94–6). She then embarks on a much more specific description of the lady herself, starting with a brief glimpse at the bed she is lying on (again referring to its enormous value):[18]

> Ele jut sur un lit mut bel –
> Li drap valeient un chastel –
> En sa chemise senglement.
> Mut ot le cors bien fait e gent:
> Un cher mantel de blanc hermine,
> Covert de purpre alexandrine,
> Ot pur le chaut sur li geté;
> Tut ot descovert le costé,
> Le vis, le col e la peitrine;
> Plus ert blanche que flur d'espine. (L 97–106)

This is the image which, as it were, 'sets' our impression of the lady at this, her first appearance, and the combination of exposed flesh and fur mantle suggests the same sort of calculated display implied in the scene at Arthur's court, the vestigial chemise even perhaps working to increase the allure for the susceptible male.[19] But the description is in fact remarkable for the cool delicacy with which Marie enumerates the details. There is no striving for effect, no heaping-up of salacious suggestion, no hint that the lady is being in any way forward or improper. This is simply how she looked. Nor is there any clue that she is anything other than a rich and splendid, but perfectly human, lady.

The translations seem by comparison heavy-handed. To deal first with the question of magic, all identify the lady as a king's daughter from a place that comes out in R (92) as *Amylion* and in P (114) as *Million* – generally taken to be garbled forms of Avalon, a name clearly redolent of the unearthly by the fourteenth century. Marie also locates the lady's home in Avalon, but, interestingly, not until the very end, by which time her unusual powers have become apparent. The reference in L is moreover extremely low-key: 'Avalun' is simply 'un isle que mut est beaus' of which 'nus recuntent li Bretun' (L 641-3) – a Wace-like acknowledgement of a place that in Marie's time is perhaps more mysterious and beautiful than explicitly supernatural.[20]

For the R redactor there is, however, no question that 'Amylion' is

> an ile of the fayre,
> In occian full faire to see. (R 93-4)

Thomas Chestre, though he calls the island 'Olyroun', is also quite clear that her father was 'kyng of Fayrye' (C 278, 280). So in these fourteenth-century redactions the lady's fairy nature is bluntly stated at the outset. Only the late Percy Folio rejects the idea, omitting the lines completely, but the idea that the lady is a 'king's daugter' is retained (P 114).

The details of the description also undergo emphatic shifts:

> There was a bede of mekyll price,
> Coverid with purpill byse.
> Thereon lay that maydyn bright
> Almost nakyd and upright.
> Al her clothes byside her lay;
> Syngly was she wrappyd parfay

> With a mauntell of hermyn:
> Coverid was with alexanderyn.
> The mantell for hete down she dede
> Right to hir gyrdill stede. (R 95–104)

This not only says bluntly what Marie says delicately; it also reduces the lady's garments to one: the rich mantle now overtly covers her naked body, and the term *senglement,* which in L (99) is applied to the chemise, now applies to the mantle (*syngly,* R 100). P more or less follows this, and its substitution of *seemlie* for *syngly* (P 120) does not do much to sanitize the impression.

Obvious as it may seem, however, it is worth pausing at this point to consider exactly what sort of image we actually have here. There is no question of either the seductiveness or the fairy origins of the lady in R, where she really does seem to be the 'forth-putting' fay of the folklorists,[21] but by suppressing the fairy element P is in danger of exchanging the houri for an exceptionally well-to-do courtesan: removing the magic also removes the 'excuse' for sexual freedom. However, as we have seen, the magical suggestions are extremely subdued in *Lanval* also, where the reader's reaction to the lady's state of undress hangs upon the fine thread of Marie's exceptional delicacy in describing it. The tent is perhaps an added complication. Beautiful ladies trysting in tents, sometimes for supernatural purposes, become quite common in later Arthurian story,[22] but they do not seem to have acquired the habit in the twelfth century. Tom Peete Cross, who has written exhaustively on the subject of fairy mistresses, does not explicitly cite any who lay out their wares in tents, so there is no magical glamour about the tent *per se.* Splendid as it is, it may well be no more than a bit of circumstantial detail; or, as Cross rather archly puts it,

> it seems ... probable that originally Lanval's mistress appeared with two attendants bathing in a stream, and that when her character as a water-fée was forgotten, she was rationalized into a twelfth-century fine lady reclining in an ornate pavilion, her original scanty attire (if, indeed, she wore any clothes) was changed into a shocking deshabille, and her fairy companions were transformed into drawers of water for my lady's hands before her twelfth-century picnic luncheon.[23]

But if the tent is simply a 'rationalization' of an original outdoor setting, does her clothing also belong more to the real than to the fairy world? Just how 'shocking' would her 'deshabille' have seemed to a sophisticated twelfth-century audience, and do we have to use Celtic folklore to excuse it? In fact, Hoepffner pointed out long ago that a number of Marie's descriptive details have not a traditional but a literary origin in those seminal forerunners of courtly narrative, the *romans d'antiquité*.[24] The *Roman de Thèbes* in particular, written only a decade or two before *Lanval*,[25] paints some pictures of female dress that are, in more ways than one, significantly revealing. Antigone, for instance, a respectable princess, pays a ceremonial visit arrayed in *porpre inde*:

>	Tot senglement a sa char nue;
>	La blanche char desoz pareit. (3808–10)[26]

True, she is not reclining in a tent, but the revealing garment is clearly not in any way 'shocking', and this is not the only example. Tents, interestingly, also attract much rhetorical attention. Hoepffner cites, among others, the tent of King Adrastus, which has an eagle of gold on the top. The poet adds:

>	Li reis David ne Salomon
>	N'ot tal aigle en son paveillon.
>	(*Roman de Thèbes* 2951–2)

Marie had cited Semiramis and Octavian at a similar moment. So far as I know, the *romans d'antiquité* do not anywhere bring together the fashionably scanty clothing and the tent, but literary sources for both exist here. Far from seeking to shock, Marie is dressing her heroine in garments which are not out of place on a Theban princess, and locating her in a tent to match: exotic, perhaps, but literary, and quite unexceptionable.

Without access to Marie's actual source for the story we cannot, of course, be precise about her procedure. She may, indeed, have worked a rationalization as sweeping as the one Cross suggests, but the result is hardly as mundane, for her literary models are 'realistic' only in the heightened, idealized mode of the newly burgeoning genre of romance.[27] Her pictures may not have the glamour of a supernatural Otherworld, but their luxurious allure is still far beyond the reach of everyday experience. This is no Kardoel known to worldly geography, but even her Avalon is the refuge not of fairies but of courtly lovers.

It is only in the R translation that the magical build-up appears, culminating in the explicit identification of her home as 'an ile of the fayre'. This is then reduced again in P, with the removal of the overt fairy references, but revealing garments are no longer in literary fashion, and the substitution of *seemly* for *singly* suggests a slightly desperate attempt by the P redactor to render coyly respectable a lady who had started out as merely exotic.

The fay's second appearance, riding through the city on her way to vindicate Lanval in the judgement scene, forms the climax to a carefully structured rhetorical effect identified by Hoepffner as '"la triple gradation" ou ... l' "emerveillement croissant"'.[28] As before, she is heralded by her handmaidens, in two pairs this time, building up to the 'increasing wonder' of her own entry. Hoepffner suggests a literary source for this 'triple gradation' in an episode from a primitive version of the Tristan legend where Iseut rides at the end of a procession, her beauty surpassing that of all who ride ahead of her.[29] The preserved materials are, of course, much later, but popular ballad tradition also makes much use of the technique:

> Some ride upon a black, lady,
> And some ride on a brown,
> But I ride on a milk-white steed,
> And ay nearest the town.[30]

The point is, of course, that the third item should both fulfil and eclipse the preceding two. Dress here forms an important part of the effect, the first pair of maidens being clad in 'cendal purpre ... tut senglement a lur char nues' (L 475–6). This clearly recalls the tightly laced purple *blians* of the encounter scene, but these are now emphatically all that the maidens are wearing, next to the bare skin. The close parallel with Antigone should remind us that this is fashion, not provocation, but the sensuous richness is even more pronounced. Marie's description of the crowd reaction is typically ambiguous: 'Cil les esgardent volenters' (L 477). The second pair, however, are simply in 'pailes freis' (L 511) but the crowd breaks out into praise of their *cors*, *vis* and *colur* (L 530).

Interestingly, the sexy purple dresses are not worn (by the maidens, that is) in any of the translations, which consistently refer to the beauty of both pairs of attendants in general terms only, avoiding mention of specific bodily features, while the crowd around the second pair is anxious to behold their *gentrise/ gentryes* in R and P, more bluntly *har clodynge* in C. Sensuous appeal gives way to chatter and speculation.

The climax to all this, though, is the lady, separated from her harbingers and riding 'by herselfe alone' (P 507). As with the damsels, the picture she presents is both familiar and different. Her palfrey, like her tent, is described in terms of costliness in both L and R, though not in P. P also fails to mention her garments, which Marie refers to as a *chainsil blanc* and a *chemise*

> Que tuz les costez li pareient,
> Que de deus parz laciez esteient. (L 561–2)

Furthermore:

> Sis manteus fu de purpre bis;
> Les pans en ot entur li mis.
> Un espervier sur sun poin tient,
> E un levrer aprés li vient. (L 571–4)

For this highly public ride she therefore wears the same combination of simple white under-raiment and opulent purple cloak as she wore for private purposes in the tent, but the blend of display and concealment is even more subtle: *chaisnil* and *chemise* seem to imply two garments, not just one, but the lacing still leaves her skin exposed. As she has drawn the skirts of her rich mantle around her, Marie may here be describing what will only become visible when she unveils in the court, though the example of Antigone again suggests that modesty need have imposed no constraint:

> Sis manteaus fu, ço m'est vis, vairs,
> Et afubla s'en en travers:
> Les panz en ot bien entroverz,
> Que li costez fu descoverz.
>   (*Roman de Thèbes* 3817–20)

Even the sparrowhawk may have a literary origin, for Antigone's sister, Ismène, rode with her, as Hoepffner points out, *en chasseresse,* with hawk on wrist.[31]

As a climax to the 'triple gradation' this is clearly a far more specific picture of beauty and leisured courtliness, not just sexual allure, than was presented by the maidens, with the purple and ermine mantle arranged so as to conceal her full beauty until it can be revealed with greatest impact in the court. Riding alone as she does, she presents a truly singular image of unadorned feminine loveliness, with no hint of either magic or royal splendour.

This singularity assumes less subtle lines in translation, though all the English texts emphasize the dramatic solitariness of her ride. The palfrey and the hawk appear in all; the greyhounds multiply to two in C, three in R and P. As for her clothing, C and R mention only purple silk, thus depriving her of the odd sense of innocence conveyed by the *chainsil blanc* of L. It is not clear in either C or R whether the purple silk belongs to her tunic or her mantle, or even both, and neither text transmits the fact of the cloak being pulled concealingly around her. R, indeed, makes the precise and individual observation:

> The pane of hir mantell inwarde
> On hir harmes she foldid owtewarde   (R 443-4)

– as if to display a rich lining, though none is mentioned in this text. The gesture, however, with its hint of ostentation, is the reverse of that described in L, where the bulk of Marie's description in fact concentrates on the lady's natural beauties of face and hair. These are also present in R and C, which, significantly, both also give her a royal crown of gold and gems. This agrees with their previous identification of her as a king's daughter, but it is only now that the visual symbol draws attention to the importance of the change.

P at this point, though distressingly garbled, nonetheless produces one of its most individual effects. As indicated, most of the physical details of hair, complexion and clothing have dropped from the text completely, leaving the lady only her hawk, hounds and jewelled crown. But to this regal picture the P redactor adds one unique detail of crowd reaction:

> Wife and child, yonge and old,
> All came this lady to beholde,
> And all still uppon her gazinge
> As people that behold the sacring.   (P 523-6)

Religious hyperbole is more frequent in this text than the others but is usually commonplace. Here, though, the lady, stripped elsewhere in P of her fairy magic, acquires a new and different mystery: by comparing the awe of the crowd to that of a congregation witnessing the elevation of the Host at the Mass, the redactor has endowed the lady with a peculiarly Christian holiness. Marie's image of her riding alone, hawk on hand, her unadorned white beauty partly concealed under a cloak of dark purple, is both womanly and enigmatic, almost suggestive of the virgin huntress. Here, regally crowned, she suggests, rather, a late medieval religious procession, occupying perhaps the position reserved for the Host at Corpus Christi, or a statue of the Virgin Mary, though neither of those would have processed unaccompanied. The odd thing is the way both images, the pagan and the Christian, insist that this 'forth-putting fay' is in some way unique, phoenix-like, even virginal.

Against this background, the final scene of the lady's unveiling in the courtroom assumes a far less salacious aura. In L, of course, she never was salacious: her maids wore tight-fitting purple silk, she only white, subtly veiled; undecked with crown or jewels, her beauty is her own; her power is mysterious, its source never stated, but her moral superiority to the vicious earthly queen is now as self-evident as her beauty. This is indeed the naked truth.

R and C, decking out the lady with so much more worldly regal glamour, could easily have vulgarized the scene. As we have seen, only C describes her removing her mantle 'þat men schuld her beholde the bet', but in fact both these fourteenth-century texts make it clear that the unveiling was not done specifically for the men: it was a woman who forced Launfal into his rash boast, and it is the women who must make public acknowledgement that he was right:

> Vp stod þe quene & ladyes stoute,
> Her forto beholde all aboute,
>   How euene sche stod vpryȝt;
> Þan wer þey wyth her also donne
> As ys þe mone ayen þe sonne.
>   Aday whan hyt ys lyȝt.   (C 985–90)

This stress on the female component of the audience is not in Marie, who, as we have seen, evidently felt quite at ease with a heroine in the habit of displaying her flesh in public. Her very restrained reference to 'Avalun' suggests, furthermore, that she did not even feel much need to provide the lady with the excuse of being a fairy. Her portrait is of the consummate Woman, in whom exceptional beauty goes with exceptional power – a fantasy figure no doubt in Marie's time, but endowed with the prime virtues of faithfulness to one man, and the integrity to wield her power justly even when wronged, though her justice has a touch of ruthlessness: she saves Lanval from death, but Marie never actually tells us that she forgave him.

This omission may also have got through to the original English translation, for there is no forgiveness in Thomas Chestre either. For him, however, sheer womanliness was not enough: power she had, so she became for him both queen and fairy, in a crown of gold, perhaps also exchanging her pure white chemise for the opulent purple tunic of her handmaidens. Sir Landevale's lady, in R, is also queenly and magical, but this is the first text in which she is explicitly forgiving, forcing her knight to plead with her before she will take him back, but eventually riding off with him to 'Amylyon', whence they never return – a consummation in tune with ideal courtly loving as well as magic, the lady graciously showing mercy to the erring but faithful knight.

Finally P, having elevated the lady to almost divine heights, transforms this scene of pleading into a sort of duet-with-chorus of near-operatic intensity, with Lambewell actually pleading on his knees with the king to intercede on his behalf with his unrelenting mistress. The picture provides an ironic comment not just on the excesses of courtly love but also on the normal gender roles in medieval literary courtrooms, in which the woman wields no power at all and is habitually presented kneeling and weeping as she begs a ruthless monarch to show mercy (as, indeed, Guenevere had done in private when making her complaint to the king, though only in the couplet version (R 242, P 278). Nor is it altogether clear that Lambewell's grovel is successful: the conversation recorded in R is not present, though the lady does ride off with him and apparently gives him all he wants. But, true to the last in its resolute rejection of all suggestion of fairies, P finally reduces her to the indignity of full human status, made worse by a particularly ill-timed scribal corruption:

> But in that iland his life he spend,
> Soe did shee alsoe tooke her end.   (P 629–30)

What these comparisons suggest, then, is a kind of progression in the representation of the lady from Woman in Marie, to Fairy in *Sir Landevale*, to an almost divine Queen in *Sir Lambewell*. Spearing's Freudian analysis is again of interest here. His interpretation of Lanval's experience as a male wish-fulfilment fantasy provides 'one reason why the tension of the trial scene is so powerful: it is hard to believe that Lanval's secret love is anything *but* a fantasy, and we do not really expect the lady to return once he has allowed public reality to impinge on his fantasy-world'.[32] The couplet texts form no part of Spearing's discussion, but it could be argued that in R the greater stress on the lady's fairy nature imparts an equal, but quite different, tension to this crucial scene. For, as *Sir Orfeo* shows, the fairies of Breton *lai* have a particularly ruthless attitude to promises. It took some sharp thinking on Orfeo's part to catch them out at their own game and make their rigid word-keeping work against them, but Landevale's situation is past hope: he has broken his word and cannot expect to be saved. It is therefore tempting in this text to see the fairy's solitary and majestic ride through the city as proof of her uniqueness: this was the one fairy who could and did forgive, her unbending nature subsumed into the capacity for mercy of an idealized, but human, courtly mistress.

In P, however, Sir Lambewell's lady is human throughout, but powerfully, regally human, with an almost divine aura which suggests both the capacity for mercy of the Virgin Mary, and the superstitious awe of late medieval devotion which reduces the penitent to a grovelling wreck before he can be graciously accepted back. Spearing acknowledges the element of female, as well as male, fantasy in the story, but the ruthless Queen of P (in her way almost as ruthless as Guenevere) is a far cry from both the gravely forgiving Fairy on the verge of humanity in R, and the mysteriously protective, enigmatic Woman of L.

Notes

1 For references and quotations, see Bliss 1960.
2 Weiss 1991: 149 n. 2.
3 For quotations and references for all her *lais*, see Ewert 1944.
4 For a useful account of Marie's dates and provenance, see Burgess 1987: ch. 1.

5 Text printed in Hales and Furnivall 1867-8: I, 144-64. For a recent account of the Percy Folio (London, British Library, MS Add. 27879), see Donatelli 1989: 1-5.
6 Mortimer J. Donovan, in Severs 1967: 139.
7 The name 'Lanval' emerges in a wide variety of forms in Middle English, which provides a useful way of distinguishing one text from another according to the predominant form used, though scholars are not entirely consistent in this: Donovan (see above n. 6) refers to the Rawlinson version as *Sir Landeval*.
8 For textual relations, see Kittredge 1889, which includes a text of *Sir Landevale;* Edwards 1954, which contains an edition of all the Middle English texts in parallel.
9 In addition to the very late Percy Folio, two printed fragments, Oxford, Bodleian Library, Malone 941 and Douce Fragments e.40, are printed in Hales and Furnivall 1867-8: I, 522-32, 533-5; and one further manuscript fragment, Cambridge University Library, MS Kk.5.30, in Furnivall 1890: xxxi. For information on the Rawlinson MS and the printed texts, see Boffey and Meale 1991; and for extensive bibliographies for all the English texts, see Severs 1967: 295-6.
10 Spearing 1993: esp. ch. 5.
11 Ibid.: 98.
12 Cross 1915; Schofield 1900.
13 Williams 1969: 87; 1991: 190-1.
14 R 35-42. Quotations from R and P are from the manuscripts, with modern punctuation, word-division, letter-forms and capitalization, abbreviations expanded and minor emendations unsignalled. For L and C, see the editions cited.
15 For references, see Patch 1950: 58 n. 75; Cross 1915: 595 n. 3.
16 The bird is actually a heron in R, probably a scribal mistake for some form of *ern*, 'eagle', the word used by Chestre (C 268). In P (line 105) it has become an even more exotic *gripe*, 'griffin'.
17 See, e.g., Bliss 1966: lines 151-2, 371-2 (Auchinleck text); Patch 1950: 56 n. 67.
18 Although her *lais* contain so little personal description, Marie rarely ignores a chance to describe a handsome bed: in addition to the present one, see, e.g., the wonderful examples in *Guigemar* 170-82 and *Yonec* 387-9, and the charming little carry-cot in *Milun* 99-104.
19 'The juxtaposition of luxurious garment and bare skin, more provocative than complete nudity, is a recurrent element in descriptions of female seductiveness' (Spearing 1993: 101).
20 For Wace as the source of Marie's knowledge of the Arthurian legend, see Hoepffner 1933: 353-6.
21 Cf. Cross 1915: 611.

22 E.g. in Malory: see Vinaver and Field 1990: 153 (human), 549 (diabolical).
23 Cross 1915: 609–10.
24 Hoepffner 1933.
25 Burgess 1987: 6.
26 Constans 1890.
27 For a similar argument, showing how Marie used literary sources to make 'those changes she considered necessary to transform the folk-tale into a courtly short story', see Stokoe 1948.
28 Hoepffner 1933: 357.
29 Ibid.: 357–8.
30 *Tam Lin* (Child 1882: no. 39, version B, st. 27).
31 Constans 1890: line 3857; Hoepffner 1933: 361.
32 Spearing 1993: 100

11

Looking behind the book: MS Cotton Caligula A.ii, part 1, and the experience of its texts

JOHN J. THOMPSON

Readers of this celebratory volume in honour of Maldwyn Mills will require little formal introduction to the fifteenth-century literary miscellany now known as London, British Library, MS Cotton Caligula A.ii, part 1 (hereafter Ca).[1] This was formerly identified as MS Cotton Vespasian D.viii until it was bound together with MS Cotton Vespasian D.xxi (Cb) sometime before the 1654 Cotton catalogue. Despite the modern fame of Ca, however, hardly any specific details of the volume's provenance have emerged. The hand of its single unnamed copyist has remained unidentified in other extant documents. And the inscription 'Donum Jo. Rogers' in a sixteenth-century hand on fo. 3^r gives the name of a possible former owner the book but no obvious means of identifying the person behind the name. The identity of other early owners or readers is completely unknown. On a slightly more positive note, however, modern editors have been able to use the identification of different dialect strata in many of the surviving texts in Ca to argue that this intriguing miscellany was copied by someone from the general south-east, or south-east Midland, area.

Modern scholars have been acutely aware of the need to 'look behind' the items gathered together in Ca.[2] The manuscript has long been recognized by Maldwyn Mills and others as an important witness to the manner in which 'mixed' collections of Middle English metrical romances continued to circulate among certain fifteenth-century readers some time after the individual items were first written in a variety of stanza forms and then widely disseminated. Comparisons have been made between Ca and a variety of other late medieval manuscript miscellanies containing Middle English romances copied by single scribes. These other medieval books are now frequently characterized as 'household' volumes, sometimes 'homemade', and usually assumed to have been prepared for devout and literate layfolk. Typical of these are the two mid-fifteenth-century 'Thornton' collections (Lincoln Cathedral Library, MS 91, and London, British Library, MS Add. 31042), which, with Ca, are the only surviving late medieval collections known to us that preserve a combination of Middle English tail-rhyme romances and Middle English romances written in alliterative verse; also Cambridge University Library, MS Ff.2.38 (of unknown provenance and copied by a single late fifteenth-century scribe, whose identity is unknown); Oxford Bodleian Library, MS Ashmole 61 (of unknown but possibly north-east Midland provenance, copied in an agenda format by a late fifteenth-century scribe called Rate); and Naples, Biblioteca Nazionale, MS XIII.B.29 (copied in the second half of the fifteenth century by one 'More').[3]

For modern scholars interested in the processes by which such fifteenth-century manuscript collections came into existence, it remains a mixed blessing that the Thornton scribe is perhaps the most 'comfortingly familiar' of the late medieval English romance copyists named above – more 'comfortingly familiar' than the Ca scribe, for example, because the Thornton scribe names himself at the end of some of his items, thereby enabling modern scholars to call upon a range of other documentary sources to build up a convincing account of his life as a member of the north Yorkshire minor gentry. But our still imperfect awareness of Thornton's identity is no substitute for our complete ignorance of the Ca scribe's, whose name, rank, gender and precise geographical origins are likely to remain completely unknown to us. This is my main justification for returning to Ca in this short paper to explore the probable manner in which the volume that now bears witness to this scribe's copying activities itself came into existence.

Physical make-up and the problems of collation

All recent attempts to describe Ca have been hampered by uncertainties concerning its original quiring. Both Ca and Cb are quarto volumes, and Ca is made up of at least four different stocks of fifteenth-century paper, none of which is shared with Cb.[4] Fos. 1–2 and 140–1 at either end of Ca consist of post-medieval paper that was probably added when the two parts of the present manuscript were finally bound together. The manuscript was rebound in 1957, at which time its leaves were guarded (that is, its individual folios were mounted on modern paper strips). As far as I can tell, no record was kept of the state of the manuscript when it was disbound, and no attempt was made to establish a physical collation for the manuscript prior to 1957. This was probably because the manuscript was considered too tightly bound to collate. It is also unfortunate that the manuscript has been so heavily cropped, since this has removed all traces of any catchwords or quire and leaf signatures that may have once existed.

While there are undoubted difficulties in attempting to describe the physical make-up of this fragmentary medieval volume, these are not insurmountable. As Figure 1 indicates, close examination of the watermarked paper stocks in Ca permits the hypothetical reconstruction of seven fifteenth-century quires. For reasons of space, I have had to present these findings in summary form, without full discussion of the many intriguing issues and problems that arise when the stocks of medieval paper that make up Ca are subjected to detailed scrutiny. It seems to me that the manner in which many of the watermarked sheets in the manuscript were originally folded (folded twice, that is) to make up the quires in this quarto volume will clearly reward some closer attention than I have been able to give them here. I must also acknowledge the characteristic generosity of Ralph Hanna, whose unpublished work to establish a partial physical collation for the book by checking the watermark sequences was completed shortly before my own. Professor Hanna sent me a summary draft of the brief manuscript description which I understand will appear in his forthcoming edition of *The Siege of Jerusalem*. In Figure 1, I offer my own identification of the watermarked folios (because this is a quarto arrangement, it should be noted that the remains of watermark designs on some of the guarded folios are sometimes quite difficult to detect).[5] I have also included my own tentative identification of the mould sides of individual leaves, since such evidence lends additional support to the collation.

There are a number of places where the suggested reconstruction of the original quires offered in the appendix must remain open to the possibility of some future revision. The original status of fos. 44–9 is unclear, for example, although for convenience I follow the line of least resistance by allowing that the physical evidence of the chain indentations in the paper (which permits the mould sides to be

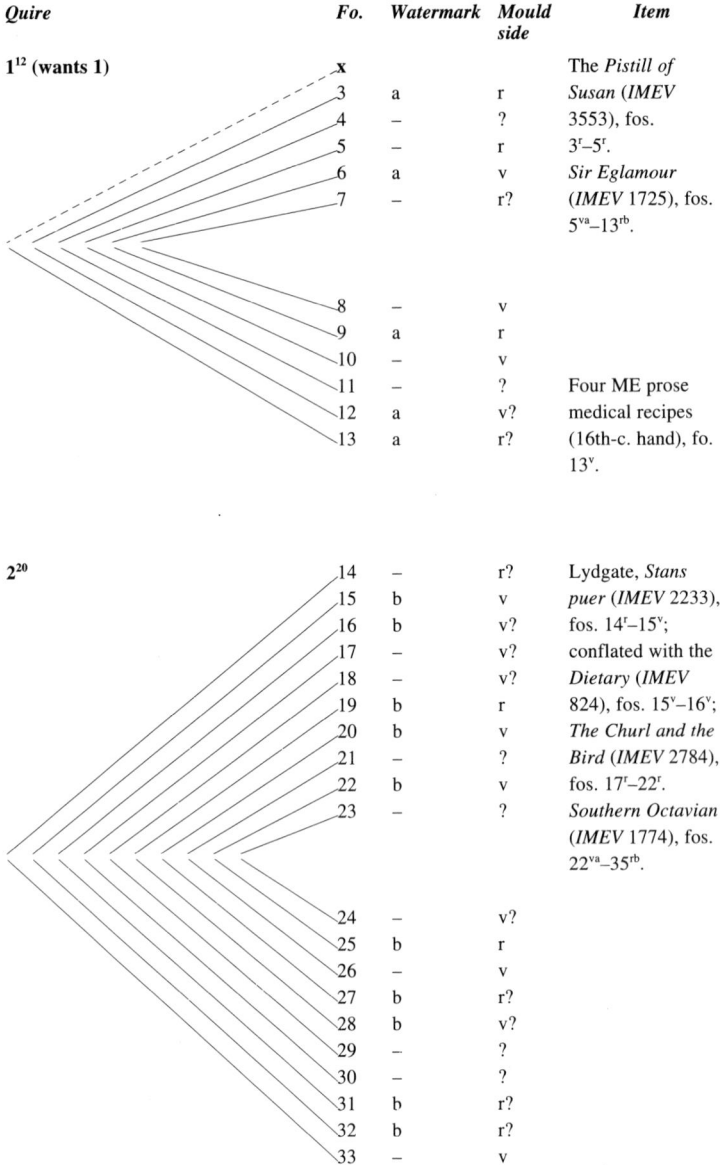

Figure 1 MS Cotton Caligula A.ii, part 1 – contents and physical make-up

MS COTTON CALIGULA A.ii, PART 1

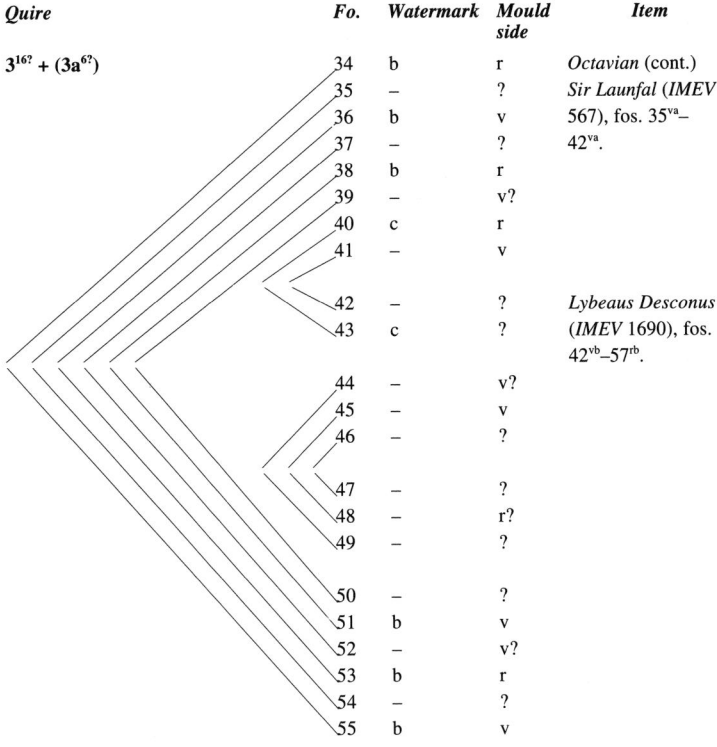

Quire	Fo.	Watermark	Mould side	Item
$3^{16?} + (3a^{6?})$	34	b	r	*Octavian* (cont.)
	35	–	?	*Sir Launfal* (*IMEV*
	36	b	v	567), fos. 35va–
	37	–	?	42va.
	38	b	r	
	39	–	v?	
	40	c	r	
	41	–	v	
	42	–	?	*Lybeaus Desconus*
	43	c	?	(*IMEV* 1690), fos.
				42vb–57rb.
	44	–	v?	
	45	–	v	
	46	–	?	
	47	–	?	
	48	–	r?	
	49	–	?	
	50	–	?	
	51	b	v	
	52	–	v?	
	53	b	r	
	54	–	?	
	55	b	v	

Figure 1 continued

176   JOHN J. THOMPSON

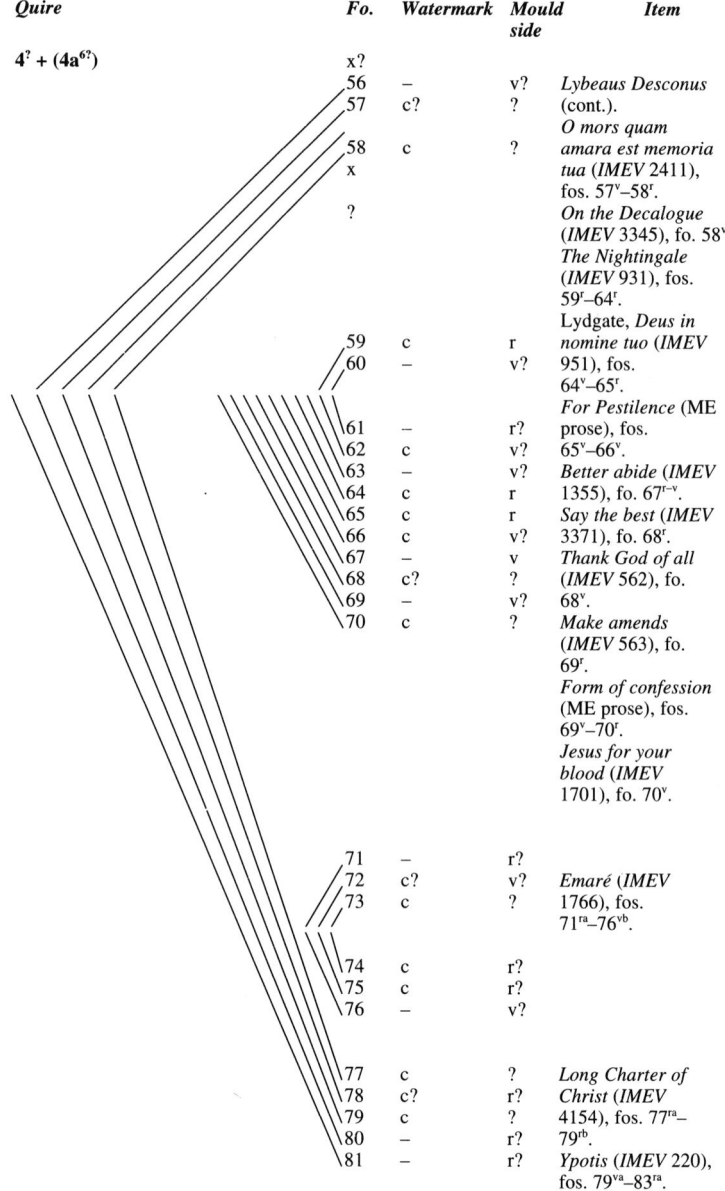

Quire	Fo.	Watermark	Mould side	Item
4⁷ + (4a⁶?)	x?			
	56	–	v?	Lybeaus Desconus (cont.).
	57	c?	?	O mors quam amara est memoria tua (IMEV 2411), fos. 57ᵛ–58ʳ.
	58	c	?	
	x			
	?			On the Decalogue (IMEV 3345), fo. 58ᵛ· The Nightingale (IMEV 931), fos. 59ʳ–64ʳ.
	59	c	r	Lydgate, Deus in nomine tuo (IMEV 951), fos. 64ᵛ–65ʳ.
	60	–	v?	
	61	–	r?	For Pestilence (ME prose), fos. 65ᵛ–66ᵛ.
	62	c	v?	
	63	–	v?	Better abide (IMEV 1355), fo. 67ʳ⁻ᵛ.
	64	c	r	
	65	c	r	Say the best (IMEV 3371), fo. 68ʳ.
	66	c	v?	
	67	–	v	Thank God of all (IMEV 562), fo. 68ᵛ.
	68	c?	?	
	69	–	v?	
	70	c	?	Make amends (IMEV 563), fo. 69ʳ. Form of confession (ME prose), fos. 69ᵛ–70ʳ. Jesus for your blood (IMEV 1701), fo. 70ᵛ.
	71	–	r?	
	72	c?	v?	Emaré (IMEV 1766), fos. 71ʳᵃ–76ᵛᵇ.
	73	c	?	
	74	c	r?	
	75	c	r?	
	76	–	v?	
	77	c	?	Long Charter of Christ (IMEV 4154), fos. 77ʳᵃ–79ʳᵇ.
	78	c?	r?	
	79	c	?	
	80	–	r?	
	81	–	r?	Ypotis (IMEV 220), fos. 79ᵛᵃ–83ʳᵃ.

Figure 1 continued

MS COTTON CALIGULA A.ii, PART 1

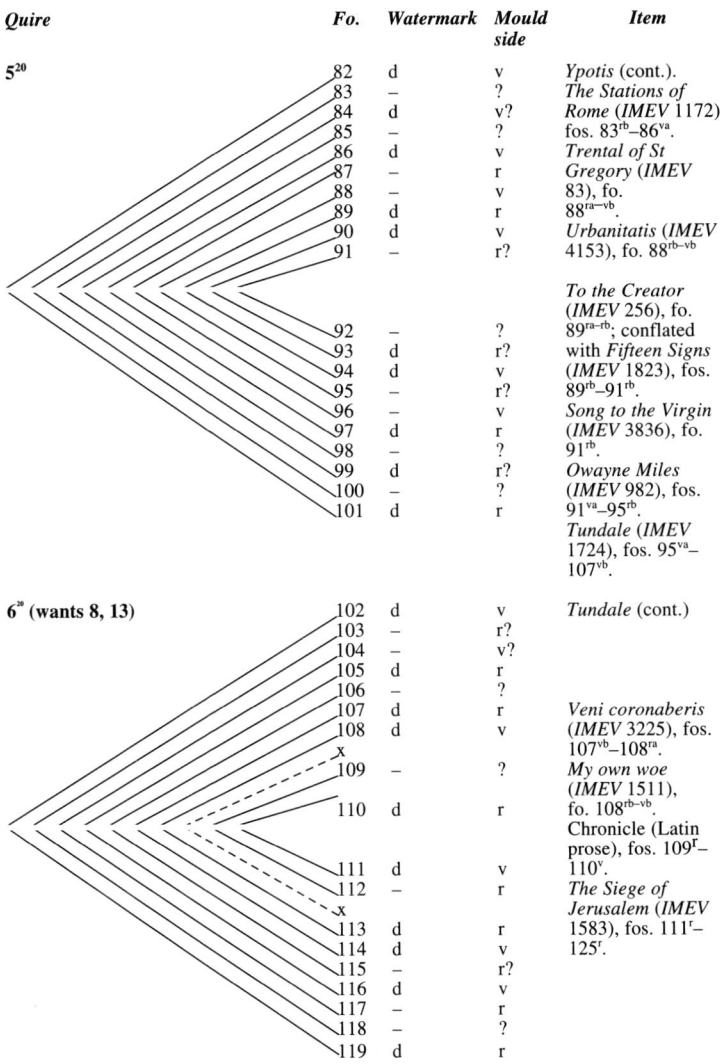

Figure 1 continued

Quire	Fo.	Watermark	Mould side	Item
7²⁰	120	d	v	The Siege of Jerusalem (cont.).
	121	–	?	
	122	d	v	
	123	–	?	
	124	d	v	
	125	–	?	Chevelere Assigne (IMEV 272), fos. 125ᵛ–129ᵛ.
	126	–	v?	
	127	d	r	
	128	d	v	
	129	–	r	Sir Isumbras (IMEV 1184), fos. 130ʳᵃ–134ʳᵇ.
	130	–	v	
	131	d	r	
	132	d	v	
	133	–	r	Lydgate, Five Wounds (IMEV 3845), fo. 134ᵛ. Five Joys (IMEV 1046), fo. 135ᵛ. Jerome (IMEV 2922), fos. 135ᵛ–137ʳ; Eustache (IMEV 2894), fos. 137ᵛ–139ᵛ.
	134	–	?	
	135	d	r	
	136	–	v	
	137	d	r	
	138	–	?	
	139	d	r	
?		x	–	Eustache (cont.) other material?

Figure 1 continued

identified) does not preclude the possibility that these leaves once formed six unwatermarked bifolia inserted in quire 3. I am also unable to resolve completely the collation difficulties presented by the fragmentary and possibly rearranged middle section of the book to my entire satisfaction. The available physical and textual evidence in fos. 56–81 does not contradict the notion that this particularly difficult section of the manuscript once consisted of a single fragmentary and composite quire. I tentatively identify the remains of at least eight bifolia and suggest that another nine singletons in this quire may have lost the leaves with which they were originally conjoint. Several of these missing leaves may well have been cancels. In order to offer a speculative reconstruction of the quire along these lines, I have been forced to concede that at least one leaf (a blank?) may have been lost before fo. 56 and that the manuscript has probably also suffered an extensive physical loss of some kind between fos. 58 and 59.

There are good grounds for assuming a textual lacuna between fos. 58 and 59. This is because the item that now begins on fo. 59^r (a short Lydgatian lyric known to modern scholars as *The Nightingale*) opens abruptly in Ca and may have lost some or all of the dedicatory lines found in one of its two other extant copies. This hypothesized textual loss is inadequate by itself to account for an extensive physical loss between fos. 58 and 59, but I am tempted by the speculation (discussed further below) that a number of other short items has been irretrievably lost from the collection at this key point. I should make clear, however, that my main goal is to deal with the seemingly intractable collation problem presented by this difficult middle section without contradicting the limited and unsatisfactory evidence at my disposal. The physical evidence is so wide open to interpretation that it would even be possible to argue for the manuscript's having suffered several other physical losses not indicated in the diagram if that would permit a more convincing collation to be proposed.[6]

My collation diagram suggests that this problematic and fragmentary fourth quire was also composite: the original quire was soon supplemented by at least one further batch of watermark c paper inserted off-centre. This insertion was probably made while the scribe was continuing to copy material that had been gathered together from diverse sources to fill out the limited remaining space in the original quire. And it is fortunate that the previous quire in the manuscript – quire 3 – provides a precedent for such practically motivated scribal activity. Unlike the situation in quire 3, however, the late insertion of paper in quire 4 may also be identified as a 'mini-quire' of six bifolia (fos. 71–6), containing the Ca scribe's text of *Emaré*.[7] This was inserted immediately before the *Long Charter of Christ* on fos. 77ra–79rb, which, I suspect, was probably the *first* item that the scribe copied in this extraordinary composite quire. If so, the original quire had to be refolded to allow the final lines of *Lybeaus Desconus* to be added.

Finally, I am reasonably certain that at least one whole quire but possibly more has now gone missing following quire 7. This would have contained the remaining lines of *Eustache* and perhaps some other related *South English Legendary* material.

Texts and textual clusters in the manuscript

In this section of the paper I want to continue the process of building up a picture of the manner in which a number of smaller clusters of material are likely to have been originally brought together by the Ca scribe.

The 'booklet' status of the first quire offers a convenient starting-point for this discussion. Since the 'booklet' was often used as a production aid by medieval compiler–copyists (the example of Robert Thornton springs to mind), it is possible to argue that the two main items originally copied in this first surviving quire (*The Pistill of Susan* and *Sir Eglamour*) have retained the kind of semi-detached relationship to the rest of the manuscript that may have once been enjoyed by other items before the quires were finally assembled in their present order. Throughout this discussion, therefore, I have assumed that the collection as a whole probably once consisted of a series of unbound, blank and partly filled quires in which items were not necessarily copied in the order in which they now survive. The four medical receipts copied by an unknown sixteenth-century hand on fo. 13^v in the first quire are perhaps the most obvious examples of items being added to the collection some time after the quires were first constructed.

The three romance items copied consecutively in quires 2–4 have already attracted much critical attention. Maldwyn Mills and others have argued in support of the view that all three items – the *Southern Octavian*, *Sir Launfal* and *Lybeaus* – are likely to represent the works of a single writer, who names himself as Thomas Chestre in *Sir Launfal* 1039. Ca preserves the only surviving copies of the *Southern Octavian* and *Sir Launfal*, while other texts of *Lybeaus* are extant in four other fifteenth-century manuscripts and a seventeenth-century copy in the Percy Folio (London, British Library, MS Add. 27879). Despite some puzzling linguistic variation between the three 'Chestre' romances, it seems probable that the Ca scribe inherited all three items from one source, and the order in which they are now preserved in Ca may also reflect the chronological sequence in which Chestre is presumed to have written them.

The Ca scribe probably went to particular lengths to ensure that Chestre's 'collected works' were presented as a single series. On fo. 22va the scribe began the process of imposing some uniformity on Chestre's poems by consistently adding marginal stanza indicators at six-line intervals in the text. These markers usefully indicate the beginnings of the six-line tail-rhyme stanzas in *Octavian*, of course, but on fos. 35va–57rb the function of such marks clearly changes, because their presence means that the twelve-line tail-rhyme stanzas in which *Sir Launfal* and the bulk of this copy of *Lybeaus* are written are systematically broken down into smaller, six-line units. *Sir Isumbras* in quire 7 is the only other item in the manuscript that has been forced to conform to this scribe's obvious desire to present some twelve-line stanzas in six-line reading-units.[8]

The cluster of 'Chestre' romances is also distinctive because the Ca scribe experimented with other features of their visual layout. On fo. 22^v, the first stanza of *Octavian* is written across the page in a single column, where each line in the manuscript represents two lines of verse. The procedure is then halted and never repeated with the other tail-rhyme items, but if the Ca scribe had persisted, this would have imposed a visual layout on the 'Chestre' romances that would have been similar to the layout used for the two alliterative romances in quires 6 and 7, or the two *South English Legendary* saints' lives in quire 7 (both written in septenary long lines), or even the three short refrain poems crowded on to fos. 68^r–69^r in quire 4 (see below). On fo. 22va, however, perhaps after some momentary hesitation, the scribe commenced presenting the *Octavian* text in double columns (the format in which all the tail-rhyme romances and a good number of other items in the manuscript are also presented). It is particularly striking, moreover, that, on fos. 31ra–57rb, but nowhere else in the manuscript, the scribe also consistently managed to copy exactly six six-line units of text (i.e. 36 lines) per column. The only exception to this rule is fo. 35rb, where the scribe only needed to copy five six-line stanzas in the column in order to complete *Octavian* before commencing to copy *Sir Launfal* on a fresh page (fo. 35^v).

As the description of items in Figure 1 demonstrates, this scribe generally ensured that the beginnings and endings of items usually coincided with the beginnings and endings of pages (or, occasionally, columns) in the manuscript. And some care has been taken to impose uniformity on the completed volume by the provision of formal headings, explicits and running titles. But the obvious concern for standardizing the visual appearance of the text of the 'Chestre' romances of fos. 31^r-57^r in quires 2-4 is still extraordinary in the context of the collection as a whole. The original make-up of quires 2-4 suggests that the concern to copy exactly the same number of lines per page, using exactly the same visual format, may well be related to some of the circumstances in which the scribe received and copied an exemplar, or exemplars, containing the 'Chestre' romances.

These items may well have been added to a growing collection that already consisted of a number of unbound and partly filled quires. The bulk of *Octavian* was added to a quire (now quire 2) which already contained a sequence of three short Lydgate poems. These are presented in single columns with marginal markers properly indicating stanza-divisions, and the two shortest texts (*Stans puer* and the *Dietary*) are presented here, as in some other Lydgatian manuscripts, as a single item. The visual presentation of this material represents the usual fifteenth-century scribal procedure for dealing with such items. It is hardly surprising, therefore, that the same general standard of presentation was maintained for some other short items in the manuscript. These include the cluster of four poems (including one by Lydgate, and two others that were written in his manner) that now survives on fos. 57^v-65^r in quire 4, and also the symmetrically presented pair of lyrics on the Five Wounds and the Five Joys (the first by Lydgate) on fos. 134^v-135^r in quire 7.

Quire 3 contains the remaining lines of *Octavian*, the complete text of *Sir Launfal* and the bulk of *Lybeaus*. This is a composite quire with its outer leaves consisting of watermark b paper to which was added a core of watermark c paper. And fos. 44-9 represent a later insertion of six unwatermarked leaves in the second half of the quire. This unusual feature implies that the scribe was forced to supplement the original quire for some reason, perhaps because of some earlier miscalculation, or even because some additional material by Chestre unexpectedly became available as he was working on this quire. But quire 3 is also made up of at least two different stocks of watermarked paper (b and c), and this is the only extant quire in the volume made up of mixed paper-stocks. Such evidence strongly suggests that the quire is likely to have been originally constructed from the limited remaining paper-stocks available to the scribe. This was perhaps after quires 2 (containing only watermark b paper) and 4 (entirely made up of paper with watermark c) had already come into existence.

I tentatively suggested in the previous section that quire 4 is probably best described as a composite quire. This originally consisted of a quire containing the *Long Charter of Christ* (presented in double columns) that may have been turned inside-out in order to permit some of the blank folios remaining in it to be used for copying the final lines of *Lybeaus*, also in double columns. My collation diagram assumes that fos. 71–6, containing the text of *Emaré* (in double columns), was inserted at some stage in the rearranged quire. At another stage in the rapidly changing history of this quire, it is easy to see how the short items on fos. 57^v–70^v – now at the heart of this collection – may well have been copied as 'fillers'.

An abrupt change in the scribe's presentation of four short refrain poems on fos. 67^r–69^r supports this hypothesis. All four items form another obviously related textual cluster. The first (*Better Abide*, on fo. 67^{r-v}) is copied using the same relatively spacious single-column format that was employed for the other short poems on fos. 57^v–65^r and also for the Lydgatian material dispersed elsewhere in the manuscript. The next three poems are then crowded in long manuscript lines on to fos. 68^r–69^r (each one containing two lines of verse). As a result, the last three refrain poems are copied at the rate of one item per page, using exactly half the amount of space that the scribe would have needed if all three had been presented similarly to the first item in this short refrain-poem sequence. The scribe's exemplar for all three items was closely related (if not identical) to one of the exemplars lying behind Princeton University Library, MS Garrett 143.[9] If that source contained other material (perhaps an extended lyric sequence), the Ca scribe may well have been inclined to 'tailor' such material for its new manuscript context.

That the scribe may also have been searching to find room for as many other short items as possible is also indicated by the probable nature of at least one 'Lydgatian' exemplar used for the material now copied on fos. 57^v–65^r in quire 4. The range of similar items found in several other fifteenth-century manuscript anthologies suggests, moreover, that a similar source may have once contained copies of a number of the other short poems now extant in quires 2, 6 and 7. The Ca scribe could easily have had access to such 'Lydgatian' material in two quite different types of exemplar: either in one of the series of booklets that Lydgate refers to in his own work and that are presumed to have been in wide circulation in fifteenth-century England; or else in one of the great 'selected works' anthologies of the type that are known to have been produced in the fifteenth century and later by Londoners such as John Shirley. Examples of the latter include Oxford, Bodleian Library, MS Ashmole 59 (by Shirley), London, British Library, MSS Add. 29729 (by Stowe) and Harley 2251 (by the so-called 'Hammond' scribe), the last two of which are probably both largely based on Shirleian exemplars. All three manuscripts include a number of the more widely copied minor poems by Lydgate that are also represented in Ca. Despite the well-documented Shirleian connections of MSS Add. 29729 and Harley 2251, however, the precise nature of the relationship of these three books to one another through their sources requires further clarification, as indeed does the possible relationship of such sources to other extant manuscripts like Ca.[10]

Our understanding of the place of Ca in this network of possible manuscript connections is still some way off, but I want to close this brief discussion by making a series of comparisons between Ca and another fifteenth-century manuscript collection containing Lydgatian material, London, British Library, MS Harley 116 (H).[11] The main item in H is Hoccleve's *Regement of Princes*, copied by a single, unnamed scribe. This is followed by a number of other items, by Lydgate or in his style, which are copied by a series of different anonymous hands. Four of the items are also represented in quires 1 and 4 of Ca. These are Lydgate's *Dietary* and his *Churl and the Bird* (copied side-by-side in quire 1 of Ca, though both poems are now more widely dispersed in H); the Middle English mortality lyric entitled *O mors quam amara est memoria tua* and Lydgate's *Deus in nomine tuo* (both copied in quire 4 of Ca but more widely dispersed in H). The textual affiliations of the H and Ca texts of these items are not always particularly close: H, unlike Ca, preserves a text of the distinctive disarranged version of the *Dietary* that was also copied in London, Lambeth Palace, MS 853, for example; and the Ca text of *the Churl and the Bird* often seems closer to some of the early prints than to H.

Set against this rather negative evidence is the fact that Ca and H now preserve the only two surviving texts of *O mors*. And the text of *O mors* in H is immediately preceded by *The Churl and the Bird*; this perhaps hints at the similar contents of one of the sources in which both the Ca scribe and the H scribes may have found their poems. Julia Boffey has also recently pointed out to me a brief scribal note in H which immediately follows this text of *O mors* and reads: 'hic scribatur conveyed by a [lure] as / rigth as an ramhorne'. Although a copy of the Lydgatian satirical poem being alluded to here (*IMEV* 199) is not preserved in either Ca or H, the survival of this brief note may enable us to piece together some further details concerning the identity of another item by Lydgate that the writer of the note in H probably expected to have been able to add to the manuscript. This was perhaps because it was already present in an earlier 'Lydgatian' source. It is not inconceivable, therefore, that the satirical item may have once been copied for Ca; if so, however, all trace of the text itself has since been lost.

Comparison of the texts of *O mors* in H and in Ca is also very revealing.[12] In H this short poem takes the form of a mortality lyric written in remembrance of Ralph, Lord Cromwell – 'this worthi lorde of veray polyce' – whose reputation and famous and ostentatious building projects, together with the tomb built following the death of his wife in 1454, are all briefly alluded to in the penultimate stanza of the poem (lines 49–56). In the final stanza both young and old are invited to 'muse in this mirrour of mortalite' before praying for the souls of the former Lord Treasurer of England and his wife. The text in Ca, by contrast, does not preserve material corresponding to lines 49–56 in H and offers a variant reading of line 60 in the final stanza. This encouraged Rosemary Woolf to argue that Ca preserves an earlier version of the poem than H and that lines 49–56, containing the direct reference to Cromwell and his family tomb, were probably a late insertion in a highly conventional 'song of mortality'.[13] Like a number of scholars, I remain unconvinced by Woolf's argument. In terms of style, vocabulary and the rhymes used, the penultimate stanza in H seems perfectly well integrated into the poem. In Ca, however, the text has been revised, presumably for readers who had no reason to be interested in, or perhaps even sympathetic to, 'these same right worthi, resting vndire the stone' (line 60 in H, altered in Ca to read 'thenk all mankende schall reste under erthe and ston').

Ralph, Lord Cromwell died childless in 1456, having enjoyed a lengthy and at times controversial political career. He left behind many bitter local and national enemies and seems to have worked hard to frustrate not only his rivals but also many erstwhile associates up to and even beyond the end of his life.[14] By April 1454, Cromwell had also unambiguously allied himself to the Yorkist cause, so it seems legitimate to wonder whether, on the one hand, the decision to erase all reference to Cromwell from the text in Ca might not also reflect some deeply held local or national political loyalties or opinions. On the other hand, a vested interest in recent English history and current affairs might well explain why, in H, the texts of *The Churl and the Bird* and *O mors* immediately follow a copy of the Middle English prose *Pettigrew of England*, which has clear Yorkist connections.

Ca contains a good number of other short texts which can be compared to similar items or clusters of items in other manuscript miscellanies reflecting their compilers' contemporary or near-contemporary interest in current events. Many such books were probably being compiled for readers living in London or having an interest in London affairs. (I am thinking, particularly, of manuscripts such as MSS Ashmole 59 and Harley 2251, mentioned briefly above; also Oxford, Bodleian Library, MS Rawlinson C.86, London, Lambeth Palace Library, MS 306, and Oxford, Balliol College, MS 354.) Strenuous scholarly efforts are now being made to 'look behind' several of these London books so that the wider socio-literary networks of shared interests and contacts represented by the people who variously compiled and read them can be better understood.[15] These, together with an informal discussion with Maldwyn Mills in York some years ago, have prompted my own tentative attempts in this paper to understand something more about the origins of Ca, the range of interests that motivated its anonymous scribe–compiler, the likely nature of some of its sources, and also the losses that the volume has unfortunately suffered (solely by accident, or perhaps also through some early acts of vandalism?). Further exploration of these intriguing issues must remain, however, a task for another chapter in a different book.

Notes

1. Previous descriptions of the manuscript include: Mills 1969: 1–2; Guddat-Figge 1976: 169–72; McSparran 1979: 10–13; Mearns 1985: 45–7; Easting 1991: xxv–xxviii.
2. See Figure 1 for a summary description of the items in Ca. For economy and ease of reference, I have identified all verse texts by their numbering in *IMEV* and *Supplement*.
3. For convenient descriptions of these manuscripts, see Guddat-Figge 1976; see also, on MS Ashmole 61, below pp. 208–20.
4. For details of the distribution of the four stocks of watermarked paper (a–d), see Figure 1. Watermark a (*raisin*) is like Briquet 12999 or 13005; watermark b (*roue*) is not unlike Briquet 13245; watermark c (*lettre B*) broadly resembles Briquet 7996; watermark d (*tête de boeuf*) resembles Briquet 15093. Without further scrutiny of many other published and unpublished tracings, it would be unwise to offer these identifications as evidence for the origin or date of the paper in Ca.
5. Hence my tentative identification of the remaining watermark fragments on fos. 57, 68, 72 and 78.
6. E.g., because of the manner in which short items in this part of Ca begin and end, one cannot completely rule out the possibility of further physical (and perhaps also textual) losses following fos. 66, 68, 70 and 76.
7. For a definition of 'mini-quire' and other examples of informal book-production methods, see Thompson 1991: esp. n. 48.
8. Perhaps this scribal policy in Ca also represents one contemporary response to the idiosyncratic manner in which some tail-rhyme romance texts were written using a variety of six-line and twelve-line stanza forms. See further Mills 1994b.
9. See Thompson 1990: esp. 214–15.
10. Julia Boffey and I are continuing our work on these fascinating literary anthologies, but see also the overview in Boffey and Thompson 1989.
11. For a summary description of the manuscript, see Seymour 1974: 265–6.
12. See the text of H, and textual notes, in Brown 1939: 243–5, 339–40.
13. Woolf 1968: 340.
14. On this last point, see particularly Friedrichs 1990.
15. See, e.g., Boffey and Meale 1991: 143–70.

12
MS Porkington 10 and its scribes
DANIEL HUWS

Announced in colour supplements of Sunday papers, awaited with curiosity by Maldwyn Mills in Aberystwyth, not to say by others, in 1991 the Porkington Press made its brief showing in the firmament. The first and only publication of the press was a facsimile edition of Aberystwyth, National Library of Wales, MS Brogyntyn I.8, an imperfect fifteenth-century manuscript of the English *Brut*.[1] The second publication was to have been a facsimile, together with transcript and translation, of MS Brogyntyn II.1, the manuscript widely known since 1839, when Sir Frederic Madden published an account of it with his edition of *Syre Gawene and the Carle of Carelyle*, as Porkington MS 10.[2] This second publication, more than the first, would have earned the Porkington Press the gratitude of scholars as well perhaps as giving gratification to collectors of limited editions. It was not to be. All that remains as a hint to future generations of the narrowly missed public appearance of Porkington 10 is a pencil note by the owner inside the upper cover recording its removal from the National Library of Wales in January 1991 'for full trans./ transcr. © Porkington Press'. In 1993 Porkington 10 found itself on a new tide. With the residue of the Brogyntyn deposit of manuscripts it was bought by the National Library.

Changes of name are upsetting. The shelfmark of Porkington 10 since 1938, little advertised and seldom acknowledged in print, has been Brogyntyn II.1, or Brogyntyn (1938 deposit) MS 1. So it is likely to remain. This study has to accept the awkward duty of being correct rather than traditional and to refer to our manuscript as Brogyntyn II.1 (Porkington 10), or, for short, Brogyntyn II.1.

By way of introduction, or reintroduction, it may be said that Brogyntyn II.1 is a miscellany, written by many scribes, which includes astrological tracts, tables of eclipses, rules for bloodletting, medical receipts, a treatise on grafting and planting trees, a treatise (of great interest, 'the earliest extensive English language treatise in print')[3] on the 'crafte of lymnynge of bokys', and a life of St Catherine; and then the poetry: religious and love lyrics, parody and satire, nonsense, carols – Brogyntyn II.1 contributes five or more poems to each of R. H. Robbins, *Secular Lyrics of the XIVth and XVth Centuries*, R. L. Greene, *The Early English Carols*, and Carleton Brown, *Religious Lyrics of the XVth Century* – not to mention its unique text of the romance *Syre Gawene and the Carle of Carelyle*, first printed by Madden.[4] What follows has little to say of the texts, most of which are in print, but offers new observations on the make-up of the book and on the hands. From the nineteen scribes identified by Kurvinen, and accepted by Guddat-Figge, but here reduced in number to sixteen, there will emerge two who between them, I suggest, gave the miscellany its character and who might even be regarded as its architects.

The contents of Brogyntyn II.1 have been listed in print five times: by Sir Thomas Phillipps, scantly, in 1837; by Madden in 1839; by Alfred Horwood for the Royal Commission on Historical Manuscripts in 1871; by Auvo Kurvinen, most fully, in 1953; and by Gisela Guddat-Figge in 1976.[5] Madden, Kurvinen and Guddat-Figge all provide comprehensive listings although they differ slightly from each other in their numeration of items. It is no part of the present intention to offer a new list of contents, but a simplified list, sufficient to serve as a guide to this paper, is incorporated in the accompanying table of collation, contents and scribes.

Brogyntyn II.1 is a small book, 140 × 105mm, written space 100–110 × 70–80mm (up to 125 × 90mm in quire 1) with nineteen to twenty-four lines (up to thirty-six in quire 1). It comprises twenty-six quires, all but the first three of them regular quires of eight leaves, and all but the first three entirely of paper, together with a singleton which is all that survives of quire 27. Kurvinen's analysis of the quiring errs in two details; in each case, as it happens, she overlooked something significant. The first concerns fo. 11.

Quire 1, one of ten leaves, is of parchment. In layout and in its didactic subject-matter it differs from the rest of the book. Kurvinen, followed by Guddat-Figge, prefers to treat this quire, together with fo. 11, whose text concludes that begun at the end of

Table 1 Collation, contents and scribes of MS Brogyntyn II.1

Quire	Sig.	Fos.	Wmk.	Texts and scribes
1^{10}	–	1–10	–	Prognostication etc., inc. table of eclipses 1461–81; on the new calendar (1463) (A–H); *Concerning þe wedurying* (I)
2^{10}	–	11–20	–	Continued (I): *Syre Gawene and the Carle of Carelyle* (*IMEV* 1888) (J)
3^6	e	21–26	W1	Continued (J, K)
4^8	–	27–34	W2	On grafting (L): *The crafte of lymnynge* (L)
5^8	g	35–42	W3	Continued (L)
6^8	h	43–50	W4	Continued (L)
7^8	–	51–58	W5	Continued (L); *Dialogue with a bird* (*IMEV* 2018) (L); *Tale of ten wives*, (*IMEV* 1852) (L)
8^8	–	59–66	W6	Continued (L); *When I slepe* (*IMEV* 1957) (O); *An old man's lament* (*IMEV* 349) (O); *Vision of Philibert* (*IMEV* 3330 and 1932) (O)
9^8	–	67–74	?	Continued (O)
10^8	–	75–82	W7	Continued (O); *Erthe upon erthe* (*IMEV* 704) (O); *Complaint of a hare* (*IMEV* 559) (O)
11^8	n	83–90	W7	Continued (O); *The knight and his wife* (*IMEV* 1641) (O); *St Martin* (*IMEV* 3289) (O); *St Anthony* (*IMEV* 3289) (O); *Ave regina celorum* (*IMEV* 2610) (O); medical receipts (O, I, O)
12^8	o	91–98	W8	*Life of St Catherine of Alexandria* (Q)
13^8	p	99–106	W8	Continued (Q)
14^8	q	107–14	W9	Continued (Q)
15^8	r	115–22	W8	Continued (Q)
16^8	s	123–30	W8	Continued (Q); parody on medical cures (O); *Be trewe and holde* (*IMEV* 479) (J); *That wons was lefe* (*IMEV* 4) (J)
17^8	t	131–38	W8	Continued (J); *The stacyons of Rome* (J); *The good wyfe wold a pylgremage* (*IMEV* 3363) (J)
18^8	v	139–46	W7	*The friar and the boy* (*IMEV* 977) (Q)
19^8	x	147–54	W7	Continued (Q); *Ever say well* (*IMEV* 369) (O); *Trutallys* (*IMEV* 1116) (O); *A love-letter* (*IMEV* 1241) (O); *Have all my hert* (*IMEV* 1120) (O)

Table 1 *continued*

20^8	y	155–62	W7	Continued (O); *Do for þiselfe, (IMEV* 341) (O); *The Siege of Jerusalem* (O)
21^8	–	163–70	W7	Continued (O)
22^8	*	171–78	?W7	Continued (O)
23^8	*	179–86	W10	Continued (O); texts occuring in Dame Juliana Berners's *Boke of Saint Albans* (O)
24^8	*	187–94	W11	Continued (O); The cock in the north (*IMEV* 4029) (J); satirical letter, *Balteser, be þe grace of Mahounde* ... (J); gifts of the lords of Venice to the Pope (J)
25^8	*	195–202	W2	*Timor mortis conturbat me* (*IMEV* 3743) (R); stanza from Lydgate (*IMEV* 674) (R); By a chapel as I came (*IMEV* 298) (S); The three kings, (*IMEV* 1785) (S); *Veritas verbi domini* (*IMEV* 4001) (O); Dear son, leave thy weeping (*IMEV* 22) (O); The boar's head (*IMEV* 3314) (O)
26^8	*	203–10	W8	Mercy and righteousness (*IMEV* 560) (J); *The Marchand* (*IMEV* 1897) (J)
27	–	211	–	Continued (J)

Letters of quire signatures are given where they survive; the asterisks represent a sequence of *ad hoc* marks. Watermarks are represented by W1, W2, etc.

quire 1 but whose physical relationship to quire 1 is left unexplained, as having belonged originally to a different manuscript. That our book was intended from the start to include quire 1 does indeed seem to be ruled out. But that quire 1 had an independent existence other than, briefly, as a loose quire appears unlikely. In any case, quire 1 need not detain us at present. It is to quires 2 and 3 that we must turn. Quire 2 is also of parchment and, now, also of ten leaves. On its fourth and fifth leaves (fos. 14 and 15) it has, however, leaf signatures iii and iv, while on the verso of its ninth leaf (fo. 19^v) it has a catchword leading to its tenth leaf (fo. 20), which, in turn, has at the foot of its recto a quire signature *e v*: originally the quire must have been one of eight leaves, fos. 12–19. Quire 3, alone in the book, is of six leaves, the inner bifolium of parchment, the other leaves of paper. What evidently happened is that fo. 20, of parchment, originally the first leaf of quire 3, was gathered with quire 2, and the conjugate leaf, originally the last leaf of quire 3, a leaf which was blank, was folded backwards to wrap around quire 2, becoming folio 11. When the catchword was written on fo. 19^v, when the quire signature *e v* was written on fo. 20, both quires 2 and 3 were quires of eight, as are all quires in the remainder of the book. Unlike quire 2, however, quire 3 had only inner and outer bifolia of parchment.

In bridging from fo. 10, the end of quire 1, to fo. 11, our reversed leaf, scribe I (to follow Kurvinen's lettering) made fo. 11 witness to the early unity of the book. By this action he joined the extraneous quire 1 to the already completed and signed but as yet unbound body of quires organized by scribe O. To scribe O and to the chronological implications we shall turn later.

Although no quire signature survives in quire 2, extrapolation from the surviving signatures shows that quire 2 must have been signed *d iiii* (see Table 1). Quire 1, we presume, formed no part of the book when the quire signatures were given. We have to conclude that three quires, signed *a i, b ii* and *c iii*, were replaced by our quire 1 soon after their being written and certainly before the book was first bound. Rejected or lost or given away: one can only guess at the fate of these three quires.

The second error in Kurvinen's account of the quiring of Brogyntyn II.1 relates to its last surviving leaf, fo. 211, the singleton. It is of parchment, not paper. This seemingly trivial fact may be significant. While quires 4–26 are entirely of paper, quires 2 and 3, the earliest in the surviving signed series, both include parchment bifolia. The return to parchment in quire 27 is probably a sign that we are approaching the end of the book. Quire 27, the last, perhaps, or one of the last quires of the book, was made up, at least in part, of parchment, to allow for the greater wear to which it would be exposed. Following the interrupted text of *The Marchand* on fo. 211^v (two more leaves should have completed it), not much is likely to have been lost from the end of Brogyntyn II.1.

In her analysis of the hands that appear in Brogyntyn II.1, Kurvinen identifies nineteen scribes, observing however that 'some hands resemble one another, e.g. hands L, M, and N'. I would reduce the number of scribes to sixteen, identifying I with P, and L with M with N (see Plate 1). Sixteen is still a large number for a small book. The upshot of the following consideration of the contributions of the sixteen scribes will be, however, to leave us with a mere three, I/P, J and O, who appear to have been there or thereabouts at the finish, and only two, J and O, who might stake a claim to have been prime movers in the enterprise.

The work of scribes A–H occurs only in quire 1. They have no bearing on the rest of the book, and it seems improbable that they would have been aware in what a literary neighbourhood their texts were destined to find themselves. I shall not discuss these scribes further. Scribe I/P, the most proficient of the scribes and the only one to write an almost unadulterated secretary hand, is a key figure; he contributed the bridging text we have already mentioned, a text which could possibly have been the last in the book to have been written. His second stint (given by Kurvinen to P), one which, chronologically, might or might not have preceded his first, comes on fo. 90 (see Plate 4). Here he contributed four medical receipts to a series begun by scribe O on fo. 89^v and ended by the same scribe on fo. 90^v. Scribe O and scribe I/P, in collaboration, were filling three blank pages at the end of a quire. The apparent differences which must have led Kurvinen to distinguish I and P arise from the two stints being done under quite different conditions: the one on parchment, the other on paper; the one thirty-four lines to the page, the other nineteen; the one in yellowish-brown ink, the other in a darker brown. Scribe I/P's *w* and his abbreviation mark may help convince the doubter of the identity of the hand.

Three of the remaining scribes each contribute only a single run of text, none of more than seven pages. Scribe K completed *Syre Gawene and the Carle of Carelyle*, which J had begun (see Plate 2). Scribe R, opening a new quire, contributed a single poem, *Timor mortis conturbat me,* and a stanza of Lydgate's; while scribe S, following on R, added two carols. None of these three appears to have played a decisive part in the making of the book.

We are left with four scribes, each of whom wrote over sixty pages. The four fall into two pairs. Scribe L/M/N, beginning with quire 4 and ending in quire 8, wrote four consecutive texts: two in prose, that on grafting and that on limning, and two poems. Scribe Q, like L/M/N starting with a fresh quire, began the life of St Catherine with quire 12 and ended in quire 16, and began his second text, *The Friar and the Boy*, with quire 18 and ended in quire 19 (see Plate 6). The three quires left partly unfilled by scribes L/M/N and Q, quires 8, 16 and 19, were each filled by scribe O, with or

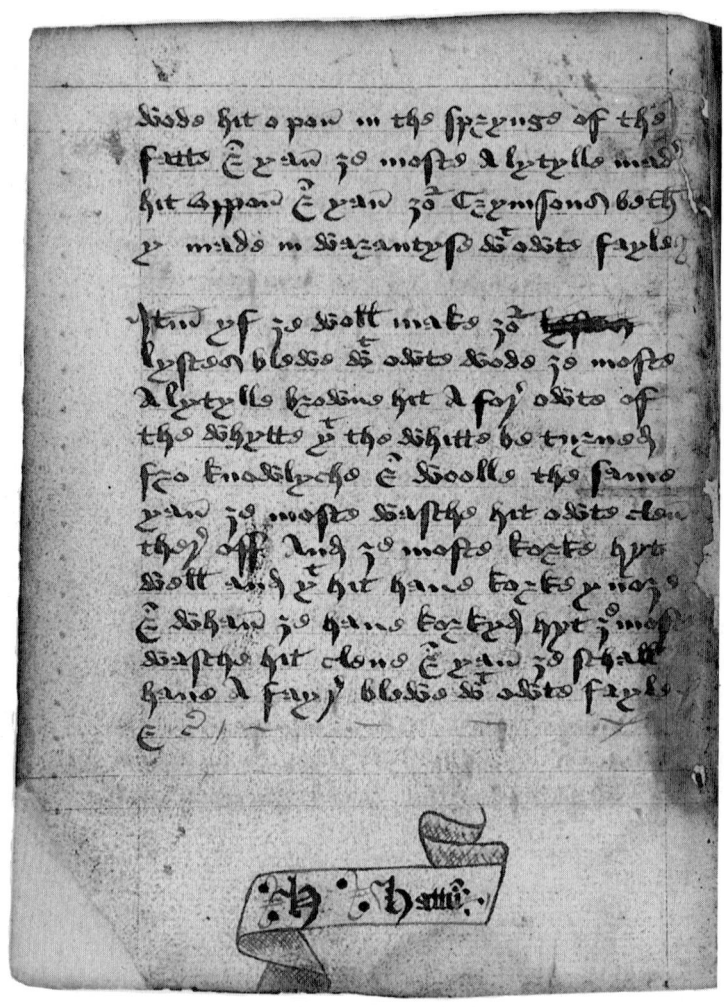

Plate 1 MS Brogyntyn II.1, fo. 52ᵛ: scribe L/M/N.

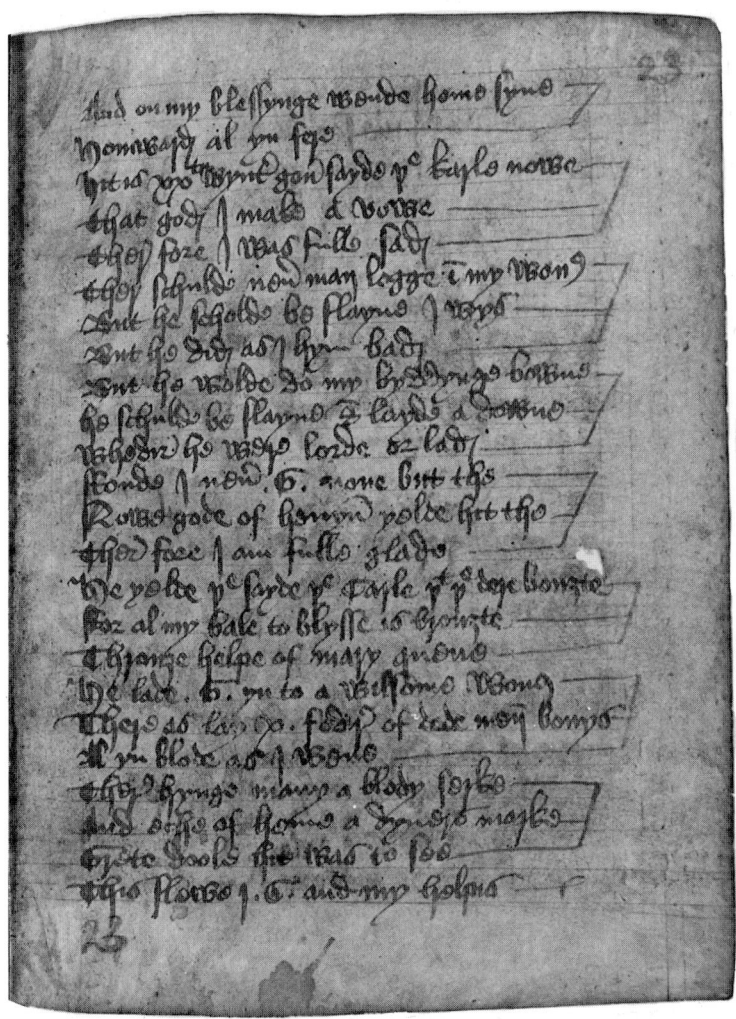

Plate 2 MS Brogyntyn II.1, fo. 23^r: scribe K.

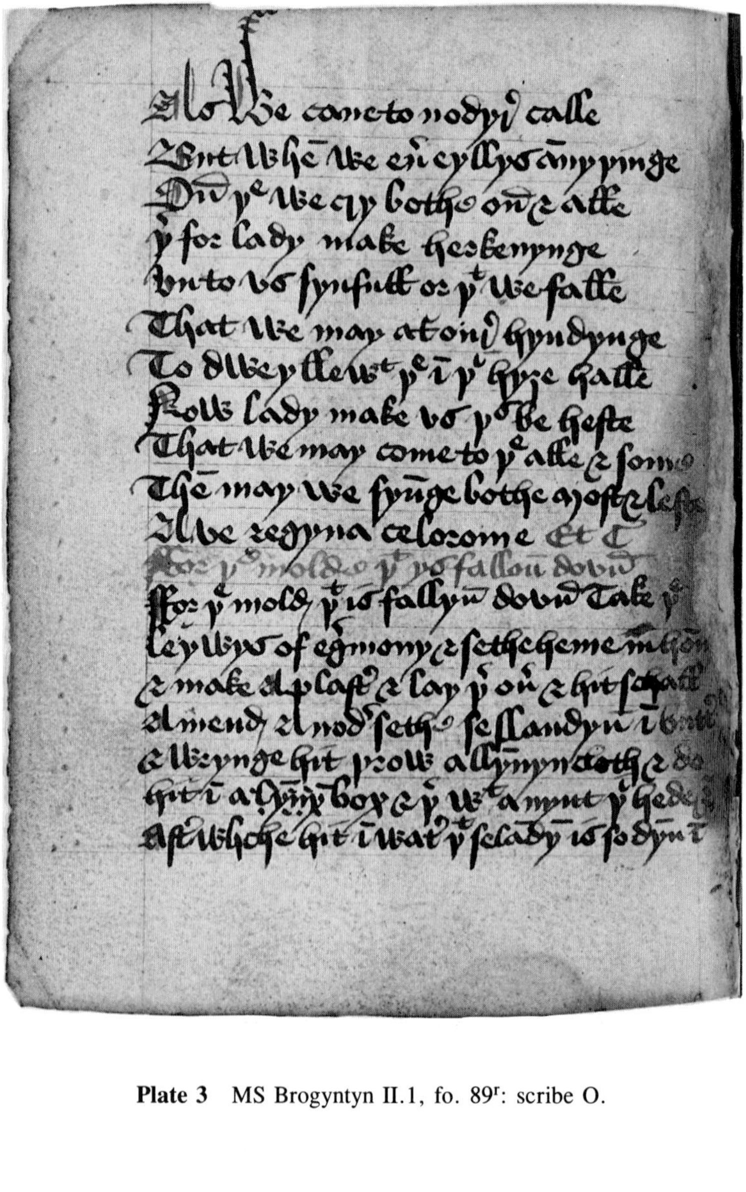

Plate 3 MS Brogyntyn II.1, fo. 89ʳ: scribe O.

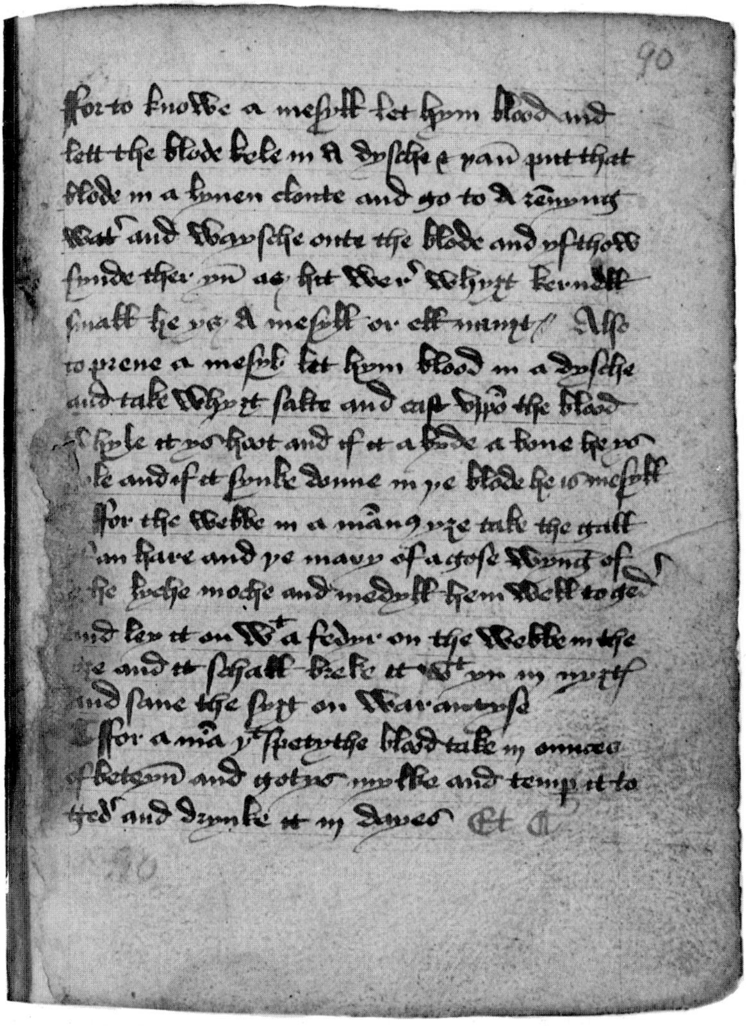

Plate 4   MS Brogyntyn II.1, fo. 90ʳ: scribe I/P.

without the help of others. Scribes L/M/N and Q in effect appear to have been piece-workers.

Scribes J and O remain. They between them wrote half the book: J 63 pages in four stints, and O 153 in five. More significantly, if we exclude from our count the extraneous quire 1, scribes J and O contributed three-quarters of the items in the book. And it is J and O alone (O once assisted by I/P) who fill the blank leaves at the end of quires: O, ever-present, in quires 8, 11, 16, 19 and 25 (see Plate 3); J, in association with O, in quires 16–17 and 24 (see Plate 5). Twice J begins a text with a fresh quire (quires 2 and 26), something O never does. Scribe O was evidently the organizer and tidier-up.

The role of scribe O, already evident, is made all the clearer by another consideration: it is he who provided most of the rubrication in the book, and it is he who wrote the quire signatures (note in particular the form of the *g* on fo. 35, though this might be mistaken for scribe J's, and that of the *v* on fo. 139, unmistakably scribe O's) (see Plate 6). Setting aside, again, quire 1, J is the only scribe other than O who wrote his own headings in red and provided his own two-line coloured initials. For the rest, the rubrication and decoration are by O. He provided headings in red for the text of scribe Q, and two-line coloured initials for all but scribe J and, possibly, scribe R. Scribe O, it may also be said, is the only scribe outside quire 1 who is demonstrably at home in Latin, although the thinness of evidence allows little weight to this observation.

The two scribes, J and O, who from our consideration of purely mechanical operations have emerged as the shapers of Brogyntyn II.1 come alive when we begin to notice which texts they added to the book in their own hands: *Syre Gawene and the Carle of Carelyle*, the love-poems, the satire and parody, most, in fact, of the short pieces which leaven the book. Their selection of pieces surely reflects personal taste, something one would not confidently assert about the contributions of scribes L/M/N and Q. There would clearly be a case, if a single controlling hand were to be sought, for preferring O. But it might be argued that O was perhaps the Martha to J's Mary. We need also to ask whether there might not have been an invisible third party whose tastes were known and whom J and O both wished to please. Whoever the arbiter may have been, whether a single or a composite person, the planning of the book seems to have been single-minded, to judge by the solitary role of scribe O in the mechanics of the editing. The end-of-quire additions made by J and O tell us a good deal about their predilections. The technical treatises – medical, astrological, even that on grafting and planting trees – tell us less; they are texts which met fairly universal interests. The exception among them is the treatise on limning. Illuminating manuscripts and making books were far from being universal interests. Was this comprehensive text on the subject copied for its practical usefulness or simply because it had theoretical appeal? If the former, we have cause to wonder with heightened curiosity about the sort of household or community that produced Brogyntyn II.1. The convenience of being able to categorize in discussion of medieval manuscripts has led to the attaching of the labels 'commonplace book' and, more recently, 'household miscellany' to Brogyntyn II.1.[6] The operation overseen by scribe O seems distinct both from the accrual of heterogeneous quires and booklets, later bound together, which lies behind some medieval miscellanies, and from the slow accumulation of favoured texts which is the usual connotation of 'commonplace book'. 'Miscellany', however, Brogyntyn II.1 certainly is.

Inevitably, from a well-cropped octavo book such as Brogyntyn II.1 the watermarks can at best be recovered only fragmentarily, and unqualified identification of the marks is almost out of the question. In each of quires 3–26 a watermark is visible. In all but quires 3 and 9 enough of the watermark survives to allow tentative identification of the type. The high number of different marks is striking; there are eleven if not twelve, only three of them occurring in more than one quire. Their occurrence is shown in Table 1. The following observations exemplify the haphazard use. Scribe L/M/N wrote his texts continuously and consecutively in five quires, yet each quire is of paper of a different watermark; the only paper used by scribe L/M/N that is also used by another scribe is that in quire 4, also used for quire 25, begun by scribe R; for four of a sequence of five quires (12–13 and 15–16) scribe Q used paper which was also used by scribe J for quires 17 and 26; scribe O for quires 10–11 and 20–1 (and perhaps 22) took the same paper as scribe Q for quires 18–19. One is given the impression of the concurrent activity of several scribes, and an air of improvisation, with regard to use of paper as well as the makeshift team of scribes. The regular ink-ruling, in octavo format, could even be taken to suggest the buying-in of batches prepared by a stationer.[7]

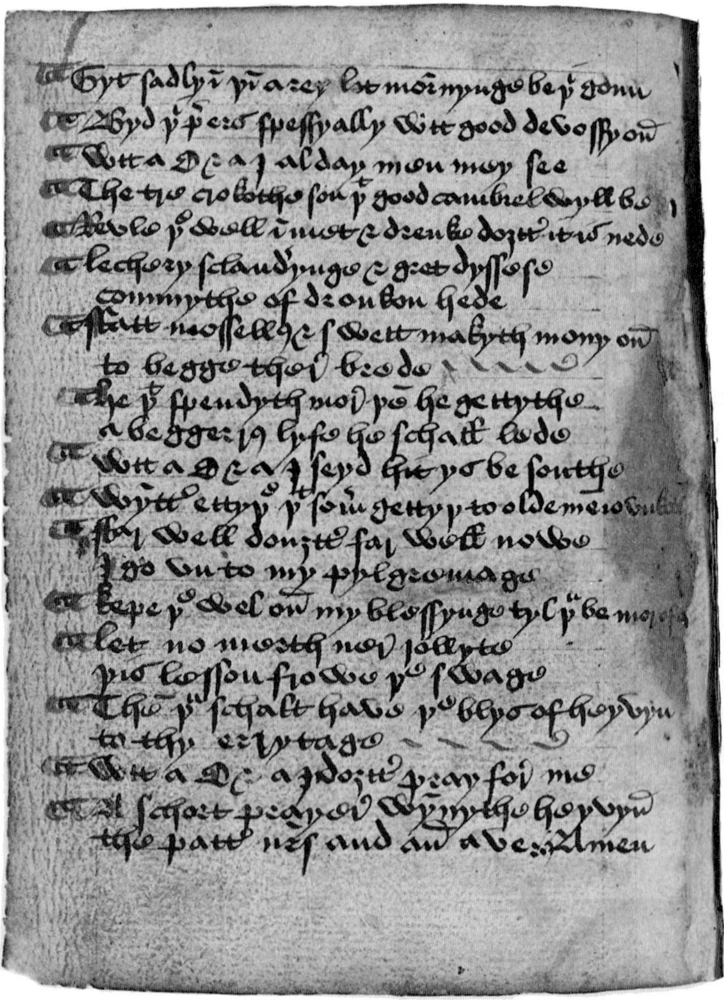

Plate 5   MS Brogyntyn II.1, fo. 138ᵛ: scribe J.

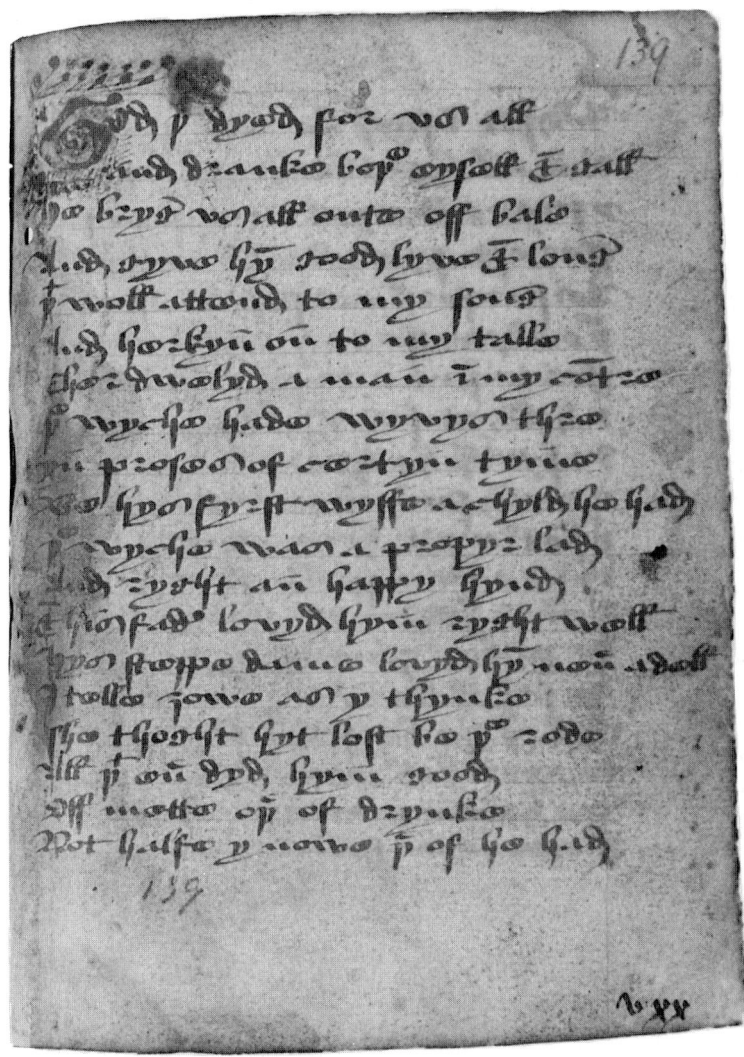

Plate 6 MS Brogyntyn II.1, fo. 139ʳ: scribe Q.

There are four different ox-head watermarks: quires 4 and 25, of type Briquet 15103-12 (1434 × 1475), Piccard 801-97; quire 5, too fragmentary to classify; quire 8, of the same type as quires 4 and 25; and quires 12-13, 15-17 and 26, again of the same type.[8] None corresponds to any of Piccard's measured examples. Quires 10-11 and 18-21 (and perhaps 22, though this appears to be a variant) have a shield-and-crown watermark, similar or even identical to Briquet 2064 (1464). Quire 6 has an ox-watermark similar or identical to Briquet 2816 (1469). Quire 14 has a cart watermark combining features of Briquet 2538 and 2539 (1466 × 1468).

The evidence for dating Brogyntyn II.1 is not conclusive but it is sufficient to dispense us from having to rely on palaeography. Quire 1 was written not before 1463; some of its contents, however, are texts whose merit resided largely in their being up to date, texts not likely to have been copied more than a few years after 1463. Quire 1 only acquired its closing text after the decision to add it to the already signed quires of the body of the book. The body of the book cannot have been completed before 1453 (Kurvinen notes the reference to the fall of Constantinople);[9] the evidence suggests that it was put together fairly quickly, by scribe O with the help of others. When quire 1 became attached, the body of the book was still unbound; there is no wear on the outer pages of quires to suggest that they remained unbound for any length of time. The watermarks, hesitantly but in unison, direct us to the late 1460s. A date *c.* 1470 for the whole book would be unexceptionable. What is ruled out is the possibility which Kurvinen allows for, taking the addition of quire 1 to be of unascertainable date, that the writing of the body of the book might have been as late as 1500.[10]

Unlike the other great north Wales manuscript collections – Hengwrt, Gwysaney, Mostyn, Wynnstay – Brogyntyn is without an early catalogue. Nor were Edward Lhuyd or Angharad Llwyd able to include Brogyntyn in their surveys of Welsh manuscripts. Angharad Llwyd in 1828 publicly recorded her pique; she lamented that, in contrast to the other north Wales owners of manuscripts, 'the present possessors of the Brogyntyn (at Porkington) collection were not influenced by the same feeling of nationality'.[11] Sir Thomas Phillipps's catalogue of 1837 briefly describes thirty-two manuscripts. MSS 1-14, he notes, were uniformly bound. All but one of these fourteen, our Brogyntyn II.1, are still in their uniform bindings. Not long after 1837, the manuscripts from 15 upwards were renumbered and the sequence extended to MS 40. This revised form of Phillipps's catalogue is recognizable in two sources, a copy by D. R. Thomas (historian of the diocese of St Asaph, 1833-1916) in Aberystwyth, National Library of Wales, MS 1197, and in the pencil revisions in a copy of Phillipps's printed catalogue.[12] The Historical Manuscripts Commission report by Alfred Horwood on 'The manuscripts of J. R. Ormsby-Gore, Esq., M.P., of Brogyntyn, co. Salop.' follows the revised numeration (with one exception, probably a misprint), provides fuller descriptions than Phillipps but omits fifteen manuscripts altogether.

The uniform bindings referred to by Phillipps (uniform in style but not in size) are a strange affair. The manuscripts were rebound in thick pigskin, but inlaid on their covers are re-used blind-tooled calf covers taken from sixteenth-century bindings. The work is perhaps late eighteenth- or early nineteenth-century. The old covers very likely came from books in the Brogyntyn library which were themselves being rebound.[13] Such must have been the binding of Brogyntyn II.1 in the first half of the nineteenth century. Its original binding had evidently been on three bands: three sets of old sewing-holes are visible. The present binding of calf probably dates from the latter part of the nineteenth century.

The third and fourth Lords Harlech more than made amends for any lack of public spirit on the part of their ancestor. In 1934 the third lord placed on deposit in the National Library of Wales thirty manuscripts, including most of those in Welsh, and including ten which had been numbered as 'Porkington MSS'; these thirty were catalogued and numbered as 'Brogyntyn MSS'.[14] In 1938 a further fifty-four manuscripts, including the remaining 'Porkington MSS', were deposited (on this and other occasions, a wealth of family archives was also deposited). These were numbered in a new sequence, the 'Second Series'.[15] The two series have since 1938 been Brogyntyn MSS I.1-30 and Brogyntyn MSS II.1-54. In 1945 the fourth Lord Harlech converted a large part of the deposited collection into a donation. In 1993 the remainder of the collection was bought by the National Library. The Library's aim is to publish a catalogue including both series of manuscripts.

The lack of early catalogues has left the whole history of the Brogyntyn library rather obscure.[16] Sir Robert Owen (d. 1698) is a known bibliophile and antiquary, and he kept up the family tradition of patronage of Welsh poets.[17] His grandfather, Lewis Anwyl of

Parc, 'the first member of the family interested in pure literature', owned his Shakespeare and his Jonson and was probably responsible for the fine collection of English drama which was at Brogyntyn. Some later members of the family were keen collectors of early printed books. But there is no manifest manuscript collector. The internal evidence of the manuscripts suggests that the collection had mostly come together, by descent or deliberate acquisition, by *c.* 1700. Brogyntyn II.1 conforms to the pattern.

The latest batch of names associated with Brogyntyn II.1 occurs in pentrials of the mid-seventeenth century. They take us into Eifionydd in Caernarfonshire. The names are John Owen (fos. 4^v, 5^r and 26^r, 'To Mr John Owen / Theise are in the name of the keepers of the Liberte of Engla[nd]'), Griffyth Owen (fos. 4^v, 5^r and 7^v, once 'of the county of Carnarvon') and William Marice (*sic*), John Williams 'Petty Constable of the parish of Llanarmon' and Robert William (all on fo. 4^v). The one fairly certain autograph among these names is that of Griffyth Owen. His hand is not irreconcilable with that in the will of Gruffyth Owen of Penmorfa, who died in 1682.[18] While the hand of John Owen of Clenennau, the Royalist, knighted in 1644, is probably not present, it is hard to resist the conclusion that our manuscript was already associated with Clenennau in the parish of Penmorfa, a house in which the reference to the Keepers of the Liberty of England would have been written with deliberate irony. Llanarmon was a nearby parish. Sir John Owen (d. 1666) was the last of the Owens to make Clenennau his home. His son William, in whose person the Clenennau and Brogyntyn estates were reunited on the death of his uncle, Colonel William Owen, lived mainly at Brogyntyn.[19]

Brogyntyn II.1 had come early into Welsh hands. The name 'John ap Dd ap Gruff' ap Holl' (John ap Dafydd ap Gruffudd ap Howell) appears twice on fo. 26, once in what might be an early sixteenth-century hand and once copied by a later hand, perhaps of *c.* 1600, a hand which also wrote on fos. 5 and 26, in the same ink, in legal script, 'per me John Owen'. John ap Dafydd, despite the four generations in his name, cannot be identified with any confidence. The same name appears, in a sixteenth-century hand quite dissimilar, in Aberystwyth, National Library of Wales, MS Peniarth 41, p. 40. The John Owen of the legal hand might be John Owen of Bodsilin (d. 1611, secretary to Sir Francis Walsingham), who married the heiress of Clenennau and Brogyntyn, or one of his nephews of the same name.[20] Other names of about the same date, *c.* 1600, are William Williams (in a note which also names Hywel Fychan, William ap Roberd and Madoc Fychan in association with sums of money), Hugh Lewes ap Thomas ('anno regni domine nostre Elizabeth &c') and John Goch, all on fo. 26ᵛ.

Under a heavy varnish of standardization, the recognizable dialect of the texts in Brogyntyn II.1 is West Midland.[21] A linguistic analysis more sophisticated that I am capable of might, with the help of the *Linguistic Atlas of Late Middle English*, determine a likely common locality for our scribes. The part of England with which north Wales in the fifteenth century had its main social and commercial links was Cheshire and northern Shropshire. A West Midland origin north rather than south of Watling Street (the present A5) may not be ruled out by more southerly features in the language of one or two scribes.[22] This area would be a natural meeting-ground for a northern poem such as *Syre Gawene and the Carle of Carelyle* and the West Midland dialect with which it is overlaid. Let us turn to a last teasing piece of evidence.

At the foot of fo. 52ᵛ, in a scroll marking the close of *The crafte of lymnynge*, is the name 'H. Hattun' (see Plate 1). The scribe is fairly certainly L/M/N, although the fere-textura used for the name is more formal than anything else by this scribe (there is indeed some resemblance to the fere-textura of scribe R, but the *a* is not R's). Accepting the writing to be that of scribe L/M/N still, however, leaves a question: was he himself 'H. Hattun' (probably) or was he writing the name of one for whom the book was intended?

The place-name Hatton is more frequent in Cheshire and north Shropshire than in any other part of England. We might venture further. In the fifteenth and sixteenth centuries there was in these two counties a single many-branched family of Hattons, deriving from the stock Hatton of Hatton (near Runcorn).[23] Contemporary with our 'H. Hattun' would have been the many sons of Peter Hatton of Quisty (Questy Birches), in the chapelry of Daresbury near Runcorn. They included Henry, who became a London merchant, another Henry (son of a second marriage) who married a Northamptonshire heiress and became the great-grandfather of Sir Christopher Hatton, and Hugh Hatton, a priest. One would like to know more about the last-named.

Perhaps 'H. Hattun' will be identified; perhaps linguistic analysis or textual affiliations will help to locate the place of origin of Brogyntyn II.1; perhaps the hands of some of our scribes will be discovered elsewhere. For the time being, although two of our scribes now stand out from the ruck, J and O must remain J and O.

Notes

1 Voaden 1991.
2 Madden 1839: lviii–lxiii.
3 Gullick 1979: 4, where our text is set in perspective.
4 Robbins 1952; Greene 1977; Brown 1939; Madden 1839: 187–206. Other editions are Ackerman 1947; Kurvinen 1951. A text based on those of Ackerman and Kurvinen is printed in Sands 1966: 348–71.
5 *Manuscripts at Porkington* 1837; Madden 1839; Royal Commission on Historical Manuscripts 1871; Kurvinen 1953; Guddat-Figge 1976.
6 See Rigg 1968: 24–6; Boffey 1985: 19–27, esp. 24; Boffey and Thompson 1989: 294.
7 I owe this suggestion to Dr Ian Doyle, to whom I am grateful for comment on a draft of this paper.
8 Piccard 1966.
9 Kurvinen 1953: 37.
10 Ibid.; Kurvinen 1969: 9, 48. Ackerman (1947: 2–3), relying on several ostensibly palaeographical judgements by others, including Madden, offers 'third quarter' of the century, or even 1460–70.
11 Llwyd 1828: 36.
12 The annotated copy of the Phillipps catalogue is in Aberystwyth, National Library of Wales, MS Brogyntyn I.23.
13 One example of these bindings is described and illustrated in Spencer and Alexander 1978. The lute book is Aberystwyth, National Library of Wales, MS Brogyntyn I.27 (Porkington 11).
14 The catalogue is typescript. See also National Library of Wales Annual Report 1933-4: 39–40.
15 See National Library of Wales Annual Report 1937–8: 59–66.
16 Harlech 1947-8 provides a useful background. The Brogyntyn Welsh manuscripts are described in a series of articles by E. D. Jones in volumes 5–8 of the *National Library of Wales Journal*. See also Denholm-Young 1950: xiv–xvi.
17 On Sir Robert Owen as an antiquary, see Roberts 1971-2: 101, 183–4, 195.
18 National Library of Wales, Bangor probate records, 1682/62.
19 On the Owen family of Clenennau and Brogyntyn, see Bulkeley-Owen 1898: 43–132; *DWB*: 709–11; Harlech 1947-8.
20 See Bulkeley-Owen 1898: 43–4; Griffith 1914: 136.

21 Kurvinen 1951: 32, and 1969: 48; Ackerman 1947: 8, 13. The glossaries in these editions provide convenient digests of the usage of scribes J, K and O. The texts of scribe L/M/N and one of those of scribe Q are printed in Halliwell 1855. Kurvinen 1953 prints short texts by scribes A, F, G and I/P. There are bizarre inconsistencies, none more striking than scribe O's resistance to standardization of the word that other scribes are content to spell *sche:* O has *sche,* s*chew, schewe, scho, schoe, schow, schowe, schw* and *schwe.*

22 Ackerman (1947: 13 n. 44) proposes 'the north-western corner of Shropshire'; Kurvinen (1951: 32) prefers the southern part of the county – this on the strength of the habits of scribes J, K and O.

23 Rylands 1882: 112–20; Grazebrook and Rylands 1889: 225–30.

13

Rate revisited: the compilation of the narrative works in MS Ashmole 61

LYNNE S. BLANCHFIELD

It is appropriate that for Maldwyn Mills's birthday volume I should contribute a companion paper on Oxford, Bodleian Library, MS Ashmole 61,[1] since it is thanks to him that I became a medievalist at all, and that I ended up a codicologist devoted to this particular manuscript. Over the course of my thirteen years' rewarding study with Maldwyn he propelled me (fired by his compelling enthusiasm) first to the field of medieval literature as an undergraduate, then to the delights of Middle English romance as an MA topic, and finally to this particular scribe, whose intriguing vagaries preoccupied me for the seven years of my doctorate. In the previous paper I described the manuscript as containing five popular romances and thirty-eight other items. It was Maldwyn himself who pointed out that when we take away the classification 'romances', we have a compilation of *twenty*[2] 'narrative works' (eleven of which occur contiguously in the middle, and, after a 'break' of five mainly religious texts, in an almost uninterrupted group of seven narratives at the end, with the remaining two opening the first two quires).

This paper provides an opportunity simply to highlight the character of the non-romance narratives that Rate compiled,[3] to complement the work previously done on the five romances.[4] Murray Evans deplores the trend in which 'literary critics make facile observations on the literary shaping of manuscripts, which ignore the compiling processes that enrich, or perhaps undercut, the patterns they propose'.[5] I previously suggested that labelling Ashmole 61 as a minstrel's holster-book, or a professional scribe's output, is inappropriate in the light of Rate's demonstrated editing of the texts, which gives them a religious and family bias. Here I suggest that even labelling the volume as a romance manuscript ignores Rate's careful building-up of a body of narratives – all displaying some romance features[6] in a variety of genres – for the same purpose. For convenience I have included a corrected version of the list of items in Ashmole 61, although there is not space in this paper to discuss the non-narrative items as I should have liked, to give a complete picture; I would just note here that many of the family and religious themes highlighted in the narrative items are also present in the lyrics and didactic pieces.

It is unfortunate that owing to an oversight in cataloguing, the great collectors of romances such as Thomas Percy, Joseph Ritson, Thomas Warton, Walter Scott and George Ellis, did not know of Ashmole 61.[7] According to Leah Dennis, Thomas Percy saw only one romance at Oxford, the 'Ashmolean' *Erle of Tolous*, which will undoubtedly have been that of Oxford, Bodleian Library, MS Ashmole 45.[8] If it had been Ashmole 61, Percy would have also found the other four romances to add to his plan of collecting romances.[9] Dennis adds: 'On July 11, 1761, Warton wrote Percy (for the second time) that the libraries at Oxford contained no such treasures as he was seeking.'[10] Since no records were kept by Ashmole himself or by the authorities at the Ashmolean Museum, where the manuscripts were housed until 1860, it appears that Ashmole 61 did not come to light until Brydges discovered it in the first decade of the nineteenth century: 'Accident, however, having thrown in my way a manuscript containing a perfect copy of this romance [*Sir Cleges*]', he decided to publish the Ashmole instead of the Edinburgh copy. His account of that discovery explains the probable reason for the manuscript's neglect in the early part of its critical history:[11]

> The manuscript from which I have extracted it is contained in the Ashmolean Collection at Oxford – By some singular oversight it has not been mentioned as a separate article in the Oxford Catalogue, the only notice of it being the following, 'No.6922, Another poem by the same author (Ric. Rolle) 60. Vide etiam num.61'. The No. 61 thus cursorily noticed has apparently no connection with the works of R. Rolle, (the writer of the *Stimulus consciencie)*[12] but is in fact a miscellaneous collection of early English poetry, chiefly of a religious or moral nature; in addition to which it contains the romances of 'The Erle of Tolous', 'Lybeus Dysconius', 'Ysumbras', 'King Orfeas' [*sic*], and 'Syr Clegys' ... The MS. is a long narrow folio on paper, written apparently about the year 1450.

The mistake was rectified in the 1830s, when Black began work on the Ashmolean catalogue for the Bodleian Library, published in 1845;[13] yet even now this error is still confusing to some modern editors.[14]

Our application of the term 'romance' has certainly changed between William Black's catalogue of Ashmolean manuscripts in 1845, and Gisela Guddat-Figge's catalogue of romance manuscripts in 1976.[15] Black also describes the saints' lives (items 1 and 37), the three debate tales (items 16, 26 and 27), and the Passion texts (items 28, 34 and 36), as 'romances'. The overlap between different types of narrative has often been remarked, since similar techniques are employed in writing religious and romance narratives.[16] Religious narratives often borrow the trappings of romance to make them more palatable. Miracle stories such as saints' legends are to biography as historical romances are to chronicle: both are imaginative expansions of factual account, in order to achieve the 'wish-fulfilment dream', to use Northrop Frye's term, characteristic of the romance mode.[17] Piero Boitani points out that, while the romances were written 'purely to please the public', part of the function of 'romanticized' religious stories was that of 'entertaining a public that would not have taken to indoctrination pure and simple'.[18]

Thus the narrator in the prologue to the *South English Legendary* (64–5) earnestly assures his audience that saints are just as exciting as romance heroes, and that apostles and martyrs are just as 'hardy kniȝtes ... / þat studeuast were in bataille and ne fleide noȝt for fere', and who suffered 'al quik hare lymes totere'.[19] Derek Brewer remarks that in religious stories 'the extravagance and variety of incident can, as with the romances, in the hands of a good writer, create an imaginative world of legitimate excitement';[20] on the other hand, Douglas Kelly observes that the excitement of romance is 'founded on emotional but inarticulate religious experience',[21] while Edmund Reiss notes that 'the didactic and the religious are the warp and woof of romance'.[22] W. R. J. Barron suggests that religious stories share a fundamental attribute with romances: 'they represent life as it is *and* as it might be, as imperfect reality *and* imagined ideal in one'.[23] As he remarked at the 1994 Romance in Medieval England conference, analysing texts in terms of romance *mode* rather than *genre* might well be a more fruitful way to study texts which in 'tone' and 'content' are more compatible than their generic boundaries suggest.

I noted previously that the romances are family-based, sharing a separation-and-reunion structure which is not reflected in the other narratives: therein lies one distinction, but it is not exclusively a 'romance' characteristic; rather, it suggests one criterion for Rate's selection of these romances. The manuscript was compiled sequentially, rather than as a series of main texts interspersed with filler items within single gatherings or booklets.[24] It falls roughly into four parts, but there is no rigid demarcation; rather, a gradual move upwards from the low-level and relatively unsophisticated 'teaching' verses to the meatier exegetical texts. Reference to the four 'parts' of the manuscript is simply for critical convenience and is not a codicological description. The lack of clearly defined sections in Rate's anthology means that there are many different ways of grouping together the texts for the purposes of discussion – as, for example, by the different types of verse in the manuscript, which fall into four broad categories: narratives, instructional verse, lyrics, and preaching texts. The different types of narrative comprise the romances (items 5, 19, 20, 24, 39), the saints' lives (items 1, 37), the exempla (items 18, 22, 23, 35a, 35b), the Passion narratives (items 28, 34, 36) and the secular tales (items 16, 21, 41). The first part of the manuscript is mainly made up of pragmatic instructional verse: the courtesy books (items 3, 4, 7, 8) and the Latin proverbs, and rules for land purchase (items 9, 10, 11ab), added later. There are few verses in the manuscript that may be described as lyrics (that is, verses which capture a mood or an emotion), rather than telling a story or giving instruction: the three poems on the Passion (items 29, 30, 38), and the two satirical poems (items 2, 40) fall into this category. The remaining texts are what might be termed 'preaching' verses, that is, meditational texts possibly used in daily worship (items 25, 26, 27, 32, 33), and functional texts possibly taught to children for learning by heart (items 6, 12, 13, 15, 17). However, the present discussion of the narrative works moves sequentially through the manuscript as it was compiled. By doing this it is possible to perceive thematic groupings of texts, even though these sequences are usually 'interrupted' by a text of contrasting character, as if Rate tried to vary the tone even while pursuing particular interests at different stages in the compilation.[25]

The first text (*St Eustace,* item 1) and the first romance (*Sir Isumbras*, item 5) in the manuscript are both redactions of the same Latin legend, saint's life and pious romance respectively, concerning the knight Placidas who became the martyr St Eustace.[26] The two redactions were probably compiled together as a mark of devotion to the saint, and apart from their common use as pious entertainment *St Eustace* may also have been recited as a commemorative text on the saint's day. When compared with the version in Oxford, Bodleian Library, MS Digby 86 – which was not done by Laurel Braswell in her study of *St Eustace*[27] – Rate's version of *St Eustace* exhibits intensified pietistic elements, coupled with a greater concentration on family relationships, a trend that is sustained throughout the manuscript. Each text begins a new quire, the only time this occurs in the manuscript.

The types of text compiled at the beginning and ending of the volume (as we have it) are similar, opening and closing with an entertaining tale: one sacred, *St Eustace* (item 1), the other profane, *King Edward* (item 41), while the second and penultimate texts (*Ram's Horn*, item 2; *Vanity*, item 40) are both satires on the vanity of gaining worldly status. The early part of the manuscript consists of a 'children's corner' of texts, with a run of courtesy books (items 3, 4, 7, 8), added filler items (items 9, 10, 11), simple religious texts and prayers (items 6, 12, 13, 15, 17), and a more sophisticated lyric, *Ram's Horn*, which satirizes fifteenth-century society, including its religious integrity, and the corruptness of human nature. The end of the first sequence includes a debate text: the satirical *Carpenter's Tools* (item 16), which is one of only three secular tales in the manuscript together with *Sir Corneus* (item 21), and *King Edward* (item 41); all of them are drinking-tales unique to Ashmole 61. *Carpenter's Tools* was probably recited at a Carpenter's Guild feast, where the satirical lampooning of drunkenness, shrewish wives and profligate masters would be fully appreciated.

The second part of the manuscript comprises a run of narratives, with exempla (items 18, 22, 23) interspersed between romances (items 19, 20, 24). Items 18, 22, 23 all exemplify the ill consequences of wrath and the reward of fidelity. Particularly striking is item 18, *Forgiving Knight*, in which blood-vengeance for the slain father is undertaken by the faithful son. But the son's fidelity to God proves the greater, and forgiveness wins over wrath. His virtue is rewarded with a miracle, as the animated crucifix embraces the good son. In my previous discussion of the two romances copied consecutively at this point, I noted the marked unsuitability of

Lybeaus (item 20)[28] in this manuscript context, especially because of its juxtaposition with the eminently suitable *Erle of Tolous*. If Rate was indeed working to a patron's orders, as a household chaplain for instance, he may simply have been ordered to copy *Lybeaus* by a man whose taste in entertaining literature was less than refined. All the other entertaining stories have some obvious moral point: *Sir Isumbras* (penance redeems pride); *Carpenter's Tools* (drink ruins industry); *Sir Corneus* (cuckoldry levels rank); *The Erle of Tolous* (fidelity rewarded); *Sir Cleges* (justice served); *Sir Orfeo* (power of love triumphs); *King Edward,* the extant text (the treachery of drink). Even by the most generous interpretative licence it would be hard to see *Lybeaus* as the story of, for example, a disadvantaged child who triumphs over his difficulties, and perhaps Barron's explanation that it is simply a popular folk-tale is better than trying to see any deeper meaning in it.[29] The short narrative following, *Sir Corneus* (item 21), is a quasi-Arthurian tale falling between romance and exemplum. Its style is that of a romance, but its nature is that of an exemplum, illustrating how cuckoldry, like death, is a great leveller of rank: when King Arthur is proved to have been deceived by Guenevere, he joins his 'brothers' in the cuckold's dance as a forfeit. The text provides a comic analogue to the more serious cautionary tales of the *Lost Soul* (item 35a) and the *Adulterous Falmouth Squire* (item 35b), where the forfeit is the everlasting torments of hell. Both *Jealous Wife* (item 22) and *Incestuous Daughter* (item 23) serve as cautionary tales of women fallen from grace, warning of the perils of sexual wrong-doing: jealousy and incest respectively. The stories also offer hope of redemption, since both women are rescued from damnation.

By contrast with the long-winded and shallow *Lybeaus*, the shortest romance in the volume, *Sir Cleges*, successfully combines the three elements of entertainment, religious morality and family unity, which run through most of the texts compiled in the first half of Ashmole 61. In a similar way to Isumbras, the generous knight commits the sin of pride by placing too much value on worldly wealth. While it is the folk-tale element of *Sir Cleges*, incorporating motifs of the miraculous cherries and the shared blows that is generally held to be its primary source of interest,[30] Barron notes that 'pious legend comes even closer to a secular saint's legend in *Sir Cleges*',[31] while Lillian Herlands Hornstein describes it as a 'pleasant combination of romance, piety and humor'.[32] It therefore serves as an appropriate link between the narrative section of exempla and romances, and the third part of the manuscript, where the texts become more discursive on religious concerns.

Items 25-7 might be termed 'Court of Heaven' texts, as each provides a vision of life after death by means of mixing imaginative and intellectual conceptions of the hierarchy of heaven. In form they are a mixture of visionary, miraculous and allegorical elements. In *All Saints* (item 25) the spirit of a good monk is given a guided tour of Hell, Purgatory and Paradise by an angel while his body appears lifeless to his brothers.[33] The beggars whom he sees at the Feast of Paradise represent all those souls who have nobody to pray for them to be released from Purgatory, and this is the reason for establishing the Feast of All Souls after the Feast of All Saints. The easy narrative style and miraculous vision framework indicate that the text served an entertaining as well as an exegetic function. *Four Daughters* (item 26) is a unique translation of part of Grosseteste's *Chasteau d'Amour*, a moral debate loosely housed in the framework of personified virtues arguing the sentence of a misbehaving servant before the Judge (God). It was evidently popular and had several outlets and audiences for its recitation.[34] It is described in Black's catalogue as a 'Romance of the Creation of the World and Fall of Man with an allegory of the King and his Four Daughters'.

Ypotis (item 27) is a more technical description of the physical make-up of the heavens, creation and man, ending with the Thirteen Reasons for Fasting on Friday. Chaucer included it in his list of 'romances of prys' simply as a rhyme-filler, and so misled Percy in 1765 into mistaking it for a romance when he found the version in London, British Library, MS Cotton Caligula A.ii.[35] This misconception persisted as late as 1939, when Ritchie Girvan cited the 'six romances' of Ashmole 61, the sixth being *Ypotis*.[36] Everett notes that there was probably an exemplar circulating in Chaucer's time, containing the texts of *Ypotis*, *Lybeaus* and *Sir Isumbras*, as these texts appear together in Cotton Caligula A.ii and in Ashmole 61.[37] Since *Lybeaus* may also have appeared with *The Erle of Tolous* and *Sir Corneus*,[38] we may also include these in that exemplar; and since Sajavaara suggests that *Ypotis* appeared in an exemplar with *Four Daughters*,[39] which seems likely to have been compiled with *All Saints*, we may posit an exemplar containing at least items 5, 19-21 and 25-7. Although such a conjecture cannot be proved, the close copying of the second and third groups in this manuscript suggests its probability; such an exemplar may have contained a different version of *Sir Isumbras* from the one Rate copied as item 5.

Items 28-30 interpret the events of the Passion in three different ways: by narrative, allegory and lyric. Black describes the narratives of items 28, 34 and 36 respectively as 'the Romance of the Passion', a 'religious romance', and the 'Romance of the Resurrection'; whereas the last romance-type tale, or burlesque romance, of *King Edward* is merely called a 'gest'. This confirms the narrative success of the Passion accounts despite their non-adventurous form. Dramatization of Christ's life and the biblical stories was a means of instructing the people through accessibly entertaining interpretations of the Gospels and Old Testament. The *Northern Passion* (item 28) is a straightforward Gospel account from Palm Sunday to the Resurrection; parts of Rate's version are omitted in favour of a unique text of the *Resurrection* (item 36), suggesting that some pre-planning may have been involved. In spite of these reductions, it is the second longest text in the volume,[40] and was recited in stages over Holy Week.[41] Rate's version is particularly interesting for the addition of anti-Semitic variants, and other anomalies. The *Passion* is followed by five non-narrative texts forming a meditational sequence 'interrupted' by Lydgate's *Dietary* (item 31): two Passion lyrics of contrasting mood (items 29, 30) and two liturgical texts (items 32, 33) probably used serially in the context of worship. After *Conscience* (item 33) the page-scoring suggests that the manuscript originally ended with this 'third' part; it then continues with *Pilgrimage* (item 34), an account of a journey to the Holy Land that may have been first-hand or else written in the tradition of imitative pilgrimage narratives.

The final part of the manuscript is a mixture of narrative types: Passion narratives (items 34, 36), exempla (items 35a, 35b), a saint's life (item 37), a romance (item 39), and a secular tale (item 41). The texts of *Lost Soul* (item 35a) and *Adulterous Squire* (item 35b) interrupt what would otherwise be a congruous placing of *Pilgrimage* (item 34) followed by *Resurrection* (item 36).[42] These exempla are grim reminders of hell won and heaven lost through lechery. The Lost Soul (identified by Rate as Sir William Basterdfeld)[43] speaks direct to the audience, lamenting his fate; while the Adulterous Falmouth Squire, languishing in Hell, cautions his son in a dream vision to follow the better example of the squire's brother, happy in Paradise above. The *Resurrection* is an account of

Table 2 Contents of MS Ashmole 61

Item	Status	Form	Quire	Folio	Short title	Type
1	2	T	1	1^r–5^r	*Legend of St Eustace*	Saint's life
2	11	E	*1*	5^v–6^r	Lydgate, *Ram's Horn*	Satirical verse
3*	6	E	1	6^{rv}	*Wise Man Taught Son*	Courtesy book
4*	V	C	1	7^r–8^v	*Good Wife Taught Daughter*	Courtesy book
5*	10	T	2	9^r–16^v	SIR ISUMBRAS	Pious romance
6*	V	Q	2	16^v–17^r	*Ten Commandments*	Doctrinal verse
7*	V	E	2/3	17^v–19^v	*Stans puer ad mensam*	Courtesy book
8*	V	C	3	20^r–21^v	*Dame Curtasy*	Courtesy book
9	V	C	3	21^v	Latin proverb: 'Tempere felici'	Added item
10	15	C	3	21^v	Rules for land purchase	Added item
11a	U	–	3	21^v	Latin oracle: 'O asside asside'	Added item
11b	V	Q	3	21^v	Latin proverb: 'Tres infelices'	Added item
12	3	Q	3	22^r	Prayer at night	Religious verse
13*	2	Q	3	22^{rv}	Prayer at morning	Religious verse
14	–	Q	3	22^v	Commandments	Partial recopy
15	51	C	3	22^v–23^r	Prayer to Mary	Religious verse
16*	U	C	3	23^r–26^r	*Carpenter's Tools*	Comic debate
17*	7	Q	3	26^{rv}	Prayer at the Levation	Religious verse
18*	3	C	3	26^v–27^v	Miracle story: *Forgiving Knight*	Exemplum
19*	4	T	3/4	27^v–38^v	THE ERLE OF TOLOUS	Chivalric romance
20*	6	T	4/6	38^v–59^v	LYBEAUS DESCONUS	Chivalric romance
21	U	T	6	59^v–62^r	*Sir Corneus*	Burlesque tale
22	U	T	6/7	62^r–65^v	Miracle story: *Jealous Wife*	Exemplum
23	3	T	6/7	66^r–67^v	Miracle story: *Incestuous Daughter*	Exemplum
24	2	T	7	67^v–73^r	SIR CLEGES	Miracle romance
25	V	C	7/8	73^r–78^v	*All Saints and All Souls*	Miracle story
26	V	C	8	78^v–83^r	*King and Four Daughters*	Religious Debate
27	14	C	8	83^r–87^v	Miracle story: *Ypotis*	Religious Dialogue
28	12	C	8/10	87^v–105^v	*Northern Passion*	Passion Narrative
29	21	C	10	106^r	*Short Charter of Christ*	Passion lyric
30*	5	E	10	106^r–107^r	Marian lament	Passion lyric
31	53	Q	10	107^r–108^r	Lydgate, *Dietary*	Instructional verse
32*	13	E	10	108^r–119^v	Maydestone, Psalms	Meditative verse

Table 2 *Continued*

Item	Status	Form	Quire	Folio	Short title	Type
33	7	E	10/11	120ʳ–128ʳ *Prick of Conscience Minor*	Meditative verse
34*	V	C	11	128ʳ–136ʳ *Jerusalem Pilgrimage*	Passion narrative
35a	6	E	11	136ʳᵛ *Lament of a Lost Soul*	Exemplum
35b*	8	Q	11/12	136ᵛ–138v *Lament of Adulterous Squire*	Exemplum
36*	V	T	12	138ᵛ–144ᵛ *Resurrection story*	Passion narrative
37*	2	C	12	145ʳ–150ᵛ *Legend of St Margaret*	Saint's life
38	11	C	12/13	150ᵛ–151ʳ *The Wounds of Christ for Sins*	Passion verse
39	11	C	13	151ʳ–156ʳ SIR ORFEO	Romance
40*	U	E	13	156ᵛ–157ʳ *On Worldly Vanity*	Romance Satirical verse
41	U	T	13	157ʳ–161ᵛ *King Edward and the Hermit*	Burlesque tale

* = signed by Rate. Status (Ashmole text one of specified number of copies): U = unique text; V = unique version. Form: T = tail-rhyme stanzas; C = couplets; Q = quatrains; E = more elaborate rhyme-scheme.

the knights guarding the tomb of Christ, and their boasts and discomfiture, a passage which is omitted from Rate's text of *Passion* (item 28).

The *Legend of St Margaret* (item 37) is a romance-type saint's life like *St Eustace*, but, by contrast to the opening text, which is a restrained and pious family tale of corporate martyrdom, Margaret exemplifies the virtues of holy virginity and fidelity to the Christian faith through a series of quite fantastic miracles designed for the conversion of her pagan tormentors. These include being swallowed by a dragon and killing it by bursting from it, and surviving subsequent deaths by boiling oil, molten lead, drowning and burning, to die finally at her own request by beheading. Brewer comments: 'Saints' legends eventually earned themselves a bad name for improbability even among the devout',[44] but he also notes their long-lasting popularity and their influence on secular romance (as illustrated by the relationship between *St Eustace* and *Sir Isumbras* in this manuscript).

Sir Orfeo (item 39) appears at the end of a long, weighty religious section. It counterbalances two types of narrative: one of excessive religious absurdity in *St Margaret* (37), the other of excessive secular absurdity in *King Edward*. Its remarkable focus on marital love and fidelity is entirely in keeping with the general trend of Ashmole 61, as are its entertaining elements of the supernatural, which light-heartedly complement the miraculous motifs of the more overtly Christian tales. This end sequence is interrupted by two lyrics: one Passion verse (item 38) and one satire (item 40). The inclusion of satirical verse in a devotional miscellany such as Ashmole 61 demonstrates the compiler's realistic awareness of human nature and of the audience for whom it was intended. As such it provides a balance with the idealistic didacticism of most of the other texts.

The end of the volume is incomplete. The extant manuscript concludes with half of a romance-type tale, the burlesque of *King Edward and the Hermit*. This was evidently recited at rowdy feasts, from the frequent requests for the audience to be quiet. As the last text in the volume, it is the most debased, a crude tale of how King Edward, incognito, indulged in a drinking competition with a lowly hermit, the substance of which revolves around their ability to shout 'fusty bandias' and 'strike panter' as they grow increasingly drunk and debauched. One speculates whether the end of the manuscript is indeed lost, or deliberately cancelled by Rate, drawing the line at this particular 'comic analogue' on drunkenness, or whether it had been included specifically to point up the absurdity and treachery of drink.

The juxtaposing of such a varied selection of narrative types – yet homogeneous in tone and 'colouring' – suggests that Rate himself was unaware of, or unconcerned about, any generic difference between, for example, *St Eustace* and *Sir Isumbras*, or *Sir Corneus* and *Sir Cleges*, or *Lybeaus* and *King Edward*. What is strongly suggested by the nature of the compilation is that he chose texts according to their content and *mode* – predominantly the romance mode – in order that they might work together as a compilation providing a comprehensive policy of pastoral care for both the spiritual and the temporal needs of its readers.

Notes

1 See Blanchfield 1991b.
2 In a loosely defined sense: items 25 and 26 are discursive, with the most tenuous of narrative frameworks. But Rate himself would not have made such fine distinctions.

3 The scribe's first name is unknown, possibly William (see Blanchfield 1991b: 85–6).
4 Items 5, 19, 20, 24 and 39.
5 Evans 1992: 19. For recent studies of manuscript collections, see Thompson 1991; Rogers 1991; Meale 1991.
6 Whether or not they take the 'adventure' format. On the colouring of religious texts with romance features, see Barron 1987: 204–5.
7 See Johnston 1964: passim.
8 Dennis 1934: 90.
9 As described in Johnston 1964: 75–99.
10 Dennis 1934: 90.
11 Brydges and Haslewood 1814: 17–19.
12 Either Brydges is not attributing the *Stimulus consciencie minor* in Ashmole 61 (item 33) to Rolle or he is not aware of its presence. However, he does highlight the overall pious nature of the compilation.
13 Black 1845.
14 The manuscript is referred to as Ashmole 60 in Ogilvie-Thomson 1988: 633.
15 Guddat-Figge 1976.
16 For recent studies, see Wogan-Browne 1994; Thompson 1994; Meale 1994.
17 Frye 1957: 186.
18 Boitani 1982: 1.
19 D'Evelyn and Mill 1956–9: I, 3.
20 Brewer 1983: 258–9.
21 Kelly 1985: 74.
22 Reiss 1985: 115.
23 Barron 1987: 6; see also Mehl 1968: 17–19.
24 See the discussion of the different methods of making up miscellanies in Boffey and Thompson 1989: esp. 290–7, 298–9.
25 Subject to the availability of exemplars.
26 Although the text of *St Eustace* in London, British Library, MS Cotton Caligula A.ii is from the *South English Legendary*, one may speculate that *St Eustace* was selected for the Cotton and Ashmole MSS owing to the presence of *Sir Isumbras* in both.
27 Braswell 1965. Braswell compares in detail the structure and motifs of other versions of *St Eustace* and *Sir Isumbras,* and concludes that the romance disseminates Christian teaching more successfully than the religious narrative, by reason of its greater accessibility to the people. Significantly, perhaps, in Rate's volume it is the religious narrative that is the opening text of the (bound) volume, though I have shown elsewhere (Blanchfield 1991a: ch. 1, section 1.6) that before binding the first gathering may have been circulated separately, leaving the romance

as the opening text of the 'main' volume. See also Childress 1978.
28 Blanchfield 1991b: 66–7.
29 Barron 1987: 166.
30 Ginn 1967.
31 Barron 1987: 200.
32 Severs 1967: 171.
33 The text is described in *MED: Bibliography* as a 'Sermon on the Founding of the Feasts of All Saints and All Souls'.
34 Including the *Cursor mundi*. For discussion of the *Cursor* poet's attitude to romance as a literary genre, see Thompson 1994: 104–5.
35 Johnston 1964: 91. Reiss (1985: 111–12) suggests that the names of Ypotis and Pleyndamour were recognized by Chaucer's audiences as those of romance heroes, and that Ypotis may have derived from 'Hippotes', meaning a knight.
36 Girvan 1939: xxxiv.
37 Everett 1930: 448.
38 Blanchfield 1991b: 67.
39 Sajavaara 1967: 187–8. Texts of *The Castle of Love* precede *Ypotis* in the Vernon and Simeon MSS (Oxford, Bodleian Library, MS Eng. Poet. a. 1; London, British Library, MS Add. 22283).
40 It has 1913 lines; *Lybeaus* (item 20) is the longest, with 2,251 lines.
41 Barratt 1975: 265.
42 Thus are the long exegetical texts alternated with shorter, pithier poems which appeal to the imagination and conscience. Similarly, the lighthearted pious romance *Sir Cleges* (item 24) is followed by the long instructive items 25–8, relieved by the shorter lyrics and verse items 29–31 before the long meditational items 32–4. This pattern probably reflects Rate's own need of relief both in copying and in reading his collection.
43 I have not been able to discover any significance in Rate's (unique) naming of this character.
44 Brewer 1983: 258.

14

'Prenes: engre': an early sixteenth-century presentation copy of *The Erle of Tolous*

CAROL M. MEALE

The Erle of Tolous is, in many respects, an unremarkable example of Middle English romance, written *c*. 1400 in twelve-line tail-rhyme stanzas; its poet claims for it the status of a Breton *lai* (1214), and it thus forms part of a small generic sub-group.[1] Its relative popularity is indicated by its survival in four manuscripts, produced over the course of a century.[2] In one respect, however, it is highly unusual, for the latest of the four copies in which it is preserved, part I of Oxford, Bodleian Library, MS Ashmole 45, is prefaced by a fine presentation miniature (Plate 7). Illustrated copies of romances in English are rare enough, but the nature of this particular miniature makes Ashmole 45 unique amongst romance manuscripts,[3] and highly unusual amongst manuscripts containing any kind of text in the English vernacular, where presentation scenes are few and far between. But the Ashmole frontispiece does not conform to any expected pattern of presentation miniatures, either. Whilst copies of Hoccleve's *Regement of Princes* or Lydgate's *Troy Book* depict the author presenting his work to a (royal) patron,[4] it is unlikely that the male figure presenting the bound volume to a woman in Ashmole 45 is meant to represent the poet of *The Erle of Tolous*. Not only is there a studied anonymity in the text (as in most English romances), but also the donor is not kneeling: his stance is that of an equal, not that of a supplicant writer seeking patronage. This impression of equality is strengthened by the fact that the couple's dress shows that they share social status as relatively wealthy members of the bourgeoisie. The frontispiece therefore raises many intriguing questions about the manuscript as a whole, from the identity of the artist to the occasion of its production.

The date of the manuscript's copying can be placed fairly certain-

Plate 7 The presentation miniature in Oxford, Bodleian Library, MS Ashmole 45, fo. 2ʳ.

ly towards the end of the decade 1520–30. It is a quarto paper volume, and one of the two watermarks which occur, folded into the gutter, of a hand emerging from a decorated cuff, an arabic numeral three in the palm, the whole surmounted by a five-petalled fleuron, is close to Briquet 11341, recorded from Lisieux in 1526.[5] The second mark is also a hand surmounted by a fleuron; although I have not as yet been able to trace this, the similarity in appearance and measurement of the two marks suggests that all the paper came from the same source. The clothing of the couple in the frontispiece also indicates a date towards 1530. In Holbein's drawing of the More family dating from 1526–8, for example, Sir Thomas wears a furred gown comparable with, though more luxurious than, that of the man in Ashmole 45, and their square caps and blunt-toed shoes are alike.[6] And the convex line of the bodice of the woman's gown, together with the tight, cuffed sleeves and tasselled girdle, and the rosary hanging from her waist, bear comparison with the clothing of a young bourgeoise in a Holbein drawing now in the Ashmolean Museum, which may also belong to the artist's first period of residence in England.[7] The question of the manuscript's provenance is more complex. The identity of the manuscript's commissioner(s) is unknown, but the drawing, together with certain features of the script employed in the copying, do offer significant clues as to its place of origin.

The quality of the craftsmanship of the frontispiece is of a high order. The drawing is executed in pen, with colour-wash applied as tint. The style is unlike that of English artists of the period, recalling, rather, contemporary Flemish work. Illuminators and craftsmen from the Low Countries had, for many years, found employment in England, and the vogue for tinted drawings was well established.[8] But in the case of Ashmole 45 the immediate point for comparison is not with other books, either vernacular or religious, but with legal documents associated with the royal administration, and with the patronage of Thomas Wolsey. Erna Auerbach, in her classic study *Tudor Artists*, noted a change which occurred in royal portraiture on plea rolls of the King's Bench during the 1520s, and, stylistically, the Ashmole drawing can be linked with this group of documents.[9] There are particularly strong connections between the frontispiece and the pen-and-wash drawing of Henry VIII which decorates the initial *H* of Wolsey's patent for Cardinal College, Ipswich, dated 20 August 1528 (Plate 8). There are marked similarities in technique, for example, in the hatching used for shading; in the execution of the folds of the long gowns worn by the king and by the woman; and in the representation of facial features: a shadow under the lower lip, for instance, is common to all three figures.

The change in royal portraiture evident in these legal records has been attributed to the arrival in England during the 1520s of a family of artists from Flanders – Gerard, Lucas and Susanna Horenbout (or Hornebolt, to use the anglicized form of their name).[10] Gerard, employed as 'paynter' by Henry VIII between 1528 and 1531, arrived in England with impressive credentials. He had long been active in the artistic circles of Ghent and Bruges, having been appointed court painter to Margaret of Austria, regent of the Netherlands, in 1515. Amongst the commissions carried out by his atelier for Margaret were sixteen 'belles ystoires, bien enlumynées' added to a book of hours given or bequeathed to her by Bona Sforza (now London, British Library, MS Add. 34294).[11] The first payment recorded for Gerard's son, Lucas, in England dates from September 1525, when in the Chamber accounts he is described as 'Lewke Hornebaud pictor maker'. Nine years later, on 22 June 1534, Lucas was appointed King's Painter, and he continued to receive a salary from Henry until the king's death in May 1544. There is less information about the artistic career in England of Lucas's sister, Susanna. Dürer bought a miniature of the *Salvator mundi* from her in Antwerp in 1521, praising her achievement in the light of her youth, but no other contemporary accounts of her work survive. It has been suggested that she may have been the first of the Horenbout family to enter the royal service in England, and there is evidence to support the idea of an early and close acquaintance with the court in her marriages and subsequent career. Her first husband, whom she married sometime during the 1520s, was John Parker, Yeoman of the King's Wardrobe and Keeper of the Palace of Westminster; and after his death in 1537 she became the wife of John Gilman, gentleman and vintner of London, later Serjeant of the King's Woodyard, and one-time Master of the Revels. In her own right she was gentlewoman to two of Henry's queens, Anne of Cleves and Catherine Parr. The only remaining artefact with which she has so far been associated, however, is a commemorative brass to her mother, Margaret de Vandere (d. 1529), in the church of All Saints, Fulham.

The surviving documentary evidence does not link any of the

'PRENES: ENGRE': *THE ERLE OF TOLOUS* 225

Plate 8 Drawing of Henry VIII from Wolsey's patent for Cardinal College, Ipswich (London, Public Record Office, Exchequer: Treasury of the Receipt, Wolsey's Patents, 24/12/1 (20 August 1528)).

Horenbout family with extant work.[12] Notwithstanding, a number of attributions to them have been made. Gerard has been credited with the series of drawings on the unfinished roll which marked the death of John Islip, abbot of Westminster, in May 1532; and with an epistolary and Gospel lectionary executed for Wolsey in 1528-9;[13] whilst a number of portrait miniatures have been attributed to Lucas, in part at least on the basis of an early tradition that he taught Holbein to illuminate.[14] It has also been suggested that Lucas was responsible for the portrait of Henry VIII in the 1528 patent for Cardinal College, Ipswich.[15] Such suggestions, in the absence of confirmatory documentary proof, must remain speculative, but the records of payments which survive are sufficient to indicate that Gerard and Lucas certainly, and Susanna probably, played an important role in the artistic life of the Henrician court. Whether they also accepted commissions from outside the court – as Holbein did – is still to be established. In the circumstances it would be rash to attempt to put a name to the artist of the Ashmole frontispiece, but I suggest that it is possible to set the drawing within an artistic context. Its foreign, and probably Flemish, style, and its affiliations with the illustrations in a group of charters and plea rolls dating from the second half of the decade 1520-30 – and in particular with the 1528 patent for Wolsey's Ipswich foundation – place the artist in London, and therefore, it would seem, within the milieu of the Horenbouts and their presumed atelier.

A metropolitan provenance is also indicated for the copying of the text. The scribe writes a variety of legal anglicana, an essentially conservative script used for administrative purposes over a number of years from the late fifteenth until well into the sixteenth century.[16] He was also responsible for the elaborate strapwork initials which appear in the title above the frontispiece; at the opening of the text on fo. 3^r (Plate 9); at the major textual break on fo. 14^v (line 475); and at the minor divisions of the text on fos. 7^r and 22^r (lines 163, 802). (The way in which the lines of verse follow the outline of these large initials proves that the calligraphic detailing was an integral part of the copying process, and not filled in by another hand at a later stage in production.) The text concludes with the word 'ffinis', accompanied by a paraph mark and the aphorism 'sic transit gloria mundi' (Plate 10). The paraph mark is interesting, in that it contains the letters *m* and *d*, which are presumably intended as a means of identifying the scribe, perhaps

Plate 9 The opening of *The Erle of Tolous* in Oxford, Bodleian Library, MS Ashmole 45, fo. 3r.

being his initials. The scribe adds a less ambiguous signature to the text in the decoration of the initial *I* with which the romance opens on fo. 3^r: here the name 'morganus' appears on a scroll entwining the stem of the letter.[17] 'Morgan', it is safe to assume, was the scribe's name, and his status as a professional scrivener may be deduced from his use of a paraph and the overall professionalism of his hand. There are close parallels to the strapwork initials, for instance, in the documents I have discussed above, which might suggest that he was used to working within the offices of the royal administration. Attempts to identify him have not, as yet, proved successful. A scribe and notary public who was made free of the Scriveners' Company in 1497 signed himself 'Morganus', but his surname was Williams, and in any case he seems to have died in 1516.[18] A trawl through the testamentary indexes of London has not produced anyone named Morgan who had a surname beginning with *D*, although I have come across a reference to a Morgan David who is noted in the *Letters and Papers of Henry VIII* as one of the individuals who owed arrears to Wolsey 'for faculties expedited' for the three years ending 23 October 1530.[19] It may be possible eventually to resolve the question of the scribe's identity and define the nature of his scribal activities more precisely. In the meantime, certain tentative conclusions concerning his involvement in the book-trade may be offered.

It is relevant to observe, for example, that manuscript-book production was apparently no more formally organized in the early sixteenth century than it had been in the fifteenth.[20] Given this situation, and taking into account the scribe's likely training, a comparison between the careers of the copyist of the Ashmole romance and Thomas Hoccleve is not out of place. Hoccleve, a clerk of the Privy Seal, was also engaged in the commercial production of at least one vernacular text; the Ashmole scribe may, in a similar fashion, have been called in on an *ad hoc* basis to carry out a particular commission.[21] Such an arrangement would almost certainly have been made with the artist responsible for the presentation miniature since, whether or not s/he were connected in some way with the Horenbout atelier, book-illustration is unlikely to have formed a major source of income, especially at a time when printed books were gaining a rapid ascendancy over handwritten ones.[22] Like a great many other manuscripts made in late medieval London, the production of which required an effort of co-ordination, Ashmole 45

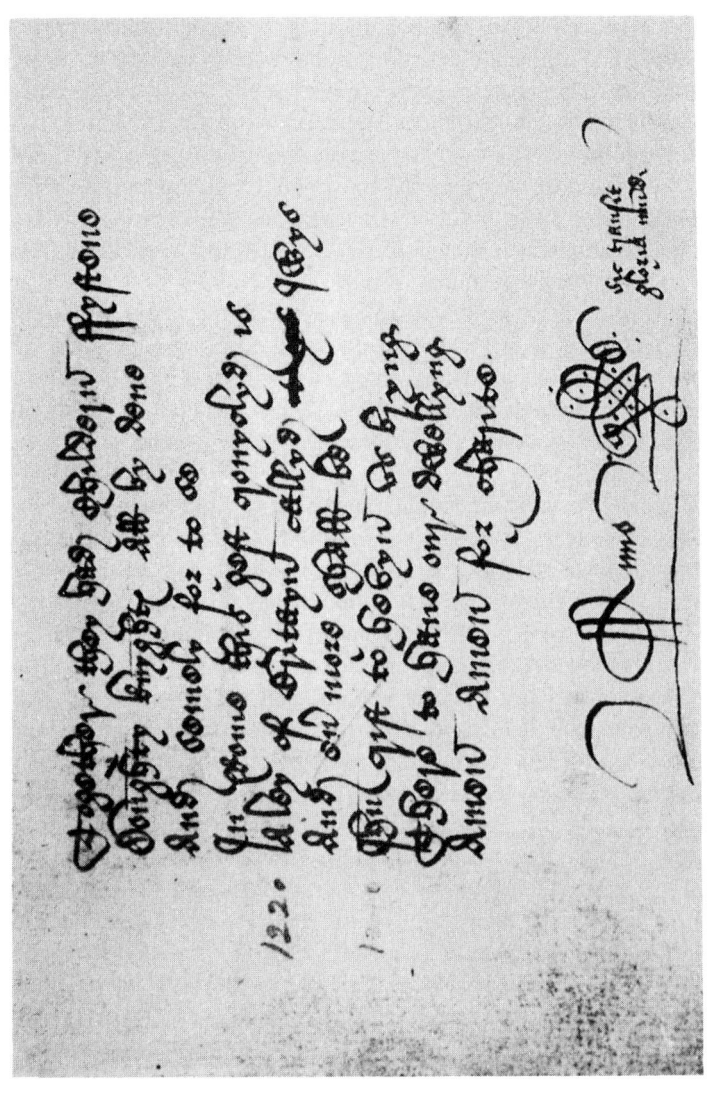

Plate 10 The conclusion of *The Erle of Tolous* in Oxford, Bodleian Library, MS Ashmole 45, fo. 31ʳ.

may have taken shape under the supervision of a stationer, working in consultation with the purchaser, or commissioner.[23]

Typical of its period though this manuscript of *The Erle of Tolous* may be in its mode of production, it is, however, extraordinary when looked at in the context of the book-trade in the 1520s, for by this time English romances had become a staple output of the early printing presses – in particular those of Wynkyn de Worde and Richard Pynson.[24] Texts of this length could be bought for a few pence, considerably less than the most conservative estimate of the cost of Ashmole 45 (copying of the text alone would probably have amounted to about 5s.), though it may be noted that no evidence has come to light to suggest that *The Erle of Tolous* itself was ever printed.[25] Manuscript copies of romances were, it is true, in circulation during the early 1500s, but many of these were produced in the preceding century. Three important romance miscellanies – Cambridge University Library, MS Ff.2.38, and Oxford, Bodleian Library, MSS Ashmole 61 and Rawlinson C.86 – have each been dated to around 1500,[26] but copies of texts newly made after this tended to be the work of antiquarian collectors like John Stow; or Edward Banyster, esquire, of Hampshire, who owned several medieval codices and who, in 1564, took a great deal of trouble to copy out several poems, including *Robert the Devil* and *The Jeaste of Sir Gawain*, from printed editions, even supplying a number of illustrations modelled on contemporary woodcuts.[27]

But Ashmole 45 is a bespoke volume, and it originally contained only one romance, which suggests that the prospective buyer was interested in this, and no other, text. Although the arrangement of the frontispiece, with the title written boldly above it, is reminiscent of, and may indeed have been modelled on, the title-pages of printed romances,[28] the content is personalized. The donor and recipient are precisely localized in terms of their social class, and it is conceivable that the device underneath the two figures, which reads 'Maid Maria', refers to the woman. (An alternative interpretation would be that it is a reference to the Virgin Mary, although there is no obvious connection between the Virgin and the content of the romance.) The man's injunction to the woman, 'Prenes: engres' ('Receive, or take [this book], with pleasure'), emphasizes its status as a gift.[29] Yet, despite both the quality of the drawing, and the pleasing presentation of the text – copying is careful and regular throughout, there are few corrections, and fo. 2^v was originally left blank, which is another feature of layout which recalls printing practice – the book does not come into the category of the *de luxe*. It is a paper manuscript, not parchment, and it is small: it measures approximately 150 × 208 mm. An altogether more curious aspect of production, however, is that a number of leaves were left blank at the conclusion of the text. The romance is copied on gatherings of four leaves, except for the first, which is a six. The text concludes on fo. 31^v, the last page of signature G. Two more complete gatherings of four leaves composed of paper from the same stock follow, and there are an additional two leaves which, in the absence of a watermark, I would hesitate to state came from the same source. The whole is prefaced by a singleton, which is clearly from a different batch of paper. All the leaves additional to those which contained the romance were originally left blank. The title-page is slightly rubbed, which could mean either that the volume lacked a protective covering for a time, or that it was left open, perhaps on display. The structure of the codex, as it stands, would seem to suggest that a number of gatherings were put together for the scribe in a semi-permanent form before copying of the text commenced. In other words, no exact calculations had been made as to how many gatherings or leaves would be required and, once the copyist had completed his task, no effort was made to remove the surplus paper.

The impression conveyed by the physical characteristics of the manuscript is that it was a special commission, but a commission executed within certain financial limits. So what could have been the occasion of its production? Now *The Erle of Tolous*, as a romance, is notable for its promotion of an ideal of virtuous womanhood: the heroine is introduced in terms of her virtues, as one who was 'gode in all thynge, / Of almesdede and gode berynge' (40–1), and the narrative functions as an exemplification of the ultimate rewards to be reaped from this mode of living: 'take hede', the author writes, of 'How a lady had grete myschefe, / And how sche covyrd of hur grefe' (10–12). Unlike the antecedent *lais* of Marie de France, this English lay takes as its theme the sanctity of the marriage bond. The empress of Almayne, 'Dame Beulybon', is married to a man who at the opening of the story is seen to be tyrannically disinheriting 'many a man' and 'falsely' winning their lands through brute force, 'Wyth maystry and wyth myght' (19–21). The moral rectitude of the empress is heightened by contrast with the proud and wilful behaviour of her husband, as she rebukes him for his actions 'agayne the ryght quarell' (143). Yet when one of the emperor's enemies, the worthy earl of Toulouse, Sir Barnard, falls in love with her, the empress remains true to her vows, and the couple do not consummate their love until they are married, following the emperor's death and Sir Barnard's election as emperor by the people. And at an earlier point in the story, when two treacherous knights attempt to seduce Dame Beulybon, her immediate response is to stress her status as a married woman (563, 568–70, 650–4).[30] Throughout, the concept of *trowthe* (282) is emphasized as the governing principle of moral behaviour. One reading of the romance would therefore be to stress its didacticism, if this may be defined as a privileging of social, legal and religious bonds over the desires of the individual.[31] Might it be appropriate to see this copy of a text which underlines the necessity of fidelity within an institution sanctioned both by society and the Church as a gift from husband to wife, or perhaps as a marriage-gift from a man to his prospective wife? Whatever the reality of the relationship between the couple depicted in the Ashmole frontispiece, the image is of considerable significance in any discussion of the audiences for romance for, whilst women as a group are known to have had an interest in the genre, and whilst both documentary evidence and that provided by surviving books demonstrate women's engagement with texts in French, this is one of the few instances where an English romance is known either to have been intended for a particular female reader, or to have been in the possession of a woman.[32]

The earliest identifiable owner of Ashmole 45, however, is William Fitzwilliam 'of the anchant hows of sprodbrovght in the covnty of yourcke' (fo. 2ᵛ). It is not clear when he acquired the romance, but he made good use of the blank pages surrounding the text, utilizing them to make a commonplace book. Amongst the items which he copied, in addition to a piece on 'The wartue of parssnypes', a list of herbs which go 'To macke a good povdynge', an anti-papal tract, various instructions on how to lead a good life, and a list of the 'ix wartus apartanynge to a knyght', was an autobiographical account of his 'hard and trovbelsome lyfe' (fo. 32ᵛ),[33] and the details of this latter not only substantiate the notion that the book was originally commissioned by a member of the middle classes, but also suggest a specifically mercantile readership for the text.[34] The autobiography is of considerable interest in its own right, as it details Fitzwilliam's career in London as an apprentice with his master, Richard Waddington (a distant relative), who served as Master of the Merchant Tailors in 1548; his apparent persecution for his Protestant beliefs following the passing of the Act of the Six Articles in 1539, and his resulting exile in Antwerp, where he gained his freedom; and his subsequent activities in Scotland, where he was during the final English campaign against the Scots in 1549 (in which he appears to have been wounded), and in Ireland, where he was for sixteen years in the service of another relative, and namesake, Sir William Fitzwilliam, Treasurer of that country, and later Lord Deputy (1559–75).[35] The account is also of value for the way in which it allows insight into London intellectual circles of the mid-sixteenth century: Waddington named as overseer of his will his 'lovinge freinde S*ir* Anthony Coke knighte', tutor to Edward VI, whose four highly educated daughters married leading scholars and statesmen, amongst them Sir Thomas Hoby, translator of Castiglione's *Il Cortegiano* and William Cecil, Lord Burleigh.[36] The William Fitzwilliam who owned Ashmole 45 described Waddington as his father's 'garmane Ramoved', and both men were related – and seem to have been close to – the branch of the Fitzwilliam family based at Gaynes Park, Chigwell, in Essex, and Milton in Northamptonshire, much of whose prosperity came about through involvement in trade. Waddington, who on the death of the first Sir William Fitzwilliam of Gaynes Park in 1534 was appointed one of the executors of his will and given the 'custodye Rule and gouernaunce' of one of his sons, may even have owed his entry to the Company of Merchant Tailors to him. This Sir William enjoyed a successful career, moving between city and court, occupying at various stages in his life the positions of Warden and Master of the Merchant Tailors; Alderman of London; successively Sheriff of London, Essex and Northamptonshire; and Treasurer and High Chamberlain to Wolsey. He was eventually appointed to the King's Council.[37] His grandson, another William, was the Treasurer and Lord Deputy of Ireland, under whom the owner of Ashmole 45 served.

The milieu which I have sketched here, in which various members of the Fitzwilliam family may be located, is one which would, I think, explain the genesis of the Ashmole copy of *The Erle of Tolous*, commissioned as it appears to have been by a prosperous member of the middle classes who had a taste for the kind of artwork in favour amongst those in power.[38] If the William

Fitzwilliam who inscribed his personal history on to the pages of Ashmole 45 would have been little more than a child at the time the manuscript was produced, and therefore in no position to have commissioned it himself, on leaving his native Yorkshire for London he entered circles in which such a book, and such a text, would have found a receptive audience a generation earlier.

Notes

1. Severs 1967: 133–43. All references to the text are to Fellows 1993c: 231–65.
2. Cambridge University Library, MS Ff.2.38; Lincoln Cathedral Library, MS 91; Oxford, Bodleian Library, MSS Ashmole 45 and 61; see Guddat-Figge 1976: 94–9, 135–42, 247–9, 249–52.
3. Meale 1994: 213–14, 222.
4. See, e.g., Lawton 1983: 56.
5. My interpretation of the paper evidence differs from that of Hülsmann 1985.
6. Ganz 1950: no. 176 and fig. 55; cf. the brass of the merchant Thomas Powder in Ipswich (1525) (Norris 1977: plate 65); the hairstyles of Powder and of the man in the drawing are also identical. I am grateful to Mrs Agathe Lewin and Dr M. Q. Smith for their assistance on the matter of costume.
7. Parker 1938: 132–3 and fig. 298. See also the costume of the daughters on the Powder brass (above n. 6).
8. Shoukri 1974; Scott 1976.
9. Auerbach 1954b: 37–46. I should like to thank Professor J. J. G. Alexander and Mr Michael Liversidge for their helpful conversations regarding this illustration.
10. The information in this passage is from Auerbach 1954b: passim, and 1954a; Paget 1959; Campbell and Foister 1986; Gunn and Lindley 1991: 40–1, 42.
11. Kren 1983: 113–22.
12. See esp. Campbell and Foister 1986, for a sceptical reassessment of the evidence.
13. Hope 1906; for the attribution, see Pächt 1953-4: no. 625. The epistolary and lectionary are now Oxford, Christ Church, MS 101, and Oxford, Magdalen College, MS Lat. 223, respectively.
14. See, e.g., Strong 1983; Backhouse 1991.
15. Paget 1959.
16. See, e.g., Johnson and Jenkinson 1915: II, plates XLI(b), XLIII; Jenkinson 1927: II, plate XIII (iii).
17. Guddat-Figge (1976: 249) is mistaken in reading the name as 'morga-

mus' and in her conclusion that the initials in the paraph mark are not *m* and *d*.

18 Steer 1968: 13, 24. See the signature and notarial mark of this man in Freshfield 1895: 253 and fig. 29; for his death, see Smith 1893-5: II, 576.
19 Brewer, Gairdner et al. (1862-1932): IV.3, 3047.
20 See Griffiths and Pearsall 1989.
21 See Burrow 1994; Doyle and Parkes 1978: 182-5 (on Cambridge, Trinity College, MS R.3.2).
22 On the diversity of commissions undertaken by artists at this time, see, e.g., 'Holbein in England' (Rowlands 1988: 229-52); Campbell and Foister 1986: 719-20.
23 For a discussion of possible methods of production of illustrated books, see Scott 1980.
24 Meale 1992.
25 For costs of printed texts, see Madan 1885 and 1890.
26 See McSparran and Robinson 1979; Blanchfield 1991b; Boffey and Meale 1991. Cf. the copy of *Melusine*, London, British Library, MS Royal 18.B.ii (*c*. 1500).
27 See, e.g., London, British Library, MS Harley 6223, one of John Stow's manuscripts containing a fragment of *Of Arthour and of Merlin;* and Seymour 1980. The Douce romances are currently being edited by Maldwyn Mills for the series Middle English Texts (Heidelberg). See also Mills 1994a.
28 See, e.g., de Worde's editions of *Kynge Rycharde cuer de lyon* (1509; *STC* 21007); *A lytel treatyse of ... Marlyn* (1510; *STC* 17841); or '*vndo your Dore*' (= *The Squire of Low Degree;* ?1520; *STC* 23111.5).
29 Mary Erler has pointed out to me that a scroll bearing the words 'Prandez en gre. moun cur' occurs in a copy of Boccaccio's *Genealogiae deorum* dated to the second half of the fifteenth century, now Exeter Cathedral Library, MS 3529; see Ker 1969-92: II, 836-7. It is unlikely that the words are a family motto, as suggested by Ker, especially since the book was a gift to St Augustine's Abbey, Canterbury.
30 Line 653 is particularly interesting in the light of the reading I am proposing, since the empress demands what the second knight had ever seen or heard of her to suggest that 'y were a hore or a scolde', thus invoking two of the jibes directed against women which the didactic construction of her character is presumably designed to undermine.
31 An alternative reading of the romance, as proposed to me by Mr Alcuin Blamires, would privilege female over male behaviour and would thus assign to the empress an independent and active virtue. But the manuscript context suggests to me that the exemplary nature of the heroine

is, rather, controlled by a system of beliefs which is essentially masculine: the empress neither stands outside nor threatens the ideology that the work embodies.
32 Meale 1994: 221–5.
33 Complete list of contents (with some inconsistencies in transcription) in Guddat-Figge 1976: 247–8.
34 For discussion of mercantile audiences for romance, see Meale 1994: 217–20.
35 On this man, see *DNB,* XIX, 232–5.
36 Waddington's will is London, Public Record Office, Prob. 11/48, fos. 218^v–220^r. On his career, see Clode 1875 and 1888.
37 See Clode 1875 and 1888; also *DNB*, XIX, 230.
38 It is interesting in this context to note that another distant relative of the owner of Ashmole, William Fitzwilliam, earl of Southampton (d. 1542) was drawn by Holbein: see Parker 1945: no. 66.

15
Robert Parry's *Moderatus*: a study in Elizabethan romance

JOHN SIMONS

When Elizabethan literature is surveyed, attention is inevitably focused on the achievements of poets and dramatists. Yet throughout Elizabeth's reign prose fiction flourished. Although there have been some fine scholarly and critical works on the enormous body of Elizabethan fiction, these have tended to focus on a relatively limited number of texts: the collections of Italianate *novelle* (often drawn from French sources and known as much for their influence on the drama as for their own merits), the Euphuistic prose of the school of Lyly, Sidney's *Arcadia*, and the picaresque stories of Nashe and Greene, among which the search for the roots of the novel is enthusiastically conducted.[1] Yet alongside these fictions and, arguably, far more widely read was a massive corpus of romances. Some of these were drawn direct from the traditions of Middle English narrative, others from more modern continental examples, especially from Spain, while others represent hybrids which draw on both of these sources as well as on elements from other English genres.

The reasons for this comparative neglect are not hard to find. First, the romances of the later sixteenth century pose a challenge to the mechanisms of periodization and canonization which construct English Literature as a usable scholarly discourse.[2] Secondly, the easy separation of literature into popular and polite which seems natural when made for the nineteenth century, where class-based analyses of the literary market and reading public retain some credibility, is badly strained by attention to Elizabethan romance.[3] Thirdly, the rarity of some of the texts and the lack of modern editions has caused them to appear obscure and unattractive. These three factors have combined to create a climate of neglect in which texts which were undoubtedly far more familiar to Elizabethans than anything commonly studied as part of the Elizabethan canon are barely known even by name. This neglect has been most startling with respect to romance, and it is typical that in Paul Salzman's excellent *English Prose Fiction 1558–1700* only four of the 109 pages devoted to the Elizabethan period are given to chivalric romances.

Chivalric romance had, in fact, proved wonderfully durable. In keeping with their predominant position among secular narratives in the Middle Ages, romances frequently appeared in the lists of the early printers, and texts of Middle English favourites such as *Guy of Warwick* and *Bevis of Hampton* were printed more-or-less unchanged well into the sixteenth century.[4] By the 1590s these texts were plainly beginning to look rather suspect, and a combination of their association with Roman Catholicism, fashionable humanistic strictures and the growth of a broad and socially stratified reading public meant that they were less frequently produced in forms which retained a close fidelity to medieval originals.[5] However, that does not mean that they went out of sight. In fact, romances closely based on Middle English texts, and retaining their narrative structures while displacing much of their chivalric content in favour of the concerns of trade and Protestant nationalism which characterized citizen culture, had begun to appear at much the time when the old reprints faded away.[6] In addition, the lengthy chivalric texts of the Iberian cycles (especially those of *Amadis* and *Palmerin*) were plainly of immense popularity not only with citizen readers but also with the elite which formed the market for other kinds of literature.[7]

However, the purpose of this contribution is not to write a brief history of sixteenth-century romance, and the above sketch must suffice to contextualize the main object of this study: *Moderatus, The most delectable and famous Historie of the Blacke Knight* by Robert Parry. Many years ago Maldwyn Mills suggested to me that an edition of this text might make a suitable core for a doctoral thesis, and although I became more interested in the general problems of the transmission of romance from the Middle Ages to the Renaissance, I have not lost sight of this idea and now present to him what I believe to be the first critical study of this interesting book, which exists in a unique copy in the Bodleian Library.[8] *Moderatus*, printed in 1595, is in many ways a typical late Elizabethan romance and it has features which demonstrate just how difficult it is to come to anything but provisional conclusions when attempting to align text and reading public in the later sixteenth century.

Before proceeding with an analysis, it will be helpful to the reader to have a synopsis of the plot, chapter by chapter:

1. Florence is besieged by the Goths. The governor, Perduratus, escapes with his wife, Flaminea, and their son, Moderatus. They wander in the wilderness of Apenninus until they come to the court of Duke Devasco in Albigena.
2. Lady Flaminea gives birth to a daughter, Verosa. Florida, Devasco's daughter, is educated by Flaminea.
3. Priscus, the son of Lothus, king of Aemulia, hears of Florida's beauty and secretly leaves his father's court to become an attendant to Devasco. He makes friends with Moderatus and courts Florida.
4. Florida rejects Priscus and he sings a madrigal of complaint. Priscus discovers his identity to Moderatus, who promises to help him in his courtship.
5. Florida falls in love with Moderatus, and Verosa overhears her private meditation. They meet Cornelius (the duke's son), Priscus, Moderatus and Pandarina, a gentlewoman of the house of Devaloyes. Priscus and Pandarina debate the nature of love while Florida censures it. The gentlemen choose by lot the three ladies who will be their mistresses for that year. They sing, dance and write poems about love. Moderatus woos Florida on behalf of Priscus but she favours Moderatus. He perseveres and she leaves in anger. They all go to Florida's chamber, where they eat.
6. Moderatus sadly decides to leave Devasco's court and writes to Florida to tell her this.
7. Moderatus leaves Albigena. Priscus intercepts the letters to Florida and reads them. He sends them to Florida, who falls in love with Priscus. Priscus becomes ill and is visited by the ladies and gentlemen.
8. Cornelius and Verosa become attached to each other. Florida promises herself to Priscus. Cornelius and Verosa confirm their mutual affection.
9. Priscus recovers, and exchanges love-poems with Florida.
10. Moderatus suffers from hunger in the forest. He passes through Umbria and the forest of Esina, where he meets a hermit, who

tells him of the imprisonment of Modesta, the daughter of King Lothus. Moderatus decides to be her champion and magically finds armour and a horse.
11. Moderatus leaves the forest and arrives at Lothus' court under the name of the Black Knight. He fights and beats Delamure, who has falsely accused Modesta.
12. Delamure confesses his intended treachery. The king is overjoyed but the Black Knight slips away from the court after sending Modesta a declaration of love. Modesta sends Moderatus a message revealing her love for him. He travels through the forest singing madrigals.
13. Moderatus has a dream. He saves the young man who is carrying Modesta's letter from a dragon and starts back to the king's court. A triumph is to be held both there and in Florence, and the victor rewarded with the king's daughter. The giant Bergamo is victorious and sets off for Florence with Modesta. Moderatus fights and beats him in the forest of Mountalt. Meanwhile Perduratus has returned to Florence.
14. Moderatus and Modesta declare their mutual love and travel to Florence. They stop at the village of Albavilla, which is plagued by the giant Albanus. Cornelius and other members of Duke Devasco's court go to Florence for the triumph.
15. Priscus loves Florida but becomes tired of her indecision and leaves Albigena to look for Moderatus. He travels through Apenninus, where he suffers from hunger but is comforted by poems engraved in the bark of trees. He meets an old man who tells him of Mersa, a beautiful shepherdess. He hears her singing and converses with her. Two shepherds sing. Albanus interrupts this scene, but Priscus fights and beats him. Priscus searches out the giant's son, Calfurnio. He meets Moderatus and they defeat Calfurnio. They recognize each other, and Moderatus tells him of his love for Modesta and his intention to go anonymously to the triumph at his father's court.
16. Priscus goes to Florence. Moderatus, Cornelius and the others from Devasco's court also arrive there. Priscus gives Perduratus Albanus' head. Moderatus does well in the first day of the triumph.
17. Cornelius falls in love with Bysantia, and Priscus with Verosa, who reciprocates.
18. Moderatus is victorious in the combat. Perduratus is reminded of

Moderatus, who asks Priscus and Modesta how best to reveal his identity. Modesta tells Perduratus about the love between Priscus and Verosa and that the Black Knight is his son, Moderatus. The marriages of both sets of lovers are celebrated.[9]

This summary makes clear the extent to which *Moderatus* consists of a compilation of motifs and episodes common to romance: a state of order disturbed, complex love-affairs, fights with powerful enemies, false accusations, disguises, journeys, honourable behaviour, and a final reconciliation. Parry's treatment of this material is heavily involved with the ethos of pastoral, and the text is shot through with poems, songs and Latin tags. *Moderatus* can thus be said to represent a hybrid in which highly traditional elements are blended with contemporary depictions, and discussions of honourable and chivalric love.

However, before moving to an analysis of some of the detail of *Moderatus* it is worth pausing to look at Parry himself and the very specific literary and bibliographical contexts in which *Moderatus* may be placed. Parry, as his name suggests, was Welsh, but *Moderatus* cannot be designated the first modern Anglo-Welsh prose fiction: this honour goes to David Rouland of Anglesey's translation of the Spanish picaresque novel *Lazarillo de Tormes* (1576). Parry is unusual among minor Elizabethan writers in that he left a diary which, in the manner of many pre-Enlightenment journals, records not private thoughts and feelings but events of the day.[10] It does, however, show that in 1600 he undertook a long tour of Italy; this is in keeping with his apparent knowledge of European literature and his styling of himself as 'Gent.'. In fact, Parry moved in what were relatively exalted circles, as he was associated with the intellectual and aristocratic Sir John Salusbury. He was related to the Salusbury family by marriage and in 1591 was among a group of gentlemen who wrote elegies, now preserved in Oxford, Christ Church, MS 184, on the death of Sir John's mother, Kathryn Thelwall.[11] In 1597 Sir John was the dedicatee of Parry's volume of poems, *Sinetes passions uppon his fortunes*.[12] *Moderatus* keeps up the Welsh connection in that it is dedicated to Henry Townshend, a Cheshire justice, in whose service Parry apparently was, having delivered Privy Council papers to him in 1599.[13] The kind of environment implied by this level of patronage and dedication is, however, curiously contradicted by *Moderatus* itself, which was produced by Richard Jones, a Welsh printer more usually associated with the lower end of the book-trade. The style and content of *Moderatus* are by no means unambiguously attractive to the popular taste, so I can only suggest that the reason Parry went to Jones was because of a Welsh connection.

Before writing *Moderatus*, Parry had been extensively engaged in the translation of Spanish romances of chivalry. It is almost certain that he was the 'R. P.' who had worked on the series titled *The mirrour of princely deeds and knighthood* by Diego Ortuñez de Calahorra. The first volume of this work had been translated by Margaret Tyler (probably the first English woman to be a professional writer) in 1578.[14] Parry added a translation of the second part of volume I in 1585, the third part (by an anonymous author) in 1586, the second volume (books 4 and 5 continued by Pedro de la Sierra) in 1583, the sixth book (now continued by Marcos Martinez) in 1598, and the ninth book (also by Martinez) in 1601. In 1597 and 1599 another translator ('L. A.') had published books 7 and 8. The dating of the translation of the third part is uncertain but there may have been earlier editions which for some reason are not noted. It is also possible that, having completed work on volume II and sensing that the full cycle would find a good market, Parry returned to fill in the gap before completing the sequence in chronological order. It is worth remarking that if R. P. and Robert Parry are the same man, then Parry was only 17 years old when he started his labours.[15] It is likely that Parry was competent in Spanish, as his diary incorporates a translation from a Spanish account of the death of King Philip II.[16]

The *Espejo de Principes y Cavalleros* is today the least known of the Spanish romances which flooded English consciousness after the appearance of Anthony Munday's translation of *Amadis de Gaule* in 1589 – the others being the cycles of *Palmerin of England* and *Palmerin d'Oliva*. Although there were relatively few English editions of these romances, they had achieved their vogue as an import from France, where between 1540 and 1582 there were no fewer than 217 editions of Herberay des Essarts's translation of *Amadis* alone.[17] In lighting upon Calahorra's work, Margaret Tyler and, subsequently, Parry were thus anticipating a vogue the importance of which remains quite unrepresented in most accounts of Elizabethan literature. The various cycles gained currency through the work of Munday and others, and also inspired domestic imitations which blended incidents and styles from the Peninsular romances with traditional English chivalric material to produce texts which appealed to a citizen audience. Interesting among these are the works of Emmanuel Forde, a man perhaps unfairly characterized by A. C. Hamilton as 'the Barbara Cartland of this grouping of romance', whose *Montelyon* (1599?), *Parismus* (1598), and *Parismenos* (1599) pay explicit homage to the Spanish cycles.[18]

The Spanish romances can be characterized as highly episodic, and relied on the effect of blending accumulated adventures with lengthy debates on love and chivalry. They do not attempt to impose on the romance mode any psychological interiorization or stylistic extravagance, as did the more courtly romances and stories of Lyly, Sidney, Lodge and Greene. In England the chivalric virtues represented in these romances seem to have been explicitly attractive to those citizens who now formed a distinctive part of the reading public. This was not the case across Europe and we learn that 'l'Amadis né en Espagne ... était selon certains la "Bible" du roi Henri IV', but in Spain itself the detailed critical analysis of *Amadis*-like texts to be found in *Don Quixote* testifies to a loss of attraction among sophisticated readers.[19] Parry was a writer who moved in courtly-intellectual circles – we know from his diary that he frequently visited London and attended court at Windsor – but he connected with the citizen reader through his choice of printer.[20] The content and structure of *Moderatus* clearly show the traces of this double life.

In *Moderatus* Parry seems to be attempting to blend the popular neo-chivalric content of the *Amadis* cycle with the more refined pastoral ethos of courtly romance and *novella*. In virtually the only critical comment I have found on *Moderatus*, it has been noted:

> The work begins in highly euphuistic fashion. But in Chapter X the narrative suddenly shifts from the vein of courtly love to that of chivalric pastoralism, and the prose style undergoes a corresponding change from decorated to plain.[21]

Certainly the book begins in learned style with a Euphuistic dedication and address to the reader and six poems (five in Latin, and one in Greek) by unidentified hands in praise of the author.[22] The text thus appears, for all its low production values, to be aiming at readers more likely to be flattered than annoyed at being confronted with classical learning. The following quotations will demonstrate just how the prose style changes:

> For even as a dwarffe standing upon the battlements of the highest Towre, is but of a small stature: and a Gyant in the depth of a dungeon, is of a huge bignesse: So a wise man, in what chaunge soever of Fortune, is ever the same. (sig. A1^v)

> When they had thus debated between themselves, of all the accidents happened unto them, after their parting they determined that Priscus should carrie the head of great Albanus into Florence, and present it unto Perduratus, making himselfe knowen unto him and no dobut [sic] he should be very welcome. (sig. T4^v)

As might be deduced from the plot summary, the plain style corresponds to that section of the text which deals with the commonplace episodes of knight errantry appropriate to chivalric romance, while the Euphuistic section deals with the business of amorous intrigue, and the obligations of friendship as they bear on a courtly gentleman. Thus we can see the legacy of Lyly and Sidney on the one hand, and the *Amadis* cycle on the other, within the same text. By the standards of Elizabethan romance, *Moderatus* is not a long text (179 pages, not including laudatory poems) and it is one which holds together without strain, so we cannot safely assume that the reasons for the change of style are to be found in any intention to produce the work on a different scale, authorial fatigue, or composite authorship (the work ends 'Finis, R. P. Gent.'). We must, therefore, take the view that Parry was fully in control of his material and that his shift from one mode to another is an observation of decorum.

The text begins with the disturbance of peace and order that precipitates every romance narrative, but the loss of his father's city does not constitute the quest in which Moderatus will win his reputation. Nor does the wandering of Perduratus and Flaminea in the wilderness begin a romance of the lost-child kind in which a young prince, having lived in the forest, suddenly discovers his courtly nature and restores his family's fortunes. In fact, Moderatus and his family do not suffer a long exile and are soon safely lodged in the Albigena under the protection of Duke Devasco. Thus the first movement of the text refuses the opportunities for narrative development that such events usually offer to the romance-writer. Instead *Moderatus* settles down to a lengthy series of conversations and debates, much interspersed by poems and songs, on the nature of love and friendship.

At this stage Moderatus is not unambiguously established as the hero. That role surely belongs as much to Priscus, the son of King Lothus, who has turned up at Devasco's court in disguise and is attempting to woo Princess Florida. Moderatus meets in Priscus a character who is acting out all the behaviours of a romance hero but whose adventures are not detailed and whose success in love will plainly depend not on chivalric prowess but on the courtly accomplishments of dancing, music, poetry, rhetoric and the cultivation of refined friendship. It appears, then, that in the first nine chapters of *Moderatus* Parry is attempting to recast the conventional events of medieval and neo-chivalric romance into a mould of Renaissance courtliness borrowed from Sidney and written in a style adapted from Lyly. This kind of strategy might have appealed to courtly readers who were beginning (at least in public) to distrust stories in which martial prowess predominated to the dereliction of gentler accomplishments, with the result that the romances proper were increasingly associated with a citizen audience which did not necessarily share in the revolution in manners and behaviour that was still sweeping in from the Continent as late as 1595.

In chapter 10 the chivalric section begins and Moderatus is shown on what will become his quest. But note two things: first, Moderatus does not have any specific object in mind when he leaves Devasco's court; secondly, the motivation for this departure is not to achieve knightly reknown but simply to help his friend win the love of Florida. The impetus that knights like Guy of Warwick or Sir Gawain have for their travels is missing here, and Moderatus sets out from Albigena still positioned wholly within a cultural world constructed by the demands of Renaissance courtliness, and anxious that his parents will worry about him while he is away:

> Moderatus betook him to his ease, who all this night tooke but small rest, beating his braines sometimes about the course of his travell, otherwhiles calling to memorie howe grievously his parents would take his absence, with divers other occurents which happened to come to his minde: and lastly resolved upon this point, that if he truely discharged the part of a friend, he did not care how his travell prospered, howe his

parents should be grieved, nor howe he should be thought of by his friend. (sig. I3ᵛ)

Once Moderatus leaves the court, both the style and the fictional world change and we begin to enter the familiar territory of the chivalric quest. In the forest Moderatus is often in danger of his life and suffers from hunger, but it is not until he reaches the cave of a hermit that he is motivated towards a real adventure: the rescue of Princess Modesta. Interestingly enough, we learn from one of Moderatus' many complaints that he considered himself to be a 'hireling to Devasco' (sig. M4ᵛ); this might have given the text a credible motivation had it been mentioned earlier, but to have expressed such a view while under Devasco's roof would, presumably, have been such a breach of style that it simply could not have been said.

Moderatus learns that Modesta has been accused by Delamure of fornication with a Florentine exile whom Delamure has killed out of jealousy and xenophobia. There is an obvious contrast here between the treatment of foreigners, and especially Florentines, in Devasco's court with that meted out to them in the court of Lothus, which is still bound by the codes of chivalry (as we should expect, as it is from there that Priscus has come). Moderatus defeats Delamure after a combat which seems to border on the burlesque and then proceeds on his way. The combat with Delamure is the longest single description of martial activity in the text and does much to establish the mode of the romance at this point. Generally, Parry does not dwell on the detail of fighting and physical suffering, preferring instead to work out their consequences in singing, conversations and letter-writing. A good example of this is the news that Perduratus has been restored (by Charlemagne!) to the governorship of Florence. Readers experienced in romance might have anticipated that this would be an ideal task for Moderatus, but, as a knight who has started his fictional existence in a comedy of courtly manners, it does not seem to cross his mind. Instead the journey to Florence serves the twofold purpose of re-uniting Moderatus with Modesta and, in a fashion typical of *Amadis*-style romances, facilitating the interlacing of the adventures of Moderatus with those of Priscus, whom he left behind at Devasco's court.

If Moderatus has passed through a romance world which was coloured by the conventions of pastoral, Priscus has passed through a pastoral world which is coloured by the conventions of romance. Whereas Moderatus' travels lead him to a genuinely bloody battle with Delamure, Priscus encounters all the trappings of full-blown Mannerism – poems carved in bark, a singing contest between two shepherds, a beautiful shepherdess described in classical terms – before he defeats a giant in a somewhat brief fight. If the court of Lothus shows up the values inherent in the genteel environment provided by Devasco, the pastoral idyll which Priscus discovers shows their insufficiency; for while Moderatus had to leave court in order to avoid a conflict of interest over Florida, Priscus finds in the forest two shepherds whose shared interest in the shepherdess is resolved in song. In the court of Lothus only blood would settle such disputes, but in Devasco's court self-imposed exile serves to avoid violence but does not provide an ethic which will offer solutions to the problems of love: this is what we see presented in the pastoral world.

Yet the pastoral world is not one for princes, and after more giant-killing the text moves into its final phase, in which Moderatus wins the hand of Modesta and is re-united with his father. Once again Parry does not exploit the moral potential which romance conventionally provides for this kind of episode. There is, after all, nothing to be reconciled, as Perduratus and Moderatus have been separated not as the result of any misunderstanding, false accusation or sin but through a choice made from good manners. When Moderatus is victorious in the tournament for Modesta's hand, Perduratus is shown attempting to balance the worlds of chivalry and courtliness when he invites his son (still unknown to him) to supper to discover 'if his skill in carper trade were equivalent with his marshall discipline' (sig. X2r). This goes some way to reconciling the two worlds which Parry presents to the reader. Neither the courtly nor the chivalric environment has been shown as sufficient to sustain a value system which can adequately confront the various challenges which a nobleman might face. In the course of his adventures Moderatus has developed from a rather spineless and silly courtier into a competent knight who is still able to conduct himself with courtesy and gentility: in this he begins to approach a model which is found in the very wide range of Renaissance conduct books but not necessarily in either the pastoral romance of a writer like Lodge (who managed to transform a rough and hearty Middle English romance like *Gamelyn* into the refined quasi-Mannerist pastoral *Rosalynde*) or the Spanish neo-chivalric cycles.

I wrote above of *Moderatus* as constituting a kind of hybrid and of the way it blends elements from courtly and more popular styles of romance. However, careful reading will show that this hybridization is not a function of any lack of control but, rather, a way of exploiting and frustrating generic expectation in order to create the contrasts that enable the text to become a commentary both on contemporary values and on the possibility that any one mode of writing is capable of articulating and analysing them. *Moderatus* has its roots very deep in the traditions of romance, which were, by the 1590s, being renewed through works like *Amadis*, but its use of courtly pastoral is not a crude attempt to make a neo-chivalric episodic structure more palatable to a new audience. On the contrary, *Moderatus* is an exploration of romance itself, and one which creates a dialogue between popular and courtly romance as the two modes most suited for the exploration of polite behaviour and all that it might entail for a sixteenth-century gentleman.[23] *Moderatus* is a text with a hero who is fundamentally unmotivated, but its narrative structure places it very clearly among the romances and particularly among the neo-chivalric popular texts, like the two parts of Richard Johnson's *Seven Champions of Christendom* (1596/7) or Christopher Middleton's *Chinon of England* (1597), which drew promiscuously on the common European stock of narrative motifs.

In conclusion, *Moderatus* is a surprisingly sophisticated and self-aware text which operates a narrative strategy far in advance of its technical execution – no one could claim that Parry is anything more than a competent writer of prose. It is a book which challenges over-rigid divisions of readership or bodies of literature into high and low, courtly and popular. The ideal reader of *Moderatus* is well educated and is able to understand the nuances of courtly behaviour as these are expressed in contemporary literary texts. At the same time, this reader is familiar with the forms and conventions of chivalric romance and is still prepared to devote time to reading about the adventures of a knight. Such a reader falls across the traditional divisions of the Elizabethan public yet is plainly implied not only by *Moderatus* but also by Parry himself, who appears quite happily to have produced poetry in a learned style alongside translations of Spanish romance. *Moderatus* offers an apparently typical example of minor Elizabethan prose, but it shows just how even an obscure work can open up interesting and tantalizing views of early modern culture. Above all, it shows the flexibility of romance as an expressive mode and how the most banal set of its narrative conventions can be treated so as to develop structural interest and stimulate reader involvement.

Notes

1 E.g. Davies 1969; Helgerson 1976; Hamilton 1982; Margolies 1985; Salzman 1985. Jusserand 1890 remains valuable, as does Schlauch 1963, but probably the best general treatment of the field is still Wright 1935.
2 On this, see Simons 1988.
3 See Burke 1978 and 1985.
4 See Crane 1919. See also below pp. 251–4.
5 In his *Anatomie of Absurditie* Nashe remarked that romances were 'the fantasticall dreames of those exiled Abbie-lubbers' (McKerrow 1958: I, 11). For detail of humanistic attitudes to chivalry more generally, see Baker-Smith 1990: 129–44; see also Watt 1991.
6 See Stevenson 1984; Simons 1983; see also Simons 1982.
7 The fullest study of these texts remains Thomas 1920. On *Amadis* and *Palmerin*, see O'Connor 1970; Patchell 1947.
8 The title-page is lost and has been replaced by a handwritten one, which looks as if it dates from the late seventeenth or the early eighteenth century and may have been written by a child; it reads: MODRATUS, / OR/ THE / ADVENTURES. OF THE / BLAC[K] KNIGHT, / LONDON PRIN[T]ED BY / RICHARD IHONES, / 1595.
9 This summary is based on abridged and modernized versions of Parry's lengthy chapter headings.
10 This has been anonymously edited (by A. Foulkes-Roberts?) as Parry 1915. In fact the diary begins in 1559 (before Parry was born), so he must have produced it as a general account of his life and times – perhaps as a memento for his children – much as did John Evelyn later in the seventeenth century. Evidence of this is also found in the fact that Parry records the death of Kathryn Thelwall, a person he presumably knew quite well, as having taken place in 1590, and then notes in the margin: `All this hapned the yere following viz 1591 & is heere mistaken' (ibid.: 118). There is no trace in the diary of Parry's literary activities or aspirations. The manuscript is now in the National Library of Wales.
11 Parry's brother married Blanche, the daughter of Edward Thelwall (Sir John Salusbury's stepfather), and John, the son of this marriage, married Sir John's daughter Oriana: see Brown 1914: xl. Parry's elegy

on Kathryn Thelwall is partially edited ibid.: 41.
12 Salusbury also contributed a substantial number of poems to *Sinetes*: see ibid.
13 Parry 1915: 123.
14 Margaret Tyler has been relatively neglected by modern critics. See Mackerness 1946. Travitsky (1981: 144–5) reproduces a portion of Tyler's claims for the education of women.
15 In his diary for 1600, where Parry is recounting his visit to Italy, we learn that he is 34 (Parry 1915: 124).
16 This section was not edited, and can be found on fos. 18–19 of the manuscript.
17 See Cooper 1990.
18 Hamilton 1982: 288.
19 Martin 1969: I, 292.
20 See Parry 1915: 120, 123.
21 O'Connor 1970: 221.
22 The poems are signed 'I. B.', 'Car. D.', 'Th. P.', 'R. O.' and 'H. T.'.
23 Hamilton (1982: 298) remarks that there is 'no place for any critical glance' in Elizabethan romance. I do not think that this is true of *Moderatus*; indeed, although Hamilton may be right in identifying 'the immediate, powerful impact on the reader of the individual episodes' as the 'defining characteristic' (ibid.: 290) of Elizabethan romance, I believe that the genre is more self-aware than he suggests.

16

Bevis redivivus: the printed editions of *Sir Bevis of Hampton*

JENNIFER FELLOWS

In recent years Maldwyn's growing interest in late texts of Middle English romances has been increasingly evident, especially in his work on Oxford, Bodleian Library, MS Douce 261.[1] What I aim to do here is to trace the fortunes of one particular romance, *Sir Bevis of Hampton*, both from a textual point of view and within the literary-historical context of the 'vogue' of medieval romance more generally in the sixteenth and seventeenth centuries.[2]

Textual history

No medieval romance seems to have enjoyed a more prolonged popular success than did *Bevis*. Its chief rival in this respect is *Guy of Warwick*,[3] and up to a point the respective histories of these two romances run parallel courses. *Bevis* and *Guy* were among the very few metrical romances to survive beyond the Middle Ages and to continue to flourish in printed form side by side with the new stock of chivalric prose romances which were first introduced to the English public by Caxton in the late fifteenth century.

Caxton was alone among the major early printers in confining himself, as far as romances were concerned, to prose works (all, with the exception of Malory's *Morte Darthur*, imported from the continent), to the exclusion of the native metrical tales;[4] but his successor, de Worde, while reissuing four of the seven romances printed by Caxton,[5] also printed slightly modernized texts of a number of the older metrical romances,[6] including (probably) *Bevis*, of which only fragments survive,[7] and *Guy*.[8] The other two giants among the early printers, Richard Pynson and William Copland, were both responsible for producing editions of *Bevis* and *Guy* – which were, indeed, the only two native metrical romances, apart from *Torent of Portyngale* and *Syr Tryamour*, to be included among Pynson's publications.[9]

The surviving de Worde texts of *Bevis* are unfortunately too fragmentary to lend themselves to textual analysis, but their relations to the later editions by Copland suggest that they belong to the mainstream of the printed *Bevis* tradition. Pynson's text of *Bevis* (*c.* 1503; hereafter O)[10] is, on the other hand, a somewhat anomalous one, varying more from most other printed editions than they vary among themselves. A large number of manuscript readings preserved in later editions has been lost from O,[11] which is much more radical than other early printed texts in its treatment of 'difficult' readings, tending not infrequently to rewrite a line or couplet entirely where other editions tend rather to keep as close as possible to the wording of what, on manuscript authority, we must assume to have been the reading of their common ancestor.[12]

In a volume dedicated to Maldwyn, I cannot leave discussion of Pynson's *Bevis* without mentioning the woodcuts. Several are used only for *Bevis* among Pynson's publications, and at least one must have been made specifically for that text, since it shows the giant Ascopard carrying Bevis, Josian and the horse Arundel towards a ship (Plate 11). Woodcuts depicting fights against a boar and against a giant may also have been made specifically for *Bevis*.[13]

Fragments of two editions attributed to Julian Notary (*c.* 1510 and *c.* 1515)[14] show every sign of having been set up from O: they almost invariably agree with it, often against other editions, and in the very few and very slight instances in which they differ from it, they stand alone, never agreeing with any other text against O.

William Copland's two editions (*c.* 1560 and *c.* 1565)[15] are more closely related to the de Worde fragments, agreeing with them in all cases where they and O differ substantially and in most instances of minor variation, even where the reading of O is the one with manuscript authority.[16] Curiously, the second of Copland's editions (hereafter Q) does not appear to have been set up from his first – at least not in its entirety; for though they share a number of clearly erroneous readings, Q contains several manuscript readings lost from the first of Copland's editions. Furthermore, it preserves a significant number of readings that have manuscript authority but that are not found in *any* of the earlier printed editions now extant (it may well be that these derive from a lost de Worde exemplar).[17]

Thomas East's edition of *c.* 1585 and an edition attributed to

Plate 11 A woodcut from Pynson's edition of *Bevis* (*c*. 1503) (Oxford, Bodleian Library, Douce B. Subt. 234, fo. 40[r]).

Snodham and dating from *c.* 1610[18] have each at least one reading that seems to have manuscript affinities not shared by earlier printed texts,[19] but in the vast majority of cases the readings of these editions are either the same as those of Q, even where Q is obviously corrupt, or can be seen to derive from them.

All the early printed editions of *Bevis* extant,[20] then, have close textual affiliations either with O or with Q. While each of these contains original features absent from the other, there is nothing (such as agreement with different manuscripts) to suggest that they might not derive ultimately from a common original, and it is at least highly probable, on both chronological and textual grounds, that that original was a de Worde print.[21] Furthermore, in the absence of evidence for the existence of any lost corpus of variant manuscripts in the tradition represented by the printed editions collectively,[22] it would seem that *Bevis* was rewritten specifically for the press, most likely at de Worde's instigation.

Once *Bevis* had attained printed status, its textual history in the sixteenth and seventeenth centuries was characterized by a marked degree of stability and continuity. There are no very substantial changes to the text of the metrical *Bevis* after the Snodham edition, apart from a handful in an edition of *c.* 1626[23] and a few of a cautious nature in Richard Bishop's 'Newly Corrected and amended' edition of *c.* 1639.[24] Apart from the occasional dropping of a line or couplet, there is a line-for-line correspondence between all the extant verse editions of the romance,[25] though minor alterations of a syntactical and lexical nature abound in all editions right up to *Bevis*'s final appearance in metrical form in 1711. This continued textual flexibility indicates the importance attached to the romance as a saleable commodity during this period and of anxiety, therefore, that it should be readily comprehensible to its readers. In its narrative and thematic essentials, however, *Bevis* remained unchanged for over two centuries. I turn now to a characterization of the version of the story that achieved this extraordinarily enduring popularity.

The printed version of 'Bevis'

Bevis is untypical of medieval romance in the way in which its hero is characterized and his role presented. The motif of revenge (for the death of Bevis's father at the hands of the hero's mother and her lover) gives some structural coherence to at least the first part of the story, but the poem as a whole is not unified in relation to any overall thematic concept, and the celebration of ideals seems not to be central to the poet's purpose;[26] in its savagery and sardonic humour, the character of the protagonist is often more reminiscent of some of the heroes of Icelandic saga than of those of the more exemplary kind of Middle English romance.

Later manuscripts of *Bevis*, especially MS C,[27] do attempt to modify the characterization of the hero in some respects, but a more sustained effort in this direction is made in the printed editions (henceforth referred to collectively as P) than in any of their predecessors. The theme of *pryse* is particularly emphasized,[28] and linked with this is the growing importance attached to honour. This latter is most clearly seen in the episode (shared by C) in which Bevis asks Bradmond to grant him fair battle instead of condemning him to a dishonourable death,[29] and in Bevis's interior monologue (peculiar to P) in which he decides against killing his stepfather, Murdure, by taking him unawares in his own hall:

> For men might wene by reasone
> That I him slewe by treasone:
> It wolde me turne to cowardyse
> Yf I him slee in this wyse.
> I wyll not [him] assayle –
> I wyll him slee in playne batayle.   (2567–72)

In P, also, the chivalric virtue of *largesse* – which, though not entirely absent from early versions, is there largely functional[30] – is constantly emphasized, for example:

> Eche man, both erle and baron,
> Loued and drad Beuis of Hampton,
> For largely woulde he spende,
> And gyftes both gyue and sende
> To euery man after his astate.   (3165–9)

Here too the virtue of courtesy is ascribed to Bevis –

> Beuis was loued with squier and knight,
> For he was curteise both daye and nyght
>   (449–50)[31]

– though other features of the narrative are not adapted with sufficient consistency radically to alter the characterization of the hero.[32]

Another feature of P consists in differences in the way in which the hero's relationship with Josian is portrayed. In *Boeve*, and even more consistently in the Middle English manuscripts,[33] Bevis's behaviour towards Josian is harsh, discourteous and domineering, and there is a marked lack of sentimentality in the English story as compared to the Anglo-Norman. The relative unimportance of the 'love element', and the presentation of the heroine as wooing rather than wooed, are more characteristic of *chanson de geste* and often meet with a certain measure of authorial disapproval in romance;[34] but the later English redactions of *Bevis* slightly modify the way in which the relationship between hero and heroine is presented. Thus, although instances of Bevis's discourtesy towards Josian are still retained here, P also hints at more tenderness between the two[35] and reduces or altogether omits Josian's expressions of unrequited passion.[36] It even suggests at one point a typically chivalric connection between love and prowess:

> Beuis loked vp to Iosyan,
> And suche a comfort toke he than
> That the to lyons gryme and lothe,
> At one stroke he slewe them both. (2125–8)

The story is thus modified in P in the direction of the courtly and chivalric; and it is a reasonable assumption, if de Worde was indeed responsible for the version that achieved such lasting success, that the changes were made in order to bring *Bevis* more into line with the romances that he inherited from Caxton. However, any change in the conception of the hero is confined to the realm of statement about him and does not really affect the ethos of the romance as a whole. The survival of *Bevis* in the face of competition from more courtly and sophisticated romance is perhaps therefore all the more remarkable.

The vogue of 'Bevis'

Up until about 1575 the attention of printers of romance – with the exception of Caxton – seems to have been fairly equally divided between the old metrical tales, particularly *Bevis* and *Guy*, and newer, more sophisticated romances of continental provenance. Since most of these early printers seem to have been fairly astute men of business,[37] it may be assumed that they were thus catering for the known demands of a twofold public: whereas Caxton's versions of continental chivalric romances were produced in expensive folio editions, de Worde and later publishers printed such tales as those of *Bevis* and *Guy* in a much cheaper format, these editions clearly being designed for a public less exacting in its demands and with less money to spend on the luxury of books. Some at least of these small quartos, which Crane describes as 'the true precursors of the chapbooks of the seventeenth century',[38] were sold to country readers: sometime before 1498 John Russhe, an itinerant bookseller, bought twenty bound copies of *Bevis* – at 10d. each, they were among the cheapest books in the lot.[39] Further evidence as to the social standing of *Bevis*'s main public is to be found in the work of George Puttenham, who describes this romance, among others, as 'made purposely for recreation of the cōmon people at Christmasse diners & brideales, and in tauernes and alehouses and such other places of base resort';[40] and later Henry Parrot, characterizing the objects of his satire by their taste in books, shows obvious contempt for the uncultured man of the lower classes whose preference is for the old romances:

> Next after him, your Countrey-Farmer viewes it [i.e.
>   Parrot's own work],
> It may be good (saith hee) for those can vse it.
> Shewe mee King *Arthur, Beuis*, or Syr *Guye*,
> Those are the Bookes he onely loues to buye.[41]

But it is not possible to see the co-existence of the romances' immense popularity and the critical disparagement with which they were regarded exclusively in terms of the uncultured predilections of the majority on the one hand and the scornful disapprobation of the highly educated few on the other: such distinguished men of letters as Sidney, Drummond of Hawthornden, Spenser, Drayton and Milton, to name but a few, manifested varying degrees of interest in and approval of medieval romance, and some of them borrowed from the romances in their own work.[42] On the whole, however, men of letters seem to have qualified their disapprobation only with regard to the newer kinds of chivalric romance: Sidney, for example, whose own work owes much to continental romance, is prepared to concede that men 'even with reading *Amadis de Gaule* (which God knoweth wanteth much of a perfect poesy) have found their hearts moved to the exercise of courtesy, liberality, and especially courage'.[43]

Although the influence of *Bevis* upon works of much higher literary quality than itself (notably Spenser's *Faerie Queene* and Drayton's *Polyolbion*)[44] indicates that the romance must have had some readers among the *literati* of the period, none of these seems to have said anything explicitly in its favour. Indeed, *Bevis* was frequently named specifically among those singled out for attack in the denunciations of the genre that became increasingly common during the sixteenth century and were roughly coterminous with the popularity of the romances in general.

Criticism of the Middle English romances on moral or aesthetic grounds was not unknown during the Middle Ages: in a well-known passage in *Speculum vitae*, for example, *Bevis* and other 'gestes' are condemned as 'nowht bot vanyte';[45] while Chaucer burlesques the romances' extravagant subject-matter and cliché-ridden style in *Sir Thopas*.[46] In the early sixteenth century, however, the work of the Spanish humanist Juan Vives gave fresh impetus to the practice of condemning romance literature both morally and aesthetically; and Richard Hyrde, translating Vives's *De institutione feminae Christianae* around 1529, adds to Vives's catalogue of harmful works a list of English romances, including *Bevis*.[47] The denunciatory tradition flourished in the work of English humanists and later in that of Puritan writers. *Bevis* is often specifically mentioned in these attacks, in which moral considerations are usually uppermost. Among the earliest is William Tyndale's in *The Obedience of a Christian man* (1528), where the author numbers *Bevis* among 'hystoryes & fables of loue and wantones, and of rybaudrye, as fylthy as harte can thynke: to corrupte the myndes of youth with all: clene contrary to the doctrine of Chryst and his apostles'.[48] Similar attacks, alluding to *Bevis* by name, are made by Edward Dering, Meredith Hanmer, Francis Meres (who mentions only *Bevis* and *Guy* of the metrical romances), Robert Ashley, William Perkins and Henry Crosse, whose outburst in *Vertues Common-wealth* (1603) is much in the spirit of Tyndale's attack:

> if a view be had of these editions ... what may we thinke? but that the

floudgates of all impietie are drawne vp, to bring a vniuersall deluge ouer all holy and godly conuersation: for there can be no greater meanes to affright the mind from honestie, then these pedling bookes, which haue filled such great volumes, and blotted so much paper, theyr sweete songs and wanton tales do rauish and set on fire the young vntempered affections, to practice that whereof they doo intreate.[49]

The authors of these attacks seem to have shown little if any discrimination in their criticisms: their targets are heterogeneous in nature and, though there are certain differences between the various denunciations as to their objects, there seems to have been something like a stock list of 'works to be denounced', the variations in which probably reflected currently prevailing tastes and fashions.

The chief grounds professed for adverse criticism of romances such as *Bevis* were that they presented bad moral examples to impressionable youth and that they distracted the mind from more serious and profitable reading: the burden of Tyndale's denunciation, for example, is that the layman is allowed to read romances but forbidden to read the Bible in the vernacular. The genre as a whole, and the metrical romances in particular, also, however, came under attack on more or less aesthetic grounds, particularly for lack of verisimilitude and crudeness of form.

Probably the earliest, and almost certainly the most entertaining, example of this kind of criticism is implicit in *Sir Thopas*: here, as far as *Bevis* is concerned, it is style rather than matter that is ridiculed, particularly in the burlesque use of the six-line tail-rhyme stanza. Probably of more considerable influence, however, were the strictures of Vives upon the improbabilities of the romances and upon the ignorance and ineptitude of their authors:

> As for lernyng, none is to be loked for in those men, whiche sawe neuer so moche as a shadowe of lernyng theym selfe. And whan they tell ought, what delyte can be in those thinges, that be so playne and folyshe lies? One kylleth .xx. hym selfe alone ... an other wounded with .C. woundes, and lefte dead, riseth vp agayne, and on the next day made hole and strong, ouer cometh .ii. gyantes ... What a madnes is it of folkes to haue pleasure in these bokes? ... Nor I neuer harde man say, that he lyked these bokes, but those that neuer touched good bokes.[50]

If the objection to the romances' lack of verisimilitude started out as an aesthetic criticism, it soon took a more moral slant, so that the genre was denounced for dishonesty. In his play *Lingua* Tomkis has the well-named Mendacio say of a variety of works, including *Bevis*, 'no doubt but they breathe in my breath up and down', to which Appetitus replies: 'Downwards, I'll swear, for there's stinking lies in them.'[51]

In similar vein Thomas Nashe, in the *Anatomie of Absurditie* (1589), accuses these 'bable bookemungers' who write romances of endeavouring 'to restore to the worlde that forgotten Legendary licence of lying, to imitate a fresh the fantasticall dreames of those exiled Abbie-lubbers,[52] from whose idle pens proceeded those worne out impressions of ... feyned no where acts'.[53] Later in the same work, however, he singles out *Bevis* for attack on more purely aesthetic grounds:

> Who is it, that reading Beuis of Hampton, can forbeare laughing, if he marke what scambling shyft he makes to ende his verses a like? I will propound three or foure payre by the way for the Readers recreation.
> "*The Porter said, by my snout,*
> *It was Sir Beuis that I let out.*"
>   or this,
> "*He smote his sonne on the breast,*
> *That he neuer after spoke with Clark nor Priest.*"
>   or this,
> "*This almes by my crowne,*
> *Giues she for Beuis of South-hamptoune.*"
>   or this,
> "*Some lost a nose, some a lip,*
> *And the King of Scots hath a ship.*"
> But I let these passe as worne out absurdities.[54]

Similar ridicule of *Bevis* is entertainingly implied in Massinger's play *The Picture* (1630), where the character Hilario, recounting Mathias's supposed exploits, claims: 'and as 'tis sayd truely / Of *Beuis*, some he quarter'd all in three'; to which Sophia not unreasonably replies: 'This is ridiculous.'[55]

The strong vein of criticism that co-existed with *Bevis*'s vogue, and whose intensity seems to have fluctuated in proportion to the romance's popularity, did nothing to diminish that popularity. Not only was *Bevis* among the several metrical romances that continued to be printed until the mid-1570s, when a fresh wave of chivalric romances imported from Spain swept many of the older romances of both kinds away,[56] but it was the only one of them – not excepting *Guy* – to survive this blow and to continue to be printed without interruption, in something closely approximating to its earliest printed form, until the mid-seventeenth century, when a decline in the vogue of romance in general took place.[57] There are several probable reasons for this enduring appeal. In the first place, it celebrates the exploits of a national hero, who was regarded as at least quasi-historical and as to whom local tradition, in the area of Southampton, was strong.[58] But perhaps the most significant factor contributing to the lasting popularity of *Bevis* was the association of its hero with St George, whose cult managed to survive even the most repressive period of the Reformation[59] and who was kept in the public eye at the level of 'popular' culture by the Mummers' Play.[60] The Mummers' Play, indeed, probably contributed significantly to the popularization and perpetuation of the association between Bevis and St George, since many of its variant forms owe a good deal to the work of Richard Johnson, whose version of the St George legend in *The Seven Champions of Christendom* (1596) is heavily indebted to the Bevis story.[61] The popularity of the *Seven Champions* itself also contributed to that of *Bevis* in all probability.[62]

Whatever the reasons for it, the popularity of *Bevis* until well into the seventeenth century cannot be doubted: the numerous references to it, both adverse and favourable, in contemporary literature attest the story's enduring appeal. Bevis is mentioned, in company with St George and other heroes, in two of the seventeenth-century Pepys Ballads,[63] and Thomas Carew refers to him as one of 'the darlings of the Gods' in the third song of *Coelum Britannicum* (1634).[64] The influence of *Bevis* upon the work of writers such as Spenser, Drayton and Bunyan also argues in favour of the story's popularity,[65] which was such that the romance continued to be printed in verse long after the other metrical romances, including *Guy*,[66] had passed into temporary oblivion.

Between 1625 and 1640 only seven Middle English romances were reprinted,[67] and although *Bevis* (the only metrical romance among them) was one of these, its long-lived popularity was by now on the point of decline. No editions of the romance in its metrical form seem to have appeared between 1667 and 1711. However, the practice of adapting romances by abridgement, and by prose renderings of those in verse, was begun at about this period.[68]

The chapbook versions of *Bevis* usually preserve the bare outlines of the narrative, but the tone, style and general 'colour' of the romance are inevitably lost, and the plot is so baldly summarized as, often, to lead to losses in sequential logic. Bevis's giant page, Ascopard, features quite prominently in these versions, where his character is developed in its comic aspects.[69]

In 1689 a much-elaborated version of *Bevis* in prose was produced (see Plate 12), perhaps by John Shurley.[70] For part at least of this work, the story follows that of the earlier romance in its broadest outlines, but it is embellished by the introduction of entirely new episodes and completely altered in tone.

The author's recommendation of his work in the 'Epistle to the Reader' provides a striking contrast to the denunciations of the romance on moral grounds so common in the sixteenth century, and is more in keeping with the patriotic fervour of some of the early seventeenth-century ballads in which Bevis is mentioned:

> I Here present you with the pleasant History of the Famous and Renowned Knight, Sir *Bevis* of *Southampton*, a Man for his Virtue and Valour, highly esteemed throughout the World: In whose many Actions and glorious Achievements, you will find things that may reasonably surmont an ordinary credit, however in perusing them, you may plainly perceive the difference between Elder times and these we live in, which are too much divolved into effeminacy ... Therfore for the honour of our Country, of which he has so well deserved, let his Memory live in the thoughts of every true English Man, and be to them a pattern of Heroick Virtue, that by imitating him, they may raise the very name of the British Empire, as formerly it was, to be the Terror of the World. (p. 4)

While some of the additions to the story simply emphasize Bevis's physical prowess, his character undergoes considerable change, so that he becomes the perfect gentleman, gallant and tender towards Josian and even 'no ways ignorant of any Learning' (p. 15) – a far cry indeed from his medieval counterpart!

That such modifications were felt to be necessary or desirable in adapting *Bevis* for a late seventeenth-century audience indicates how alien to generally held canons of taste the manner and ethos of the Middle English romance had by this time become. What the author has done in fact is to make the story as much as possible like the prose romances of continental provenance by which the native tales of the *Bevis* type had largely been displaced during the previous two centuries.

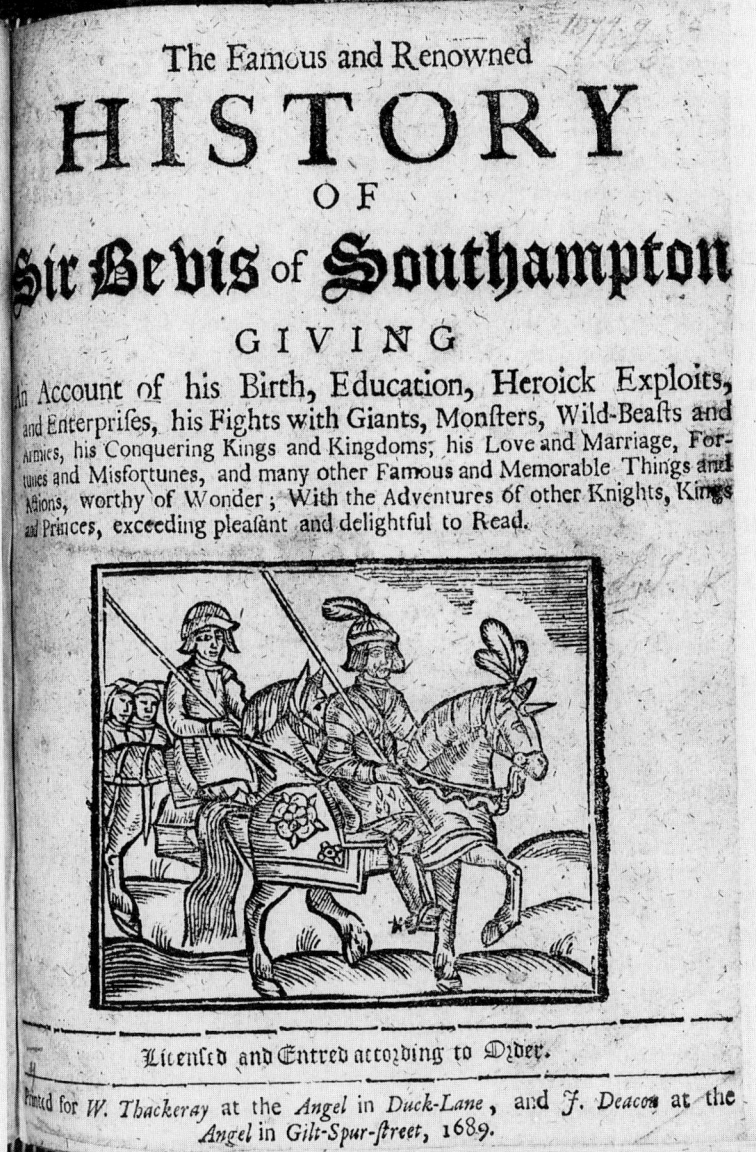

Plate 12 The title-page of *The Famous and Renowned History of Sir Bevis of Southampton* (1689) (London, British Library, 1077g 35 (3)).

This version of *Bevis* was reprinted, with some additions, by T. Baker of Southampton in 1775, but it is evident that the story was by this time largely forgotten, for Baker's edition is justified on the grounds that 'the great Achievements and noble Actions of this famous Champion were equal, if not superior, to those of any Hero of Antiquity, *and very little known*'.[71]

By the end of the eighteenth century interest in Bevis was virtually extinct, except from an antiquarian point of view,[72] but the evidence afforded both by the romance's literary influence and by the amount of comment, favourable or otherwise, that it excited during the sixteenth and seventeenth centuries is sufficient to suggest that *Bevis* was very much a 'living' story for some four centuries after its first translation into English.

Notes

1 See Mills 1994b: n. 40.
2 See Crane 1915 and 1919; also Cooper forthcoming.
3 See Crane 1915: passim.
4 Crane 1919: 2-3; Bennett 1969: 15-18.
5 Crane 1919: 2-3; Bennett 1969: 239-76.
6 See the list in Bennett 1969: 239-76; to this might be added *The Squire of Low Degree* (*STC* 23111.5).
7 *STC* 1987, 1987.5 (both *c*. 1500) and 1988.6 (*c*. 1533) are all attributed to de Worde. A printed edition of *Bevis,* now lost, was clearly in existence before 1498: see Plomer 1909: 122, 126-8.
8 For *Guy*, see *STC* 12541.
9 See Duff 1895-1905: II, 3-16; but cf. *STC* 24301.5, an edition of *Syr Tryamour* not listed in Duff.
10 *STC* 1988.
11 See Fellows 1980: I, 45; V, 185-250.
12 See, e.g., Fellows 1980: III, lines 767-70 (references to the text of the printed *Bevis* will be by line-number to this edition); and cf. ibid.: IV, lines 703-6.
13 See Hodnett 1973: 387-9, esp. nos. 1939 and 1941.
14 *STC* 1988.2 and 1988.4.
15 *STC* 1988.8 and 1989.
16 See, e.g., line 3237: O's superior reading *catel* (as against *castell*) is shared by all manuscripts.
17 See Fellows 1980: I, 43-4.
18 *STC* 1990 and 1992.

19 See Fellows 1980: I, 44 n. 146.
20 Thomas Marshe, John Tysdale and John Alde each secured a licence for *Bevis* between 1558 and 1569 (Crane 1919: 36-8), but no editions from any of their presses have apparently survived.
21 Cf. my remarks above as to the relationships between Q and the surviving de Worde fragments; and see above n. 7.
22 Although MS M (Manchester, Chetham's Library, MS 8009) has much in common with the printed texts in the opening and closing sections of the romance, there is at least a distinct possibility that these were copied from a non-extant printed *Bevis* to supplement a defective exemplar: cf. Fellows 1980: I, 40-3, though I have slightly modified the views expressed there at p. 43 – I now believe that, although the inception of the textual tradition attested by the *Bevis* prints must antedate M and any *extant* printed text, it need not antedate *Bevis*'s introduction into print.
23 *STC* 1993.
24 *STC* 1996.
25 Twenty-one in all, including fragments: see Fellows 1980: I, 25-32.
26 This is also true of the Anglo-Norman *Boeve de Haumtone*, from which the Middle English *Bevis* derives: see Martin 1968: 126-31; Fellows 1980: I, 59.
27 Cambridge University Library, MS Ff.2.38.
28 See, e.g., lines 701, 2463.
29 Lines 1275-86; cf. lines 209-14, where Guy's conduct is analogous to that of his son in the later episode.
30 It serves as the means whereby Josian recognizes her mistake in calling Bevis 'cherl' and thus effects her reconciliation with him (Fellows 1980: II, lines 1312-19; cf. Stimming 1899: lines 747-51.
31 Cf. lines 701-2.
32 See, e.g., Bevis's discourtesy towards Josian at lines 564-6.
33 See Martin 1968: 164-7.
34 See Weiss 1991: passim.
35 E.g. line 754.
36 See lines 624, 697-8, and Commentary ad loc. (in Fellows 1980: V).
37 Crane 1919: 4; Bennett 1969: 54-5.
38 Crane 1919: 9-10.
39 Ibid.: 10.
40 Willcock and Walker 1936: 83-4. Watt (1991: 13-14) suggests that minstrel versions of romances 'cannot have been unaffected by the circulation of printed copies'.
41 Henry Parrot, *The Mastive* (1615), sig. I1; quoted Wright 1935: 96; Watt 1991: 257.
42 Shepherd 1965: 114; MacDonald 1971: 131-4; Fellows 1980: I, 134-8;

Parker 1968: I, 75, 619. The young Milton's favourable attitude towards chivalric romance was later modified (Parker 1968: I, 330). Milton's father wrote a sonnet of commendation on *Guy of Warwick* (ibid.: I, 16).

43 Shepherd 1965: 114.
44 See above n. 42. *Bevis* is also quoted in *King Lear*, III.iv.142–3.
45 Ullmann 1884: line 48; cf. the similar judgement implied in C*ursor mundi* 1–28 (Bennett and Smithers 1968: 185–6).
46 See Brewer 1966: 11–15.
47 Hyrde 1529?: fo. 10^v.
48 Duffield 1964: 331. Ironically, William Copland, who produced more editions of Middle English romance than any other sixteenth-century printer, also published Tyndale's *Obedience* – a real case of running with the hare and hunting with the hounds! Or perhaps he felt that a little notoriety might improve sales of the romances.
49 Dering 1572: sig. A2^v; Hanmer 1576: sig. *iii^r; Meres 1598: fo. 268^v; Crane 1913–14: 271; Perkins 1590: sig. A2^r; Grosart 1878: 102–3.
50 Hyrde 1529?: fos. 10^v–11^r. The earlier type of romance was clearly felt to be more susceptible to criticism of this kind: see Leach 1957: v; and see above pp. 257–8.
51 Dodsley 1874–6: IX, 365.
52 An implied charge of 'popery' is also brought by Dering and by Ascham: see Dering 1572: sig. A2^v; Giles 1864–5: II, *Toxophilvs*, 7–8, and III, 159; but cf. Lewis 1954: 29.
53 McKerrow 1958: I, 11.
54 Ibid.: I, 26.
55 *The Picture*, II.i.120–3 (ed. Edwards and Gibson 1976: 193–292). I am grateful to Mrs Elsie Duncan-Jones for drawing my attention to this passage. Massinger's allusion is to line 4145.
56 Crane 1919: 7.
57 Nearly fifty years separate the last two editions of the metrical *Bevis*, that of 1711 being, therefore, an isolated phenomenon.
58 See Fellows 1986: passim. On the use of Bevis traditions 'to bolster civic prestige' in Southampton in the sixteenth century, see Rance 1986: 151–2.
59 See Baring-Gould 1873: 315; Chambers 1933: 172–4; Fellows 1993b: 42.
60 See Chambers 1933: passim; Tiddy 1923: passim; Brody 1970: 46–52; Helm 1980: 4–8.
61 See Helm 1980: 4–5.
62 See Fellows 1993b: 36 and n. 49.
63 Rollins 1929–32: I, no. 6; II, no. 56.
64 Dunlap 1949: 181.
65 See Fellows 1980: I, 123–39.

Plate 13 An illustration from Andrew Lang's *Red Romance Book* (1905). (See n. 72.)

66 *Guy* had not, however, died out in other forms: see Crane 1915: 165-94.
67 Crane 1919: 28.
68 Ibid.: 29.
69 That Ascopard retained his imaginative appeal is also indicated by his survival in local Bevis tradition until a late date: see Fellows 1986: esp. 142; Rance 1986: passim. On the readership of the chapbook *Bevis,* see Spufford 1981: esp. 50-1. See also Watt 1991: 262, and 270, where *Bevis* is listed among the 'top ten' chapbooks in the seventeenth century.
70 Wing F359. The 'Epistle to the Reader' is signed 'S. J.'; the work is ascribed to Shurley without comment in Johnston 1964: 29.
71 *The History of the Famous and Extraordinary Sir Bevis of Southampton* ... (Southampton, T. Baker, 1775), sig. [A1]^v; the italics are authorial.
72 See Fellows 1986: 140-1; Johnston 1964. *Bevis* may also have enjoyed a kind of afterlife as a children's book: at the beginning of the eighteenth century Richard Steele had alluded to it as part of 'the Learning on t'other side Eight Years Old' (*Tatler,* 17 Nov. 1709; quoted Johnston 1964: 31), and it may well be that it continued to be read by children (in chapbook form?) for some time after the decline of its popularity amongst an adult public (cf. Fellows 1980: I, 124 n. 135 on the later fortunes of Johnson's *Seven Champions*). In 1905 Andrew Lang produced a somewhat bowdlerized version ('Sir Bevis the Strong') of the first part of the story (Lang 1905: 267-86; see Plate 13), based on the re-telling by George Ellis (1805: II, 95-168) but lacking the tongue-in-cheek quality of Ellis's rendering. (I am indebted to Mrs Elaine Loades for the Lang reference.)

Bibliography

Ackerman, Robert W. (ed.) (1947). *Syre Gawene and the Carle of Carelyle*, University of Michigan Contributions in Modern Philology 8 (Ann Arbor, University of Michigan Press, 1947).
Alexander, Flora (1975). 'Late medieval Scottish attitudes to the figure of King Arthur: a reassessment', *Anglia*, 93 (1975), 17-34.
Allen, Dorena (1964). 'Orpheus and Orfeo: the dead and the *taken*', *Medium Ævum*, 33 (1964), 102-11.
Allen, Rosamund (1987). 'Some sceptical observations on the editing of *The Awntyrs off Arthure*', in Derek Pearsall (ed.), *Manuscripts and Texts: Editorial Problems in Later Middle English Literature* (Cambridge, D. S. Brewer, 1987), 5-25.
Allen, R. S. (1968). 'A textual study of *The Awntyrs off Arthure*' (Univ. of London MA thesis, 1968).
Amours, F. J. (ed.) (1897). *Scottish Alliterative Poems in Riming Stanzas*, 2 vols., STS 27, 38 (Edinburgh, Blackwood, 1897).
—— (ed.) (1908). *The Original Chronicle of Andrew of Wyntoun*, Vol. VI, STS (Edinburgh and London, Blackwood, 1908).
Archibald, Elizabeth (1985-6). 'The flight from incest: two late classical precursors of the Constance theme', *Chaucer Review*, 20 (1985-6), 259-72.
Arendt, Hannah (1958). *The Human Condition* (Chicago, Ill., University of Chicago Press, 1958).
Armstrong, A. M. et al. (1950-2). *The Place-Names of Cumberland*, 3 vols., Publications of the English Place-Name Society 20-2 (Cambridge, Cambridge University Press, 1950-2).
Armstrong, E. C., D. L. Buffum, Bateman Edwards and L. F. H. Lowe (1965). *The Medieval French Roman d'Alexandre*, II: *Version of Alexandre de Paris: Text* (New York, Kraus Reprints, 1965).
Arthur, R. G. (1989). 'Emare's cloak and audience response', in Julian N. Wasserman and Lois Roney (eds.), *Sign, Sentence, Discourse: Language in Medieval Thought and Literature* (New York, Syracuse University Press, 1989).

Auerbach, Erna (1954a). 'Notes on Flemish miniaturists in England', *Burlington Magazine*, 96 (1954), 51–3.
—— (1954b). *Tudor Artists* (London, Athlone Press, 1954).
Backhouse, Janet (1991). 'Illuminated manuscripts and the development of the portrait miniature', in David Starkey (ed.), *Henry VIII: A European Court in England* (London, Collins and Brown in association with the National Maritime Museum, 1991), 88–93.
Bain, J. (ed.) (1881–8). *Calendar of Documents relating to Scotland*, 4 vols. (Edinburgh, HM General Register House, 1881–8).
Baker-Smith, Dominic (1990). '"Inglorious glory": 1513 and the humanist attack on chivalry', in Sydney Anglo (ed.), *Chivalry in the Renaissance* (Woodbridge, Boydell Press, 1990), 129–44.
Baring-Gould, S. (1873). *Curious Myths of the Middle Ages* (London, Oxford and Cambridge, Rivingtons, 1873).
Barratt, Alexandra (1975). 'The Prymer and its influence on fifteenth-century English Passion lyrics', *Medium Ævum*, 44 (1975), 264–79.
Barron, W. R. J. (1967). '*Chevalere Assigne* and the *Naissance du Chevalier au Cygne*', *Medium Ævum*, 36 (1967), 25–37.
—— (1974). '*Golagrus and Gawain*: a creative redaction', *Bibliographical Bulletin of the International Arthurian Society*, 26 (1974), 173–85.
—— (1982). 'Alliterative romance and the French tradition', in David Lawton (ed.), *Middle English Alliterative Poetry and its Literary Background* (Cambridge, D. S. Brewer, 1982), 70–87.
—— (1987). *English Medieval Romance* (London and New York, Longman, 1987).
Baxandall, Michael (1972). *Painting and Experience in Fifteenth-Century Italy* (Oxford, Clarendon Press, 1972).
Bennett, H. S. (1969). *English Books & Readers 1475 to 1557* ..., 2nd edn. (Cambridge, Cambridge University Press, 1969).
Bennett, J. A. W., and G. V. Smithers (eds.) (1968). *Early Middle English Verse and Prose*, 2nd edn. (Oxford, Clarendon Press, 1968).
Benson, Larry D. (1976). *Malory's 'Morte Darthur'* (Cambridge, Mass., Harvard University Press, 1976).
—— (ed.) (1987). *The Riverside Chaucer* (Boston, Mass., Houghton Mifflin, 1987).
Black, William H. (1845). *Catalogue of the Manuscripts of Elias Ashmole* ... (Oxford, Clarendon Press, 1845).
Blanchfield, Lynne S. (1991a). '"An idiosyncratic scribe": a study of the practice and purpose of Rate, the scribe of Bodleian Library MS Ashmole 61' (University College of Wales, Aberystwyth, Ph.D. thesis, 1991).
—— (1991b). 'The romances in MS Ashmole 61: an idiosyncratic scribe', in Maldwyn Mills, Jennifer Fellows and Carol M. Meale (eds.), *Romance in Medieval England* (Cambridge, D. S. Brewer, 1991), 65–87.

Bliss, A. J. (ed.) (1954). *Sir Orfeo*, Oxford English Monographs (London, Oxford University Press, 1954).
—— (ed.) (1960). *Sir Launfal*, Nelson's Medieval and Renaissance Library (London and Edinburgh, Nelson, 1960).
—— (ed.) (1966). *Sir Orfeo*, 2nd edn. (Oxford, Clarendon Press, 1966).
Boffey, Julia (1985). *Manuscripts of English Courtly Love Lyrics in the Later Middle Ages* (Cambridge, D. S. Brewer, 1985).
Boffey, Julia, and Carol M. Meale (1991). 'Selecting the text: Rawlinson C. 86 and some other books for London readers', in Felicity Riddy (ed.), *Regionalism in Late Medieval Manuscripts and Texts* (Cambridge, D. S. Brewer, 1991), 143-69.
Boffey, Julia, and John J. Thompson (1989). 'Anthologies and miscellanies: production and choice of texts', in Jeremy Griffiths and Derek Pearsall (eds.), *Book Production and Publishing in Britain 1375-1475* (Cambridge, Cambridge University Press, 1989), 279-315.
Boitani, Piero (1982). *English Medieval Narrative in the Thirteenth and Fourteenth Centuries*, tr. Joan Krakover Hall (Cambridge, Cambridge University Press, 1982).
Bosworth, A. B. (1988). *From Arrian to Alexander: Studies in Historical Interpretation* (Oxford, Clarendon Press, 1988).
Brasseur, Annette (ed.) (1989). *La Chanson des Saisnes* (Geneva, Droz, 1989).
Braswell, Laurel (1965). '"Sir Isumbras" and the legend of St Eustace', *Mediaeval Studies*, 27 (1965), 128-51.
Brémond, Claude, Jacques Le Goff and Jean-Claude Schmitt (1982). *L'Exemplum*, Typologie des sources du moyen âge occidental 40 (Brepols, Catholic University of Louvain, 1982).
Brereton, Georgine E., and Janet M. Ferrier (eds.) (1981). *Le Menagier de Paris* (Oxford, Clarendon Press, 1981).
Brewer, D. S. (ed.) (1966). *Chaucer and Chaucerians* (London, Nelson, 1966).
—— (1980). *Symbolic Stories: Traditional Narratives of the Family Drama in English* Literature (Cambridge, D. S. Brewer, 1980).
—— (1983). *English Gothic Literature* (London, Macmillan, 1983).
—— (1988). 'Escape from the mimetic fallacy', in D. S. Brewer (ed.), *Studies in Medieval English Romances: Some New Approaches* (Woodbridge, D. S. Brewer, 1988), 1-10.
Brewer, J. S., J. Gairdner, et al. (eds.) (1862-1932). *Letters and Papers, Foreign and Domestic, of the Reign of Henry VIII*, 22 vols. (London, HMSO, 1862-1932).
Briquet, C. (1968). *Les Filigranes*, 4 vols., reproduced with supplementary material, ed. Allan Stevenson (Amsterdam, Paper Publications Society, 1968).

Brody, Alan (1970). *The English Mummers and their Plays: Traces of Ancient Mystery* (London, Routledge and Kegan Paul, [1970]).
Bromwich, Rachel, A. O. H. Jarman and Brynley F. Roberts (eds.) (1991). *The Arthur of the Welsh* (Cardiff, University of Wales Press, 1991), 171–82.
Brooks, Peter (1984). *Reading for the Plot: Design and Intention in Narrative* (Oxford, Clarendon Press, 1984).
Brown, Carleton (ed.) (1914). *Poems by Sir John Salusbury and Robert Chester*, EETS, ES 113 (London, Oxford University Press for the EETS, 1914).
—— (1939). *Religious Lyrics of the XVth Century* (Oxford, Clarendon Press, 1939).
Brown, Carleton, and Robbins, Rossell Hope (eds.) (1943). *The Index of Middle English Verse* (New York, Columbia University Press for the Index Society, 1943).
Brown, Michael (1994). *James I*, The Stewart Dynasty in Scotland 1 (Edinburgh, Canongate Academic, 1994).
Bryant, Nigel (tr.) (1978). *The High Book of the Grail* (Cambridge, D. S. Brewer, 1978).
Brydges, Samuel E., and Joseph Haslewood (eds.) (1814). *The British Bibliographer*, Vol. IV (London, Bensley, 1814).
Bulkeley-Owen [Fanny M. C.] (1898). *History of Selattyn Parish* (Oswestry, Woodall, Minshall and Co., 1898).
Burgess, Glyn S. (1987). *The 'Lais' of Marie de France: Text and Context* (Manchester, Manchester University Press, 1987).
Burke, P. (1978). *Popular Culture in Early Modern Europe* (London, Temple Smith, 1978).
—— (1985). 'Popular culture in seventeenth-century London', in B. Reay (ed.), *Popular Culture in Seventeenth-Century England* (London, Croom Helm, 1985), 31–58.
Burrow, J. A. (1982). *Medieval Writers and their Work: Middle English Literature and its Background 1100–1500* (Oxford, Oxford University Press, 1982).
—— (1994). *Thomas Hoccleve*, Authors of the Middle Ages: English Writers of the Late Middle Ages 4 (Aldershot, Variorum, 1994).
Bynum, Caroline Walker (1987). *Holy Feast and Holy Fast: The Religious Significance of Food to Medieval Women* (Berkeley, University of California Press, 1987).
Campbell, Lorne, and Susan Foister (1986). 'Gerard, Lucas and Susanna Horenbout', *Burlington Magazine*, 128 (1986), 719–27.
Carlin, Martha (1983). 'The urban development of Southwark c1200–1550' (Centre for Medieval Studies, Toronto, thesis, 1983).
Carmody, Francis J. (ed.) (1948). *Brunetto Latini: 'Li Livres dou Tresor'*

(Berkeley and Los Angeles, University of California Press, 1948).
Cary, George (1956). *The Medieval Alexander*, ed. D. J. A. Ross (Cambridge, Cambridge University Press, 1956).
Cerquiglini, Bernard (1989). *Eloge de la variante: Histoire critique de la philologie* (Paris, Seuil, 1989).
Chambers, Sir Edmund (1933). *The English Folk-Play* (Oxford, Clarendon Press, 1933).
Charles-Edwards, Gifford (1980). 'The scribes of the Red Book of Hergest', *National Library of Wales Journal*, 21 (1980), 246–56.
Charles-Edwards, T. M. (1970). 'The date of the four branches of the Mabinogi', T*ransactions of the Honourable Society of Cymmrodorion* (1970), 263–98.
Child, F. J. (1882). *The English and Scottish Popular Ballads*, Vol. I (Boston, Mass., 1882).
Childress, Diana (1978). 'Between romance and legend: secular hagiography in Middle English literature', *Philological Quarterly*, 57 (1978), 311–22.
Clode, C. M. (1875). *Memorials of the Merchant Taylors' Company* (London, Harrison and Sons, 1875).
—— (1888). *The Early History of the Guild of Merchant Taylors*, 2 vols. (London, Harrison and Sons, 1888).
Colgrave, Bertram, and R. A. B. Mynors (ed. and tr.) (1969). *Bede's 'Ecclesiastical History of the English People'* (Oxford, Clarendon Press, 1969).
Constans, Léopold (ed.) (1890). *Le Roman de Thèbes*, SATF (Paris, Firmin-Didot, 1890).
Cooper, Helen (forthcoming). 'Romance after 1400', in David Wallace (ed.), *The Cambridge History of Medieval English Literature: Writing in Britain 1066–1547* (Cambridge, Cambridge University Press, forthcoming).
Cooper, R. (1990). '"Nostre histoire renouvelée": the reception of the romances of chivalry in Renaissance France', in Sydney Anglo (ed.), *Chivalry in the Renaissance* (Woodbridge, Boydell Press, 1990), 175–238.
Coward, Rosalind (1984). *Female Desire: Women's Sexuality Today* (London, Paladin, 1984).
Crane, R. S. (1913–14). 'The reading of an Elizabethan youth', *Modern Philology*, 11 (1913–14), 269–71.
—— (1915). 'The vogue of "Guy of Warwick" from the close of the Middle Ages to the Romantic revival', *PMLA*, 30 (1915), 125–94.
—— (1919). *The Vogue of Medieval Chivalric Romance during the English Renaissance* (Menasha, Wis., University of Wisconsin Press, 1919).
Cross, Tom Peete (1915). 'The Celtic elements in the lays of *Lanval* and *Graelent*', *Modern Philology*, 12 (1915), 585–644.

Davies, Sioned (1989). *Pedeir Keinc y Mabinogi* (Caernarfon, Gwasg Pantycelyn, 1989).

Davies, Walter R. (1969). *Idea and Act in Elizabethan Fiction* (Princeton, NJ, Princeton University Press, 1969).

Davis, Norman (ed.) (1971-6). *Paston Letters and Papers of the Fifteenth Century*, 2 vols. (Oxford, Clarendon Press, 1971-6).

Denholm-Young, N. (ed.) (1950). *The 'Liber Epistolaris' of Richard de Bury* (n.p., Roxburghe Club, 1950).

Dennis, Leah (1934). 'Percy's essay "On the Ancient Metrical Romances"', *PMLA*, 49 (1934), 81-97.

Dering, Edward (1572). *A bryefe and necessary Catechisme or Instruction. Very nedefull to be knowne of al Housholders* ... (1572; London, J. Charlewood, 1577 [*STC* 6679.7]).

de Sélincourt, Aubrey (tr.) (1958). *The Life of Alexander the Great*, Penguin Classics (Harmondsworth, Penguin, 1958).

D'Evelyn, Charlotte, and Anna J. Mill (eds.) (1956-9). *The South English Legendary*, 3 vols., EETS 235-6, 244 (London, Oxford University Press for the EETS, 1956-9).

Dodsley, Robert (ed.) (1874-6). *A Select Collection of Old English Plays*, 4th edn., rev. W. C. Hazlitt, 15 vols. (London, Reeve and Turner, 1874-6).

Donatelli, Joseph M. P. (ed.) (1989). *Death and Liffe* (Cambridge, Mass., The Medieval Academy of America, 1989).

Doob, Penelope B. R. (1974). *Nebuchadnezzar's Children: Conventions of Madness in Middle English Literature* (New Haven and London, Yale University Press, 1974).

Doyle, A. I. (1982). 'The manuscripts', in David Lawton (ed.), *Middle English Alliterative Poetry and its Literary Background* (Cambridge, D. S. Brewer, 1982), 88-100.

Doyle, A. I., and M. B. Parkes (1978). 'The production of copies of the *Canterbury Tales* and the *Confessio Amantis* in the early fifteenth century', in M. B. Parkes and Andrew G. Watson (eds.), *Medieval Scribes, Manuscripts and Libraries: Essays presented to N. R. Ker* (London, Scolar Press, 1978), 163-210.

Duff, E. Gordon (1895-1905). *Hand-Lists of English Printers 1501-1556*, Bibliographical Society, 3 vols. (London, Bibliographical Society, 1895-1905).

Duffield, G. E. (ed.) (1964). *The Work of William Tyndale*, Courtenay Library of Reformation Classics 1 (Appleford, Sutton Courtenay Press, 1964).

Duggan, Hoyt N., and Thorlac Turville-Petre (eds.) (1989). *The Wars of Alexander*, EETS, SS 10 (Oxford, Oxford University Press for the EETS, 1989).

Dunlap, Rhodes (ed.) (1949). *The Poems of Thomas Carew with his Masque 'Coelum Britannicum'* (Oxford, Clarendon Press, 1949).

Easting, Robert (ed.) (1991). *St Patrick's Purgatory*, EETS, OS 298 (Oxford, Oxford University Press for the EETS, 1991).

Echard, Sian (1990). 'Expectations and experimentation in medieval Arthurian narrative: a study of Anglo-Latin, Middle English and Middle Welsh texts' (Univ. of Toronto thesis, 1990).

Edwards, Mary C. (1954). 'An edition of the early English versions of the *Lai de Lanval*' (Univ. of London MA thesis, 1954).

Edwards, Philip, and Colin Gibson (eds.) (1976). *The Plays and Poems of Philip Massinger*, Vol. V (Oxford, Clarendon Press, 1976).

Ellis, F. S. (ed.) (1900). *The Golden Legend, or Lives of the Saints as Englished by William Caxton*, 7 vols. (London, Dent, 1900).

Ellis, George (1805). *Specimens of the Early English Metrical Romances ...*, 3 vols. (London, Longman, Hurst, Rees and Orme, 1805).

Evans, Ivor H. (ed.) (1970). *Brewer's Dictionary of Phrase and Fable*, 12th edn. (London, Cassell, 1970).

Evans, J. Gwenogvryn (ed.) (1909) *Facsimile of the Chirk Codex of the Welsh Laws* (Llanbedrog, the editor, 1909).

Evans, J. Gwenogvryn and R. M. Jones (eds.) (1973), *Llyfr Gwyn Rhydderch* (Cardiff, University of Wales Press, 1973).

Evans, Murray J. (1992). 'Manuscript studies: new directions for appreciating Middle English romance', in John Simons (ed.), *From Medieval to Medievalism* (Basingstoke, Macmillan, 1992), 8–23.

Everett, Dorothy (1930). 'A note on "Ypotis"', *Review of English Studies*, 6 (1930), 446–8.

Ewert, Alfred (ed.) (1944). *Marie de France: Lais* (Oxford, Blackwell, 1952).

Fellows, Jennifer (1980). '*Sir Beves of Hampton*: study and edition', 5 vols. (Univ. of Cambridge Ph.D. thesis, 1980).

—— (1986). 'Sir Bevis of Hampton in popular tradition', *Proceedings of the Hampshire Field Club and Archaeological Society*, 42 (1986), 139–45.

—— (1991). 'Editing Middle English romances', in Maldwyn Mills, Jennifer Fellows and Carol M. Meale (eds.), *Romance in Medieval England* (Cambridge, D. S. Brewer, 1991), 5–16.

—— (1993a). 'Mothers in Middle English romance', in Carol M. Meale (ed.), *Women and Literature in Britain, 1150–1500*, Cambridge Studies in Medieval Literature 17 (Cambridge, Cambridge University Press, 1993), 41–60.

—— (1993b). 'St George as romance hero', *Reading Medieval Studies*, 19 (1993), 27–54.

—— (ed.) (1993c). *Of Love and Chivalry: An Anthology of Middle English*

Romance, Everyman's Library (London, Dent; Rutland, Vt, Charles E. Tuttle, 1993).

Fenster, Thelma (1982). 'Beaumanoir's "La Manekine": kin d(r)ead: incest, doubling, and death', *American Imago*, 39 (1982), 41–58.

Fetterly, Judith (1978). *The Resisting Reader* (Bloomington and London, Indiana University Press, 1978).

Fichte, Joerg (1989). '*The Awntyrs off Arthure*: an unconscious change of the paradigm of adventure', in U. Böker, M. Markus and R. Schönerling (eds.), *The Living Middle Ages: Studies in Medieval English Literature and its Tradition: A Festschrift for Karl Heinz Göller* (Stuttgart, Belser, 1989), 129–36.

Field, P. J. C. (1971). *Romance and Chronicle* (London, Barrie and Jenkins, 1971).

—— (1982). 'Malory and *The Wedding of Sir Gawain and Dame Ragnell*', *Archiv für das Studium der neueren Sprachen und Literaturen*, 219 (1982), 374–81.

—— (1991). 'Malory and Chrétien de Troyes', *Reading Medieval Studies*, 17 (1991), 19–30.

—— (ed.) (1978). *Le Morte Darthur: The Seventh and Eighth Tales*, The London Medieval and Renaissance Series (London, Hodder and Stoughton, 1978).

—— (1993a). 'Author, scribe, and reader in Malory: the case of Harleuse and Peryne', in Eiléan Ní Cuilleanáin and J. D. Pheifer (eds.), *Noble and Joyous Histories: English Romances, 1375–1650* (Blackrock, Co. Dublin, Irish Academic Press, 1993), 137–55.

—— (1993b). 'Malory and *Perlesvaus*', *Medium Ævum*, 62 (1993), 259–69.

Fisher, Sheila, and Janet E. Halley (eds.) (1989). *Seeking the Woman in Late Medieval and Renaissance Writings* (Knoxville, University of Tennessee Press, 1989).

Flinn, John (1963). *Le Roman de Renart dans la littérature française et dans les littératures étrangères au moyen âge* (Paris, Presses Universitaires de France, 1963).

Foster, B. O. (ed. and tr.) (1919). *Livy*, Vol. I, Loeb Classical Library (Cambridge, Mass., Harvard University Press, 1919).

Foulet, Lucien (1914). *Le Roman de Renard* (Paris, Champion, 1914; repr. 1968).

Foulon, Charles (ed.) (1958). *L'Oeuvre de Jehan Bodel* (Paris, Presses Universitaires de France, 1958).

Frappier, Jean (ed.) (1936). *La Mort le Roi Artu* (Paris, Droz, 1936).

—— (1961). *Etude sur 'La mort le roi Artu'* (Paris, Droz, 1961).

French, W. H., and C. B. Hale (eds.) (1930). *Middle English Metrical Romances* (1930; repr. New York, Russell and Russell, 1964).

Freshfield, Edwin (1895). 'Some notarial marks in the "common paper" of the Scriveners' Company', *Archaeologia*, 54 No. 2 (1895), 239–54.

Freud, Sigmund (1960). *Totem and Taboo*, tr. James Strachey (London, Routledge and Kegan Paul, 1960).

Friedman, Albert B., and Norman T. Harrington (eds.) (1964). *Ywain and Gawain*, EETS 254 (London, Oxford University Press for the EETS, 1964).

Friedman, John Block (1970). *Orpheus in the Middle Ages* (Cambridge, Mass., Harvard University Press, 1970).

Friedrichs, Rhoda L. (1990). 'The two last wills of Ralph Lord Cromwell', *Nottingham Medieval Studies*, 34 (1990), 93–112.

Friedwagner, Mathias (ed.) (1909). *La Vengeance de Raguidel* (Halle, Niemeyer, 1909).

Frye, Northrop (1957). *Anatomy of Criticism* (Princeton, NJ, Princeton University Press, 1957).

Furnivall, Frederick J. (ed.) (1890). *Captain Cox, his Ballads and Books* (Hertford, Ballad Society, 1890).

Ganz, Paul (1950). *The Paintings of Hans Holbein* (London, Phaidon Press, 1950).

Gates, Robert J. (ed.) (1969). *The Awntyrs off Arthure at the Terne Wathelyne*, Haney Foundation Series 5 (Philadelphia, University of Pennsylvania Press, 1969).

Giles, J. A. (ed.) (1864–5). *The Whole Works of Roger Ascham*, Library of Old Authors, 3 vols. in 4 (London, J. R. Smith, 1864–5).

Ginn, Rosemary K. (1967). 'A critical edition of the two texts of *Sir Cleges*' (Queen's University, Belfast, thesis, 1967).

Girvan, Ritchie (ed.) (1939). *Ratis Raving*, STS, 3rd ser. 11 (Edinburgh, Blackwood, 1939).

Glanville, Lucia (ed.) (1958). 'A new edition of the Middle English romance *The Weddyng of Syr Gawen and Dame Ragnell*' (Univ. of Oxford B. Litt. thesis, 1958).

Gordon, E. V., and Eugène Vinaver (1937). 'New light on the text of the alliterative *Morte Arthure*', *Medium Ævum*, 6 (1937), 81–98.

Gowans, Linda (1988). *Cei and the Arthurian Legend*, Arthurian Studies 18 (Cambridge, D. S. Brewer, 1988).

Graves, Robert (1955). *The Greek Myths*, 2 vols. (Harmondsworth, Penguin, 1955).

Grazebrook, G., and J. P. Rylands (eds.) (1889). *The Visitation of Shropshire*, Harleian Society 28 (London, Harleian Society, 1889).

Greene, Richard Leighton (ed.) (1977). *The Early English Carols*, 2nd edn. (Oxford, Clarendon Press, 1977).

Griffith, J. E. (1914). *Pedigrees of Anglesey and Carnarvonshire Families* (Horncastle, for the author, 1914).

Griffiths, J. J. (1982). 'A re-examination of Oxford, Bodleian Library, MS

Rawlinson C.86', *Archiv für das Studium der neueren Sprachen und Literaturen*, 219 (1982), 381–8.

Griffiths, Jeremy, and Derek Pearsall (eds.) (1989). *Book Production and Publishing in Britain 1375–1475* (Cambridge, Cambridge University Press, 1989).

Grosart, A. B. (ed.) (1878). *Vertue's Commonwealth by Henry Crosse (1603)* (Manchester, Charles E. Simons, 1878).

Gruffydd, W. J. (1928). *Math vab Mathonwy* (Cardiff, University of Wales Press, 1928).

Guddat-Figge, Gisela (1976). *Catalogue of Manuscripts containing Middle English Romances* (Munich, Wilhelm Fink, 1976).

Gullick, Michael (introd.) (1979). *The Art of Limming: A Reproduction of the 1573 Edition* (London, The Society of Scribes and Illuminators, 1979).

Gunn, S. J., and P. G. Lindley (eds.) (1991). *Cardinal Wolsey: Church, State and Art* (Cambridge, Cambridge University Press, 1991).

Hales, J. W., and F. J. Furnivall (eds.) (1867–8). *Bishop Percy's Folio Manuscript: Ballads and Romances*, 4 vols. (London, Trübner, 1867–8).

Halliwell, J. O. (1855). *Early English Miscellanies*, Warton Club (London, for the Warton Club, 1855).

Hamel, Mary (ed.) (1984). *Morte Arthure*, Garland Medieval Texts 9 (New York, Garland, 1984).

Hamilton, A. C. (1982). 'Elizabethan romance: the example of prose fiction', *English Literary History*, 49 (1982), 287–99.

Hanmer, Meredith (1576). *The Avncient Ecclesiasticall Histories of the First Six Hundred Yeares after Christ ...* (1576; London, T. Marsh, 1585 [*STC* 10573]).

Hanna, Ralph, III (ed.) (1974). The *Awntyrs off Arthure at the Terne Wathelyn*, Old and Middle English Texts (Manchester, Manchester University Press, 1974).

Harlech, Lord (1947–8). 'The Brogyntyn library of printed books', *National Library of Wales Journal*, 5 (1947–8), 165–74.

Heffernan, Carol Falvo (ed.) (1976). *Le Bone Florence of Rome*, Old and Middle English Texts (Manchester, Manchester University Press, 1976).

Helgerson, R. (1976). *The Elizabethan Prodigals* (Berkeley, University of California Press, 1976).

Helm, Alex (1980). The *English Mummers' Play* (Cambridge, D. S. Brewer; Totowa, NJ, Rowman and Littlefield; for the Folklore Society, 1980).

Herbert, J. A. (1910). *Catalogue of Romances in the Department of Manuscripts in the British Museum*, Vol. III (London, British Museum, 1910).

Herman, J., and L. Hirschman (1977). 'Father–daughter incest', *Signs*, 2

(1977), 735-56.

Herrtage, Sidney J. H. (ed.) (1879). *The Early English Version of the 'Gesta Romanorum'*, EETS, ES 33 (London, Oxford University Press for the EETS, 1879).

Hill, D. M. (1961). 'The structure of "Sir Orfeo"', *Mediaeval Studies*, 23 (1961), 136-53.

Hodnett, Edward (1973). *English Woodcuts 1480-1535* (Oxford, Oxford University Press, 1973).

Hoepffner, E. (1933). 'Pour la chronologie des lais de Marie de France', *Romania*, 59 (1933), 353-6.

Hope, W. H. St John (1906). *The Obituary Roll of John Islip, Abbot of Westminster, 1500-1532*, Vetusta Monumenta 7:4 (London, Society of Antiquaries, 1906).

Horney, Karen (1973). 'The problem of feminine masochism', in Jean Miller (ed.), *Psychoanalysis and Women* (Harmondsworth, Penguin, 1973).

Hülsmann, Friedrich (1985). 'The watermarks of four late medieval manuscripts containing *The Erle of Tolous*', *Notes and Queries*, n.s. 32 (1985), 11-12.

Huws, Daniel (1991). 'Llyfr Gwyn Rhydderch', *Cambridge Medieval Celtic Studies*, 21 (1991), 1-37.

—— (1992). *Llyfrau Cymraeg 1250-1400* (Aberystwyth, National Library of Wales, 1992).

Hyrde, Richard (1529?). *A Very Fruteful and Pleasant boke callyd the Instruction of a Christen woman ... tourned into Englysshe* (1529?; London, T. Berth[eleti], 1541 [*STC* 24858]).

Jackson, W. A., F. S. Ferguson and K. A. Pantzer (eds.) (1976-91). *A Short-Title Catalogue of Books printed in England, Scotland, & Ireland, and of English Books printed Abroad, 1475-1640*, rev. edn., 3 vols. (London, The Bibliographical Society, 1976-91).

Jenkinson, Hilary (1927). *The Later Court Hands in England: From the Fifteenth to the Seventeenth Century*, 2 vols. (Cambridge, Cambridge University Press, 1927).

Johnson, Charles, and Hilary Jenkinson (1915). *English Court Hand A.D. 1066 to 1500*, 2 vols. (Oxford, Clarendon Press, 1915).

Johnston, Arthur (1964). *Enchanted Ground: The Study of Medieval Romance in the Eighteenth Century* (London, Athlone Press, 1964).

Jusserand, J. J. (1890). *The English Novel in the Time of Shakespeare* (London, T. Fisher Unwin, 1890).

Kelly, Douglas (1985). 'Romance and the vanity of Chrétien de Troyes', in Kevin Brownlee and Marina S. Brownlee (eds.), *Romance: Generic Transformations from Chrétien de Troyes to Cervantes* (Hanover and London, University of New England Press, 1985), 74-90.

Kelly, Thomas E. (1974). *Le Haut Livre du Graal: Perlesvaus. A Structural Study* (Geneva, Droz, 1974).
Kennedy, Elspeth (ed.) (1980). *Lancelot do Lac: The Non-Cyclic Old French Prose Romance*, 2 vols. (Oxford, Clarendon Press, 1980).
—— (1986). *Lancelot and the Grail: A Study of the Prose 'Lancelot'* (Oxford, Clarendon Press, 1986).
Ker, N. R. (1969-92). *Medieval Manuscripts in British Libraries*, 4 vols. (Oxford, 1969-92).
Kestenberg, J. (1975). *Children and Parents: Psychoanalytic Studies in Development* (New York, Aronson, 1975).
Kittredge, George Lyman (1889). 'Launfal (Rawlinson version)', *American Journal of Philology*, 10 (1889), 1-33.
Kren, Thomas (ed.) (1983). *Renaissance Painting in Manuscripts: Treasures from the British Library* (New York and London, Hudson Hills Press and J. Paul Getty Museum in association with the British Library, 1983).
Kurath, Hans, Sherman M. Kuhn et al. (eds.) (1952-). *A Middle English Dictionary* (Ann Arbor, University of Michigan Press, 1952-).
Kurvinen, Auvo (ed.) (1951). *Sir Gawain and the Carl of Carlisle in Two Versions,* Series B, 71 Pt. 2 (Helsinki, Suomalaisen Tiedeakatemian Toimituksia Annales Academiae Scientiarum Fennicae, 1951).
—— (1953). 'MS Porkington 10: description with extracts', *Neuphilologische Mitteilungen,* 54 (1953), 33-67.
—— (ed.) (1969). *The Siege of Jerusalem in Prose*, Mémoires de la Société Néophilologique de Helsinki 34 (Helsinki, Société Néophilologique, 1969).
Lacy, Norris J. (ed.) (1993). *Lancelot-Grail: The Old French Arthurian Vulgate and Post-Vulgate in Translation*, Vols. I and II (New York, Garland, 1993).
Lang, Andrew (ed.) (1905). *The Red Romance Book* (London [etc.], Longmans, Green, 1905).
Lawton, David (1989). 'The diversity of Middle English poetry', *Leeds Studies in English*, n.s. 20 (1989), 145-53.
Lawton, Lesley (1983), 'The illustration of late medieval secular texts, with special reference to Lydgate's "Troy Book"', in Derek Pearsall (ed.), *Manuscripts and Readers in Fifteenth-Century England* (Cambridge, D. S. Brewer, 1983), 41-69.
Leach, MacEdward (ed.) (1957). *Paris and Vienne*, EETS, OS 234 (London, Oxford University Press for the EETS, 1957).
Leitzmann, Albert (ed.) (1965). *Wolfram von Eschenbach*: *'Parzival'*, Altdeutsche Textbibliotek 13 (Tübingen, Niemeyer, 1965).
Lerer, Seth (1985). 'Artifice and artistry in *Sir Orfeo'*, *Speculum*, 60 (1985), 92-109.

Lewis, C. S. (1954). *English Literature in the Sixteenth Century excluding Drama*, Oxford History of English Literature 3 (Oxford, Clarendon Press, 1954).
Lloyd-Morgan, Ceridwen (1978). 'A study of *Y Seint Greal* in relation to *La Queste del Saint Graal* and *Perlesvaus*' (Univ. of Oxford D. Phil. thesis, 1978).
—— (1981). 'Narrative structure in *Peredur*', *Zeitschrift für celtische Philologie*, 38 (1981), 187-231.
—— (1991). '*Breuddwyd Rhonabwy* and later Arthurian literature', in Rachel Bromwich, A. O. H. Jarman and Brynley F. Roberts (eds.), *The Arthur of the Welsh* (Cardiff, University of Wales Press, 1991), 183-208.
—— (1994). 'Lancelot in Wales', in Karen Pratt (ed.), *Shifts and Transpositions in Medieval Narrative: A Festschrift for Dr Elspeth Kennedy* (Cambridge, D. S. Brewer, 1994), 169-79.
Llwyd, Angharad (1828). 'Catalogue of Welsh manuscripts, etc., in North Wales', *Transactions of the Honourable Society of Cymmrodorion*, 2 (1828), 36-58.
Longsworth, Robert M. (1982). 'Sir Orfeo, the minstrel, and the minstrel's art', *Studies in Philology*, 79 (1982), 1-11.
Loomis, C. Grant (1938-9). 'Two miracles in *The Chevelere Assigne*', *Englische Studien*, 73 (1938-9), 331-3.
Loomis, Laura Hibbard (1941). 'Chaucer and the Breton lays of the Auchinleck Manuscript', *Studies in Philology*, 38 (1941), 14-33.
Lot, Ferdinand (1918). *Etude sur le Lancelot en prose* (Paris, Champion, 1918).
Louis, Kenneth R. R. Gros (1967). 'The significance of Sir Orfeo's self-exile', *Review of English Studies*, n.s. 18 (1967), 245-52.
Lovecy, Ian (1991). '*Historia Peredur ab Efrawg*', in Rachel Bromwich, A. O. H. Jarman and Brynley F. Roberts (eds.), *The Arthur of the Welsh* (Cardiff, University of Wales Press, 1991), 171-82.
Macaulay, G. C. (ed.) (1900-1). *The English Works of John Gower*, 2 vols., EETS, ES 81-2 (London, Oxford University Press for the EETS, 1900-1).
MacDonald, Robert H. (ed. and introd.) (1971). *The Library of Drummond of Hawthornden* (Edinburgh, Edinburgh University Press, 1971).
Mackerness, E. D. (1946). 'Margaret Tyler: an Elizabethan feminist', *Notes and Queries*, 190 (1946), 112-23.
McKerrow, R. B. (ed.) (1958). *The Works of Thomas Nashe*, 2nd edn., rev. F. P. Wilson, 5 vols. (Oxford, Blackwell, 1958).
McSparran, Frances (ed.) (1979). *Octovian Imperator*, Middle English Texts 11 (Heidelberg, Carl Winter, 1979).
McSparran, Frances, and P. R. Robinson (introd.) (1979). *Cambridge University Library MS Ff.2.38* (London, Scolar Press, 1979).

Madan, Falconer (1885). 'The day-book of John Dorne, bookseller in Oxford, A.D. 1520', *Collectanea*, 1 (1885), 73–177.
—— (1890). 'Supplementary notes', *Collectanea*, 2 (1890), 454–78.
Madden, Sir Frederic (ed.) (1839). *Syr Gawayne: A Collection of Ancient Romance Poems* ..., Bannatyne Club 61 (1839; repr. New York, AMS Press, 1971).
Manuscripts at Porkington (1837). *Manuscripts at Porkington, the Seat of William Ormsby Gore Esq.* ([Middle Hill], [Middle Hill Press], 1837).
Marchalonis, Shirley A. (1980–1). 'Above rubies: popular views of medieval women', *Journal of Popular Culture*, 14 (1980–1), 87–93.
Margolies, David (1985). *Novel and Society in Elizabethan England* (London, Croom Helm, 1985).
Martin, H. J. (1969). *Livre, pouvoir, et société à Paris au XVIIe siècle*, 2 vols. (Geneva, Droz, 1969).
Martin, Judith E. (1968). 'Studies in some early Middle English romances' (Univ. of Cambridge Ph.D. thesis, 1968).
Matthews, William (1960). *The Tragedy of Arthur: A Study of the Alliterative 'Morte Arthure'* (Berkeley, University of California Press, 1960).
Meale, Carol M. (1991). 'The Morgan Library copy of *Generides*', in Maldwyn Mills, Jennifer Fellows and Carol M. Meale (eds.), *Romance in Medieval England* (Cambridge, D. S. Brewer, 1991), 89–104.
—— (1992). 'Caxton, de Worde, and the publication of romance in late medieval England', *The Library*, 6th ser. 14 (1992), 283–98.
—— (1994). '"gode men / Wiues maydnes and alle men": romance and its audiences', in Carol M. Meale (ed.), *Readings in Medieval English Romance* (Cambridge, D. S. Brewer, 1994), 209–25.
Mearns, Rodney (ed.) (1985). *The Vision of Tundale*, Middle English Texts 18 (Heidelberg, Carl Winter, 1985).
Medary, Margaret P. (1916). 'Stanza-linking in Middle English verse', *Romanic Review*, 7 (1916), 243–70.
Mehl, Dieter (1968). *The Middle English Romances of the Thirteenth and Fourteenth Centuries* (London, Routledge and Kegan Paul, 1968).
Meres, Francis (1598). *Palladis Tamia ... Being the Second Part of Wits Commonwealth* (London, P. Short for C. Burbie, 1598 [*STC* 17834]).
Merkelbach, Reinhold (1954). *Die Quellen des griechischen Alexanderromans* (Munich, C. H. Beck'sche Verlagsbuchhandlung, 1954).
Micha, Alexandre (ed.) (1978). *Cligés*, Les romans de Chrétien de Troyes 2, CFMA 84 (Paris, Champion, 1978).
Mills, Maldwyn (ed.) (1969). *Lybeaus Descunus*, EETS, OS 261 (London, Oxford University Press for the EETS, 1969).
—— (ed.) (1973). *Six Middle English Romances*, Everyman's University Library (London, Dent; Totowa, NJ, Rowman and Littlefield, 1973).

— (ed.) (1988). *Horn Childe and Maiden Rimnild*, Middle English Texts 20 (Heidelberg, Carl Winter, 1988).

— (ed.) (1992). *Ywain and Gawain, Sir Percyvell of Gales, The Anturs of Arther*, Everyman's Library (London, Dent; Rutland, Vt, Charles E. Tuttle, 1992).

— (1994a). 'The illustrations of British Library MS Egerton 3123A and Bodleian Library MS Douce 261', in Tegwyn Jones and E. B. Fryde (eds.), *Essays and Poems presented to Daniel Huws* (Aberystwyth, National Library of Wales, 1994), 307–27.

— (1994b). '*Sir Isumbras* and the styles of the tail-rhyme romance', in Carol M. Meale (ed.), *Readings in Medieval English Romance* (Cambridge, D. S. Brewer, 1994), 1–24.

Moi, Toril (1988). *Sexual/Textual Politics* (London, Routledge, 1988).

Morris-Jones, J., and J. Rhŷs (eds.) (1894). *Llyvyr Aglcyr Llandewivrevi* (Oxford, Clarendon Press, 1894).

Mosher, J. A. (1911). *The Exemplum in the Early Religious and Didactic Literature of England* (New York, Columbia University Press, 1911).

Musgrove, Frank (1990). *The North of England: A History from Roman Times to the Present* (Oxford, Blackwell, 1990).

Nelson, Jan A. (ed.) (1977). *La Naissance du Chevalier au Cygne*, introd. Geoffrey M. Myers, The Old French Crusade Cycle 1 (University Park, University of Alabama Press, 1977).

Nicolas, N. H. (ed.) (1834). *Proceedings and Ordinances of Privy Council*, Vol. III (London, Record Commission, 1834).

Nitze, William A., and T. Atkinson Jenkins (eds.) (1972). *Le Haut Livre du Graal: Perlesvaus*, 2 vols. (New York, Phaeton Press, 1972).

Norris, Malcolm (1977). *Monumental Brasses: The Craft* (London and Boston, Faber and Faber, 1977).

O'Connor, John J. (1970). *Amadis de Gaule and its Influence on Elizabethan Literature* (New Brunswick, NJ, Rutgers University Press, 1970).

Oesterley, Hermann (ed.) (1872). *Gesta Romanorum* (Berlin, Weidmannsche Buchhandlung, 1872).

Ogilvie-Thomson, S. J. (ed.) (1988). *Richard Rolle: Prose and Verse from MS Longleat 29 and related Manuscripts,* EETS 293 (London, Oxford University Press for the EETS, 1988).

O'Loughlin, J. L. N. (1959). 'The English alliterative romances', in R. S. Loomis (ed.), *Arthurian Literature in the Middle Ages* (Oxford, Clarendon Press, 1959), 520–7.

Owen, D. D. R. (tr.) (1987). *Chrétien de Troyes: Arthurian Romances*, Everyman's Library (London and Melbourne, Dent, 1987).

Owen, Lewis J. (1971). 'The recognition scene in *Sir Orfeo*', *Medium Ævum*, 40 (1971), 249–53.

Pächt, Otto (1953-4). *Flemish Manuscripts at Burlington House* (London, for the Royal Academy, 1953-4).
Paget, Hugh (1959). 'Gerard and Lucas Hornebolt in England', *Burlington Magazine*, 101 (1959), 396-402.
Paris, Gaston, and Jacob Ulrich (eds.) (1886). *Merlin: Roman en prose du XIIIe siècle*, 2 vols., SATF (Paris, Firmin-Didot, 1886).
Parker, K. T. (1938). *Catalogue of the Collection of Drawings in the Ashmolean Museum*, Vol. I (Oxford, Clarendon Press, 1938).
—— (1945). *The Drawings of Hans Holbein at Windsor Castle* (Oxford and London, Phaidon Press, 1945).
Parker, William Riley (1968). *Milton: A Biography*, 2 vols. (Oxford, Clarendon Press, 1968).
Parry, Robert (1915). 'Robert Parry's diary', ed. anonymously, *Archaeologia Cambrensis*, 6th ser. 15 (1915), 109-39.
Parry, Thomas (ed.) (1979). *Gwaith Dafydd ap Gwilym*, 3rd edn. (Cardiff, University of Wales Press, 1979).
Patch, Howard Rollin (1950). *The Other World according to Descriptions in Medieval Literature* (Cambridge, Mass., Harvard University Press, 1950).
Patchell, M. (1947). *The Palmerin Romances in Elizabethan Fiction* (New York, New York University Press, 1947).
Pearsall, Derek (1977). *Old English and Middle English Poetry*, The Routledge History of English Poetry 1 (London, Henley and Boston, Routledge and Kegan Paul, 1977).
—— (1981). 'The origins of the Alliterative Revival', in Bernard S. Levy and Paul E. Szarmach (eds.), *The Alliterative Tradition in the Fourteenth Century* (Kent, Ohio, Kent State University Press, 1981), 1-24.
Penguin Freud Library, The, Vol. XIV (London, Penguin, 1985).
Perkins, William (1590). *The Fovndation of Christian Religion* (1590; Cambridge, [J. Orwin] for J. Porter and J. L[egat], 1595 [*STC* 19711]).
Phillips, Helen (ed.) (1988). *The Awntyrs off Arthure at the Terne Wathelyne: A Modern Spelling Edition* (Lancaster, University of Lancaster Department of English, 1988).
—— (1989). 'The ghost's baptism in *The Awntyrs off Arthure*', *Medium Ævum*, 58 (1989), 48-58.
—— (1993). '*The Awntyrs off Arthure*: structure and meaning. A reassessment', *Arthurian Literature*, 12 (1993), 63-88.
Piccard, G. (1966). *Die Wasserzeichenkartei Piccard im Hauptstaatsarchiv Stuttgart: die Ochsenkopfwasserzeichen* (Stuttgart, W. Kolhammer, 1966).
Pickford, Cedric E. (1959). *L'Evolution du roman arthurien en prose vers la fin du moyen âge* (Paris, Nizet, 1959).
—— (ed.) (1978). *L'Hystoire du Sainct Greaal 1516* (London, Scolar Press, 1978).

Plomer, H. R. (1909). 'Two lawsuits of Richard Pynson', *The Library*, n.s. 37 Vol. 10 (1909), 115-33.
Pratt, Karen (ed.), *Shifts and Transpositions in Medieval Narrative: A Festschrift for Dr Elspeth Kennedy* (Cambridge, D. S. Brewer, 1994).
Rance, Adrian B. (1986). 'The Bevis and Ascupart panels, Bargate Museum, Southampton', *Proceedings of the Hampshire Field Club and Archaeological Society*, 42 (1986), 147-53.
Record Commission (1814-18). *Rotuli Scotiae*, 2 vols. (Edinburgh, Record Commission, 1814-18).
Reiss, Edmund (1985). 'Romance', in Thomas J. Heffernan (ed.), *The Popular Literature of Medieval England* (Knoxville, University of Tennessee Press, 1985).
Rice, Joanne A. (1987). *Middle English Romance: An Annotated Bibliography, 1955-1985* (New York and London, Garland, 1987).
Richards, Melville (ed.) (1990). *Cyfreithiau Hywel Dda yn ôl Llawysgrif Coleg yr Iesu LVII Rhydychen* (Cardiff, University of Wales Press, 1990).
Rigg, A. G. (1968). *A Glastonbury Miscellany of the Fifteenth Century* (London, Oxford University Press, 1968).
Robbins, Rossell Hope (ed.) (1952). *Secular Lyrics of the XIVth and XVth Centuries* (Oxford, Clarendon Press, 1952).
Robbins, Rossell Hope, and John L. Cutler (1965). *Supplement to the Index of Middle English Verse* (Lexington, University of Kentucky Press, 1965).
Roberts, B. F. (1971-2). 'Llythyrau John Lloyd at Edward Lhuyd', *National Library of Wales Journal*, 17 (1971-2), 88-104, 183-206.
Robertson, William (1908). *Ayrshire: Its History and Historic Families*, 2 vols. (Kilmarnock, Dunlop and Drennan; Ayr, Stephen and Pollock, 1908).
Rogers, Gillian (1991). 'The Percy Folio manuscripts revisited', in Maldwyn Mills, Jennifer Fellows and Carol M. Meale (eds.), *Romance in Medieval England* (Cambridge, D. S. Brewer, 1991), 39-64.
Rollins, H. E. (ed.) (1929-32). *The Pepys Ballads*, 8 vols. (Cambridge, Mass., Harvard University Press, 1929-32).
Roques, Mario (ed.) (1948-72). *Le Roman de Renart*, CFMA, 7 vols. (Paris, Champion, 1948-72).
—— (ed.) (1955). *Erec et Enide*, CFMA (Paris, Champion, 1955).
Rosenstein, Roy (1993). 'D'Eden à Armageddon, ou La pomme et le serpent: Sir Thomas Malory, *laudator temporis acti*', in *Fin des temps et temps de la fin dans l'univers médiéval* (Aix en Provence, Publications de CUER MA, 1993), 459-74.
Rowlands, John, with the assistance of Giulia Bartrum (1988). *The Age of Dürer and Holbein: German Drawings 1400-1550* (London, British Museum, 1988).

Royal Commission on Historical Manuscripts (1871). *Second Report* (London, HMSO, 1871).
Ryan, William (tr.) (1993). *Jacobus de Voragine: The Golden Legend*, 2 vols. (Princeton, NJ, Princeton University Press, 1993).
Rylands, J. P. (ed.) (1882). *The Visitation of Cheshire*, Harleian Society 18 (London, Harleian Society, 1882).
Rymer, Thomas (ed.) (1739-45). *Fœdera, conventiones, literæ* ..., 10 vols. (1739-45; repr. Farnborough, Gregg Press, 1967-).
Sajavaara, Kari (ed.) (1967). *The Middle English Translations of Robert Grosseteste's 'Château d'Amour'*, Mémoires de la Société Néophilologique de Helsinki 32 (Helskini, Société Néophilologique, 1967).
Salzman, Paul (1985). *English Prose Fiction 1558-1700: A Critical History* (Oxford, Clarendon Press, 1985).
Sandred, Karl Inge (ed.) (1971). *A Middle English Version of the 'Gesta Romanorum'*, Acta Universitatis Upsaliensis: Studia Anglistica Upsaliensia 8 (Uppsala, Almqvist & Wiksell, 1971).
Sands, Donald B. (ed.) (1966). *Middle English Verse Romances* (New York [etc.], Holt, Rinehart and Winston, 1966).
Schlauch, Margaret (1941). 'The Man of Law's Tale', in W. F. Bryan and Germaine Dempster (eds.), *Sources and Analogues of Chaucer's 'Canterbury Tales'* (Chicago, Ill., University of Chicago Press, 1941), 155-206.
—— (1963). *Antecedents of the English Novel* (London, Oxford University Press, 1963).
Schofield, William Henry (1900). 'The lays of *Graelent* and *Lanval*, and the story of Wayland', *PMLA*, 15 (1900), 121-80.
Scott, Kathleen L. (1976). *The Caxton Master and his Patrons*, Cambridge Bibliographical Society Monographs 8 (Cambridge, Cambridge Bibliographical Society, 1976).
—— (introd.) (1980). *The Mirroure of the Worlde – MS Bodley 283 (England c. 1470-1480)* (Oxford, for the Roxburghe Club, 1980).
Serjeantson, M. S. (ed.) (1938). *Osbern Bokenham: Legendys of Hooly Wummon*, EETS, OS 206 (Oxford, Oxford University Press for the EETS, 1938).
Severs, J. Burke (ed.) (1967). *A Manual of the Writings in Middle English, 1050-1500*, Fasc. I (New Haven, Conn., The Connecticut Academy of Arts and Sciences, 1967).
Seymour, M. C. (1974). 'The manuscripts of Hoccleve's *Regiment of Princes*', *Edinburgh Bibliographical Society Transactions*, 4 Pt. 7 (1974), 253-97.
—— (1980). 'MSS. Douce 261 and Egerton 3132A and Edward Banyster', *Bodleian Library Record*, 10 (1980), 162-5.
Shepherd, Geoffrey (ed.) (1965). *Sir Philip Sidney: 'An Apology for*

Poetry', Old and Middle English Texts (1965; repr. Manchester, Manchester University Press, 1977).

Shepherd, Stephen H. A. (ed.) (1995). *Middle English Romances*, A Norton Critical Edition (New York and London, W. W. Norton, 1995).

Shoji, Kuniko (1993). 'The failed hero: Mordred, Gawain's brother', *Poetica* (Tokyo), 37 (1993), 53-63.

Shoukri, Doris Enright-Clark (ed.) (1974). *Liber apologeticus de omni statu humanae naturae* ... *A Moral Play by Thomas Chaundler* (London and New York, Modern Humanities Research Association and the Renaissance Society of America, 1974).

Simons, John (1982). 'Medieval chivalric romance and Elizabethan popular literature' (Univ. of Exeter Ph.D. thesis, 1982).

—— (1983). *Realistic Romance: The Prose Fiction of Thomas Deloney*, Contexts and Connections 12 (Winchester, King Alfred's College, 1983).

—— (1988). 'Open and closed books: a semiotic approach to the history of Elizabethan and Jacobean popular romance', in C. Bloom (ed.), *Jacobean Poetry and Prose* (London, Macmillan, 1988), 8-24.

Sisam, Kenneth (ed.) (1921). *Fourteenth Century Verse and Prose* (Oxford, Clarendon Press, 1921).

Smith, J. C. C. (ed.) (1893-5). *Index of Wills proved in the Prerogative Court of Canterbury 1383-1588*, 2 vols., British Record Society, Index Library 10-11 (London, British Record Society, 1893-5).

Spearing, A. C. (1970). *The Gawain-Poet* (Cambridge, Cambridge University Press, 1970).

—— (1982). 'Central and displaced sovereignty in three medieval poems', *Review of English Studies*, n.s. 33 (1982), 247-61.

——(1987). *Readings in Medieval Poetry* (Cambridge, Cambridge University Press, 1987).

——*(1993). The Medieval Poet as Voyeur: Looking and Listening in Medieval Love-Narratives* (Cambridge, Cambridge University Press, 1993).

Speed, Diane (ed.) (1993). *Medieval English Romances*, 3rd edn., Durham Medieval Texts 8 (Durham, University of Durham, 1993).

—— (1994). *'Havelok* and the great code', paper read at the fourth conference on Romance in Medieval England, Winchester, April 1994.

Spencer, R., and J. Alexander (introd.) (1978). *The Brogyntyn Lute Book* (Kilkenny, Boethius Press, 1978).

Spufford, Margaret (1981). *Small Books and Pleasant Histories: Popular Fiction and its Readership in Seventeenth-Century England* (London, Methuen, 1981).

Steer, Francis W. (ed.) (1968). *Scriveners' Company Common Paper 1357-1628*, London Record Society Publications 4 (London, London Record Society, 1968).

Stephen, Sir Leslie et al. (eds.) (1885–). *The Dictionary of National Biography* (London, Smith, Elder & Co., 1885–).

Stevenson, L. C. (1984). *Praise and Paradox: Merchants and Craftsmen in Elizabethan Popular Literature* (Cambridge, Cambridge University Press, 1984).

Stimming, Albert (ed.) (1899). *Der anglonormannische Boeve de Haumtone ...,* Biblioteca Normannica 7 (Halle, Niemeyer, 1899).

Stokoe, William C., Jr (1948). 'The sources of *Sir Launfal: Lanval* and *Graelent*', *PMLA*, 63 (1948), 392–404.

Strong, Roy (1983). *Artists of the Tudor Court* (London, Victoria and Albert Museum, 1983).

Summerson, Henry (1993). *Medieval Carlisle: The City and the Borders from the Late Eleventh to the Mid-Sixteenth Century*, 2 vols., Cumberland and Westmorland Antiquarian and Archaeological Society, extra ser. 25 (Kendal, Cumberland and Westmorland Antiquarian and Archaeological Society, 1993).

Sumner, Laura (ed.) (1924). *The Weddynge of Sir Gawen and Dame Ragnell*, Smith College Studies in Modern Languages 5 No. 4 (Northampton, Mass., Smith College, 1924).

Swanson, A. B. (1934). *A Study of the 1516 and 1523 Editions of the 'Perlesvaus'* (Chicago, Ill., University of Chicago Press, 1934).

Thomas, Henry (1920). *Spanish and Portuguese Romances of Chivalry* (Cambridge, Cambridge University Press, 1920).

Thompson, John J. (1990). 'The textual background and reputation of the Vernon lyrics', in Derek Pearsall (ed.), *Studies in the Vernon Manuscript* (Cambridge, D. S. Brewer, 1990), 201–24.

—— (1991). 'Collecting Middle English romances and some related book-production activities in the later Middle Ages', in Maldwyn Mills, Jennifer Fellows and Carol M. Meale (eds.), *Romance in Medieval England* (Cambridge, D. S. Brewer, 1991), 17–38.

—— (1994). 'The *Cursor Mundi*, the "Inglis tong", and "romance"', in Carol M. Meale (ed.), *Readings in Medieval English Romance* (Cambridge, D. S. Brewer, 1994), 99–120.

Thomson, R. L. (ed.) (1968). *Owein* (Dublin, Institute of Advanced Studies, 1968).

Tiddy, R. J. E. (1923). *The Mummers' Play* (1923; repr. Chicheley, Paul P. B. Minet, 1972).

Tolkien, J. R. R., and E. V. Gordon (eds.) (1967). *Sir Gawain and the Green Knight*, rev. Norman Davis (Oxford, Clarendon Press, 1967).

Travitsky, B. (ed.) (1981). *The Paradise of Women: Writings by English Women of the Renaissance* (Westport, Conn., and London, Greenwood Press, 1981).

Ullmann, J. (1884). 'Studien zu Richard Rolle de Hampole' [including text

of *Speculum vitae*], *Englische Studien*, 7 (1884), 415–72.
Vinaver, Eugène (1971). *The Rise of Romance* (Oxford, Clarendon Press, 1971).
Vinaver, Eugène, and P. J. C. Field (eds.) (1990). *Sir Thomas Malory: The Works* (Oxford, Clarendon Press, 1990).
Voaden, Rosalynn (tr. and transcribed) (1991). *Brogyntyn Manuscript No. 8*, introd. Felicity Riddy (Moreton-in-Marsh, Porkington Press, 1991).
Vorontzoff, Tania (1937). 'Malory's story of Arthur's Roman campaign', *Medium Ævum*, 6 (1937), 99–121.
Watt, Tessa (1991). *Cheap Print and Popular Piety, 1550–1640* (Cambridge, Cambridge University Press, 1991).
Weiss, Judith (1991). 'The wooing woman in Anglo-Norman romance', in Maldwyn Mills, Jennifer Fellows and Carol M. Meale (eds.), *Romance in Medieval England* (Cambridge, D. S. Brewer, 1991), 149–61.
Wheatley, Henry B. (ed.) (1891). *Thomas Percy: Reliques of Ancient English Poetry*, 3 vols. (London, Sonneschein, 1891).
Whitelock, Dorothy (1950). 'The interpretation of The Seafarer', in C. Fox and B. Dickins (eds.), *Early Cultures of North-West Europe: H. M. Chadwick Memorial Studies* (Cambridge, Cambridge University Press, 1950), 259–72.
Whitford, Margaret (ed.) (1991). *The Irigaray Reader* (Oxford, Blackwell, 1991).
Willcock, Gladys Doidge, and Alice Walker (eds.) (1936). *George Puttenham: 'The Arte of English Poesie'* (Cambridge, Cambridge University Press, 1936; repr. 1970).
Williams, Elizabeth (1969). '*Lanval* and *Sir Landevale*: a medieval translator and his methods', *Leeds Studies in English*, n.s. 3 (1969), 85–99.
—— (1991), 'Hunting the deer: some uses of a motif-complex in Middle English romance and saint's life', in Maldwyn Mills, Jennifer Fellows and Carol M. Meale (eds.), *Romance in Medieval England* (Cambridge, D. S. Brewer, 1991), 187–206.
Williams, G. J., and E. J. Jones (eds.) (1934). *Gramadegau'r Penceirddiaid* (Cardiff, University of Wales Press, 1934).
Williams, Ifor (ed.) (1974). *Pedeir Keinc y Mabinogi* (Cardiff, University of Wales Press, 1974).
Williams, Robert (ed.) (1876). *Y Seint Greal (Selections from the Hengwrt Manuscripts)*, Vol. II (London, Thomas Richards, 1876; repr. Pwllheli, Jones, 1987).
Williams, Stephen J., and J. Enoch Powell (eds.) (1961). *Cyfreithiau Hywel Dda yn ôl Llyfr Blegywryd* (Cardiff, University of Wales Press, 1961).
Wilson, Robert H. (1934). 'Characterization in Malory: a comparison with his sources' (University of Chicago Ph.D. thesis, 1934).
—— (1950a). 'Malory's early knowledge of Arthurian romance', *University*

of Texas Studies in English, 29 (1950), 33-50.

—— (1950b). 'Malory's "French book" again', *Comparative Literature*, 2 (1950), 172-81.

Wing, Donald G. (ed.) (1948-51). *Short-Title Catalogue of Books printed in England, Scotland, Ireland, Wales, and British America and of English Books printed in Other Countries 1641-1700*, 3 vols. (New York, Columbia University Press for the Index Society, 1948-51).

Withrington, John (1987). 'The Arthurian epitaph in Malory's "Morte Darthur"', *Arthurian Literature*, 7 (1987), 103-44.

—— (ed.) (1991). *The Wedding of Sir Gawain and Dame Ragnell: A Modern Spelling Edition* (Lancaster, University of Lancaster Department of English, 1991).

Wogan-Browne, Jocelyn (1994). 'Bet ... to ... rede on holy seyntes lyves: romance and hagiography again', in Carol M. Meale (ed.), *Readings in Medieval English Romance* (Cambridge, D. S. Brewer, 1994), 83-97.

Woledge, Brian (1954-75). *Bibliographie des romans et nouvelles en prose française antérieurs à 1500*, 2 vols. (Geneva and Lille, Droz, 1954-75).

Woolf, Rosemary (1968). *The English Religious Lyric in the Middle Ages* (Oxford, Clarendon Press, 1968).

Wright, Louis B. (1935). *Middle-Class Culture in Elizabethan England* (Chapel Hill, University of North Carolina Press, 1935).

Index of manuscripts cited

Aberystwyth, National Library of Wales

Bangor Probate Records, 1682/62, 206 (n. 17); **MS 1197**, 203; **MS Brogyntyn I.8**, 188; **MS Brogyntyn I.23**, 206 (n. 12); **MS Brogyntyn I.27** (= Porkington 11), 206 (n. 13); **MS Brogyntyn II.1** (= Porkington 10), 188–207; **MS Peniarth 4–5** (the White Book of Rhydderch), 37, 38, 39; **MS Peniarth 11**, 50 (n. 25); **MS Peniarth 29** (the Black Book of Chirk), 36; **MS Peniarth 41**, 204; **MS Porkington 10** (see Brogyntyn II.1); **MS Porkington 11** (see Brogyntyn I.27).

Cambridge, Trinity College

MS R.3.2, 235 (n. 21).

Cambridge University Library

MS Add. 7071, 91 (nn. 8, 12 and 14); **MS Ff.2.38**, 172, 230, 234 (n. 2), 255, 265 (n. 27); **MS Kk.5.30**, 169 (n. 9).

Durham Cathedral Library

MS Cosin V.iii.9, 142 (n. 42).

Edinburgh, National Library of Scotland

MS Advocates' 19.2.1 (the Auchinleck MS), 52, 61 (n. 4).

Exeter Cathedral Library

MS 3529, 235 (n. 29).

Lincoln Cathedral Library

MS 91 (the Lincoln Thornton MS), 83, 84, 132, 136, 137, 140 (nn. 1, 18), 141 (nn. 33 and 36), 172, 234 (n. 2).

London, British Library

MS Add. 22283 (the Simeon MS), 220 (n. 39); **MS Add. 27879** (the Percy Folio), 110 (n. 7), 114, 116, 156, 169 (n. 9), 181; **MS Add. 29729**, 184; **MS Add. 31042** (the London Thornton MS), 172; **MS Add. 34294**, 224; **MS Add. 38117** (the Huth MS), 91 (nn. 8, 12 and 14); **MS Cotton Caligula A.ii**, 148, 156, 171-87, 214, 219 (n. 6); **MS Cotton Vespasian D.viii**, 171; **MS Cotton Vespasian D.xxi**, 171, 172-3; **MS Harley 116**, 184-6; **MS Harley 2251**, 184, 186; **MS Harley 3810**, 52, 60, 61 (n. 4); **MS Harley 6223**, 235 (n. 26); **MS Lansdowne 757**, 50 (n. 32); **MS Royal 18.B.ii**, 235 (n. 26).

London, Lambeth Palace

MS 306, 186; **MS 491**, 136, 137, 140 (nn. 1 and 18), 141 (nn. 33 and 36); **MS 853**, 185.

London, Public Record Office

Prob. 11/48, 236 (n. 36).

Manchester, Chetham's Library

MS 8009, 265 (n. 22).

Naples, Biblioteca Nazionale

MS XIII.B.29, 172.

Oxford, Balliol College

MS 354, 186.

Oxford, Bodleian Library

MS Ashmole 45, 209, 221-36; **MS Ashmole 51**, 52, 60, 61 (n. 4); **MS Ashmole 59**; 184, 186; **MS Ashmole 61**, 172, 187 (n. 3), 230, 234 (n. 2); **MS Digby 86**, 212; **MS Douce 261**, 251; **MS Douce 324**, 127, 135, 136, 137, 140 (nn. 1 and 18), 141 (nn. 33 and 36); **MS Eng. Poet. a. 1** (the Vernon MS), 220 (n. 39); **MS Jesus College 111** (the Red Book of Hergest), 37, 38, 39, 43, 49-50 (n. 25); **MS Jesus College 119** (the Book of the Anchorite of Llanddewibrefi), 38; **MS Rawlinson C.86**, 117, 127 (n. 1), 156, 186, 230.

Oxford, Christ Church

MS 101, 234 (n. 13); **MS 184**, 241.

Oxford, Magdalen College

MS Lat. 223, 234 (n. 13).

Paris, Bibliothèque Nationale

MS f. fr. 375, 40; **MS f. fr. 751**, 50 (n. 32).

Princeton, New Jersey, Princeton University Library

MS Garrett 143, 183.

Princeton, New Jersey, Robert H. Taylor Collection

Former Ireland-Blackburne MS, 129, 136, 137, 140 (nn. 1 and 18), 141 (nn. 28, 33 and 36).

General index

Ackerman, Robert W. 206-7 (nn. 4, 10, 21, 22)
Adulterous Falmouth Squire, The 213, 215
Albany, Murdac, duke of 133
Alde, John 265 (n. 20)
Alexander, Flora 110 (n. 6)
Alexander, J. 206 (n. 13)
Alexander, J. J. G. 234 (n. 9)
Alexander the Great 12, 13, 15, 22-35
Alexandre de Paris: *Roman d'Alexandre* 23, 49 (n. 19)
Allen, Dorena 62 (n. 18)
Allen, Rosamund 5 (n. 1), 13-14, 18, 140 (nn. 2, 4)
All Saints and All Souls 214
Amadis de Gaule 238, 242, 243, 246, 248, 249 (n. 7), 258
Amours, F. J. 110 (n. 1), 140-1 (nn. 5, 13, 26)
Anjou, Louis d' 137
Anne of Cleves 224
Anwyl, Lewis, of Parc 203-4
ap Dafydd, John 204
ap Gwilym, Dafydd 49 (n. 5)
ap Roberd, William 205
ap Thomas, Hugh Lewes 205
Archibald, Elizabeth 68, 75 (n. 16)
Arendt, Hannah 63 (n. 19)
Aristobulus 22, 27
Aristotle 15, 22, 24, 35 (n. 6)
Armstrong, A. M. 141 (n. 20)
Armstrong, E. C. 49 (n. 19)
Arrian (Flavius Arrianus Xenophon) 13, 22-3, 24, 25, 26, 27, 29, 30, 33
Arthur, R. G. 75 (n. 10)
Ascham, Roger 266 (n. 52)
Ashley, Robert 258
Ashmole, Elias 209

Auerbach, Erna 223, 234 (nn. 9-10)
Augustine, St (of Hippo) 28
Avowynge of King Arthur, The 14, 114
Awntyrs off Arthure, The 4, 13-15, 83, 92 (n. 20), 94, 96, 97, 98, 103, 109-10, 110-11 (nn. 5, 9, 12, 16), 114, 115, 116, 117, 121, 122, 129-42

Backhouse, Janet 234 (n. 14)
Bain, J. 140 (n. 14)
Baker, T. 264, 268 (n. 71)
Baker-Smith, Dominic 249 (n. 5)
Banyster, Edward 230
Baring-Gould, S. 266 (n. 59)
Barratt, Alexandra 220 (n. 41)
Barron, W. R. J. 12, 20 (n. 1), 35 (n. 6), 104, 111 (n. 11), 144, 152 (nn. 1, 2), 210, 213, 219-20 (nn. 6, 23, 29, 31)
Basterdfeld, Sir William 215
Baxandall, Michael 61 (n. 7)
Beatrix 153 (n. 1)
Beaufort, Joan 132, 135, 142 (n. 42)
Beaumont, Lord 131
Bede: *Historia ecclesiastica gentis Anglorum* 147, 153 (n. 8)
Bedford, John, duke of 136, 137
Bekyrton (knight) 131
Bennett, H. S. 264-5 (nn. 4-6, 37)
Bennett, J. A. W. 266 (n. 45)
Benson, Larry D. 92 (n. 20), 128 (n. 23)
Berry, Jean, duc de, 137
Bible 147, 259
  Ruth 53
  I Samuel 154 (n. 14)
Bishop, Richard 254
Black, William H. 209-10, 215, 219 (n. 13)

Black Prince 137
Blamires, Alcuin 235 (n. 31)
Blanchfield, Lynne S. 12, 18, 218–20 (nn. 1, 3, 27–8, 38), 235 (n. 26)
Bliss, A. J. 5 (n. 1), 51, 58, 61 (nn. 1, 4, 6), 62 (n. 8), 128 (n. 26), 168–9 (nn. 1, 17)
Boccaccio, Giovanni: *Genealogiae deorum* 235 (n. 29)
Bodel, Jehan 41
Boeve de Haumtone 265 (n. 26)
Boffey, Julia 169 (n. 9), 187 (nn. 10, 15), 206 (n. 6), 219 (n. 24), 235 (n. 26)
Boitani, Piero 210, 219 (n. 18)
Bokenham, Osbern 76 (n. 25)
Bone Florence of Rome, Le 66, 72, 74–5 (n. 9)
Bosworth, A. B. 35 (n. 1)
Brasseur, Annette 49 (n. 16)
Braswell, Laurel 219 (n. 27)
Brémond, Claude 153 (n. 5)
Brereton, Georgine E. 50 (n. 36)
Breudwyt Macsen Wledig: see *Mabinogi*
Brewer, D. S. 20 (n. 2), 61 (n. 3), 210, 217, 219–20 (nn. 20, 44), 266 (n. 46)
Brewer, J. S. 235 (n. 19)
Bright, Philippa 153 (n. 6)
Briquet, C. 187 (n. 4), 202, 223
Britton, G. C. 5 (n. 1)
Brody, Alan 266 (n. 60)
Brooks, Peter 75 (n. 17)
Brown, Carleton 187 (n. 12), 189, 206 (n. 4), 249 (n. 11)
Brown, Michael 141–2 (nn. 26–7, 29, 31–2, 39)
Bryant, Nigel 111 (n. 15)
Brydges, Samuel E. 209, 219 (nn. 11–12)
Buchan, earl of 137
Bulkeley-Owen, Fanny M. C. 206 (nn. 19, 20)
Bunyan, John 261
Burgess, Glyn S. 168 (n. 4), 170 (n. 25)
Burgundy, duke of 137
Burke, P. 249 (n. 3)
Burleigh, William Cecil, Lord 233
Burrow, J. A. 153 (n. 4), 235 (n. 21)
Burton, Sir Thomas 141 (nn. 19, 37)
Bynum, Caroline Walker 75 (n. 15)

Callisthenes 22, 240
Campbell, Lorne 234–5 (nn. 10, 12, 22)
Carew, Thomas: *Coelum Britannicum* 261
Carle off Carlile, The 110 (n. 7)
Carmody, Francis J. 50 (nn. 28, 35)
Carpenter's Tools 212, 213
Cary, George 35 (nn. 2–3)
Castle of Love, The 220 (n. 39)
see also Grosseteste, Robert
Caxton, William 251, 256–7
Cerquiglini, Bernard 52, 61 (n. 5)
Cervantes, Miguel de: *Don Quixote* 243
Chambers, Sir Edmund 266 (nn. 59–60)
Charles-Edwards, Gifford 50 (n. 25)
Charles-Edwards, T. M. 50 (n. 38)
Chaucer, Geoffrey 214
  Franklin's Tale 62 (n. 15), 63 (n. 19)
  Knight's Tale 57
  Man of Law's Tale 16, 64, 91 (n. 2), 148
  Miller's Tale 91 (n. 15)
  Physician's Tale 76 (n. 25)
  Sir Thopas 258, 259
  Wife of Bath's Tale 14, 112, 114, 116, 118–20, 121, 128 (nn. 20, 23, 31), 138
Chestre, Thomas: *Sir Launfal* 17, 19, 155–70, 180–3
Chevelere Assigne 13, 15, 143–54
Child, F. J. 170 (n. 30)
Chrétien de Troyes: *Cligés* 76 (n. 24)
  Erec et Enide 95, 109, 111 (n. 8)
  Perceval 98
  see also *Perceval*
  Yvain 92 (n. 29)
Clark, Aidan 91 (n. 1)
Cleitarchus 22–3
Clifford, family of 139
Clode, C. M. 236 (nn. 36–7)
Cockburn (knight) 131
Coke, Sir Anthony 233
Coleridge, Samuel Taylor: *The Rime of the Ancient Mariner* 58
Colgrave, Bertram 153 (n. 8)
Colloque sur le roman arthurien en prose au 13ème siècle 49–50 (nn. 19, 31)
Colville, Thomas, of the Dale 131
Constans, Léopold 49 (nn. 14, 15), 170 (nn. 26, 31)
Cooper, Helen 264 (n. 2)

INDEX

Cooper, R. 250 (n. 17)
Copland, Robert: *History of Helyas, Knight of the Swanne* 154 (n. 17)
Copland, William 251–4, 266 (n. 48)
Coward, Rosalind 67, 75 (n. 13)
Crane, R. S. 249 (n. 4), 257, 264–8 (nn. 2–5, 20, 37–9, 49, 56, 66–8)
Cranstone (knight) 131
Cromwell, Ralph, Lord 19, 185–6
Cross, Tom Peete 161, 162, 169–70 (nn. 12, 15, 21, 23)
Crosse, Henry: *Vertues Common-wealth* 258–9
Cursor mundi 220 (n. 34), 266 (n. 45)

Dacre, family of 139
Dante Alighieri: *Inferno* 59
Davies, Sioned 37, 49–50 (nn. 4, 38)
Davies, W. R. 249 (n. 1)
Davis, Norman 91 (n. 15)
de la Sierra, Pedro 242
Dennis, Leah 209, 219 (nn. 8, 10)
Dering, Edward 258, 266 (nn. 49, 52)
de Sélincourt, Aubrey 35 (n. 4)
des Essarts, Herberay 242
de Vandere, Margaret 224
D'Evelyn, Charlotte 153 (n. 10), 219 (n. 19)
de Worde, Wynkyn 154 (n. 17), 230, 235 (n. 28), 251–4, 256–7, 264–5 (nn. 7, 21)
Diogenes 24
Dodsley, Robert 266 (n. 51)
Donatelli, Joseph M. P. 169 (n. 5)
Donovan, Mortimer J. 169 (nn. 6–7)
Doob, Penelope B. R. 61–2 (nn. 6, 10)
Douglas, earls of 132, 134, 139
Doyle, A. I. 140 (n. 1), 206 (n. 7), 235 (n. 21)
Drayton, Michael 257, 261
  Polyolbion 258
Drummond, William, of Hawthornden 257
Duff, E. Gordon 264 (n. 9)
Duffield, G. E. 266 (n. 48)
Duggan, Hoyt N. 35 (n. 5)
Duncan-Jones, Elsie 266 (n. 55)
Duncan of the Lennox 133
Dunlap, Rhodes 266 (n. 64)
dü Pré, Galiot 50 (n. 33)
Dürer, Albrecht 224

East, Thomas 252–3

Easting, Robert 187 (n. 1)
Echard, Sian 142 (n. 40)
Edward III (king of England) 137
Edward VI (king of England) 233
Edwards, A. S. G. 5 (n. 1)
Edwards, Mary C. 169 (n. 8)
Edwards, Philip 266 (n. 55)
Ellis, F. S. 76 (n. 25)
Ellis, George 209, 268 (n. 72)
Emaré 16–17, 64–76, 91 (n. 2), 148, 180, 183
Erle of Tolous, The 16, 65, 209, 213, 214, 221–36
Erler, Mary 235 (n. 29)
Estoires del Saint Graal, Li 45
Eustace, St, The Legend of 211–12, 217, 218, 219 (nn. 26–7)
Evans, Ivor H. 91 (n. 15)
Evans, J. Gwenogvryn 48 (n. 1), 49 (n. 12)
Evans, Murray J. 12, 208, 219 (n. 5)
Evelyn, John 249 (n. 10)
Everett, Dorothy 214, 220 (n. 37)
Ewert, Alfred 168 (n. 3)

Fellows, Jennifer 5 (n. 1), 20, 21 (n. 6), 61 (n. 5), 67, 75 (n.14), 91 (n. 2), 154 (n. 16), 234 (n. 1), 264–8 (nn. 11–12, 17, 19, 22, 25–6, 30, 36, 42, 58–9, 62, 65, 69, 72)
Fenster, Thelma 70, 75 (n. 21)
Ferrier, Janet M. 50 (n. 36)
Fetterly, Judith 66, 74 (n. 7)
Fichte, Joerg 140 (n. 2)
Field, P. J. C. 15, 91–3 (nn. 1, 9, 11, 13, 17, 19, 24, 26–9, 37–9, 41, 44–7), 112, 117, 127–8 (nn. 4–5, 21, 31, 35–6), 170 (n. 22)
Field, Rosalind 91 (nn. 1, 10)
Fisher, S. 21 (n. 4)
Fitzwilliam, William 232–4, 236 (n. 38)
Flinn, John 49 (n. 18)
Florys and Blaunchefour 152
Foister, Susan 234–5 (nn. 10, 12, 22)
Forbes (knight) 131
Forde, Emmanuel 243
Forgiving Knight, The 212
Foster, B. O. 153 (n. 8)
Foulet, Lucien 49 (n. 18)
Foulkes-Roberts, A. 249 (n. 10)
Foulon, Charles 49 (n. 16)
Frappier, Jean 92 (nn. 18, 29)
French, W. H. 75 (n. 11)

INDEX

Freshfield, Edwin 235 (n. 18)
Freud, Sigmund 62 (n. 18), 71, 76 (n. 23)
Friedman, Albert B. 128 (n. 25)
Friedman, John Block 62 (n. 9)
Friedrichs, Rhoda L. 187 (n. 14)
Friedwagner, Mathias 50 (n. 34)
Frye, Northrop 35 (n. 6), 210, 219 (n. 17)
Furnivall, F. J. 110–11 (nn. 7, 10), 169 (nn. 5, 9)
Fychan, Hywel 49–50 (n. 25), 205
Fychan, Madoc 205

Gairdner, J. 235 (n. 19)
Gamelyn 247
Ganz, Paul 234 (n. 6)
Gaskell, Elizabeth: *North and South* 75 (n. 15)
Gates, Robert J. 110 (n. 1), 127–8 (nn. 18, 27), 140 (n. 1)
Gawain poet 54, 102
  Sir Gawain and the Green Knight 4, 18, 52, 56, 58, 102, 110 (n. 7), 114, 116, 138–9, 245
Geoffrey of Monmouth: *Historia regum Britanniae* 92 (n. 25), 94, 130
George, St 261
Gereint: see *Mabinogi*
Gesta Romanorum 146–7
Gibson, Colin 266 (n. 55)
Giles, J. A. 266 (n. 52)
Gilman, John 224
Ginn, Rosemary K. 220 (n. 30)
Girvan, Ritchie 220 (n. 36)
Glanville, Lucia 127 (n. 15)
Goch, John 205
Godfrey of Bouillon 143
Golagros and Gawane 13–14, 94, 96, 98–110, 110–11 (nn. 3, 13, 16)
Golden Legend, The 76 (n. 25)
Gordon, E. V. 92 (n. 22), 110 (n. 7), 127 (n. 14)
Gowans, Linda 92 (n. 36)
Gower, John 16
  Tale of Florent 117, 128 (n. 20), 138
Graham, Sir Robert 141 (n. 32)
Gramagedau'r Penceirddiaid 38, 46
Graves, Robert 75 (n. 12)
Grazebrook, G. 207 (n. 23)
Greene, Richard Leighton 189, 206 (n. 4)
Greene, Robert 237, 243

Grene Knight, The 102
Griffith, J. E. 206 (n. 20)
Griffiths, J. J. 127 (n. 1), 235 (n. 20)
Grimm brothers 71
Grosart, A. B. 266 (n. 49)
Grosseteste, Robert: *Chasteau d'Amour* 214
  see also *Castle of Love, The*
Gruffydd, W. J. 37, 49 (n. 4)
Guddat-Figge, Gisela 187 (nn. 1, 3), 189–90, 206 (n. 5), 210, 219 (n. 15), 234–6 (nn. 2, 17, 33)
Guienne, duke of 137
Gullick, Michael 206 (n. 3)
Gunn, S. G. 234 (n. 10)
Guy of Warwick 2, 5 (n. 1), 20, 238, 245, 251, 256–7, 258, 261, 264–8 (nn. 8, 42, 66)

Hale, C. B. 75 (n. 11)
Hales, J. W. 110–11 (nn. 7, 10), 169 (nn. 5, 9)
Halley, J. E. 21 (n. 4)
Halliwell, J. O. 207 (n. 21)
Halyborton, William de 131
Hamel, Mary 92–3 (nn. 19, 27–8, 30–3, 40, 43), 111 (n. 14), 140 (n. 8), 142 (n. 41)
Hamilton, A. C. 243, 249–50 (nn. 1, 18, 23)
Hanmer, Meredith 258, 266 (n. 49)
Hanna, Ralph, III 131, 140 (nn. 1, 9), 173
Hardy, Thomas: *Far from the Madding Crowd* 53
Harlech, Lord 203, 206 (nn. 16, 19)
Harrington, Norman T. 128 (n. 25)
Haslewood, Joseph 219 (n. 11)
Hatton, family of 205–6
Havelok the Dane 4, 81, 152
Heffernan, Carol Falvo 74 (n. 9)
Helgerson, R. 249 (n. 1)
Helm, Alex 266 (nn. 60–1)
Henry IV (king of England) 131, 140 (n. 11)
Henry V (king of England) 136, 137, 142 (n. 42)
Henry VI (king of England) 133, 135
Henry VIII (king of England) 223, 224, 226
Henryson, Robert: *Morall Fabillis* 116
Herman, J. 75 (n. 19)
Herrtage, Sidney J. H. 153 (n. 6)

INDEX

Hilary, Christine Ryan 128 (n. 23)
Hill, D. M. 62 (n. 12)
Hirschman, L. 75 (n. 19)
Historia de preliis Alexandri: see Leo, archpresbyter of Naples
Hoby, Sir Thomas 233
Hoccleve, Thomas 142 (n. 42), 228
  Regement of Princes 184, 221
Hodnett, Edward 265 (n. 13)
Hoepffner, E. 162, 163, 169-70 (nn. 20, 24, 28-9, 31)
Holbein, Hans 223, 226, 236 (n. 38)
Hope, W. H. St John 234 (n. 13)
Horenbout, family of 224-6, 228
Horn Childe 1, 2, 4, 5 (n. 1), 12
Horney, Karen 66, 74 (n. 8)
Hornstein, Lillian Herlands 213
Horwood, Alfred 189, 203
Hülsmann, Friedrich 234 (n. 5)
Huws, Daniel 3, 18-19, 48 (n. 1), 49 (n. 10)
Hyrde, Richard 258, 266 (nn. 47, 50)

Incestuous Daughter, The 213
Irigaray, Luce 76 (n. 24)
Islip, John 226

James I (king of Scotland) 14, 132-4, 139, 141 (n. 32)
James II (king of Scotland) 139
Jealous Wife, The 213
Jeaste of Sir Gawain, The 230
Jenkins, T. Atkinson 49 (n. 20)
Jenkinson, Hilary 234 (n. 16)
Jerusalem Pilgrimage 215
Johnson, Charles 234 (n. 16)
Johnson, Richard: *The Seven Champions of Christendom* 248, 261, 268 (n. 72)
Johnston, Arthur 219-20 (nn. 7, 9, 35), 268 (nn. 70, 72)
John the Fearless (duke of Burgundy) 136
Jones, E. D. 206 (n. 16)
Jones, E. J. 49 (n. 9)
Jones, R. M. 49 (n. 12)
Josephus 28
Julius Valerius 23-4
Jusserand, J. J. 249 (n. 1)

Kelly, Douglas 210, 219 (n. 21)
Kelly, Thomas E. 49 (n. 21), 50 (n. 26)

Kennedy, Elspeth 50 (nn. 30, 31)
Ker, N. R. 235 (n. 29)
Kestenberg, J. 75 (n. 18)
King and Four Daughters, The 214
King Edward and the Hermit 212, 213, 215, 217-18
King Horn 91 (n. 2), 152
Kittredge, George Lyman 169 (n. 8)
Kren, Thomas 234 (n. 11)
Kurvinen, Auvo 189-90, 192-3, 202, 206-7 (nn. 4, 5, 9, 10, 21, 22)
Kynge Rycharde cuer de lyon 235 (n. 28)

Lament of a Lost Soul 213, 215
Lancelot, Prose 44-5, 47, 50 (n. 37), 82
Lang, Andrew 268 (n. 72)
Langland, William: *Piers Plowman* 55
Latini, Brunetto 46
Lawton, David 140 (n. 3)
Lawton, Lesley 234 (n. 4)
Lay Le Freine 65, 75 (n. 15)
Lazarillo de Tormes 238
Leach, MacEdward 266 (n. 50)
Leitzmann, Albert 49 (n. 13)
Le Noir, Michel 50 (n. 33)
Leo, archpresbyter of Naples: *Historia de preliis Alexandri Magni* 23, 24-5, 33, 35 (n. 3)
Lerer, Seth 62 (n. 16)
Lewin, Agathe 234 (n. 6)
Lewis, C. S. 266 (n. 52)
Lhuyd, Edward 202
Libro de Alexandre 32
Lindley, P. G. 234 (n. 10)
Lindsey, Alexander 131, 140 (n. 12)
Linguistic Atlas of Late Middle English 205
Liversidge, Michael 234 (n. 9)
Livy: *Ab urbe condita* 147, 153 (n. 8)
Lloyd-Morgan, Ceridwen 15, 49-50 (nn. 6, 12, 22-5, 37)
Lludd a Llefelys: see Mabinogi
Llwyd, Angharad 202, 11?
Loades, Elaine 268 (n. 72)
Lodge, Thomas 243
  Rosalynde 247-8
Loomis, C. Grant 153-4 (n. 11, 13)
Loomis, Laura Hibbard 63 (n. 19)
Lot, Ferdinand 44, 50 (n. 29)
Louis (dauphin) 137
Louis, Kenneth R. R. Gros 62 (n. 11)

Lovecy, Ian 49 (n. 12)
Lowry, Thomas 141 (n. 19)
Lybeaus Desconus 2, 3, 5 (n. 1), 12, 180–3, 213, 214, 218, 220 (n. 40)
Lydgate, John 193
  The Churl and the Bird 184–5
  Deus in nomine tuo 185
  Dietary 184–5, 215
  The Nightingale 179
  Ram's Horn 212
  Troy Book 221
Lyly, John 20, 237, 243, 244, 245
Lytel treatyse of . . . Marlyn, A 235 (n. 28)

Mabinogi 15, 36, 37, 38, 39, 40, 41, 42, 43
  Breudwyt Macsen Wledig 39
  Gereint 39, 43
  Lludd a Llefelys 39
  Owein 39
  Pedeir Keinc y Mabinogi 36, 37, 38, 39, 40, 41–2, 43, 47, 50 (nn. 25, 38)
  Peredur 39, 43, 49 (n. 25)
Macaulay, G. C. 128 (n. 20)
MacDonald, Robert H. 265 (n. 42)
Mackerness, E. D. 250 (n. 14)
McKerrow, R. B. 249 (n. 5), 266 (nn. 53–4)
Macqueen, John 141 (n. 28)
McSparran, Frances 187 (n. 1), 235 (n. 26)
McTurk, R. W. 5 (n. 1)
Madan, Falconer 235 (n. 25)
Madden, Sir Frederic 110 (n. 7), 188, 189, 206 (nn. 2, 4, 5, 10)
Malory, Sir Thomas: *Morte Darthur* 15, 18, 77–93, 127 (n. 1), 170 (n. 22), 251
Mar, earl of 131, 137
Marchalonis, Shirley 64, 65, 74 (nn. 2, 6)
Margaret, St, The Legend of 217
Margaret of Austria 224
Margolies, D. 249 (n. 1)
Marice, William 204
Marie de France 231
  Chevrefoil 16
  Guigemar 169 (n. 18)
  Lanval 16, 17, 156–68, 169–70 (nn. 14, 18, 20, 27)
  Milun 169 (n. 18)

Yonec 16, 169 (n. 18)
Marriage of Sir Gawaine, The 114, 116, 117, 123, 138
Marshe, Thomas 265 (n. 20)
Martin, H. J. 250 (n. 19)
Martin, Judith E. 265 (nn. 26, 33)
Martinez, Marcos 2420
Massinger, Philip: *The Picture* 260, 266 (n. 55)
Matthews, William 92 (nn. 23, 42)
Meale, Carol M. 16, 18–19, 169 (n. 9), 187 (n. 14), 219 (nn. 5, 16), 234–6 (nn. 3, 24, 26, 32, 34)
Mearns, Rodney 187 (n. 1)
Medary, Margaret P. 127 (n. 16)
Mehl, Dieter 64, 65, 74–5 (nn. 3, 5, 15), 219 (n. 23)
Melusine 235 (n. 26)
Menagier de Paris, Le 46
Meres, Francis 258, 266 (n. 49)
Merkelbach, Reinhold 35 (n. 1)
Merlin: *Prose Merlin* 81
  Suite du Merlin 78–9, 82, 84, 86, 87, 89, 90, 91 (n. 8), 95
  Vulgate *Merlin* 14, 95, 110 (n. 2)
  see also *Lytel treatyse of . . . Marlyn, A*; *Of Arthour and of Merlin*
Meyer, Paul 49 (n. 19)
Micha, Alexandre 76 (n. 24)
Middleton, Christopher: *Chinon of England* 248
Mill, Anna J. 153 (n. 10), 219 (n. 19)
Mills, Maldwyn 1–9, 11, 12, 20, 68–9, 74–5 (nn. 1, 20, 22), 91–2 (nn. 2, 20–1), 129, 140–1 (nn. 1–2, 5, 25), 153 (n. 9), 171, 186, 187 (nn. 1, 8), 188, 208, 235 (n. 27), 251, 252, 264 (n. 1)
Milton, John 257, 266 (n. 42)
Moi, Toril 65, 74 (n. 4)
More, Sir Thomas 223
Morgan (scribe) 228
Morris-Jones, J. 49 (n. 8)
Mort Artu 82, 83, 85, 88
Morte Arthur, Le (stanzaic) 82–3
Morte Arthure (alliterative) 15, 52, 82–93, 101, 102, 106–7, 109, 111 (nn. 9, 12), 130–1, 137, 138–9, 142 (n. 41)
Mosher, J. A. 153 (n. 5)
Mowbray, John 139, 142 (n. 39)
Mummers' Play 261
Munday, Anthony 242

INDEX

Musgrove, Frank 140-1 (nn. 16-17, 29)
Mynors, R. A. B. 153 (n. 8)

Nashe, Thomas 237
 Anatomie of Absurditie 249 (n. 5), 260
National Library of Wales 203, 206 (nn. 14-17)
Nearchus 22
Nelson, Jan A. 153 (n. 1)
Nesle, Perrot de 40
Neville, family of 14, 131-3, 135, 137, 138-9, 140-2 (nn. 16, 18, 19, 39)
Nicolas, N. H. 141 (n. 34)
Nitze, A. 49 (n. 20)
Northern Passion 215
Notary, Julian 252

O'Connor, John J. 249-50 (nn. 7, 21)
Octavian 148, 180-2
Oesterley, Hermann 153 (n. 6)
Of Arthour and of Merlin 235 (n. 27)
Ogilvie-Thomson, S. J. 219 (n. 14)
O'Loughlin, J. L. N. 92 (n. 22)
Onesicritus 22
On Worldly Vanity 212
Ormsby-Gore, J. R. 203
Ortuñez de Calahorra, Diego: *Espejo de Principes e Cavalleros* 242
Owein: see Mabinogi
Owen, D. D. R. 76 (n. 24), 110-11 (nn. 4, 8)
Owen, family of 203-4, 206 (n. 19)
Owen, Lewis J. 62 (n. 17)

Pächt, Otto 234 (n. 13)
Paget, Hugh 234 (nn. 10, 15)
Palmerin d'Oliva 238, 242-3, 249 (n. 7)
Palmerin of England 238, 242-3, 249 (n. 7)
Paris, Gaston 91 (nn. 8, 12, 14)
Parker, John 224
Parker, K. T. 234-6 (nn. 7, 38)
Parker, William Riley 266 (n. 42)
Parkes, M. B. 235 (n. 21)
Parr, Catherine 224
Parrot, Henry: *The Mastive* 257, 265 (n. 41)
Parry, Robert: *Moderatus* 13, 237-50
 Sinetes passions uppon his fortunes 241
Parry, Thomas 49 (n. 5)

Patch, Howard Rollin 169 (nn. 15, 17)
Patchell, M. 249 (n. 7)
Pearsall, Derek 11, 15, 16, 112, 113, 122, 127 (n. 3), 142 (n. 40), 235 (n. 20)
Pedeir Keinc y Mabinogi: see Mabinogi
Pepys Ballads 261
Perceval: First Continuation 106, 108
 Second Continuation 141 (n. 30)
 see also Chrétien de Troyes
Percy, family of 139
Percy, Henry 131
Percy, Thomas 117, 209
Peredur: see Mabinogi
Perkins, William 258, 266 (n. 49)
Perlesvaus 42, 43-4, 45, 47, 49 (n. 22), 92 (n. 38), 111 (n. 15)
Petit, Jehan 50 (n. 33)
Pettigrew of England 186
Philip II (king of Spain) 242
Philip of Burgundy 136
Phillipps, Sir Thomas 202-3, 206 (n. 12)
Phillips, Helen 140-1 (nn. 2, 7, 30)
Piccard, G. 202, 206 (n. 8)
Pickford, Cedric 43-4, 50 (nn. 27, 33)
Plomer, H. R. 264 (n. 7)
Porkington Press 188
Post-Vulgate Cycle 78-9, 88
Powell, J. Enoch 48 (n. 2)
Powell, S. 5 (n. 1)
Pownder, Thomas 234 (nn. 6, 7)
Prick of Conscience, The 18, 215
pseudo-Callisthenes 23-4, 25, 26, 27
Ptolemy 22
Puttenham, George 257
Pynson, Richard 230, 251-4

Queste del Saint Graal, La 42, 45, 88
Quintus Curtius Rufus 23, 31-2

Rance, Adrian B. 266-8 (nn. 58, 69)
Rank, Otto: *La Manekine* 70
Rate (scribe) 18, 172, 208-20
Redemane, Richard de 131, 140 (n. 11)
Reiss, Edmund 210, 219-20 (nn. 22, 35)
Resurrection 215-17
Rhŷs, J. 49 (n. 8)
Rice, Joanne A. 127 (n. 2)
Richard II (king of England) 131, 140 (n. 11)
Richards, Melville 48 (n. 2)

Richemont, Arthur de (duke of Brittany) 136-7, 141 (n. 37)
Rigg, A. G. 206 (n. 6)
Ritson, Joseph 209
Robbins, Rossell Hope 189, 206 (n. 4)
Robert III (king of Scotland) 133
Robertson, William 141 (n. 26)
Robert the Devil 230
Robinson, P. R. 235 (n. 26)
Robson, Margaret 16-17
Rogers, Gillian 13, 14, 15, 127 (n. 8), 219 (n. 5)
Rolle, Richard: *Stimulus consciencie minor* 219 (n. 12)
Rollins, H. E. 266 (n. 63)
Roman d'Alexandre: see Alexandre de Paris
Roman de Renart 15, 41-2, 43, 46, 47
Roman de Thèbes 40, 42, 47, 162
Roman de toute chevalerie: see Thomas of Kent
Roman de Troie 40
Roques, Mario 49 (n. 17), 92 (n. 29), 110-11 (nn. 4, 8)
Rosenstein, Roy 91 (n. 6)
Ross, A. S. C. 42
Rouland, David, of Anglesey 241
Rowlands, John 235 (n. 22)
Royal Commission on Historical Manuscripts 189, 203, 206 (n. 5)
Russhe, John 257
Ryan, William 91 (n. 10)
Rylands, J. P. 207 (n. 23)
Rymer, Thomas 140 (nn. 12, 15)

Sajavaara, Kari 214, 220 (n. 39)
Salusbury, Sir John 241, 249-50 (nn. 11, 12)
Salzman, Paul 238, 249 (n. 1)
Sandred, Karl Inge 153 (n. 6)
Sands, Donald B. 112-13, 122, 123, 127-8 (nn. 6-9, 28, 33), 206 (n. 4)
Scattergood, V. J. 5 (n. 1)
Schlauch, Margaret 91 (n. 2), 249 (n. 1)
Schofield, William Henry 169 (n. 12)
Scott, Kathleen L. 234-5 (nn. 8, 23)
Scott, Sir Walter 209
Seafarer, The 56
Seint Greal, Y 42-3, 50 (n. 25)
Seneca 24
Serjeantson, M. S. 76 (n. 25)

Severs, J. Burke 110 (n. 1), 169 (nn. 6, 9), 219 (n. 32), 234 (n. 1)
Seymour, M. C. 187 (n. 11), 235 (n. 27)
Shakespeare, William: *King Lear* 57, 266 (n. 44)
The Tempest 56
Shepherd, Geoffrey 265-6 (nn. 42-3)
Shepherd, Stephen H. A. 13-14, 18, 127-8 (nn. 13, 29)
Shirley, John 184
Shoji, Kuniko 91 (n. 5)
Shoukri, Doris Enright-Clark 234 (n. 8)
Shurley, John 262, 268 (n. 70)
Sidney, Sir Philip 243, 244, 245, 257-8
Arcadia 237
Siege of Jerusalem, The 173
Simons, John 13, 20, 249 (nn. 2, 6)
Sir Bevis of Hampton 12, 20, 238, 251-68
Sir Cleges 209, 213, 218, 220 (n. 42)
Sir Corneus 212, 213, 214, 218
Sir Degare 52
Sir Gawain and the Green Knight: see Gawain poet
Sir Isumbras 181, 211-12, 213, 214-15, 217, 218, 219 (nn. 26-7)
Sir Lambewell 17, 156-61, 163, 164, 165, 167, 168, 169 (nn. 14, 16)
Sir Landevale 17, 156, 158-61, 163, 164, 165, 167, 168, 169 (nn. 14, 16)
Sir Launfal: see Chestre, Thomas
Sir Orfeo 16, 17, 18, 51-63, 121, 152, 213, 217
Sir Percyvell of Gales 4
Sisam, Kenneth 58, 62 (n. 17)
Smith, J. C. C. 235 (n. 18)
Smith, M. Q. 234 (n. 6)
Smithers, G. V. 266 (n. 45)
Snodham, T. 253-4
South English Legendary, The 153 (n. 10), 180, 181, 210, 219 (n. 26)
Spearing, A. C. 61-2 (nn. 2, 8, 14, 16), 116, 127 (n. 17), 140 (n. 6), 157, 169-70 (nn. 10-11, 19, 32)
Speculum vitae 258
Speed, Diane 12, 13, 91 (n. 16), 153-4 (nn. 1, 15)
Speed, John: *Theatre of the Empire of Great Britain* 141 (n. 20)
Spencer, R. 206 (n. 13)
Spenser, Edmund 257, 261

INDEX

The Faerie Queene 258
Spufford, Margaret 268 (n. 69)
Squire of Low Degree, The 235 (n. 28), 264 (n. 6)
Steele, Richard 268 (n. 72)
Steer, Francis W. 235 (n. 18)
Stevenson, L. C. 249 (n. 6)
Stimming, Albert 265 (n. 30)
Stokoe, William C., Jr 170 (n. 27)
Stow, John 230, 235 (n. 27)
Strong, Roy 234 (n. 14)
Summerson, Henry 140–2 (nn. 10, 11, 14, 16, 18, 21, 43)
Sumner, Laura 110 (n. 1), 127 (n. 15)
Swanson, A. B. 50 (n. 33)
Swynbourne, Thomas 141 (n. 37)
Syre Gawene and the Carle of Carelyle 19, 110 (n. 7), 188, 193, 198, 205
Syr Tryamour 252, 264 (n. 9)

Tam Lin 170 (n. 30)
Thelwall: family of 249 (n. 11)
  Kathryn 241, 249–50 (nn. 10–11)
Thomas, D. R. 203
Thomas, H. 249 (n. 7)
Thomas of Kent: *Roman de toute chevalerie* 23–4, 32
Thompson, John J. 18–19, 187 (nn. 9, 10), 206 (n. 6), 219–20 (nn. 5, 16, 24, 34)
Thomson, R. L. 49 (n. 11)
Thornton, Robert 172
Tiddy, R. J. E. 266 (n. 60)
Tolkien, J. R. R. 110 (n. 7), 127 (n. 14)
Tomkis, Thomas: *Lingua* 260
Torent of Portyngale 252
Townshend, Henry 241
Travitsky, B. 250 (n. 14)
Trentals of Gregory 138
Tristan: *Folie Tristan* 16
  Prose Tristan 88
Turke and Gowin, The 110 (n. 7)
Turville-Petre, Thorlac 35 (n. 5)
Tydeman, W. M. 91 (n. 1)
Tyler, Margaret 242, 250 (n. 14)
Tyndale, William: *The Obedience of a Christian man* 258–9, 266 (n. 48)
Tysdale, John 265 (n. 20)

Ullmann, J. 266 (n. 45)
Ulrich, Jacob 91 (nn. 8, 12, 14)

Vengeance Raguidel, La 46

Vinaver, Eugène 15, 21 (n. 3), 82, 85, 91–3 (nn. 1, 9, 11, 17, 19, 22, 24, 26–8, 38–9, 41, 44–6), 128 (n. 36), 170 (n. 22)
Vives, Juan: *De institutione feminae Christianae* 258, 259
Voaden, Rosalynn 206 (n. 1)
Vorontzoff, Tania 92 (n. 22)
Vulgate Cycle 46, 81, 82, 88, 95
  see also Merlin

Wace 169 (n. 20)
Waddington, Richard 233, 236 (n. 36)
Walker, Alice 265 (n. 40)
Walsingham, Sir Francis 204
Wars of Alexander, The 22–35
Warton, Thomas 209
Watt, Tessa 249 (n. 5), 265–8 (nn. 40–1, 69)
Weddynge of Sir Gawen and Dame Ragnell, The 13–14, 18, 94, 96, 97, 112–28, 138
Weiss, Judith 168 (n. 2), 265 (n. 34)
Westmorland, earl of 131, 135
Wheatley, Henry B. 127 (n. 19)
White, T. H.: *The Once and Future King* 76 (n. 24)
Whitelock, Dorothy 62 (n. 13)
Whitford, Margaret 76 (n. 24)
Willcock, Gladys Doidge 265 (n. 40)
William, Robert 204
William of Malmesbury: *Gesta regum Anglorum* 94, 110 (n. 5)
Williams, D. J. 5 (n. 1)
Williams, Elizabeth 16, 144, 153–4 (nn. 3, 12), 169 (n. 13)
Williams, G. J. 49 (n. 9)
Williams, Ifor 49 (nn. 3, 7, 25)
Williams, John 204
Williams, Robert 49 (nn. 22, 25)
Williams, Stephen J. 48 (n. 2)
Williams, William 205
Wilson, Robert H. 91–2 (nn. 3, 7, 23, 30, 37)
Wing, Donald G. 268 (n. 70)
Withrington, John 92 (n. 41), 113, 117, 122, 127–8 (nn. 10–12, 21–2, 33–4)
Wogan-Browne, Jocelyn 21 (n. 5), 219 (n. 16)
Woledge, Brian 92 (n. 18)
Wolfram von Eschenbach: *Parzival* 40
Wolsey, Thomas 223, 226, 233

Woolf, Rosemary 185–6, 187 (n. 13)
Wright, Louis B. 249 (n. 1), 265 (n. 41)

York, Richard, duke of 135, 137, 139
Ypotis 214, 220 (nn. 35, 39)
Ywain and Gawain 4, 121

Tabula gratulatoria

Rosamund Allen, Queen Mary and Westfield College, London
Flora Alexander, University of Aberdeen
Malcolm Andrew, Queen's University, Belfast
Elizabeth Archibald, University of Victoria, Canada
Geraldine Barnes, University of Sydney
Peter Bement, Wycliffe Hall, Oxford
Paul Bibire, Crail, Fife
Alcuin Blamires, University of Wales, Lampeter
Lynne S. Blanchfield, Cambridge
Julia Boffey, Queen Mary and Westfield College, London
A. C. Breeze, University of Navarre, Pamplona
Derek Brewer, Emmanuel College, Cambridge
Geoffrey Bromiley, University of Durham
David Burnley, University of Sheffield
J. A. Burrow, University of Bristol
Tom Burton, University of Adelaide
Margaret Locherbie-Cameron, University of Wales, Bangor
Joseph and Gertrude Clancy, Aberystwyth
Helen Cooper, University College, Oxford
Peter Coss, University of Northumbria
Janet Cowen, King's College, London
Susan Crane, Rutgers University, New Brunswick
Rees Davies, University of Wales, Aberystwyth
Walford Davies, University of Wales, Aberystwyth
Marie Denley, King's College, London
Armel Diverres, Swansea
Penelope Cowell Doe, Gerrards Cross
Roger Ellis, University of Wales College of Cardiff
Murray J. Evans, University of Winnipeg

Eleanor Fellows, Cambridge
P. J. C. Field, Bangor
Rosalind Field, London
Alan J. Fletcher, University College Dublin
David C. Fowler, University of Washington
E. B. Fryde, Aberystwyth
Marion Glasscoe, University of Exeter
Linda Gowans, Eastbourne
Richard Hamer, Christ Church, Oxford
Brean S. Hammond, University of Wales, Aberystwyth
Isobel Harvey, Cambridge
K. M. Hodder, University of York
Nouha Homad, Yarmouk University
Jeremy Hooker, Frome
Tadahiro Ikegami, Fujisawa-Shi, Japan
Nicolas Jacobs, Jesus College, Oxford
Lesley Johnson, University of Leeds
Arthur Johnston, Altrincham
Simon Meecham Jones, Swansea
Elspeth Kennedy, Reading
Stephen Knight, De Montfort University, Leicester
Catherine La Farge, University College Galway
†Pat Lewis, University of Wales, Swansea
Gwyneth Llewellyn, Wimbledon
Peter J. Lucas, University College Dublin
John Mac Innes, University of Edinburgh
William and Janet Marx, Lampeter
Peter Meredith, University of Leeds
Douglas A. Moffat, Ann Arbor, Michigan
Veronica O'Mara, University of Hull
Derek Pearsall, York
Helen Phillips, Nottingham University
Oliver Pickering, Leeds University Library
Erich Poppe, Marburg
Sue Powell, University of Salford
Anna Hubertine Reuters, Herzogenrath-Kohlscheid
Gillian E. Rogers, Cambridge
Alyson Round, Newport, Gwent
Desmond Slay, Aberystwyth
Diane Speed, Waverley, New South Wales

Brian Stone, Open University
Toshiyuki Takamiya, Tokyo
Ned Thomas, University of Wales Press
Elizabeth Urquhart, Leeds
R. A. Waldron, Chelmsford
S. Carole Weinberg, University of Manchester
Judith E. Weiss, Cambridge
Colin Wilcockson, Pembroke College, Cambridge
Anne D. Wilson, University of Birmingham
John Withrington, University of Lancaster
Jocelyn Wogan-Browne, University of Liverpool

English Department, University of Wales, Aberystwyth
English Department, University of Wales, Bangor
English Faculty Library, Cambridge
Everyman Paperbacks, London
Girton College Library, Cambridge
Hugh Owen Library, University of Wales, Aberystwyth
Jesus College, Meyricke Library, Oxford
Leeds University Library
The Librarian, University of London Library
The Library, University of Exeter
The Library, University of Sheffield
The Library, University of Wales, Cardiff
Queen Mother Library, University of Aberdeen